Applied General Equilibrium and Economic Development

Present Achievements and Future Trends

Edited by
Jean Mercenier and T. N. Srinivasan

With a Foreword by
Herbert E. Scarf

Ann Arbor

THE UNIVERSITY OF MICHIGAN PRESS

Copyright © by the University of Michigan 1994
All rights reserved
Published in the United States of America by
The University of Michigan Press
Manufactured in the United States of America

1997   1996   1995   1994   4   3   2   1

A CIP catalogue record for this book is available from the British Library.

Library of Congress Cataloging-in-Publication Data

Applied general equilibrium and economic development : present
    achievements and future trends / edited by Jean Mercenier and T. N.
    Srinivasan ; with a foreword by Herbert E. Scarf.
        p.   cm.
    Includes bibliographical references and index.
    ISBN 0-472-10382-2 (alk. paper)
        1. Economic development—Mathematical models—Congresses.
    2. Economic development—Case studies—Congresses. 3. Equilibrium
    (Economics)—Congresses. 4. Agriculture and state—Developing
    countries—Mathematical models—Congresses. 5. Economic
    stabilization—Developing countries—Mathematical models—
    Congresses. 6. Economies of scale—Developing countries—
    Mathematical models—Congresses.   I. Mercenier, Jean.
    II. Srinivasan, T. N., 1933– .
    HD73.A67   1993
    338.9'001'51—dc20   93-9643
                                                                    CIP

Applied General Equilibrium
and Economic Development

Foreword

Herbert E. Scarf

One of the most significant uses of economic theory is to explore the consequences of a change in economic policy, or a change in the environment in which the economy is situated, for the economic well-being of the members of society. If the cost of imported oil rises dramatically, will there be a shift away from those manufacturing industries using substantial quantities of energy as inputs; will there be a rise or fall in wage rates or the price of capital, and which groups of consumers will gain or lose in the process? If a tariff is imposed on imports from abroad, will the gains in employment more than offset the loss in the quality of consumer goods for a substantial proportion of the population? Will the discovery of a new manufacturing technique improve the welfare of all members of society or merely for a privileged subset?

To resolve such questions requires an analytical instrument capable of predicting the choice of productive techniques, the prices of goods and services in the economy, the distribution of income, and their consequences for levels of consumer utility. For certain fields of economics—in the theory of international trade and in public finance—the general equilibrium model has long been the instrument of choice. In a model of international trade, the menu of productive techniques for each country can be described by an activity analysis model or a collection of production functions, the distribution of ownership of factors of production or inventories of manufactured goods are easy to deplete in principle, and consumer preference—to the extent that they are stable—can be rendered by means of utility functions in the aggregate or for a variety of subgroups.

A major preoccupation of mathematical economists during the 1950s and 1960s was to establish the existence of equilibrium prices equating supply and demand in the general Walrasian model. A competitive equilibrium will exist under modest assumptions about the preferences of consumers and under the much more restrictive assumption that production takes place under constant or decreasing returns to scale. These demonstrations, originally offered at a formidable level of mathematical argument, have been sufficiently simplified over the years, so that they are now suitable for presentation in undergraduate courses.

The preoccupation with demonstrations of existence inevitably carried theorists farther and farther away from confrontations with practical economic issues. A concern with simplifications and refinements of mathematical arguments tended to focus attention away from the possibility of using a disaggregated general equilibrium model, with definite numerical values of the many parameters required to specify the model, as an analytical instrument for the evaluation of economic policy. The predisposition in our profession during these two decades was to adopt a large-scale econometric model, in which relative prices rarely entered, as the primary analytical engine. But, if nothing else, the oil shocks of the 1970s were a striking reminder to the profession of the importance of differential scarcities and of both the origins and consequences of changes in relative prices.

Of course, the Leontief model is a disaggregated version of a general equilibrium model, and one that had been used with great regularity since the 1930s. But the input-output model is deficient in its treatment of consumer demand as a function of price and allows only the most limited incorporation of joint production and of a multiplicity of scarce factors of production. To my knowledge, the first disaggregated general equilibrium model focusing on issues of economic policy was the model of the Norwegian economy introduced by Leif Johansen in 1960. Johansen's approach of estimating the consequences of changes in economic policy by linearizing the model (in logarithms) about a presumed equilibrium and solving the resulting system of linear equations for proportionate changes has been followed with great skill and energy by many of the originators of the field of applied general equilibrium analysis.

If, however, the contemplated changes in policy are large and if several of them are expected to be executed simultaneously, a local linearization may lead to unrealistic conclusions. It may then become advisable to attempt to solve the general equilibrium model by global methods that do not require the Johansen assumption that the postchange equilibrium values are close to their prior values. Such global algorithms were first presented, in the middle 1960s, by Hansen, Kuhn, Merrill, McKinnon, Eaves, and myself, and were rapidly followed by a variety of contributions that have dramatically extended our ability to solve such models. At the present time, numerical methods are no longer a serious constraint for applied general equilibrium analysis; the challenge is now in the construction of the model with judgment and insight, in proposing proper levels of aggregation, and in the selection of the many critical parameters required to specify the model.

The present volume, edited by Jean Mercenier and T. N. Srinivasan, is a remarkable testimony to the progress made during the last twenty years. The studies are carried out with the highest professional skill and deal with a variety of topics, countries, and methods of analysis. Some of the models are static, others explicitly dynamic in their account of the evolution of an economy over time. A multiplicity of important issues are explored, ranging from agricultural policies to the unintended effects of economic decisions on the environment. In several of the models, financial instruments are explicitly introduced, leading to departures from the conventional Walrasian model. One chapter explores the subtle issue of the choice of numéraire in an oligopolistic variant of the general equilibrium model, and another allows for the important possibility of economies of scale in production.

The institutional knowledge, concern for significant economic issues, and profound investment in the details of the subject displayed by the chapters in this volume call on a set of talents that are extraordinarily different from those required to invent numerical algorithms. I am awed by these talents, which are necessary to transform the Walrasian model into a useful tool of economic analysis.

Acknowledgments

The majority of the chapters in this volume were first presented and discussed at the conference on Applied General Equilibrium and Economic Development: Present Achievements and Future Trends, held at the Université de Montréal, February 2–4, 1990, and organized by the Centre de recherche et développement en économique (C.R.D.E.). We thank all the authors and commentators for their enthusiastic collaboration and we are extremely grateful to Marie-Christine Thirion who made every effort to make the conference a success. We also wish to thank the Social Sciences and Humanities Research Council of Canada (SSHRC) and the following departments and divisions of the Université de Montréal: the C.R.D.E., the Département de sciences économiques, the Faculté des Arts et des Sciences, and the Vice-rectorat à l'enseignement et à la recherche.

Organizing a conference is one thing, producing a book is another. The production of this volume would not have been possible without the continuous collaboration of the C.R.D.E. secretariat. We owe a particular debt to Sharon Brewer-Moscato for her skilled and dedicated help in the preparation of the manuscript. We also wish to thank Colin Day, Laurie Ham, and the staff of the University of Michigan Press for their efforts in making a speedy publication possible.

Finally, the first editor wishes to express his gratitude to Jean-Marie Dufour, Director of the C.R.D.E., and to André Martens, Deputy Director for International Development, as well as to his colleagues of the C.R.D.E. and the Département de sciences économiques of the Université de Montréal for providing him with a most stimulating research environment.

Contents

Introduction

Jean Mercenier and T. N. Srinivasan

This volume presents some recent applications of a versatile tool for public policy analysis, applied general equilibrium methods, to a wide range of important policy issues in developing countries. It is organized around four major themes: agricultural and food policy, macrostabilization programs, economies of scale in production and the associated market imperfections, and modeling intertemporal trade-offs. Policy analysis using a rich variety of static, recursive, and intertemporal dynamic models is illustrated with policy problems from a number of developing countries in Africa, Asia, and Latin America. They range widely in their institutional features, stages of development, and the size of their economies.

Modeling an economy empirically as a set of interrelated markets in which price-responsive demands and supplies for goods, services, and primary factors clear at equilibrium, that is, as a general equilibrium system, was stimulated by the early and remarkable contribution of Johansen (1960). By making rather restrictive simplifying assumptions about tastes and technology, this pioneering study represented the equilibrium prices as the solution of a set of simultaneous equations that were linear in the logarithms of prices. Thus, standard matrix-inversion was all that was needed to compute the equilibrium prices and quantities. The development of powerful fixed-point methods of computation of equilibrium by Scarf (1967) and Scarf (with T. Hansen 1973) dispensed with the need for severely restricting the functional forms of production and utility functions for reasons of computational feasibility.

Early policy applications of general equilibrium modeling following

We thank Victor Ginsburgh, Michiel Keyzer, André Martens, Elisabeth Sadoulet, John Shoven, and John Whalley for their constructive comments on a previous version of this text. We also thank the participants at the Montréal Conference on Applied General Equilibrium and Economic Development: Present Achievements and Future Trends (Montréal, January 1990) for stimulating discussions. We bear full responsibility for any remaining weaknesses.

Scarf's breakthrough focused on the efficiency of the fiscal system (Shoven and Whalley 1972), followed by applications to international trade. These are surveyed in Shoven and Whalley 1984. The analytical power, flexibility, and versatility of computable general equilibrium (CGE) models for analyzing development policy were recognized early on by Adelman and Robinson (1978). Since then developing country applications have grown exponentially. A recent and already outdated survey is by Robinson (1989).

Many features of developing economies made CGE models particularly attractive. First, most markets in these economies are heavily distorted by systematic government interventions, and policy changes alter distortions in several markets simultaneously. From theory it is well known that reducing or eliminating some distortions while leaving others in place need not improve welfare in general. This means that one can hope to evaluate the actual welfare effect of such policy changes only with an empirical model that can tackle the joint effects of changes in several distortions. CGE models provide such a rigorous tool. Second, because of their ability to analyze the joint effects of several policy instruments, CGE models enable the analyst to quantify the efficiency and distributional implications of policies. This has proved extremely important from a political point of view as it helped to dispel the simplistic assertion, often made by some policymakers and even economists, that a trade-off between efficiency and equity is inevitable.

Modeling Agricultural Policy Issues

CGE models, besides being feasible with limited data, have the important virtue that they impose consistency: there can be no sources of supply other than domestic production, inventories, or imports and no demand destinations other than consumption, investment, inventory accumulation, and exports. Incomes and expenditures have to match: budget constraints, public and private, have to be respected. In particular this implies that the cost of any subsidization or transfers has to be financed and, equally, revenue from any taxes has to be allocated. The feasibility of building a CGE model with limited data does not, of course, justify limited attention to data and parameters. Indeed, the model itself could and should be used to identify the critical parameters and lacunae in the data through sensitivity analyses. Several chapters in this volume include such sensitivity analyses. The two chapters in Part 1, focused on agricultural pricing and policies, share this modeling concern. They emphasize the need to restrict models to well-understood theoretical structures and to concentrate efforts on improving the description of the institutional characteristics under which markets operate and social classes interact. Furthermore, compared to the literature on CGE models, they pay more attention to data issues and incorporate as many econometrically estimated parameters as possible. They strive for a high degree of disaggregation. To stress this difference, these authors call their approach applied (AGE) rather than computable (CGE) general equilibrium modeling.

These points are made most forcefully by Michiel Keyzer and Wim van Veen in their analysis of food policies in Indonesia. The background is the fifth Five-Year-Plan (1989–93), which is briefly described in the chapter. The authors address two basic questions. Are current policies compatible with maintaining rice self-sufficiency? What would be the consequences of pursuing current deregulation policies on income distribution and food consumption?

The authors find that, given current policies and the absence of climatic variation, the self-sufficiency pattern for rice is stable, with no wild shifts from imports to exports, and domestic price movements ensure that these shifts remain within acceptable bounds. Interestingly, they find that neither the abolition of the rice export subsidy nor the withdrawal of a rice import ban affected the trade surplus adversely. Again, they do not find any dramatic effects of deregulation except a short-run conflict between consumer welfare and balance of payments objectives. The authors recognize that, as formulated, the model is best suited for studying the impact of relatively small changes in government policy and, as such, their results should not be over-interpreted as showing a lack of sensitivity to policy changes.

In his chapter on agricultural pricing policy in India, Kirit Parikh focuses our attention on the public distribution system (PDS) in which the government procures and supplies several essential commodities (such as rice, wheat, sugar, edible oils, and kerosene) at nonmarket prices. The issues raised by this policy intervention are twofold. What are its consequences on the welfare of different income groups, and, in particular, are the poor gaining from such a policy? What would be the effect on agricultural output, and more generally on the country's growth, of changes in domestic terms of trade between agriculture and nonagriculture, and who among the different groups in the economy would gain or lose? Parikh also analyzes the impact of withdrawing the subsidy currently being offered on the use of fertilizers and using part of the revenue saved in a combination of investment in irrigation and in a public works program to provide additional employment opportunities to the rural poor.

A version of the current PDS with respect to foodgrains is compared with a scenario in which it is abolished, with its effect on public revenue offset by changing other taxes so that public investment is unaffected. From this comparison Parikh concludes that the overall effect of the PDS is to benefit the urban population both because it is the only recipient of subsidized grain and because the PDS, on balance, generates positive revenue to the government. Its abolition helps all rural classes—while increasing in number, the poorest would enjoy a higher real income. The scenarios reflecting policy-induced changes in terms of trade differ in their impact depending on the welfare indicator used. The use of resources saved from the withdrawal of the fertilizer subsidy for rural works programs and investment in additional irrigation constitutes an unambiguously superior policy from the points of view of welfare and growth.

Clearly, answering important questions that focus on the equity and efficiency implications of policy changes requires not only a multisector-multiclass apparatus, but also a very careful description of institutional arrangements that constrain the functioning of the market economy. The models by Keyzer and van Veen and Parikh are particularly noteworthy in this respect.

Analysis of Stabilization Programs

The adverse foreign shocks experienced by most developing countries during the early 1980s—depressed export demand/declining terms of trade, high interest rates, and increased debt burden due to dollar appreciation, together with the decline of new lending by commercial banks, called for drastic adjustments. Programs of adjustment were often drawn up with the active involvement of the IMF and the World Bank, separately as well as together. These programs have been characterized by a simultaneous emphasis on demand-management actions in order to reduce short-term imbalances, and on supply-side measures aiming at efficiency improvements through structural adjustments. The two components of the strategy—stabilization and structural adjustment—are, however, not easily separated, in part because of the amplitude of the adjustments required (for instance, in exchange rates).

Macromodels and standard CGE models both proved equally unsuitable in dealing with the problem: highly aggregated macromodels typically fail to take into account intersectoral and interclass resource shifts; on the other hand, in standard CGE models, money is neutral and only relative prices matter. There is no theoretically satisfactory way to study inflation, nominal wage rigidities, or nominal exchange rate policies with standard CGE models. For this reason, some researchers have developed models that are sometimes referred to as "financial CGE" models. These models attempt to integrate money and financial assets in the multisector-multiclass structure of CGEs. The aim is to capture the underdeveloped character of financial markets in semi-industrialized economies. This important feature, they argue, is responsible for strong interactions between financial and real phenomena so that growth and welfare evaluations of policies would be seriously biased if these were neglected. There is as yet no consensus, to say the least, about how money and financial assets should be introduced in general equilibrium theory or about what we really learn from these models. After all, the major concern of general equilibrium models is resource allocation in the medium and long run and not short-term forecasting. Still, there is no doubt modeling money in general equilibrium is an extremely challenging issue. Two chapters in the volume contribute to this modeling effort: Jeffrey Lewis on Turkey, and André Fargeix and Elisabeth Sadoulet on Ecuador.

In Lewis's chapter, the financial sector has no forward-looking features—expectations about the future course of nominal variables do not enter into the determination of current demands and supplies of financial assets. The latter are specified in a more-or-less ad hoc fashion with no explicit link to any optimization on the part of households or firms so that nonneutrality of money is built-in. It would appear that eliminating rigidities associated with the financial sector, by allowing exchange rates to be flexible, freeing the interest rates and time deposits, while maintaining a 2 percent growth in real wages in the face of adverse external shocks and the ratio of fiscal deficit to GDP at its no-shock pattern, enables the economy to grow faster (by 2 percent per year on the average) and to reduce the rate of inflation to less than one-fourth its value as compared to no financial liberalization.

Fargeix and Sadoulet's model of Ecuador explicitly introduces an apparently forward-looking behavior by letting wages adjust through an inflation-augmented Phillips curve. However, the expected inflation rate entering the curve is based on an adaptive mechanism, thereby almost eliminating forward-looking behavior. In the long-run steady state, however, the expected and actual inflation rates are the same. It would appear that nonneutrality of monetary changes arise primarily through the wage-adjustment mechanism. The inflationary process affects both capital flight and domestic investment. The simulation exercise consists in comparing alternative adjustment policies to foreign shocks consisting of a 40 percent reduction in the government's borrowing and a 30 percent decrease in primary exports (oil). Three adjustment policies are considered: (1) a devaluation of the exchange rate accompanied by an increase in the money supply (relative to its no-shock path) to accommodate the inflation generated by devaluation while current government expenditures and public investment grow at the same rate as in the no-shock path; (2) fiscal adjustment in the form of a reduction in the public expenditure in the shock year to maintain the government deficit at the same level in the no-shock case while resuming its no-shock growth subsequently (money supply grows at the same rate as in the devaluation scenario); (3) a monetary adjustment consisting of an annual growth in money supply reduced (approximately) to its preshock level while government expenditures are maintained at their levels in the no-shock path. It is concluded that failing to adjust has a high opportunity cost in terms of growth. In the long run, fiscal adjustment is better for growth. Adjustment through devaluation results in a smaller decrease in GDP growth in the short run than monetary adjustment, which in turn sacrifices less growth than fiscal adjustment. Monetary adjustment seems to be relatively neutral in its incidence on welfare costs among socioeconomic groups, while fiscal adjustment shifts most of the cost to urban households.

Almost a decade ago, Ron McKinnon expressed his skepticism about financial CGEs in the following words: ". . . how can we evaluate the efforts . . . to graft financial and monetary specifications onto micro general equilibrium models? Although perhaps useful to explore tentatively, at this stage it does not appear to me to be a promising future line of research. . . . Too much excess baggage must be carried along when the two (micro and macro) are joined for analyzing any specific problem. There is much to be said for the implicit traditional wisdom that has, hitherto, kept micro and macro analysis separate" (McKinnon 1984, 273–74). Since then, progress has no doubt been made, as the chapters by Lewis and Fargeix and Sadoulet illustrate. Whether these efforts have been successful enough to make McKinnon's skeptical note sound somewhat outdated is for the reader to decide.

Modeling Imperfect Competition

Policy analysis founded on neoclassical economic theory is based on the existence of a competitive equilibrium, albeit a tax-distorted one, and on its efficiency and Pareto optimality implications. Many, though not all, of the results from this theory of decentralized, price-guided resource allocation require that the production set of each producer and the consumption sets and preferences of each consumer be convex, and that there are no technological externalities in production and interdependencies and externalities in consumer preferences. Convexity in production precludes increasing returns to scale. However, scale economies and externalities could be consistent with price-taking behavior by individual producers as long as these were external to their decisions, that is, they perceive the effect of their individual choices on the factors that induce such economies or externalities to be negligible. A standard example is one in which the output of a producer of some commodity depends not only on the amounts of the inputs he or she uses to produce it but also on the aggregate output of all producers of the commodity. Clearly, as long as there are a large number of producers, it is natural to postulate that the effect on the aggregate output of the change in any one producer's output is perceived to be negligible. Thus, industry output is an unperceived externality to each producer and, in some versions where such aggregation is possible, industry output will show scale economies as a function of the aggregate input vector of the industry. Since laissez-faire competitive equilibrium in such an economy will be Pareto inefficient, appropriate intervention to internalize the externality in each producer's decisions will ensure efficiency.

Errata

P. v, line 21: "deplete" should read "depict" and "preference" should read "preferences"

Price-taking, profit-maximizing behavior of individual producers would be inconsistent with the existence of significant economies of scale or externalities that are perceived by them. For instance, in an economy closed to foreign trade or in the production of nontraded goods, if scale economies continue to be significant at levels of output beyond the size of the market for such a product, not more than one producer would be expected to produce that product and that producer will surely recognize his or her market power.

Once it is recognized that a noncompetitive structure is a more appropriate description of some markets in an economy, whether or not such a structure is induced by technology and tastes (e.g., scale economies and product differentiation) or by policy (e.g., import quotas and licensing of production capacity as in many less developed countries) it should be no surprise that a laissez-faire (e.g., free trade) equilibrium would not be Pareto optimal. What is more, piecemeal interventions, such as, for example, reducing concentration and restoring competitive behavior in one market, need not be welfare improving over laissez-faire if other markets continue to be oligopolistic. Policy design therefore would have to take into account the nature of the oligopolistic competition, including barriers to entry.

Recent developments under the rubric of a "new" or "strategic" theory of international trade in a world in which markets are oligopolistic, consumers prefer variety, production technologies exhibit indefinite economies of scale, and so forth, have generated a number of propositions that go beyond, and sometimes invalidate, the conclusions of conventional theory based on the Heckscher-Ohlin-Samuelson model of trade. For example, two countries identical in every respect will gain from trade if consumers prefer to consume a variety of products produced under scale economies. To take another example, in oligopolistic competition between home and foreign firms in a third market (for a product that is not consumed at home) in an industry closed to entry, appropriate government intervention can shift oligopoly rents to home firms from foreign firms. Unfortunately, the nature of optimal policy, and, indeed, whether policy intervention is needed at all, depends crucially on what is assumed about the nature of oligopolistic competition, assumptions that are difficult, if not impossible, to test in the real world.

Development economists early on emphasized economies of scale due to indivisibilities and also externalities and the constraints of limited size of domestic markets in early stages of industrialization of less developed countries (LDCs). However, their pessimism about the prospects of manufactured exports from LDCs led them to focus on the size of home markets. They failed to realize that scale economies are likely to be irrelevant for commodities for which the size of the world market was large. In any case, their perception of externalities and scale economies operated at an industry rather than a firm level, in which case the question of strategic behavior by firms is moot. It is a debatable issue whether the new or strategic trade theory and its sometimes protectionist policy implications have much relevance to LDCs (Helpman 1989; Srinivasan 1989a and 1989b). Be that as it may, more and more empirical models based on the theory for LDC economies are being developed.

The chapter by Jaime de Melo and David Roland-Holst illustrates the kind of issues that have been raised by this literature. More specifically, using a multisector general equilibrium model of the Korean economy, they examine whether import tariffs and export subsidies may be combined to promote the development of sectors with increasing returns to scale and oligopolistic behavior in domestic markets. Their chapter confirms, to a certain extent, the conclusions of strategic trade theory: the incorporation of imperfect competition features in general equilibrium models results in policy prescriptions that contradict some well-established propositions of classical welfare theory. However, they also confirm that such models are extremely fragile and one ought to be careful when deriving policy conclusions from them: such results appear highly sensitive to competing assumptions that are empirically difficult to distinguish.

A flavor of this extreme fragility can be seen from the following results: given increasing returns to scale in some sectors and contestable market-pricing behavior by oligopolists (a behavior that in effect ensures that profits are zero without actual entry but with the threat of potential entry), an import tariff leads to welfare losses while the same tariff under a Cournot-type behavior rule results in welfare gains. When an export subsidy at the same rate is offered in an attempt to neutralize the incentive to sell in domestic markets under a tariff, the combination leads to welfare *gains* under contestable pricing and *losses* under Cournot-type behavior. In all of these cases, the welfare gains or losses are much greater than would obtain under constant returns to scale in all sectors. As the authors point out, this last result is the least surprising: with unrealized scale economies and oligopolistic distortions, the effects of protection can greatly exceed estimates based on conventional models with constant returns to scale.

In competitive general equilibrium models, the choice of the numéraire (i.e., unit of account in which prices, profits, and incomes are defined) has no influence on the equilibrium: only *relative* prices matter. The structure of *relative prices* and the quantities of supplies and demands in any equilibrium are independent of the choice of the numéraire. However, the issue is more consequential and delicate in models of general equilibrium with oligopoly. It is known (Gabszewicz and Vial 1972; Dierker and Grodal 1986) that whether an equilibrium exists, and whether it is unique if it exists, may depend on the choice of the numéraire. The intuition behind this result is clear enough. For a price-taking and profit-maximizing producer it does not matter in what units prices are defined. Changing units simply changes profits by an exogenous scale factor. Hence it does not affect his or her optimal choice. On the other hand, if a producer who perceives that his or her decisions affect the price at which he or she sells products or purchases inputs, then his or her profits as a *function* of his or her *choice variables* will depend in an essential way on the choice of the numéraire. Hence, simply requiring producers to maximize profits is not a well-specified behavioral rule. Put another way, the separation of a firm's decision on profits and the decision of the firm's owners on the use of profits generated by the firm is inappropriate if price-taking behavior is abandoned. For example, for a monopolist-cum-owner of a firm producing gadgets who consumes only widgets, the only relevant profit function is that designated in units of widgets.

Victor Ginsburgh's chapter illustrates the dependence of equilibrium on the choice of numéraire in a two-commodity model in which each commodity is produced by a monopolist using the other commodity as an input under constant returns to scale. Both monopolists behave à la Cournot—taking the other's output and price as given. Initially there is a consumption tax (possibly at different rates) on the two goods and the policy experiment comprises the abolition of the tax. Two natural choices of numéraire, namely, one or the other of the two commodities, are considered. It is shown that under one choice of numéraire welfare increases over the status quo equilibrium from this abolition, and under the other welfare may increase less or even decrease.

It should be pointed out that most general equilibrium trade models that introduce imperfect competition assume Chamberlinian monopolistic competition of a large group with free entry. In such models, each producer is assumed to ignore the income effect of his or her choices on his or her perceived demand. At least in some of these models, for example, the simple differentiated product model of Krugman (1979), in which utility from each variety is an isoelastic function of its consumption (and aggregate utility is the sum of utilities from consuming each of the varieties available), as long as income effects are ignored, the equilibrium is independent of numéraire choice. It is an open issue whether this independence is specific to the particular features of the Krugman-type model or whether it generalizes to other CGE models with imperfect competition. None of the contributors to this literature appear to be aware of this potentially serious problem.

Modeling Intertemporal Trade-offs

The chapters discussed previously assume backward-looking expectations: only past and/or present events are taken into account by individual agents when making intertemporal choices. The resulting models are either static or recursive, that is, a sequence of static one-period solutions are linked in some ad hoc fashion. This treatment of intertemporal trade-offs and decision making has the advantage of being simple and, some may even argue, not that unrealistic. The problem with this approach is that it can lead to dynamically inefficient (and in many cases unstable) solutions. Putting this differently, these models are focused on intersectoral and interclass resource shifts induced by a change of economic environment (be it through government or foreign action), and ignore their intertemporal reallocation through forward-looking decisions of agents about investment and savings. There are many reasons why this might not be entirely satisfactory, as the chapters in Part 4 demonstrate.

The modeling strategies adopted by the authors differ significantly. The most important difference is in the treatment of forward-looking expectations. There are two options here. One is to assume that agents form model-consistent expectations, that is, expectations that are consistent with the predictions of the model. The rationale behind this is that small agents make their intertemporal decisions taking into account the complete sequence of signals they expect to face in the future, and that the expectations they form on endogenous variables will be self-fulfilling for a given exogenous environment. This is the approach pursued by all of the authors except Nancy Benjamin. For developing countries, she rejects, as inappropriate, the implicit assumption that futures markets exist and have to be cleared by futures prices. Her framework is in the spirit of Grandmont's temporary equilibrium: agents form forward-looking expectations using a restricted information set so that they need not be (and will in general not be) self-fulfilling. The dynamics are then provided by a sequence of such temporary equilibria.

Benjamin's objective is to explore the implications of private decisions based on imperfect foresight. Three models based on alternative assumptions regarding the formation of expectations are considered. The first is a "no expectations" framework in which only current period outcomes determine the level and structure of investment. The second is a framework of "rigid expectation" in which foresight about future foreign earnings is myopic in that current conditions are expected to continue, but investment responds to the structure of incentives even though existing capital stock is sector specific. The last is an "endogenous expectations" framework in which output targets are based on changes in current sales from their value at the beginning of that period's solution. All three frameworks are used in modeling three countries, Bolivia, Cameroon, and Indonesia, that differ in their structures of intermediate and final demands.

Benjamin finds that, for Indonesia, the conclusion that foreign capital flow will hurt industries that are net exporters more than import-substituting industries is robust across models. However, for the "no expectations" model this conclusion does not hold for Cameroon. The Bolivian case highlights the demand pressure that endogenous investment responding to favorable foreign shocks can exert on nontraded services such as construction and thus exacerbate the upward pressure on domestic prices.

There has been a growing concern for environmental issues (such as the so-called greenhouse effect) in policy circles during the last five years. Obviously, the costs of environmental damages cannot be correctly evaluated in a partial or static equilibrium framework, as they affect, by their very nature, other sectors and periods of activity than those in which they were generated. The same is true of policies designed to deal with environmental traumas: pollution control measures, for instance, will restrict the set of available technologies to firms and therefore affect relative prices, intersectoral resource allocations, and growth. The chapter by Charles Blitzer and his coauthors is intended as a demonstration of the potential uses of multisectoral, intertemporal programming models embodying significant nonlinearities in production and consumption to analyze the effects of environmental policies. The setting of the model was somewhat special and its design was meant for purposes other than environmental analysis. It is also restricted to quantifying the consequences of legal restrictions in carbon emissions on the growth prospects of Egypt. Although its numerical results are illustrative rather than definitive, it is clear that the methodology is general enough to be adapted to deal with a wide variety of problems involving externalities.

Among the potential uses of the model, the most important and obvious one is the analysis of trade-offs between emissions restrictions and economic performance. Two types of restrictions are considered: a global constraint on total emissions and a set of constraints on the emissions of each sector separately. In general, both types of constraints are made increasingly restrictive over time. As is to be expected, the burden of sectoral constraints are more onerous compared to global constraints. The restrictiveness of the global constraint increases from 95 percent of the emissions in the no restrictions scenario in 1992 to 70 percent in 2012. In a more restrictive scenario, the change is from 85 percent in 1992 to 45 percent in 2012. In the first scenario, the average annual rate of growth of GDP falls from 3.51 percent during 1987–2012 to 3.40 percent (2.05 percent in the second scenario). The corresponding reduction in total carbon emissions was 6.3 percent in the first and 18.9 percent in the second scenario. The nonlinearity implied in this trade-off is rather striking; the elasticity of reduction in GDP growth with respect to reduction in carbon emissions more than *quadrupled* from 0.5 in the first scenario to 2.2 in the second.

This model is an optimizing model: a centralized viewpoint is adopted, as if there were a single decision maker maximizing an economywide objective function subject to technical and behavioral constraints. This is clearly appropriate for calculations of economic efficiency in situations in which solutions to a centralized planning problem can be given a decentralized, competitive market equilibrium interpretation and vice versa. However, it suppresses the analysis of equity issues among socioeconomic groups; when dealing with market imperfections, it might be preferable to study the equilibrium solution rather than the optimal path of the economy: centralized and decentralized solutions will generally, in this case, not coincide. Given that rigidities and market imperfections are a characteristic feature of developing countries, and that these exert considerable constraints on policy-making, a decentralized representation of the economic environment is more appropriate for many purposes. This is the viewpoint adopted by Jean Mercenier and Maria da Conceiçao Sampaïo de Souza in their chapter on structural adjustment issues in a highly indebted economy (Brazil). In this computable, intertemporal general equilibrium (CIGE) framework, investment and saving decisions, based on model-consistent expectations, are independently made by firms and households to maximize their individual intertemporal criterion (sum of discounted profits or of instantaneous utilities) subject to their respective intertemporal constraints. The framework is designed to embed short-term features such as price and wage rigidities into a long run characterized by market clearing.

The model is used to evaluate alternative growth strategies (with and without short-term real-wage rigidities) in the environment of the early 1980s in which, because of its huge foreign debt, Brazil suffered more than many other countries from adverse foreign shocks. It is shown that, contrary to conventional wisdom, trade liberalization does not provide an impetus to recovery and growth in Brazil. A strategy based on subsidizing investment in most competitive, outward-oriented industries is found to be superior. It should be stressed, however, that the Mercenier-Sampaïo model assumes that the Brazilian economy is embedded in a world evolving along a balanced growth path that does not respond to Brazilian policy shifts. While such nonoptimizing behavior by the rest of the world is commonly assumed in most static CGE models, it is problematic in an intertemporal framework. Although alternative procedures of calibration that ensure that base year data represent an equilibrium may not affect the policy conclusions of static models, calibration is more complex and delicate in intertemporal models. It is an open question whether the policy conclusions of Mercenier-Sampaïo are robust to changes in their calibration procedures.

The last chapter in this volume, by Jean-Claude Berthélémy and François Bourguignon, deals with the dynamics of the North-South-OPEC interactions. This is an extremely complex issue, and the model developed is accordingly ambitious from a methodological point of view. Obviously, because oil is traded for and enters the production of other products produced by other countries, the approach has to be multisectoral and decentralized. In addition, the model has to be truly intertemporal: basic to the problem is the fact that oil reserves are limited and known to be so by producers and consumers who make their current decisions accordingly. This is the object of a large body of theoretical literature on exhaustible resources. Among the difficulties, one may note the fact that steady state growth may not exist in such models. The chapter shows how to introduce an exhaustible resource in dynamic, multisector general equilibrium models, no doubt an important issue for developing countries. The most challenging questions, however, arise from the noncompetitive structure of the oil market. The difficulty comes from the fact that, in modeling OPEC behavior, one can hardly justify a partial approach to monopoly pricing (as usually adopted when dealing with trade issues—see de Melo and Roland-Holst in this volume). Rather, the problem requires full monopolistic equilibria to be investigated: monopolist oil producers must be aware of the fact that their policy choices will affect the evolution of the whole world economy, including, in particular, the prices that clear competitive markets. This departure from perfect competition raises formidable difficulties; no general theorem of existence is available in the theoretical literature and the contribution by Berthélémy and Bourguignon is therefore a pioneering effort in an extremely promising direction of research.

Berthélémy and Bourguignon first present a finite-horizon, competitive, perfect foresight model with exogenously imposed terminal conditions on each agent since it is obviously impossible to numerically compute an infinite-horizon model. It turns out, not surprisingly, that the computed equilibria are sensitive to the terminal conditions. Three regions (North, South, OPEC) and four goods (three region specific and one universal or standard) are recognized in the model. Two policy experiments with the competitive–perfect foresight model, namely, a unilateral asset transfer from the North to South and an accelerated (exogenous and neutral) technical progress in the South, lead to expected results. Southern welfare increases (Northern welfare decreases) in the first experiment. In the second, while all regions benefit, South benefits the least because the positive impact of accelerated technical progress in its exports is partially offset by a terms-of-trade loss.

The analysis of *full* monopoly equilibria turned out to be complex, even though the authors avoid the potential problems (Ginsburgh in this volume) of nonexistence and of nonunicity of equilibrium that might arise depending on their choice of numéraire by assuming that the monopolist's policy choice is oriented toward maximizing the welfare of a single representative agent for the whole economy. In the case of North exercising its monopoly on the market for its specific good, equilibrium exists. The time profile of world growth and trade changes drastically in this case compared to the competitive–perfect foresight base run. The price of northern goods is higher by about 47 percent initially and by 68 percent at the end of five periods of three years each. North, while initially importing the standard good, eventually becomes an exporter. The attempt to compute an equilibrium for the case in which South and OPEC exercised monopoly power over their specific goods failed to converge. The authors suggest that this failure is due to the fact that, in production, there is little substitutability between southern and OPEC goods on the one hand, and capital-labor combinations on the other. However, equilibria exist when the exercise of monopoly power is restricted to some subperiods. For example, the exercise of monopoly power in period 2 by OPEC raises oil prices by 159 percent, but the anticipated return to competition lowers the price by roughly 24 percent in periods 3–5 as compared to the base run.

Where Do We Go from Here?

The research reported in this volume reflects continuous and fruitful interaction between the needs and concerns of policymakers and the responses of academic researchers. The policy problems facing the former continue to proliferate in number and complexity. Understandably, policymakers wish to have analyses that truly incorporate the features of their economic reality, including politico-economic-social constraints that they cannot ignore. Incorporating some of these features and constraints have led researchers to move farther and farther away from the frictionless Walras-Arrow-Debreu framework in devising new model structures and broadening the scope of applications. While these efforts have been successful to a certain extent, they have also raised a number of questions for future research to address.

Foremost among these questions is the modeling of the behavior of governments. Indeed, the actions of governments are represented in a surprisingly crude and simplistic way in most models, even though it is well recognized that these go far beyond a mere manipulation of tariffs, tariff equivalents or lump-sum taxation, even in the least advanced developing countries. Yet, for instance, Keyzer and van Veen (chap. 1) represent the government's price stabilization policy through tariffs, while such a price policy is implemented through buffer stocks in the real world; de Melo and Roland-Holst (chap. 5) and Mercenier and Sampaïo (chap. 9) rely on lump-sum taxation and transfers. Government procurement policies are responsible for major distortions and inefficiencies in most LDCs; yet an adequate model capturing the complexities of such policies in the real world is as yet unavailable. Furthermore, the combination of import quotas and investment licensing that applies to domestic capacity expansion often shelters some domestic producers from foreign competition as well as from the competition of local producers who failed to obtain capacity licenses. It is evident that such government interventions create a market structure that is far from Walrasian pure competition. However, modeling such a structure as Chamberlinian monopolistic competition from among the many possibilities, as available models do, is not very convincing.

Progress is also needed in modeling government spending. In most models, government consumption is exogenous and a waste, since public services seldom affect consumer welfare directly or indirectly; government-financed education and infrastructure are rarely recognized as influencing overall economic efficiency. A small step in the right direction is the work of Mercenier and Sampaïo (chap. 9), who introduce public infrastructure as an externality in firms' production functions.

In all market economies with some form of representative government, economic policy-making is subject to lobbying by interest groups through the political process. In many situations—in Latin American countries for instance—public policy is perhaps determined as the equilibrium outcome of the political market, that is, the result of a competitive struggle for political office. Only very recently has this been recognized in CGE models by Rutherford and Winer (1990), who model a democratic political economy in which equilibrium tax rates and the level of public services take on values that maximize a political support function subject to the general equilibrium structure of the private economy. This seems a promising avenue of research for modeling developing country policies, now that more and more developing countries are moving toward a multiparty, democratic political system.

Another important issue is the modeling of the rest of the world in single-country models. It would seem unnecessary and unduly complicated to abandon the "almost" small open economy assumption—that is, an open economy that has some monopoly power on the export side—by fully endogenizing rest-of-the-world prices and incomes. But, as Long observes in his comment on de Melo and Roland-Holst (chap. 5), if a policy of "strategic" trade protectionism seems appropriate, evaluating its consequences would call for a detailed understanding and modeling of how other countries react to the protective measures of the country in question.

A third item for future research is to determine the true relevance of increasing returns to scale-induced imperfect competition in models for policy-making in developing countries. First, it is generally recognized that, in LDCs, imperfect competition in markets is largely policy induced rather than the result of indefinite scale economies in production. Second, the design and implementation of beneficial strategic trade policies is extremely demanding in terms of information about the nature of imperfect competition; it is not extravagant to believe that collecting the necessary information could be prohibitively costly, if not infeasible altogether. The hypothetical returns from such a policy could be swamped by information costs. Third, it is not unreasonable to believe that the gains from the exploitation of underutilized scale economies by expanding the markets for domestic producers by reducing imports through tariff protection may be more than offset by the loss of real resources used in contesting the potential rents created and assigned by the political process. These considerations, while undoubtedly important from a developing country policy perspective, do not make such CGE models as the ones reported in this volume mere curiosities. The reason is simply that abandoning analysis because of the fear that it might prove costly relative to benefits gained confers an unwarranted advantage to the status quo. Instead, the effort should be to build more relevant models that incorporate considerations of political economy rather than abandoning modeling altogether.

Some important technical questions remain to be explored. One is related to the choice of numéraire in general equilibrium models with imperfect competition. As mentioned earlier, behind this apparently technical issue lay a number of unresolved problems regarding the specification of an oligopolist's objective function. Besides, there is also the issue of characterizing the interaction among oligopolists, that is, the specification of the oligopoly game. Some models assume a "conjectural-variations" framework, in which each oligopolist "conjectures" the response of the other oligopolists to changes in his or her strategic variable (i.e., his or her output in Cournot-type behavior and his or her price in Bertrand-type behavior). Such conjectures may or may not be consistent in that the assumption of one oligopolist about the response of another to a change in the strategic variable need not be the same as the actual response. Although the conjectural variations approach is technically convenient and tractable, it is questionable for analyzing policy change because the conjectures are assumed to be unaffected by the policy change. Besides, from behavioral and informational perspectives, this approach is unsatisfactory: more satisfactory alternatives drawing on game-theoretic formulations should be explored.

It is usual for CGE modelers to use the degrees of freedom that they have in the choice of values of some of the unknown parameters of their model to "calibrate" it, that is, to ensure that the base-period data represent a general equilibrium of the economy under consideration. The policy conclusions derived from the model could be, in principle, though unlikely in practice, sensitive to changes in procedures of calibration in static constant returns to scale models. In truly forward-looking intertemporal models, the problem of calibration is more complex and delicate. Ensuring that the base data set represents an *intertemporal* equilibrium requires that the values of all forward-looking variables (e.g., investment) represent equilibrium responses to the *future* evolution of other variables affecting them. Thus, a calibration procedure not only would specify the values of unknown parameters but also a future path for exogenous or forcing variables of the system. It is an open question whether the insensitivity of policy conclusions to the choice of calibration procedures continues to hold, as in static models. Progress on these issues will depend on the appropriate use of dynamic aggregation and finite-horizon approximations (see Keyzer 1990; Mercenier and Michel 1991b). As is well known, modeling an infinite-horizon economy as an indefinite sequence of economies populated by overlapping generations could lead to indeterminacies (Kehoe and Levine 1985) and Pareto nonoptimality of equilibria. On the other hand, modeling the economy as populated by infinitely lived dynasties of agents is obviously unrealistic. A suitably chosen mix between the two might avoid the problems of both and is worth exploring.

An important task for future research is to bridge the gap between growth theory and the CGE apparatus. Among the most promising avenues is the endogenization of technical progress, which, in developing countries, is particularly linked to international trade and trade policy (see Rivera-Batiz and Romer 1991 on modeling the effects of trade restrictions on technical progress). Also, the analysis of the dynamic effects of rent-seeking activities generated by restrictive trade policies would no doubt be of major importance for policy-making in LDCs. Another area that may prove most rewarding is the role of human capital in the process of growth (see Lucas 1988) and the interaction between government policies and human-capital accumulation.

We close this introduction by mentioning the problem of uncertainty. It manifests itself in a significant way through the expectations about the future that drive the intertemporal decisions of consumers, producers, and governments. Most of the existent models assume either that uncertainty is absent altogether or that intertemporal decisions are guided by perfect foresight about the future. Neither assumption is satisfactory though the latter is in the spirit of the general equilibrium approach (see Adelman, Roland-Holst, and Sarris 1990, which attempts to introduce uncertainty in a CGE framework). Uncertainty is no doubt a major component of real-world decision making. However, the issue is extremely complex: to be consistent with general equilibrium, it is not enough that agents know the model of the economy and their expectations are rational. In addition, the distributions of the relevant random variables arising from the decisions of agents have to be consistent with the distributional assumptions made by the agents in making these decisions (Anderson and Sonnenschein 1982). For example, from a partial equilibrium perspective, the popular assumption in finance theory, namely that returns to financial assets follow a Wiener diffusion process, may be perfectly adequate. But from a general equilibrium perspective, one has to ensure that the assumed Wiener process would, in fact, obtain in an equilibrium of the asset markets embedded in a general equilibrium of the economy. Given these difficult problems, it seems wise to divide and conquer: more returns may be expected from mastering complex deterministic systems first. No doubt, there is plenty of work ahead.

Part 1
Modeling Agricultural
Policy Issues

CHAPTER 1

Food Policy Simulations for Indonesia: The Fifth Five-Year Plan Period, 1989–93

Michiel A. Keyzer and Wim C. M. van Veen

Some Country Background

Indonesia—with its 180 million inhabitants, 27 percent of which live in urban areas, and a total area of 1.9 million km²—covers a vast archipel that spans 5,000 kilometers from east to west. It is a resource-rich country with crude oil, minerals, forestry products, and plantation crops as its main export goods. The main island, Java, with only 7 percent of the land, is the homeland of 60 percent of the population. The Indonesian government pursues an active policy of transmigration in order to achieve a more even spread of the population over the territory and to promote agricultural and rural development outside Java on the so-called Outer Islands. However, natural population growth currently exceeds 2 percent annually and the transmigration programs have in the past only marginally contributed to an alleviation of the increasing population pressure on Java. As the archipel structure generates a coastline of almost astronomic length, a strict tariff or quota policy on foreign trade is virtually impossible to implement.

Per capita gross national product amounted to about 450 U.S. dollars in 1988[1], ranking Indonesia among the low-income countries by World Bank standards. The GDP composition was roughly as follows in 1988: agriculture 24 percent, declining steadily; manufacturing 15 percent, increasing; construction 6 percent, stationary; mining 13 percent, fluctuating with prices of oil and gas; and services 42 percent, steadily increasing. Over the past decade the balance of payments has shown a surplus on merchandise trade and a current account deficit. The deficit was caused by profit outflows, which are largely related to the oil sector and by increasing interest payments on public

---

1. Statistical information in this section is based on World Bank (1989a and 1989b), supplemented with calculations. Indonesia was classified as a middle-income country between 1981 and 1987.

external debt. Soft loans from foreign aid play an important role in meeting the financing requirement. Export earnings, over 40 percent of which are obtained from oil and gas, remain characterized by a low share of manufactured products, 27 percent in 1987, of which half consists of semi-industrial wood products. In addition to official duty payments, nontariff barriers are serious impediments to trade, protecting domestic industry prices and negatively affecting exporting sectors.

In the early 1980s government current revenues were highly dependent on oil, amounting to around 70 percent in some years. Since then, government seriously embarked on restructuring and broadening the tax system. New income and land tax laws were imposed and value added taxes were introduced in the mid-1980s. Nevertheless, the decline in oil prices after 1981 necessitated severe adjustments in public expenditures. Public investments declined and public consumption stagnated.

This policy enabled government to keep external public debt within manageable bounds. By the end of 1988, outstanding public and publicly guaranteed medium and long-term debt totaled 41 billion U.S. dollars, requiring about 35 percent of export earnings for debt-servicing. Government also initiated a process of liberalization and deregulation with reduction of nontariff barriers as one of the focal activities. Active domestic pricing policies continue to exist, mainly for rice, wheat, sugar, fertilizer, and oil products. Also, the key role of over 200 public corporations in strategic sectors of the economy will remain unaffected in the near future. It seems that there is international confidence in the general directions of Indonesia's economic policies, which since 1969 are laid down in five-year plans, especially as far as policy responses to the financial problems of the early 1980s are concerned. This confidence is reflected in a steady flow of donor assistance and in increasing foreign direct investments.

More than half of the population depends on agriculture as its main source of livelihood. Rice is the main crop. Other important food crops are maize, cassava, sweet potatoes, soybeans, and peanuts, in addition to vegetables and fruits. All these food crops are produced by smallholders. However, Indonesian agriculture consists of much more than food crops, which account only for half of agricultural value added. The other half is more or less equally spread between nonfood crops and the remainder, including livestock, fisheries, and forestry. Nonfood crops are generally referred to as "estate crops" in Indonesian statistics, due to the considerable involvement of large estates, which are either publicly or privately owned, some with access to foreign capital. However, in general, smallholders produce the largest part of the nonfood crops, sometimes in relation with an estate that serves as processing and service center. Smallholders dominate in the production of sugarcane, tobacco, coconuts, coffee, rubber, spices, and kapok, whereas estate production prevails for tea and palm oil.

The major success for agriculture has been the achievement of self-sufficiency in rice in the mid-1980s, with the contribution of nonfood crops to the recent diversification of export earnings as a second area of achievement. On the negative side, upland degradation through erosion and loss of forest land must be mentioned.

Average calorie intake improved considerably over the past 25 years. It increased from 1800 to more than 2500 kcal/capita/day. Rice accounts for about 55 percent of calorie intake, other staple crops—maize, cassava, sweet potato—for another 15 percent. Protein intake averages 59 gram/capita/day, of which about 18 percent is of animal origin. The improvement of the nutritional situation is also reflected by estimates of the share of the population below the poverty level, which is based on an average nutritional requirement of 2100 kcal/capita/day. The share decreased sharply from 33 percent in 1978 to 22 percent in 1984, rather uniformly for urban and rural areas, although average urban income levels are considerably higher than rural incomes (BPS 1987). According to the most recent BPS poverty estimate, for 1987, 18 percent of the population, or about 30 million people, are below the poverty level. Ravallion and Huppi 1989 also arrive unambiguously at the conclusion that poverty decreased in the 1980s. From a nutritional point of view, Indonesia ranks quite well among the Southeast Asian countries. However, in other areas Indonesia falls below the performance of its neighbors. Life expectancy at birth stands relatively low at 57 years, and the infant mortality rate is relatively high at 83 per thousand. Nevertheless, these indicators also show a considerable improvement over the past 20 years. School enrollment ratios are rather satisfactory: almost 100 percent for primary and 40 percent for secondary education.

Reaching and maintaining self-sufficiency in rice at a more or less stable domestic price has been a primary concern of Indonesian food policy over the past decades. Even after the success of the mid-1980s it still features prominently in the Fifth plan for the years 1989–93.

The only institutionalized food distribution scheme was oriented to civil servants and the army as a wage indexation device in years of high inflation. Rather than extending the coverage of population groups under this distribution, Indonesian government opted in the 1970s for a food price policy as a major element of distributive policy. It aimed at maintaining relatively low and stable food prices in urban areas, compensating the farmers via public investment in agriculture, support and credit facilities, and fertilizer subsidies.

In this chapter we perform scenario simulations with a recursively dynamic applied general equilibrium (AGE) model of the Indonesian economy to address two questions:

(1) With its current policies, can Indonesia expect to maintain rice self-sufficiency in the next five years, and if so is a large surplus to be expected?

(2) How would a strengthening of the current policies of deregulation affect income distribution and food consumption?

Here, rice self-sufficiency is defined as the absence of the need to import rice to satisfy domestic demand, unless caused by extreme situations like a severe crop failure.

The two questions are of a different nature. The first has a narrow focus on a single commodity, rice, while the second relates to the whole economy and all commodities. They serve a dual purpose. We genuinely want to study both topics, which we think are of current interest, but we also want to illustrate how a narrowly and a more broadly focused topic can be analyzed within the same model, and why it may be informative to do so. We want in particular to point out that such an analysis is made possible because the AGE-model used was not designed for a single purpose only. This is an underlying theme of the chapter to which we shall return in the final section. For this reason we concentrate in this chapter on the use of the AGE-model in relation to the two questions rather than on AGE-modeling technique.

The chapter proceeds as follows. First we describe food policy in Indonesia in more detail. Then we give an outline of the model, present scenarios, and discuss current limitations of the model and orientation for further work. We conclude with our views on the role of applied general equilibrium modeling in relation to development policy analysis. Further details on the model can be found in the Appendix.

A Short Sketch of Food Policy in Indonesia

Past Policies

We take a brief look at Indonesia's specific food policies in the recent past as documented in papers by Ellis (1988), Hutabarat (1988), Pearson et al. (1988), and Timmer (1988).

Three types of food policies may be distinguished: pricing policies, crop support programs, and investment in land improvement. Regular food rationing programs to vulnerable groups do not exist, but a national food security stock is maintained for emergency cases. Food policy is dominated by rice policy. Although pricing and intensification policies exist for other crops, they have significantly less effect on the overall economy than rice policies.

First, nonrice policies are summarized. Price protection for sugar and soybeans has been quite strong since the late 1970s and is supplemented by farmer support programs, for soybean since 1986. For sugar there is an intensification campaign begun in the early 1980s, which also seems to include some forced planting. Nevertheless, for both crops domestic production lags behind consumption, and additional imports are necessary. These imports, combined with stockpiling activities, are fully controlled by the government and permit maintenance of the desired domestic price. Domestic production is not sufficient to meet the demand for maize and groundnuts. However, the degree of effective government involvement is much less here. The production of cassava and sweet potatoes, vegetables and fruits, and meat and fish is relatively free of government interventions. Wheat is a special case; it is not produced domestically but nevertheless is an important source of calories. Wheat consumption is generally considered to be subsidized, both through input subsidies to the mills and through direct consumer subsidies, but information is scarce and direct subsidies seem to have been abolished recently.

Government investments in land development mainly pertain to rehabilitation, improvement, and extension of irrigated areas and to the transformation of tidal swamps, fallow, and forest land into agricultural land. A substantial part of the Outer-Java land development is implemented through Nucleus Estate Schemes, in which private smallholder plots are combined with central estate facilities for marketing and processing. They typically cover palm oil, rubber, sugarcane, and coconuts. The intensity of government investments in land development varied considerably in the 1980s, depending as it did on government's financial position. The period from 1982–87 showed a severe decline in real investments, which recovered, later, in line with overall government investments but also partly due to a higher priority ranking. Recently, these investments have been estimated at 10 and 20 percent of overall public investment for irrigation and estate crops, respectively. This amounts to .5 and .9 percent respectively of gross domestic product at market prices.

The main targets of rice policies were formulated in the mid-1960s when the economy was in bad shape. They relate to self-sufficiency and price stabilization. To this end irrigation investments were increased, rice intensification programs were launched, and the National Logistics Agency (BULOG) was established. The intensification programs, which have been maintained until the present day, aim at rapid adoption by farmers of high yielding varieties (HYVs) by providing modern input packages, access to credit, and management training and input subsidies, especially on fertilizer. The main tasks of BULOG are:

—price stabilization: interyear, interseasonal, and interregional, through floor and ceiling prices;
—creation of a national food security stock, in addition to the working inventories;
—provision of monthly rations to the military and to civil servants (wages in kind).

Initially, the rations received priority, at the expense of the other tasks. The price level was kept rather low, depressing production incentives to farmers. In the second half of the 1970s policies were adjusted: defending the floor prices became the primary task and the price level was raised. Generally, BULOG succeeded in defending both floor and ceiling price by actually carrying out around 10 percent of the transactions. Imports were fully controlled. Compared to international prices, the Indonesian price in the 1980s was at an autarky level: in most years, both imports and exports were, or would have been, profitable with subsidies only.

The combined effect of irrigation, intensification, and price policy led to significant achievements, rice production doubled from 12 to 24 million tons between 1969 and 1983, and self-sufficiency was attained in 1985. After that government ordered an import ban that led to rather strong price increases in 1987 and 1988, under adverse weather conditions.

Current Debate

Contrary to the expectations at the time self-sufficiency was reached, rice has once again become a key issue in the ongoing food policy debate. There is a general concern whether it will be possible to maintain self-sufficiency in the future. Crop diversification away from rice is treated as a matter of secondary importance, in spite of its relevance in meeting the growing demand by the food processing and livestock sectors. Even more radical opinions can be heard that claim that government incentives for sugar and soybean production are socially wasteful and should be reduced in favor of rice. However, that discussion is not clear with respect to measurement concepts: should one measure operating surplus or total value added, how should long-term stable international prices be determined, and how should one apply a proper welfare criterion, instead of cost comparisons?

Concerns about the ability of rice production to keep up with consumption are related to acreage availability, yield per hectare, and pricing. The negative consequences of the reduction of irrigation efforts in the mid-1980s are currently being felt; many believe that such a cut should not be allowed again and that present efforts should be stepped up. This is even more necessary because a substantial acreage of wetland is lost for agriculture each year, due to increased urbanization and industrialization, especially on Java. Estimates vary roughly from 20,000 to 40,000 hectares annually, or 0.25 to 0.5 percent of total wetland. Adequate irrigation efforts will provide a basic source for improvement in cropping intensity and yields per hectare. Nevertheless, improved farm management techniques and continued research efforts need to be pursued, to provide additional yield growth and to counter the effect of increased vulnerability to pests. Even then, it is expected that average yield increases will not exceed 2 percent annually, which is below the 6–8 percent achieved around 1980.

Abolishing fertilizer subsidies was highly controversial in the past but the discussion seems to have calmed down. Knowledge of fertilizer application is widespread by now and fears for falling yields after abolition have diminished, as the costs of fertilizer appear to constitute only a small part of the crop values, at the present level of the rice price, even without subsidies.

The appropriate width of the marketing margin between floor and ceiling price constitutes a further element of the rice policy debate with direct consequences for the size of public stocks, the possibilities for private traders, and BULOG's financing requirements. The inadequate transmission of quality signals in the market system and the role of BULOG, which developed into a huge network with unclear assessments of the cost-effectiveness of its separate tasks, are also subject to criticism. However, the central theme of the discussion is whether Indonesia should go for a long-term production trend that is below, equal to, or above the domestic consumption requirement. Continuous substantial imports are considered politically unacceptable. For the time being, exports are considered feasible only with a subsidy. This is for quality reasons and because the international rice market is too small to absorb significant surpluses from Indonesia without a severe fall in prices. Hence, one generally opts for the middle track of long-term self-sufficiency with occasional imports and exports to deal with climatic variation. A structural reliance on trade to cope with these variations would reduce domestic stock holding costs but has its dangers due to the thinness of the international rice market. It could be very costly to obtain the required imports in time in case of a sudden shortfall, or to sell exports at a reasonable price in case of surplus. Population growth is projected at a rate of at most 2.15 percent, and demand elasticity for rice with respect to per capita income is highly income dependent but generally low (well below 0.3, on average). Thus, at a per capita real growth of around 2 percent, roughly 2.8 percent production growth would be required. Still, there is some disagreement on this rate. For instance, Ellis (1988) mentions 2.5 percent but Pearson et al. (1988) consider 3 percent necessary.

A final remark on the food policy debate relates to its participants. As may be inferred from the above cited references, most of the opinions are expressed by foreigners. Although this seems undesirable, it must be admitted that this chapter reinforces this unfortunate trend.

Before proceeding with a discussion of the simulation runs we provide a short outline of the model used.

An Outline of the Model

Main Features

- —The Indonesia-model is an applied general equilibrium model, built on a complete Social Accounting Matrix (SAM) for the year 1980.
- —It distinguishes six socioeconomic groups, two incorporated business categories, and a general government.
- —Price formation is specified for 39 commodity markets. The clearing price of each market is defined as consumer price minus value-added tax.
- —The model is operated in a deterministic mode without explicit representation of uncertainty, and all fluctuations in, say, yields can only be imposed through exogenous shocks.
- —Consumer demand follows a restricted two-level AIDS-LES specification, with income parameters obtained from cross section estimation, assuming a fixed distribution of income over households within each socioeconomic group. There are 23 subgroups in total.
- —Agricultural supply is described for four farm categories (wetland, dryland, estates, smallholders estates), the landbase of which is adjusted via a land development module. For wetland and dryland yield, input demand and acreage allocation functions were estimated that fit within a net revenue maximizing, nonlinear programming framework, implemented in dual form via land allocation functions. Thus, land balances are met, and inequality constraints, say on input availabilities, can be imposed.
- —For nonagriculture, production capacity develops according to econometrically estimated incremental capital output ratios with sector specific gestation lags and depreciation rates.
- —Labor demand follows via exogenous, but time-dependent, coefficients. Wages are set through functions by sector groups and affect income formation only.

—The model can accommodate inequality constraints and its simultaneous part solves within each year of simulation as a nonlinear complementarity problem.

—Trade and transportation margins are distinguished in production, import, and export of all commodities. Regime switches between import, autarky, and export can occur for commodities that are internationally tradeable. Import and export occur only if they can be operated without a loss.

—Private investment and savings behavior is specified in a simple way, that is, through (not necessarily equal) exogenous rates.

—Foreign trade prices are exogenous, with one exception: rice export f.o.b. price depends on Indonesia's export volume.

—The model is recursively dynamic. Production capacities are set with a lag of at least one year. Capacity utilization is set within the year for services and construction ("IO"-sectors) and with a lag of at least one year for manufacturing and agriculture.

—The balance of payments contains trade in commodities (endogenous), private current and capital flows (endogenous), government debt servicing (lagged), and new government loans (endogenous). Each year the overall closure is obtained by adjusting new public commercial loans from abroad. Bounds on the latter may be introduced. If effective, they require changes in other policy variables that lead, largely through influence on the private sector, to the desired pattern of the endogenous items on the balance of payments. The nominal exchange rate has to be kept exogenous since the model does not include monetary elements.

—Further description is given in the Appendix.

Empirical Basis

An elaborate empirical basis is a particular characteristic of this model. This is a reflection of the cooperation with the Indonesian Central Bureau of Statistics (BPS) as well as of the biases of its authors. In developing this empirical basis three stages may be distinguished: construction of the base year data set, time series analysis, and estimation and calibration. We briefly discuss each stage.

Base-year Data Set
An SAM can be considered to be the natural empirical counterpart of a general equilibrium model for a base year. The SAM provides the picture of the base year; the model shows the development of the economy from the base-year onward.

The 1980 Input-Output table of BPS and the 1980 SAM, constructed in cooperation between BPS and the Institute of Social Studies (ISS), provide the core of the base-year data set for the model. They are described in BPS 1984 and BPS 1986. However, they were not sufficient. Apart from reclassifications, substantial extensions were necessary: commodity volume balances and commodity prices; disaggregation of the corporations account, the balance of payments and the (national) capital account; derivation of investments by sector of destination; and derivation of crop production by land types.

The resulting data set is fully in accordance with model structure and model definitions. Hence, base-year model outcomes should be an exact replication of the base-year data set, provided that all exogenous variables are set at their observed value and that econometrically estimated behavioral functions replicate the base-year observation. Then, statistical work for the base year, specification and estimation of functional relations, and the development of model software can be executed as separate, relatively independent tasks, once the overall model specification has been established. Furthermore, this procedure offers a check on appropriate communication of definitions between model and SAM and of the internal consistency of each of them.

Time-series Analysis and Estimation
A dynamic model that aims at analyzing economic developments cannot be initialized with a base-year data set only. Description of behavior and technology requires time-series analysis. To this end the following additional steps were performed.

—Collection of time-series of government policy variables for the period 1980–88. Direct transformation into policy parameters, year by year, without econometric estimation.
—Construction of time-series of crop production on each land type for the period 1971–83, followed by econometric estimation of the crop decision modules.
—Econometric estimation of the consumer demand system from a cross-section data set of 23 subclasses, hence only using base-year information (time-series was not considered to be sufficiently reliable).
—Construction of time-series of real production and real investment for each of the nonagricultural sectors, period 1975–84, and derivation of technical investment parameters, such as pipelines and scrapping rates.
—Construction of time-series of government investments in cropland and time-series of productive use of cropland, period 1975–87, and derivation of technical investment parameters.

—Construction of time-series of external public borrowing and debt for the period 1980–87, and derivation of initial debt composition and borrowing conditions.

—Construction of time-series of wages and labor productivity for seven aggregated sector groups (food agriculture, estate crops, mining and manufacturing, construction, electricity, private services, and social services) and a time-series of the consumer price index, 1975–86, and econometric estimation of a wage equation for each sector group.

—Construction of time-series of intermediate input costs, paid wage input costs, and output price for each of the IO-sectors, period 1980–86, and econometric estimation of their respective output price functions.

—Specification of trends for exogenous variables.

Calibration

Once the structure of the model is determined, the time patterns of the exogenous variables have been set, and numerical values of the parameters have been obtained, the model can be solved in a recursively dynamic way. The modules listed above can be tested relatively well in a stand-alone way. However, this does not apply to all modules. Some modules contain parameters that are based on only one observation. Furthermore, the interaction between the modules still has to be validated, both within one year and between years. In other words, the performance of the complete model should be tested in a final stage. Formal econometrics does not apply here.

Therefore, a more informal and hence more subjective approach had to be followed. For this, several time-series of endogenous variables (production volumes, trade values, clearing prices, national accounts, balance of payments, and so forth) were collected from available statistics for the period 1981–87 and as far as was possible for 1988. Model outcomes for each of these years were compared with the observations at a fairly detailed level. In performing the calibration runs, the exogenous variables were set at their observed values. Unacceptable differences between outcomes and observations usually led to reconsideration of information at commodity or sector level. This process cannot be documented easily. Decisions depend on the relative strength of various data sources. Some of the more fundamental adjustments were:

—treating a large part of imports of nonfactor services as profit transfer in the balance of payments;

—introducing time-dependency of input-output and employment coefficients;

—introducing time-dependency also in the (behavioral) saving and investment rates; and

—adjusting some estimated parameters of the crop supply module due to observed trends outside the period covered in the estimation process.

This calibration toward an acceptable replication of the past is a time-consuming process. However, it is absolutely necessary as a way to strengthen, or at least test, the empirical basis of the modeling exercise.

Further details on model specification and its empirical elaboration can be found in SOW 1990b.

Scenario Simulations

The Indonesia model was in its original form a purely SAM-based, static AGE, constructed in cooperation with the Central Bureau of Statistics, Jakarta, and the Institute of Social Studies, The Hague (see BPS/ISS/SOW 1986). It gradually developed into a recursively dynamic AGE-model that was used to investigate alternative agricultural policy scenarios on behalf of the Indonesian Central Planning Bureau (see SOW 1988). Recently, an assessment of the process of structural adjustment was performed that made use of the model (see SOW 1990a). In this chapter we perform some further exercises. As it was written by SOW-staff, without direct Indonesian involvement, these new runs should be seen as illustrative only.

The Base Run

The base run is initialized with 1980–88 as calibration period and subsequently solves for the Repelita V period 1989–93.

After 1988, the base run proceeds with assumed patterns for exogenous and policy variables to describe the base scenario. Trade prices and the exchange rate remain at the level of 1988 with an exception for oil. Oil prices are increased in 1989 by 8 percent, leading to a crude export price of 16.75 U.S.$/barrel. Government direct and value-added tax rates increase steadily, as do government consumption and investments. The export subsidy on rice is set at 25 percent. The level of soft loans decreases sharply, partly offset by increased foreign direct investments. Technical input-output coefficients remain largely unaltered. Employment coefficients keep falling, albeit slightly less than before 1987, corresponding to an aggregate employment-output elasticity of around 0.6. Exogenous trends on crop yields grow moderately. Capital goods requirements per unit of increased production capacity are kept constant, except for investments in land, where a 2 percent annual increase is assumed. Annually, an additional 16 thousand hectares or 0.2 percent of wetland are lost to urbanization, as compared to the calibration period. Furthermore, the autonomous trend terms in the wage equations are reduced compared to the estimations for the period before 1987.

The main base run outcomes for the period 1988–93 will be mentioned when discussing the alternative scenarios. For the sake of completeness we mention here that the debt service ratio falls to 0.26 in 1993, according to the usual definition, whereas government tax receipts as a share of GDP at market prices amount to 8.9 percent for corporation taxes, 4.4 percent for household income tax, and 5.9 for net indirect taxes in 1993.

Finally, some worrying features of the base run need to be mentioned:

—Export diversification progressed throughout the historical period and is planned to continue in Repelita V. Nevertheless, if one counts forestry products among the nonrenewable resources, the share of nonrenewables in total exports is still very large. Also, the share of pharmaceuticals (e.g., cosmetics, soap), food industries (e.g., margarine) and chemical products (e.g., car tires) in total exports is smaller than one might expect, given the availability of raw materials to produce these manufactured goods. The growth in estate crops is sustained, but in view of the long gestation lags for these tree crops, this clearly has little to do with policies in recent years.

—The trade surplus is impressive but the fact that Indonesia, in spite of this comfortable position, still has a current account deficit and needs serious efforts to reduce its public foreign debt indicates that there is a problem somewhere else: that is, a sizeable outflow of profits[2] against a modest inflow of private savings from abroad. It then becomes hard to implement a consistent macroeconomic policy. Foreign companies have invested in the past and are still providing technical expertise, in the field of geological exploration for example, and are closely associated to public corporations and private business. They are largely engaged in the exploitation of nonrenewables. This poses a classical dilemma to the Indonesian economic policy:

(1) Are the foreign companies getting too much?

(2) Should they be allowed to move out all these profits?

(3) Is the level of exploitation of the nonrenewable resources desirable in an intergenerational sense? It must also be observed that what is recorded as profit outflow may actually cover a significant amount of private savings by Indonesians who prefer to keep bank ac-

---

2. One should mention that this includes wage remittances by employees of foreign companies.

counts in Singapore in foreign currency rather than in rupiah. According to recent press articles the Indonesian Ministry of Finance estimates these deposits at 20 billion dollars in 1989. It is as if Indonesian government had been borrowing and incurring a debt to compensate for these outflows. This puts some question marks around the policies of relative austerity followed over the past decade.

We cannot further address this issue here due to both a lack of detailed information and also to some weaknesses in the treatment of dynamics. We shall return to this later in the chapter. All we can mention now is the well-known point that for a country with ample nonrenewable resources, a narrow focus on reduction of the level of public foreign debt may lead to over-exploitation of these resources, especially when a large share of the revenue from these resources leaves the country.

A Closer Look at Rice in the Base Run

Against the background of the food policy debate the base run development of supply and demand for rice will be given some further explanation. On the production side, intensified and nonintensified paddies are distinguished. The former grows only on wetland, the latter on both wetland and dryland. The actual production volume on each land type is determined in competition with other crops, depending on relative profitabilities. Production plans are formulated one year in advance and assumed to be realized. The amount of available wetland and dryland depends on government investments and on annual losses due to urbanization and industrialization. The effects of increased cropping intensity are treated as changes in available land. Yields per hectare are largely exogenous, but there is some endogenous influence from the crop allocation process. Standard assumptions are made for the conversion factor from paddy to milled rice, as well as for seed use, feed use, and waste percentages. Consumption, stock changes, and foreign trade are treated at the level of milled rice, without distinction between intensified and nonintensified. Foreign trade prices are exogenous, based on observations, with the qualification that export price is assumed to fall when export exceeds a given threshold (see the Appendix for further details). The average CIF-FOB margin amounts to 30 percent. Government's pricing policy, which is in reality implemented through stock changes, is represented as a tariff policy. Stock changes are exogenous. Thus the pricing aspects of stockholding are covered adequately, but the link between price policy and the costs of its implementation is missing. During the calibration period both tariff rates and stock changes are set at observed values. From 1980 through 1984 imports are actual. On average they are subject to a subsidy of 5 percent. In 1985 and 1986 imports are prohibited, whereas exports are subsidized by 50 percent. In each year the foreign trade regime and volume are derived endogenously.

The base run results obtained in this way give a fairly realistic overall picture of the rice market in the years 1980 through 1986. Since then yield growth stagnated and a drought occurred in 1987. The stagnation is implemented in the base run since it is considered to have structural effects, but drought is not. Correspondingly, stock changes are kept small, contrary to reality, and government's willingness to support exports is assumed to be continued after 1986, albeit at lower subsidy rates. These rates gradually fall to 25 percent in 1989, whereas the import tariff rate is lowered to 10 percent (import ban lifted). Then, the base run production figure for 1988 amounts to 26.8 million tons of milled rice (net of seed), which is well below the generally used production estimate of 28.3 million tons (including seed). After 1988 it increases by 3.2 percent annually. This exceeds the minimum rate of 2.8 percent mentioned earlier. Average consumption increases gradually up to 136 kg per capita per year in 1993 (net of waste), starting from a level of 132 kg in 1987. This is in accordance with BPS-estimates (see Ellis 1988, 10). In each year a moderate net export volume results, increasing from 244,000 tons in 1987 to 685,000 tons in 1993. Exports would be much higher had the high production estimate been used for 1988.

Given the inconsistencies among the published statistics, it would be quite simple to adjust the base run parameters so as to have exports disappear. Exports are the result of the difference between two large, but more or less equal, values of production and consumption and alter considerably when one of the flows is adjusted only slightly. However, adjustments in waste or in the conversion rate would be unjustified, given the performance in reproducing import and export flows over the calibration period.

Rice Self-sufficiency Runs

Because rice is a main staple food in Indonesia, the policy of maintaining a secure availability of rice, at reasonably stable prices, may be understood as a means to avoid hardship for the poor urban population. To ensure this via imports may be costly, especially due to the thinness of the international rice market. Also, an export orientation for rice may be difficult due to the lack of an outlet. Thus, a policy focus on rice self-sufficiency may seem reasonable as long as it is handled in an undogmatic way. Import bans in years of shortage, and refusal to pay export subsidies in years of surplus, may lead to large fluctuations in prices or otherwise require unnecessarily elaborate stockpiling programs. We shall illustrate this with some simulation runs performed for the years 1989–93.

TABLE 1. Main Outcomes of Alternative Rice Self-sufficiency Runs Compared to the Base Run

	BASE RUN	NO RICESUBS	WET LOSS	RICE STAG	CROP FAIL	FAIL AND SUBS
1. Medium and long-term debt outstanding and disbursed, beginning of year 1993 (Rp. billions)*	76,283	75,990	76,285	76,659	77,305	76,981
2. Trade surplus, goods and non-factor services, 1993 (Rp. billions)	12,508	12,746	12,536	12,287	12,535	12,542
3. Net profit outflow to abroad, 1993 (Rp. billions)	8,320	8,329	8,314	8,286	8,318	8,319
4. GDP at 1980-factor costs (average annual % growth, 1988-1993)	4.69	4.69	4.63	4.51	4.69	4.69
5. Value added at 1980-factor costs (Rp. billions), 1993:						
agriculture	17,417	17,397	17,322	17,136	17,416	17,416
manufacturing	13,036	13,039	12,996	12,904	13,033	13,035
construction	4,159	4,158	4,149	4,129	4,157	4,159
mining	14,261	14,264	14,261	14,255	14,260	14,261
services	32,792	32,788	32,697	32,531	32,779	32,783
Total	81,666	81,647	81,425	80,955	81,646	81,655
6. Total employment (thousand manyears), 1993	80,620	80,583	80,237	79,502	80,596	80,606

7. Real per capita income (class-wise deflators), '000 Rp, 1980-prices), 1993:						
agric. labourers	165.8	166.2	165.0	163.0	165.7	165.7
agric. operators	186.9	184.3	185.9	187.5	186.9	186.9
non-agric. rural low income	207.5	208.7	206.8	203.6	207.4	207.4
non-agric. rural high income	296.4	296.9	295.5	292.9	296.3	296.3
non-agric. urban low income	402.5	403.6	401.3	397.8	402.3	402.4
non-agric. urban high income	1,160.0	1,163.6	1,157.1	1,146.2	1,159.5	1,159.7
Total population	301.4	301.3	300.3	298.3	301.3	301.4
8. GINI-coefficient, 1993	.32	.32	.32	.31	.32	.32
9. Rice production ('000 MT), 1993	31,408	31,366	30,946	29,436	31,416	31,412
10. Net rice imports ('000 MT), 1993	-685	-	-267	-	-689	-683
11. Rice price (domestic clearing, Rp/kg), 1993	450	420	450	500	450	450
12. Rice consumption (kg/cap./year), net of waste, 1993:						
rural population	129.7	132.4	129.5	124.5	129.8	129.7
urban population	156.8	160.9	156.8	148.8	156.9	157.0
Total population	136.0	138.9	135.8	130.1	136.0	136.0
13. Calory intake (Kcal/cap./day), 1993:						
rural population	2,478	2,493	2,473	2,436	2,478	2,478
urban population	3,023	3,049	3,022	2,969	3,023	3,024
Total population	2,604	2,620	2,599	2,558	2,604	2,604

*Exchange rate: 1US$ = 1681 Rupiah

The runs are primarily meant to test the effects of policy changes, parametric variations, and weather shocks on the rice trade regime, but at the same time the consequences for growth, employment, income distribution, nutritional intake, and external debt are considered. The alternative scenarios contain several elements of the Indonesian food policy debate described earlier: pricing policy, loss of land, investment in land improvement, yield stagnation, sudden crop failures, and crop diversification. They are formulated as follows:

NO RICESUBS: The export subsidy on rice is abolished from 1990 onward. In the base run it amounts to 25 percent. The question posed is: could exports still be profitable in the absence of a subsidy and if not, would this seriously destabilize the rice market?

WET LOSS: The base run has an extra annual wetland loss of 16,000 hectares, starting in 1989. In the WET LOSS–scenario the additional annual loss is increased from 16,000 to 48,000 hectares, from 1990 onward. This could alternatively be interpreted as a decrease of 25 percent in the effectivity of government investment in wetland from 1988 onward, compared to the preceding period. Now the question posed is: to what extent would the loss undermine rice self-sufficiency?

RICE STAG: The yield per hectare of intensified paddy stagnates in 1990: the average annual growth rate in the period 1989–93 equals zero percent, compared to 2 percent in the base run. As in the previous scenario the question posed is whether this would undermine self-sufficiency and how this compares with loss of land.

CROP FAIL: A single, general crop failure in 1990 reduces the yields per hectare of all crops on all types of land by 5 percent compared to the base run. After 1990 yields equal the base run levels again. Here the question is: should self-sufficiency be adhered to also after crop failure or should imports be subsidized, as is done in the following scenario?

FAIL AND SUBS: The same crop failure happens in 1990 as in CROP FAIL, but now accompanied by an import subsidy on rice of 15 percent (instead of the import tax of 10 percent, as in the base run). Thus government maintains the same domestic price level as in the base run. Evidently, the export subsidy is cancelled now. After 1990 subsidy rates are back to base run level.

Tables 1 and 2 contain the main outcomes of base run and alternative self-sufficiency scenarios. First, some general features are described. Then, each run will be discussed briefly.

In the absence of climatic variation, the self-sufficiency pattern for rice is

TABLE 2. Main Outcomes for 1990 of Crop Failure Runs Compared to the Base Run

	BASE RUN	CROP FAIL	FAIL AND SUBS
1. Medium and long-term debt outstanding and disbursed, beginning of year 1990 (Rp. billions)*	74,648	74,648	74,648
2. Trade surplus, goods and non-factor services, 1990 (Rp. billions)	9,577	8,490	8,902
3. Net profit outflow to abroad, 1990 (Rp. billions)	7,322	7,245	7,270
4. GDP at 1980-factor costs (average annual % growth, 1988-1990)	4.21	3.21	3.25
5. Value added at 1980-factor costs (Rp. billions), 1990:			
agriculture	15,555	14,977	14,949
manufacturing	11,079	10,930	10,930
construction	3,514	3,501	3,484
mining	12,565	12,565	12,565
services	27,800	27,188	27,286
Total	70,514	69,160	69,214
6. Total employment (thousand manyears), 1990	73,147	70,908	70,948
7. Real per capita income (class-wise deflators, '000 Rp, 1980-prices), 1990:			
agric. labourers	152.5	145.7	147.1
agric. operators	174.4	177.8	170.9
non-agric. rural low income	198.2	189.3	193.1
non-agric. rural high income	281.6	274.0	275.8
non-agric. urban low income	379.7	370.4	373.4
non-agric. urban high income	1,093.9	1,061.8	1,073.8
Total population	280.9	275.0	274.9
8. GINI-coefficient, 1990	0.32	0.30	0.32
9. Rice production ('000 MT), 1990	28,520	27,094	27,094
10. Net rice imports ('000 MT), 1990	-150	-	1,241
11. Rice price (domestic clearing, Rp/kg), 1990	450	530	450
12. Rice consumption (kg/cap./year), net of waste, 1990:			
rural population	127.7	122.1	127.2
urban population	155.5	147.2	156.7
Total population	133.9	127.7	133.8
13. Calory intake (Kcal/cap./day), 1990:			
rural population	2,434	2,382	2,405
urban population	2,987	2,926	2,981
Total population	2,558	2,504	2,534

*Exchange rate: 1US$ = 1681 Rupiah

rather stable. There are no wild shifts from imports to exports. Domestic price movements perform a stabilizing role, generally within acceptable bounds. Only in a year of crop failure would imports be necessary to prevent the domestic price from exceeding the zero import tariff level, which amounts to 520 Rp/kg. On the other hand, subsidies are necessary to make exports profitable. Otherwise, autarky results and the domestic price declines.

Income distribution effects are relatively small. To explain this, one may argue that the shocks, although directed at the heart of the rural economy, are rather moderate, but it is also a sign of the operation of stabilizing forces in the economy: substitution possibilities for producers (crops) and consumers (food), and wage increases to meet rice price increases. Furthermore, for agricultural laborers and operators, rice is important both on the earnings side (18 and 30 percent of value added, respectively), and on the expenditure side (25 and 23 percent of total consumption, respectively). However, when discussing effects on income distribution one should note that the classification of the population shown here is crude. This applies especially to the class of agricultural operators, which includes more than 70 million people with a wide variation within the class. Even a fall in calorie intake of 5 percent could be very severe for a considerable number of these people.

Effects on trade surplus and external public debt are not large. Nevertheless, although small in size, they are interesting due to a subtle interplay of several factors, such as changes in crop production, real income effects in consumption, substitution effects in consumption, and adjusted growth of IO production sectors leading to changes in their intermediate demand. Hence, overall effects on trade surplus are sometimes surprising. Thus, abolition of the rice export subsidy or withdrawal of the rice import ban both lead to increased trade surpluses (in spite of their immediate effect) due to demand changes implied by the lower rice prices.

We now turn to a brief separate discussion of the outcomes of each scenario.

NO RICESUBS
Abolition of the rice export subsidy implies that rice exports are no longer profitable. The rice market enters autarky and the domestic rice price declines, but the fall is not dramatic. Nutritional intake improves. Real income increases for all classes, except for agricultural operators. In spite of vanishing rice exports, trade surplus and the external debt situation improve due to substitution effects in consumption. Growth in agriculture is hardly influenced; there is a small diversification away from rice. The cumulated sum of vanishing rice exports over 1989 through 1993 equals approximately 1.7 million tons. It seems that under the assumptions made, which are modest

with respect to increases in the rice yield, the economy could do without the subsidy.

WET LOSS

Effects of the extra loss of wetland are rather straightforward and relatively small. They can be seen to produce a modest contraction. Agricultural growth decreases somewhat, rice production slightly more due to its prevalence on wetland. Some contraction of production by IO sectors follows. Real income of each class falls somewhat, but this is hardly observable in nutritional intake. Rice remains an export regime because the supply shortfall is partly matched by a drop in income and demand.

RICE STAG

Stagnation of rice yields has far more severe effects. The yield of intensified paddy in 1993 is 4.38 metric ton per hectare as compared to 4.73 tons in the base run. Hence rice production is severely hit and ends 2 million tons below the base run level. As a consequence, rice exports disappear and domestic prices increase considerably. This price increase prevents farmers from switching to other crops (paddy acreage even increases slightly in spite of the yield stagnation) and hence mitigates the fall in production. Rice consumption in 1993 declines by 4.5 percent but substitution in food consumption reduces the nutritional effect to 1.8 percent. The reduction in agricultural growth leads to lower growth in manufacturing (rice milling) and construction and services (demand-driven contraction). In 1993 the resulting total employment is 1.5 percent below the base run. Nominal incomes are uniformly higher, but real income of all classes falls with the exception of agricultural operators. The latter is even reflected in an improvement of the crude six-class GINI-measure. Mixed foreign trade effects result in increased external debt, albeit moderately. Thus, in the medium term, maintaining yield growth seems to be of higher importance than avoiding losses of land. Unfortunately, this cannot be expected to hold true in the long run. Urbanization is irreversible ("asphalt is the land's last crop") while agricultural yield may catch up later. Also, further yield increase may be undesirable from an environmental point of view.

CROP FAIL

The crop failure in 1990 implies a severe shock in that year. Agricultural production, with consequences for nonagriculture, and nutritional intake are substantially lowered. Rice comes in autarky with substantial price increases. However, the prices of most other food crops also increase for this reason. The consumer price index rises by 8 percent. Wages and nominal incomes rise also, but real incomes are lower for all classes except the agricultural operators. Trade surplus declines markedly. After 1990 most effects disappear. In 1991 there are still some consequences of crop substitution by farmers, generating one more year of rice autarky but with a hardly increased price. Prices of service sectors and wages also return to base run levels. Hence, with the exception of increased public external debt due to the higher 1990 trade deficit, there are no permanent consequences. Although revenue shortfalls in the private sector lead to reduced private investment, this appears to have been largely compensated by public investment, with a higher debt.

FAIL AND SUBS

The government's decision to keep the 1990 rice prices equal to the base run level through subsidized imports necessitates an import volume of more than 1.2 million tons. Stable rice prices also reduce the pressure on consumption of other food crops, which implies that for them price increases are also mitigated. Hence, the advantage for agricultural operators disappears. Now they also are worse off than in the base run. Production of the service sectors improves compared to the CROP FAIL run, arising from improved real incomes as well as from trade and transportation requirements of the rice imports. In spite of this, the 1990 trade surplus is higher than in the crop failure run without rice subsidy. Again, this is caused by substitutions in consumption that save demand for commodities with a higher ratio of border to retail value than imported rice. After 1990 the effects of the shock disappear with the exception of increased public external debt, which ends at a level between the base run and the CROP FAIL run. This experiment suggests that an import subsidy would be desirable in years of sudden shortfall, unless rice can be procured from available stocks.

While reiterating the qualifications on the validity of the model, we summarize the outcomes from the five scenarios in three points:

—Loss of wetland has in the medium term less negative impact than stagnation of rice yield.
—Rice imports are only required in years of crop failure when stock levels are inadequate; then they should be subsidized.
—The subsidy on rice export may be unnecessary and costly in the long run. The prevailing level of crop diversification and the crop substitution possibilities away from rice seem to offer sufficient alternatives for the farmers as a whole to mitigate the impact of a falling rice price. However, some farm groups with less alternatives might be hurt badly, but the model is too aggregated to show this at present.

Trade Liberalization with Improved Competition
on the Domestic Market

Food is not the only preoccupation of economic policy in Indonesia. Fiscal restructuring and the development and diversification of exports have received even more attention in the recent past. This is also reflected in the current Five-Year Plan. The heavy dependence on oil revenues in the 1970s, followed by a drop in oil prices in the early 1980s, has forced Indonesian economic policies into this direction. The general policy may be summarized as one that aims at reducing distortions in the economy. It has already been partly implemented, as reflected in the base run. Here we view possible consequences of further steps, in particular on the food demand situation. With respect to deregulation we confine ourselves to liberalization of domestic and foreign trade in commodities and must disregard financial reform. We specify two scenarios.

FLATTAX

First, we study further fiscal reforms by reducing tariffs and subsidies on international trade as well as excise taxes, compensating the revenue loss by a further increase in value added at a flat rate tax so as to maintain the base level public debt at the end of the plan. More specifically we specify from 1990 onward:

> —25 percent per year reduction in tariffs and subsidies on international trade (except for refined oil and cement where the export subsidies actually reflect transfer pricing);
> —30 percent per year reduction of excise tax except for tobacco products;
> —.0075 extra increase of value added tax each year;
> —50 percent annual reduction in producer subsidies on rice, wheat products, and fertilizer.

COMPETE

In the second scenario, we add a reduction of nontariff barriers and features of improved competition to the changes in tariffs and taxation. These may need some further discussion.

The nontariff barriers (cf. Fane and Phillips 1987) can include a quota rent as well as a monopoly premium on licenses. The quota rent is present, even under competitive conditions, as long as the quota (license) is binding with respect to volume. If the licenses were auctioned by the government, then the rent would accrue to government. Otherwise, it accrues to the holder of the license. However, when there is no free auction, the license is assigned to selected traders only, who may gain monopoly power via it. Thus, the license has two aspects: who gets it and how much may be imported under it? Increasing the import quota may not lead to increased imports when the ownership of licenses is heavily concentrated, as the traders may wish to maintain their monopolistic rent.

In Indonesia the licenses are heavily concentrated and a policy of deregulation would require open auctioning or abolition of these licenses.[3] To reflect this in the model, rather than imposing import quotas and obtaining a rent via market clearing prices, there are price wedges via trade margins on imports. However, as the licenses operate on very specific commodities, it is not possible to measure them precisely at a relatively aggregate level as distinct from other margins due to true costs of trading.

Also, within the country with its huge geographical spread, marketing margins are far from competitive. Again, although the rent aspect cannot be distinguished from the cost aspect at the aggregate level, improved competition can be expected to reduce these margins. This leads to the following scenario, in addition to FLATTAX:

—All intermediate demand coefficients for trade services are reduced by 2 percent annually.
—Trade margins on imports and exports are also reduced by 2 percent annually.[4]
—For categories with nontariff barriers an additional reduction of 3 percent in trade margins is imposed (rice, wheat, estate crops, basic metals, metal products).

Outcomes are summarized for 1993 in table 3. On the tariff side, it must first be mentioned that (formal) tariffs are already relatively modest in the base run. They constitute less than five percent of government receipts, in contrast to many other developing countries where tariffs are not only used to affect domestic prices, but also, and often mainly, to generate public revenue. Tariffs are mainly imposed on the import of chemicals and metal products and on the export of plywood. Thus, a reduction of tariffs is relatively easy from a budgetary point of view.

---

3. To this one might object that the licenses are required to cover the increasing returns to scale in trade: organize the marketing channels, collect information on the international market, and so forth, but even then government could limit itself to subsidies on these setup costs.

4. We observe that, had foreign and domestic goods been treated as heterogeneous in the traditional Armington way, there would have been no trade margin to reduce.

TABLE 3. Main Outcomes of Flat Tax and Compete Run Compared to the Base Run

	BASE RUN	Absolute differences from base run	
		FLATTAX	COMPETE
1. Medium and long-term debt outstanding and disbursed, beginning of year 1993 (Rp. billions)*	76,283	-25	-386
2. Trade surplus, goods and non-factor services, 1993 (Rp. billions)	12,508	793	1,149
3. Net profit outflow to abroad, 1993 (Rp. billions)	8,320	129	153
4. GDP at 1980-factor costs (average annual % growth, 1988-1993)	4.69	0.07	0.02
5. Value added at 1980-factor costs (Rp. billions), 1993:			
agriculture	17,417	6	155
manufacturing	13,036	45	523
construction	4,159	31	8
mining	14,261	49	72
services	32,792	129	-702
Total	81,666	258	56
6. Total employment (thousand manyears), 1993	80,620	140	-886
7. Real per capita income (class-wise deflators, '000 Rp, 1980-prices), 1993:			
agric. labourers	165.8	-3.0	-3.0
agric. operators	186.9	-0.8	0.1
non-agric. rural low income	207.5	-3.3	-5.6
non-agric. rural high income	296.4	-5.5	-7.8
non-agric. urban low income	402.5	-5.8	-11.4
non-agric. urban high income	1,160.0	9.0	4.4
Total population	301.4	-2.0	-3.6
8. GINI-coefficient, 1993	.32	0	0
9. Rice production ('000 MT), 1993	31,408	-78	-80
10. Net rice imports ('000 MT), 1993	-685	685	685
11. Rice price (domestic clearing, Rp/kg), 1993	450	-40	-50
12. Rice consumption (kg/cap./year), net of waste, 1993:			
rural population	129.7	2.5	2.6
urban population	156.8	3.7	3.3
Total population	136.0	2.7	2.7
13. Calory intake (Kcal/cap./day), 1993:			
rural population	2,478	1	0
urban population	3,023	8	-3
Total population	2,604	1	-2

*Exchange rate: 1US$ = 1681 Rupiah

Excise tax is mainly levied on tobacco products and trade services. There is a producer subsidy on rice (one percent only), wheat products, and fertilizer. Reduction of fertilizer subsidies is effectuated already in the base run, so that a gradual replacement of excise by value-added tax in the FLATTAX-run largely amounts to a reduction of the excise on trade services compensated by a flat value-added tax, that is, a tax on consumption. This change in indirect tax rates reduces the clearing price for imported goods. On the export side the effect is the opposite. These effects are reinforced by the tariff cuts (unless tariffs are negative, as in the case of rice exports). Thus, the impact on clearing prices is diverse. Furthermore, reduction of excise on trade services raises producer prices relative to clearing prices because trade margins fall. It also appears to contribute to a modest reduction of prices in the IO-sectors. This reinforces the fall in trade and transportation costs. The fact that producer prices come closer to border level implies that the export orientation is promoted, so that in the longer run growth may increase. For the consumer, the extra income is in part taxed away via the increased value-added tax.

This reduction in trade margins and input costs is promoted further when the trade requirements are reduced in the COMPETE-run, in part to reflect informal tariffs. However, such a reduction also leads to a fall in value added in the service sector, with multiplier effects to other sectors. Still, the COMPETE-scenario can be seen as a further step in the direction of deregulation. The trade surplus shows a noticeable increase; terminal debt is lower but part of the benefits is lost via a profit outflow.

Both scenarios appear to be employer-oriented over the period of simulation. All the classes, except the urban rich and agricultural operators, lose due to price change, and in the COMPETE-scenario due to the cut in trade services. Corporations gain. Overall growth improvement is modest. Still, it is interesting to see that in the FLATTAX-scenario, all value-added aggregates rise and that this rise is even more pronounced in the COMPETE-scenario, except, of course, for the service (trade) sector. It must be recognized that this is in part due to the method of calculation of value added at constant prices in relation to the scenario specification. Had a reduction in trade margins been implemented fully via a reduction in the price of the trade service, rather than a reduction in intermediate demand volume, then the value added at constant 1980 prices would have been affected much less, as trade service price would have kept its 1980 value. Now the fall in the intermediate requirement for trade services is immediately reflected in value added at constant prices.

Employment effects reflect these changes in sectoral growth rates. One may recall that within a sector the model has no endogenous substitution between factors of production. However, demand for four types of labor is distinguished in each of the 64 sectors, described by time-dependent coefficients to represent increases in labor productivity. Hence, differences in sectoral growth rates lead, on the aggregate, to substitution between labor types. Thus, the base run shows higher growth rates for clerical, professional, and managerial labor than for agricultural and manual labor. In the liberalization runs the changes in this pattern are modest, at least in the (relatively short) period under consideration. In the COMPETE-run they are even dominated by the loss of employment in the trade sector.

The reduction in export subsidies appears to make rice exports unprofitable in both runs, in spite of a fall in the export trade margin. Also, the price of rice falls deeper in the second run but this is mainly attributable to a general reduction in marketing costs and purchasing power. Rice consumption improves and is about the same in both runs but calorie consumption is worsened in the COMPETE-scenario as compared to the base run. This is largely attributable to the drop in real incomes of most classes combined with a rise in the price of exported foods—corn, cassava and tubers, estate crops, fish—relative to nonfood.

To summarize, again with due qualification, we conclude that the impacts shown in the FLATTAX and the COMPETE-run are nondramatic but that they do point to a conflict between consumer interests and balance of payments objectives, at least in the short run. In the longer run the combination of increased investments and reduced external debt will benefit all classes. The effects may even be larger than is shown by the straightforward extension of the model runs after 1993, due to aspects of flexibility not contained in the model. It was already mentioned that there is no endogenous factor substitution within a sector. It must also be admitted that changes in profitability have no direct effect on utilization rates and investment allocation. However, a numerical assessment of such phenomena is extremely difficult, and one should warn against excessive optimism in this respect. Observed rigidities must be explained first.

In Indonesia the current share of consumption in GDP amounts to about 70 percent only. Clearly, there is a foreign debt and a public finance problem, but this is hardly attributable to excessive consumption since a comfortable trade surplus has been there for quite some time now. Therefore there seems to be little economic justification to have the consumer pay the price of further deregulation, not even in the short run. In the past the rice self-sufficiency policy has contributed to consumer welfare in a spectacular way. In the near future food policy may have to emphasize employment issues.

In fact, the impact on food demand of the deregulation scenarios is more pronounced than the impact of direct shocks on food supply in most of the self-sufficiency scenarios. This does not suggest, let alone prove, that they are more important, but it does illustrate the importance of looking at food policy in a broader context.

Limitations of Current Specification and Orientation
for Further Research

It may be fair to say that the present model formulation is best suited to study the impact of relatively small changes in current government policy. The model is thought to be descriptive. The policy variants that are investigated can at best be seen to be more or less realistic attempts to improve welfare during the period of simulation. This immediately has two implications. First, in successful runs welfare is improved but not necessarily maximized over the period of simulation. Second, welfare implications that reach beyond 1993 are disregarded. In particular the intertemporal efficiency of the investment and production plans is questionable.

This is particularly relevant for Indonesia, which derives a major share of its export receipts from nonrenewable resources and forestry, so that resource depletion may be a serious issue. Also, in Indonesian agriculture any major productivity increase can be expected to require significant investment in irrigation, agricultural processing, and infrastructure, which are to a large extent public investments with relatively long gestation lags. The model in its present form is not suited for such long-run analysis, not only because it lacks a mechanism to select investment projects in an intertemporally efficient manner but also because these projects themselves are not described with sufficient accuracy. This would be a priority for further model development for which initial steps have been taken (cf. van den Boom 1989; Keyzer 1991). In that context it will be necessary to regionally disaggregate agricultural production. Such a research project currently is being prepared in cooperation with the Centre for Agro-economic Research in Bogor.

There are many other limitations as well, dealing with which would require improving of the empirical content of the model: more complete data sets, replacing shifters on parameters by estimated functions, a more endogenous treatment of substitution and utilization rates in the nonagricultural sector, the study of externalities such as increasing returns to scale, more detail on employment and education, and so on. These are directions for further work. We conclude with some remarks on a general point that we would like to submit for discussion.

Empirically based AGE models have generated criticism by the theoretical GE-modelers and by the applied policy analysts as well. The theoretician prefers to make a clean-and-tidy model for which clear theorems, say on turnpike properties, can be derived. The policy analyst often feels more comfortable in a partial, issue-oriented study in which the data collected relate directly to the issue at hand. Three alternative consequences may be drawn from this: either stop AGE modeling, keep it oriented to a single purpose, or go on along a more multipurpose track. We propose to go on and would like to motivate this as follows:

(a) An economywide model may be useful either as a background or as an integral part of a more narrowly focused study, although many issues will require specialized empirical and analytical work that do not need to be incorporated within an economywide model and cannot be in a balanced way.

(b) The empirically based AGE-model is a workable kind of economywide model with definite advantages.

(c) Such an AGE-model must possess multipurpose features. Economics as an integrative discipline should avoid producing a different model for every question. Moreover, the primary objective of economywide modeling should be to draw a realistic and theoretically understandable picture of the economy under consideration. Therefore, if the model is to be more than an illustration of the preconceptions of its authors and allow rejection of hypotheses, it should be empirically based. Finally, it is unrealistic to expect that economywide models will be fully tailored to deal with specific issues and at the same time have a solid empirical basis. Issues change over time, and the time and manpower required to provide a solid empirical basis for an economywide model will often mean that a model designed to serve a single question will be outdated when it reaches maturity.

The need is for comprehensive models which have a variable focus, that permit focus on a topic in the foreground as well as in the background. Therefore, we submit that AGE-modeling should be an ongoing activity of improving empirical and methodological underpinnings of a standard, multipurpose version. Special policy questions may require adjustment and refinement of this standard version, but they should not guide its overall design. Due to its ongoing nature, the activity should be institutionalized at the national level. Expatriate researchers could have an initiating, innovative, and supporting role, but they should minimize their involvement in day-to-day use, maintenance, and improvement of the model, once it has been set up. Unfortunately, we are far from such an ideal state of affairs.

APPENDIX: CHARACTERISTICS OF THE MODEL

Classifications

Agents

The model distinguishes six socioeconomic classes, two incorporated business classes, and the general government. Agricultural population is subdivided into households of operators and of laborers. The nonagricultural population is classified by job level for rural and urban areas. On the consumption side, income is allocated in fixed proportions to subclasses within each class. There are 23 subclasses in total. Population growth is specified exogenously for each class. Public corporations and foreign companies are treated as separate agents. Private domestic incorporated business is included in the urban high-level socioeconomic class. Government comprises both central government, local governments, the Bank Indonesia, and the state logistics agency BULOG.

Commodities

Thirty-nine commodities are distinguished. They are considered to be homogeneous, irrespective of origin or destination. Import and export processing margins generate price wedges between foreign and domestic levels. Commonly used quantity units are chosen, such as rice in metric tons, electricity in gigawatt hours, and plywood in cubic meters. Foreign origin is not a sufficient criterion for a commodity to be classified as a separate commodity.

A distinction is made between IO and non-IO commodities. For IO commodities there is limited possibility for stock building and foreign trade. Their supply adjusts fully, within capacity bounds in the corresponding sector, to changes in demand. IO commodities can also be seen as demand-driven commodities. The concept typically applies to services and construction. Non-IO commodities cannot be produced with perfect elasticity. In the present model version, their production is set with a lag of at least one year.

Production Sectors

There are sixty-four sectors. Each sector produces one commodity, hence some sectors produce the same commodity. The IO concept also applies to sectors. There is a single IO sector per IO commodity. For the 17 crop sectors a further disaggregation is made according to four land types (smallholder wetland with seasonal crops, smallholder dryland with seasonal crops, estate land, smallholder land with permanent crops). There is no regional disaggregation.

Labor

Labor is classified by type of occupation: agricultural, manual, clerical/sales, and professional/managerial. Paid and unpaid labor are shown separately.

Operation of the Model

The model possesses a recursively dynamic structure. Two components can be distinguished: an exchange component and a dynamic adjustment component. Both components take each others' results as given. After the exchange process of year t, the dynamic adjustment is executed resulting in updated variables for $t + 1$. Then the exchange process of $t + 1$ can start.

The dynamic adjustment component contains capacity updates for sectors and land types, sectoral production plans assumed to be realized for non-IO sectors, and other updates like population and external debt.

The exchange component consists of several simultaneous processes with major elements:

—private and public consumption and investment demand
—confrontation of supply and demand
—price formation, simultaneously under the influence of government policies and exogenous trade prices
—determination of wages
—income formation
—determination of production volume of IO sectors and foreign trade volume of non-IO commodities.

Production

Production Volumes

Quantities produced are determined separately for each sector and then mapped to the corresponding commodity. The mapping may include a unit conversion. Determination of the production volumes of IO sectors was already discussed above: as an adjustment, within capacity bounds, to changes in demand. For non-IO sectors there is a lag: production volumes are planned one year in advance, and plans are assumed to be realized.

Five types of non-IO sectors are being distinguished: crops, crop processing, specialized construction, sectors with exogenous capacity utilization, and sectors with production on trend. Production of seasonal crops is represented through land allocation modules for smallholder wetland and smallholder dryland separately. Crop decisions are related to net revenue expectations per crop and land availability. Yields per hectare depend on an exogenous trend that is modified by the land allocation pattern reflecting decreasing returns under specialization. On estate land and on smallholder land with permanent crops the crop allocation and yield are not described by competition between crops. Both follow an exogenous pattern depending on trends and on land availabilities. Production levels of crop processing sectors are determined by crop production. Output of specialized construction sectors (public works in agriculture, public infrastructural works) are directly linked to real government investment targets. Most manufacturing sectors have an exogenous utilization rate. The sectors with production on trend are inland fishery, firewood, and livestock (excluding poultry, which is treated as IO-sector).

Intermediate Demand and Employment

Intermediate input of commodities into each production sector is described through fixed quantity coefficients of the Leontief-type that follow trends. The same applies to labor use that is described through time-dependent sectoral demand coefficients for each of the eight labor types. In the crop module, only fertilizer demand is specified separately by land type as a function of yield.

Capacity Expansion

A distinction must be made between investments in cropland and investments in other sectors. For the latter both government and nongovernment investments increase sectoral production capacity. This is specified via fixed commodity requirements per unit of sectoral expansion and a fixed gestation lag. No basic distinction is made between the effects of government and nongovernment investments, even though the composition of commodity requirements is different. For each sector and each year an incremental capital-output ratio (ICOR) can be calculated by applying the prevailing prices. Due to price changes the ICOR's need not be constant over time. An annually fixed, sector-specific percentage of the existing production capacity is being scrapped.

Available cropland is influenced only through government investments. Nongovernment investments are assumed to be complementary. They have an effect only on demand for investment commodities and do not lead to extra available land. Government investments are specified separately for each of the four land types. Productive capacity of a land type is represented through the number of productive hectare months per year (one productive hectare month = productive use of one hectare for one month). This concept incorporates both land expansion and increases of cropping intensity. Using this concept the technical aspects of government investment in a land type are set analogously to other government investments: fixed commodity requirement per unit of increase in productive capacity, fixed gestation lag, and fixed scrap factor.

Revenue

Income from Production

When all prices are known, gross value added of a sector can be calculated by subtracting the retail value of intermediate inputs from the farmgate/ex-factory value of output. Paid wage rates are distinguished for each sector and occupation. For seven aggregated sectors a wage equation is specified that explains changes in wages from changes in the consumer price index, sectoral deflators, and real sectoral labor productivity. Detailed sectoral and occupational wages follow the pattern of the relevant sector group. Total wage payments are allocated with fixed, constant shares to the socioeconomic classes. These shares are only occupation specific, not sector specific. This specification was opted to reflect the noncompetitive features of the Indonesian labor market, where the share of paid-wage employment is relatively small and wages tend to fluctuate more or less with sectoral income. The remaining value added, which includes unpaid wages, is treated as entrepreneurial income and allocated to the socioeconomic classes with constant, sector-specific shares.

Remaining Income Items

Education and health subsidies, workers-remittances from abroad, and domestic transfers are represented exogenously for each agent, though indexed endogenously.

Final Demand and Savings

Nongovernment Consumption and Savings

Savings are specified as a fixed share of income (excluding education and health subsidies). Profit flows to abroad are treated the same way. For the incorporated business classes their savings rates and rates of profit flow add to one. For the socioeconomic classes the sum is well below one: the difference is the private consumption expenditure. Within each socioeconomic class, each subclass derives its consumption demand (for 27 consumable commodities) from utility maximization, given the total available budget and the commodity retail prices. The decision process is described at two levels. First, total expenditures are allocated to five commodity groups with an almost ideal demand system (AIDS), then group totals are further allocated to expenditures on the individual commodities with a linear expenditure system (LES). Since the population sizes of the classes and nutritional contents of the commodities are known, the outcomes can be used to calculate nutritional indicators like calorie and protein intake per caput per day.

Nongovernment Investment Behavior

Investment outlays of socioeconomic classes and incorporated business is modeled through fixed shares of income that are specified separately for each production sector in which the class invests. Changes in stocks are set exogenously. Net capital outflows to abroad, which may be negative, are represented like profit flows, savings, and investments, that is, through fixed shares of income.

Government Behavior

Public consumption is specified by commodity, investment by sector, direct tax through actor-specific rates (separately for household and corporation tax), and indirect taxes through commodity-specific rates. Government stock changes are specified exogenously and price policies are implemented through (ad-valorem) tariff rates on foreign trade. Monetary policies are not included. The exchange rate is exogenous. External public medium and long-term debt are recorded each year separately for soft and hard debt, each distinguished by maturity, interest rate, and dollar-yen composition. Hence, interest and amortization obligations follow endogenously. The annual amount of new soft loans is exogenous, whereas new hard loans are determined residually. Changes in foreign reserves are exogeneous. Bounds can be imposed on the size of the new hard loans, to represent a range that is acceptable for the government. When these bounds become effective, other government policy variables have to adjust in order to obtain, largely indirectly through influence on the private sector, the desired change in external borrowing requirements. Specification of alternative bounds and policy orderings means specification of alternative model closure mechanisms.

Prices

Price Linkages

For each commodity, several prices are represented: farmgate/ex-factory price, retail price for domestic buyers, market clearing price, import trade price (CIF), and export trade price (FOB). The prices differ from each other due to trade and transportation margins and indirect taxes. Trade and transportation requirements are represented through fixed quantity coefficients (Leontief input-output type), indirect taxes through proportional rates. There is no class-specific distinction of prices, nor are prices regionalized. The farmgate/ex-factory prices are specified separately for each sector. Retail and clearing prices differ only because of value-added tax. Taxes between farmgate/ex-factory and clearing are excise or sales taxes; taxes on foreign trade are ad-valorem tariffs.

Price Formation

Price formation is specified for each commodity on a nationwide (nonregionalized) market. Import CIF and export FOB prices are exogenous, except for rice where a FOB price is assumed to be decreasing with export volume whenever this volume rises above a threshold level (of 300,000 tons). This is to reflect the limited absorption capacity of the international rice market. The clearing price is the central price of each commodity market. The other domestic prices can be derived from it by taking into account taxes and costs of trade and transportation. Two different market clearing processes must be distinguished, one for non-IO commodities and one for IO commodities.

For non-IO commodities the production is lagged and cannot adjust within the year. As long as quotas on trade are not effective, imports and exports can adjust. In that case the clearing price of the commodity will not be higher than the import CIF price plus import tariff plus trade and transport margin on imports. Nor will it be lower than the export FOB price minus export tariff minus trade and transport margin on exports. Suppose that there is a situation of imports. When, for some reason, demand decreases, the price remains the same and imports adjust until autarky is reached. Then, there is a situation in which neither imports nor exports are profitable and the price adjusts to clear the market. However, when the price has fallen sufficiently, the surplus will be exported and the price remains at the lower bound. These so-called "regime" switches (from import to autarky, from autarky to export) are determined endogenously.

The price range between import and export equivalent prices represents the self-sufficiency band. Its width depends on the CIF-FOB difference, the tariffs, and trade and transportation margins. A wide band means that it is difficult to switch from imports to exports and vice versa. One may note that there will never be imports and exports of the same commodity in the same year, unless one imposes it exogenously. This assumes that commodities are homogeneous.

Farmgate or ex-factory prices of the sectors producing the commodity follow by subtracting the trade and transportation margin and indirect tax from the clearing price. Hence, prices of sectors that produce the same commodity move in parallel.

For IO commodities foreign trade is fixed exogenously. Each IO sector adjusts to changes in demand, unless an upper bound on its production capacity is reached. As long as the capacity bound is not reached, the resulting clearing price equals a markup price plus indirect tax. The markup price is set as the sum of intermediate input and paid wage costs per unit of production of the IO sector, multiplied by a given proportional rate plus indexed nonwage factor costs per unit (these costs are taken to be scale independent). When output reaches a capacity bound the markup rate is adjusted upward.

Miscellaneous

Homogeneity of Degree Zero

It should be mentioned that all equations are set up in a way which ensures that the model is homogeneous of degree zero in all foreign trade prices. In other words, a proportional change in all foreign trade prices will not affect real model outcomes, whereas all domestic prices and incomes will rise by the same proportion.

Domestic Capital Flows and Money

Money is not included in the model, nor are domestic assets and liabilities. Furthermore, domestic borrowing or lending is calculated for each actor, but it has no consequences on the allocation of value added. Domestic interest rates are not treated explicitly, neither in real nor in nominal terms.

Accounts Shown in the Printout

Commodity Balances

Thus, for each commodity and in each year a complete quantity balance of supply and utilization is determined. Net imports plus domestic production are in balance with the sum of intermediate and final demand (consumption, fixed investments, stock changes). By evaluating each flow at the appropriate price the commodity balance is obtained in value terms. By aggregating those, the national accounts result.

Accounts of Revenue and Expenditure

For each agent and each year, a complete budget account is produced. Receipts of socioeconomic classes consist of value added from production, domestic transfers, remittances from workers abroad, and education and health subsidies from government. Current expenditures comprise direct taxes, consumption, and profits to abroad (only for urban high incomes). Savings of each class make up the balance. Capital expenditures consist of fixed investments, stock increases, and net capital flows to abroad (only for the class called urban high). The gap between savings and capital expenditures is bridged through domestic borrowing, or lending. The incorporated business classes have analogous budget items, albeit that consumption, worker remittances, and education and health subsidies are absent.

Government current receipts consist of direct and indirect taxes (including tariffs), government current expenditures of public consumption, education and health subsidies, domestic transfers, and interest on external debt. The resulting savings are complemented with (net) domestic borrowing and external soft and hard loans to finance government fixed investments, stock increases, amortizations on external debt, and increases in foreign exchange reserves. By aggregating the agents' budget accounts the national accounts and balance of payments are obtained.

Further Information

A formal description can be found in SOW 1990b. The general approach is described in Fischer et al. 1988, chapter 2.

Comment

Jeffrey D. Lewis

My comments on the chapter by Keyzer and van Veen are from two different perspectives: first, as a fellow CGE modeler, and second, as an economist residing in Indonesia for the last four years while working as an advisor in the Indonesian Ministry of Finance.

The latter vantage point leads to two immediate comments. First, I can confirm readily that the problems of rice policy and trade deregulation that are investigated in the Keyzer–van Veen chapter are at the forefront of current policy debate in Indonesia. Second, the authors have amassed and synthesized an enormous amount of data and evidence in the process of constructing and calibrating their CGE model. Having struggled myself with these same sources and issues, and been frustrated by the inconsistencies and holes that exist, I congratulate them on their very capable efforts on this front.

Turning to the topic of rice policy, the authors address a concern that has been central to Indonesian development over the last two decades. Indonesia's transition from the world's largest importer of rice to self-sufficiency over a 15-year period is viewed as one of the crowning achievements of the New Order government, culminating with the awarding of a special FAO medal to President Suharto in recognition of Indonesia's success. Growth in rice output has been more important than the oil boom in generating higher rural incomes.

As their chapter outlines, the heart of Indonesia's rice policy has been a set of floor and ceiling prices, subsidization of key inputs (fertilizer and pesticides), and the creation of BULOG, the national food logistics agency charged (where rice is concerned) with maintaining the nation's rice stocks and carrying out procurement and/or sales of rice to defend the established floor and ceiling prices.

In the CGE model, the specification and detail of the agricultural production options and technologies is extensive. Cultivable land allocation and input demand relationships are econometrically estimated, and the model permits land development activities. Consumer demand is based on an estimated AIDS-LES specification for 23 different groups.

The alternative scenarios for the 1988–93 period presented in the chapter yield no great surprises. The only sizable effects come from the "climactic variation" or crop failure experiments. It is interesting that while a hypothesized 1990 crop failure does lower average GDP growth for 1988–90 by a percentage point compared to the base run, over the full five-year period there is no effect on average growth and virtually none on employment (I return to this in a discussion of model structure below).

Given its strong empirical base, the major weakness of the model as applied to rice policy would appear to be in the modeling of government *policies*. As the authors acknowledge, "Government's pricing policy, which is in reality implemented through stock changes, is represented as a tariff policy. Stock changes are exogenous." The implication of this assumption is that the government's policy *instruments* are the tariff on rice imports or subsidy on rice exports. This instrument can be used to change the price at which exports or imports will occur, in other words, by changing the width of the "self-sufficiency" or "autarky" band.

This treatment would appear to suggest that world export and import prices provide upper and lower bounds on the (flexible) domestic price, with the government able to affect these bounds through tariff/subsidy policy. However, reality is different. The government usually *chooses* the domestic procurement and sales prices, rigorously *controls* exports and imports, and has pursued a deliberate and largely successful policy of *insulating* the domestic market from world price variability, while endeavoring over time to match the *long-term* trend in international rice prices. To correctly capture the policy issues associated with rice policy, the model should more thoroughly incorporate other government instruments: stockpiling strategy and its costs, defining and tracking long-run international rice prices. In some ways, the issues are analogous to those in an exchange rate regime in which the government picks an exchange rate at which it promises to buy/sell foreign exchange as necessary. In the short run, this exchange rate may be overvalued or undervalued; in the long run, as long as the rate is adjusted in line with the "equilibrium" rate, the short-term deviations will be less important.

Turning to the second set of experiments on trade deregulation, several comments on aspects of the model structure seem appropriate.

Macro closure: The nominal exchange rate is the model's numéraire, and the foreign exchange market clears via changes in government commercial foreign borrowing. However, even with the nominal exchange rate assumed fixed, the model still has in it a *real* exchange rate. Indeed, one of the central concerns of Indonesian macroeconomic policy-making in the last decade or more has been concern about the exchange rate. Some greater emphasis on the role of the real exchange rate in affecting trade and resource allocation would be useful, especially since exchange rate policy has been a key feature of the trade deregulation efforts.

Exports and imports: One of the model's distinctive features is its treatment of international trade. Eschewing the imperfect substitutability (or Armington) assumptions that are common in many CGEs, this model instead adopts an approach in which export and import prices for each commodity (together with appropriate taxes, tariffs, and trade margins) provide upper and lower bounds for the domestic price. This range defines a "self-sufficiency" band, within which no trade will occur (unless imposed exogenously). If the domestic price falls too low, then exports become profitable; if the domestic price rises too high, imports will occur.

The debate over which trade specification is most sensible cannot usefully be entered here. But the treatment adopted by Keyzer and van Veen, which looks only at *net* trade in each sector, does run into one important challenge: two-way trade (that is, both exports and imports in the same sector) is an *empirical* fact in most countries, including Indonesia. Even in the most disaggregated input-output table (170 sectors) from which this Indonesian data is derived, two-way trade occurs. For some model applications, this empirical concern would not be very important; however, for looking at the impact of trade liberalization it seems that it is central to the questions being addressed. In a model such as this one, with relatively few (around 10) manufacturing sectors, looking only at *net* trade means that much of the action is likely to be missed.

Resource allocation: Several other model features also limit the usefulness of deregulation or liberalization experiments. First, most manufacturing sectors have an exogenous utilization rate. Second, labor demand is specified via sectoral labor/output ratios (including a time trend). Because of the fixed labor coefficients and exogenous capacity utilization rates, the model has little capability to portray the flow of resources (labor in particular) from one sector to another in response to changing incentives. Little supply response occurs, and the broader resource movements (such as labor movement from agriculture to industry) are not captured.

The liberalization scenarios examined in the chapter suffer from these model limitations, as well as several others imposed by the available instruments. As with the simulation of rice policy, the trade liberalization instruments work primarily by reducing the size of the self-sufficiency band, by lowering tariffs and subsidies and by reducing trade margins. But in Indonesia *average* tariffs were already low; the benefits from tariff reform were mostly from the reductions in the dispersion of tariff rates. Probably more important were reductions in the number and size of nontariff barriers (NTBs), together with measures to provide world-priced inputs to export-oriented industries through a series of exemption and drawback schemes. Deregulation of investment licensing was of key importance as well, as the government moved away from long lists of approved sectors and turned instead to a fairly short negative list of sectors in which investment was prohibited.

As a result of the model's specification, the dominant channels and mechanisms through which liberalization and deregulation affected the Indonesian economy are not represented. Consequently, the results fail to capture the resource shifts and dynamic response of the Indonesian economy as it underwent tremendous structural changes and a fundamental shift in its trade orientation. The benefits to liberalization calculated through model simulations are minuscule, with average annual growth improving by only 0.02–0.07 percent in the two experiments. Structural change is limited as well, with only a small reallocation of real value added from the services (nontraded) to agriculture and manufacturing (traded) sectors.

As a concluding point, I want to address the theme, proposed by the authors at the outset and returned to at the end of the chapter, that applied general equilibrium models should not deal with a single topic, but rather be designed to address many topics. As anyone who has gone through the process of building and calibrating a CGE model can attest, it is indeed tempting to extend its application from one topic to another. With the rich empirical underpinnings and theoretical sophistication (such as AIDS-LES consumption functions, and detailed agricultural production specifications) of this Indonesia model, the temptation is almost irresistible. But I would argue that it is inappropriate to confuse the richness of the *data* with the adequacy of the model *structure*. With its detailed disaggregation and modeling of the agriculture, this model is readily applied to issues of food policy. Its application to issues of industrial deregulation and trade liberalization is less compelling, because simplifying assumptions and specifications originally made about industry when the model was applied to food policy are not so sensible when the focus is trade and industrial policy and its impact on growth and structural change. A simpler three-sector model that focused specifically on trade and industrial policies and their impact might well yield more insight than a 60-sector model with an agricultural focus applied to the same topic.

Comment

Shantayanan Devarajan

This chapter represents a *tour de force* in policy-oriented economic modeling of a developing country. The authors have chosen a detailed and versatile framework, incorporated some novel features in the agricultural sector, used a blend of econometric and calibration techniques for estimating the model, and picked some compelling policy issues—food security and trade reform—to study with their model.

However, the very ambitiousness of the enterprise may also be its greatest limitation. As the authors themselves acknowledge, this chapter is an attempt to show the value of an *all-purpose model over "issue-specific" models* in policy analysis. Yet they never show this. They demonstrate that an all-purpose model *can* be used to look at two different policy issues. But whether it would have been better to build separate models for each question is not discussed. From a modeler's perspective, there is no debate: simple, tailored models are always preferred to large, multipurpose ones. Occam should be our patron saint, not Rube Goldberg.

The case for all-purpose models, then, rests on communication. Policymakers are suspicious of models that abstract too much from reality. By building a model that incorporates more of this reality, Keyzer and van Veen stand a better chance of being listened to by the policymakers. This is not a minor consideration. Many more AGE models of developing countries are built than used, partly because of this gap between the modeler's interest and the policymaker's requirements. Keyzer and van Veen are attempting to bridge this gap. Nevertheless, in so doing, they forgo another aspect of the communication process. In addition to performing policy analyses, models are useful in teaching policymakers about the crucial mechanisms by which policies affect the economy. These mechanisms are more easily seen in models designed to illustrate one particular effect. In the Keyzer–van Veen model, there are so many things going on that it is difficult to see the precise channel through which trade liberalization, for example, affects the economy. Thus, in attempting to build a model that better reproduces the Indonesian

61

reality, Keyzer and van Veen may have sacrificed the communication or educational benefit of modeling.

Having commented on the modeling strategy, I turn now to the model itself. The model contains several features that depart from the standard Walrasian system. While all AGE models do this, the particular deviations in the Keyzer–van Veen model have a bearing on how we interpret their results.

1. The model has no profit-maximizing behavior among producers: In the nonagricultural sector, production capacity is determined by econometrically estimated capital-output ratios, and labor demand by exogenous, time-dependent coefficients. Neither capacity nor labor demand responds to prices that are endogenously determined in the model. In the agricultural sector, land and input demands follow a "net revenue-maximizing" framework. However, labor input continues to be price- (and wage-) independent. At the very least, much of the consistency of the Walrasian system is lost by all this. Furthermore, policies like trade liberalization depend on the response of profit-maximizing producers for their intended success. By leaving out this effect, Keyzer and van Veen have assumed away the major mechanism through which trade liberalization affects the economy. Finally, by not allowing substitution among labor groups within a sector, the authors have built a model that, under full employment, will generate no changes in the output mix of an economy.

2. The model is closed by endogenous foreign capital inflows: In a recursive, dynamic model like the present one, this closure can be problematic. First, there is no intertemporal budget constraint, so we cannot properly compare the base run with an experiment since the two have different foreign capital inflows (and hence different future repayment streams). Second, this particular closure rule can lead to some perverse results (Ahluwalia and Lysy 1979; Devarajan and de Melo 1987; and Devarajan and Lewis 1991). For example, a reduction in tariffs can lead to a decline in exports. While the Keyzer-van Veen paper avoids this by replacing the lost tariff revenue with an increase in the value added tax, any shortfall in revenue could trigger such a response.

3. The model assumes Indonesia has market power in rice exports: While this may be realistic, it leads to difficulties in interpreting the results of a decrease in the rice export subsidy. Market power in rice exports implies that there is an optimal export tax on rice. Reducing export subsidies, therefore, will have an effect over and above the usual one of removing a distortion: it actually brings Indonesia closer to the "first-best" solution of an export tax. Again, it is not clear how this effect operates in the present model, as the current account is endogenous, and no welfare calculations are offered, but it is an important factor in deriving policy implications from the experiments.

4. The treatment of import quotas is ad hoc: The authors claim another benefit of trade liberalization is the induced competition among import licence holders. They model this by (exogenously) reducing the trade margins on imports. This is equivalent to assuming the answer rather than allowing the model to give you one. Furthermore, as there now exist ways of modeling imperfect competition in AGE models (including some of the chapters in this volume), it is not clear why the authors had to resort to this ad hoc approach.

To conclude, all applied modeling involves a trade-off between theoretical purity and empirical realism. By their choice of model specification, careful estimation, and policy-relevant experiments, Keyzer and van Veen have clearly chosen to err on the side of empirical realism. In so doing, they have shown us that the choice is not costless.

CHAPTER 2

Agricultural Price Policy in India: Some Explorations

Kirit S. Parikh

The Issues

For India, as for other developing countries, agricultural price policy is important for many reasons. Agriculture occupies a major part of the population (nearly 70 percent), contributes significantly to GDP (around 32 percent in recent years), and the expenditure on food is the predominant part of the total consumption expenditure of almost all persons (more than 75 percent for the bottom 50 percent of the population). Agricultural prices thus critically affect the real incomes of many. High prices provide incentives to producers but low prices increase the real incomes of net buyers of food, and a large part of the poor are net buyers of food. The dilemma for price policy is classical but still very important. Governments often devise a range of interventions to resolve, often with undesirable consequences, this conflict.

The Indian government also follows a variety of policies to provide incentives to farmers while at the same time guarding the food consumption levels of the poor. Policies have included dual markets involving a public food distribution system, public control over foreign trade of agricultural products, domestic bufferstock operation, and subsidized inputs for agriculture.

Under the public distribution system (PDS), the Central Government procures and supplies seven essential commodities to the States/Union Territories. These are wheat, rice, sugar, edible oil, soft coke, kerosene oil, and controlled cloth.

The procurement price (the price at which government buys food grains) and the issue price (the price at which food grains are issued to the state for sale in the ration and fair price shops) are fixed on the recommendation of the Commission for Agricultural Costs and Prices (formerly the Agricultural Prices Commissions). The procurement price which is announced in advance of the crop output, ensures a minimum support price. The free market price is usually not allowed to fall below this level. In good years, the procurement operations provide an implicit subsidy to the farmers. In years of poor harvest, however, if the procurement price is below the open market harvest price, levies are imposed and farmers are forced to sell part of their production at the procurement price to government agencies. Also, sometimes movement of grains out of surplus zones is restricted either directly or indirectly (through tightening credit or denying rail wagons to private traders) to facilitate procurement. Whereas a compulsory levy constitutes an implicit tax on the farmers on the amount sold as levy, such movement restriction imposes an implicit tax in surplus regions on the entire marketable surplus, as the movement restriction depresses the open market harvest price as well but provides a subsidy to the producers in the deficit regions as it raises the price there.

As part of the public food distribution system, consumers in major cities are provided ration cards that entitle them to purchase a certain quantity of grains at prices below the open market prices. Where such cards are issued, no means test is usually applied, and all consumers, rich and poor, are issued such ration cards.

In addition to the urban ration shops, fair price shops are opened in urban peripheral and rural areas to provide food grains at fair prices. However, these shops do not cover the entire rural population, nor do they distribute as much food grains on a per capita basis as the urban ration shops do.

The government reimburses Food Corporation of India (FCI) the difference between the costs of procurement, storage, and distribution and the proceeds of issue of grains. Since the issue prices have been in general 20 percent above the procurement prices, Sirohi (1984) has argued that this 20 percent margin would be more than adequate for private traders to cover the costs of distribution and selling. For FCI it has not been so. To the extent that private traders could have met the same distribution objectives as met by FCI at lower costs, a part of the amount of reimbursement that the FCI gets from the central budget is really a subsidy for its inefficiency and not a subsidy to the consumers. The consumers do get a subsidy as the ration shop price is still below the open market price. Part of this subsidy may be offset if they have to pay a higher price for their open market purchases. The consumer food subsidy rate is the difference between the weighted average price paid by consumers for purchases from the ration shop and open market and the open market price that would have prevailed in the absence of any public food distribution system.

The procurement and public food distribution programs do affect the open market prices and quantities, which in turn affect farmers' incomes and consumers' expenditures. The true effect of government operations on farmers' income is the difference between the income they receive under the present system and the income they would have received in the absence of any government intervention through PDS. One needs an applied general equilibrium model of the kind presented here to estimate such subsidies or costs. The relationships among the various prices, budgetary subsidies, and the economic subsidy rates are shown schematically in figure 1. The impact on farmers' incomes is shown schematically in figure 2.

The price support and PDS operations lead the government to operate bufferstocks that carry food grains from a relatively good year to a bad year. Government also controls the foreign trade of agricultural products. Together these operations affect the domestic open market prices and determine the wedges introduced between the world market prices and domestic prices. These government policies get reflected in the terms of trade between agriculture and nonagriculture.

The main policy issues that arise from the foregoing are the following:

(1) What is the impact of the present PDS on the welfare of the different groups in the economy, and in particular on the poor in the country?

(2) What would be the impact of changes in domestic terms of trade between agriculture and nonagriculture on the growth of agriculture, growth of the economy, and welfare of different groups in the economy?

The major producer subsidies relating to the food and agriculture sector are those for fertilizer, irrigation, electricity, and credit for farmers. These subsidies serve the purpose of promoting agricultural growth and of providing cheaper food. They thus help the consumers, particularly the poor ones. On

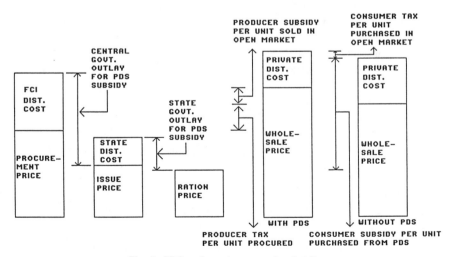

Fig. 1. PDS, prices, taxes, and subsidies

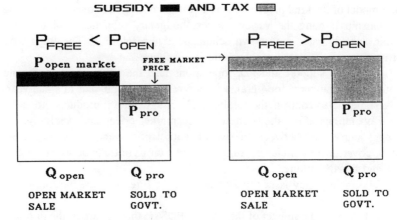

SUBSIDY ■ AND TAX ▨

$P_{FREE} < P_{OPEN}$ $P_{FREE} > P_{OPEN}$

$P_{open\ market}$ FREE MARKET →
                     PRICE
                     ↓

P_{pro} P_{pro}

Q_{open} Q_{pro} Q_{open} Q_{pro}
OPEN MARKET SOLD TO   OPEN MARKET SOLD TO
SALE   GOVT.   SALE   GOVT.

Fig. 2. PDS and farmers' income

the other hand, they put a considerable strain on the government budget and reduce investable surplus and consequently the growth rate of the economy.

We have addressed the following specific issues raised by this complex of subsidies for food and agriculture:

(1) If the prices of the subsidized inputs are raised to reduce government budgetary allocations, what would be the impact on agricultural output, food grains production, prices, and the incomes and welfare of different groups in society? In the short run and over time?

(2) If part of the amount spent on such subsidies by the government is used instead to operate a nationwide employment guarantee program, part for additional investment in irrigation, and the remaining for additional investment, how would it affect the welfare of different groups in the short run and over time?

These issues, at the heart of agricultural price policy debate in India, are explored with the help of an AGE model. One needs an AGE model to account for the importance of prices in determining production, income, and consumption, as well as the macroeconomic feedbacks on government budget, investment, and growth.

In the end, the outcome of any set of policies, subsidies, and taxes has to be judged by its impact on the welfare of society. In the absence of a well-defined, generally agreed-upon social welfare function one has to look at the constituents of such a function, on which perhaps a much greater degree of consensus is likely. The real incomes and consumption levels of different groups in society and their distribution over time are obviously very important determinants of social welfare. We judge policy in terms of its impact on them. Though comparing two alternative situations in these terms raises some other methodological problems, we will address them later when we come to such comparisons. This chapter is organized as follows. In section 2, the AGE model is briefly described. Section 3 describes the reference run and policy scenarios. Simulation results are given in section 4 and concluding comments are given in section 5.

A Brief Description of the Features of the AGE Model for India

The analytical model is of the sequential applied general equilibrium (AGE) genre, in which an equilibrium price vector is computed for each year in succession. Unlike other such models, a number of behavioral functions relating to demand and supply have been econometrically estimated with data mostly from the period 1950–51 to 1973–75. In the running of the model, for the period up to 1980, outputs, imports, and exports were set equal to their actual values, and the actually observed prices were generated as equilibrium prices by ensuring market clearance at these prices through stock accumulation or decumulation. Indeed, the fact that such a procedure did not lead to implausible values of changes in stocks was viewed as a validation of the model. The period after 1980 was the simulation period. Great simplification was achieved by imposing a one-year lag between production and market sale. Thus, in effect the economy became an exchange economy for the purpose of computing equilibrium prices. The economy is divided into ten sectors, of which the first nine produce agricultural commodities and the tenth produces the only nonagricultural good. The nine agricultural commodities are rice, wheat, coarse grains, bovine and ovine meats, dairy products, other animal products, protein feeds, other food, and nonfood agriculture. There are three sets of agents: producers, consumers, and government. Consumers are classified by their residence as rural or urban. Rural as well as urban consumers are divided into five expenditure classes, each according to their monthly per capita household consumption expenditure. Means of production (capital), natural resources (land), human resources (labor), and livestock (draft and milch animals, poultry, and so forth) generate income through production activities that is distributed to consumers. Thus, the behavior of producers (that is, their production activities) determines commodity supplies and incomes. Consumer behavior generates commodity demands (and implicitly resource supplies). The government sets policies (e.g., investment targets, taxes, tariffs, quotas, rations, price supports and ceilings). Finally, equilibrium is achieved through exchange in which domestic demands, together with export demand by the rest of the world for each sector's output, is equated to the sum of domestic supply (emerging from the previous year's production net of changes in stocks) and (foreign) import supply.

Per capita consumer demand of each of the ten classes of consumers for the output of each sector is modeled as a Stone-Geary linear expenditure system. The growth of total population and number of households (rural and urban) is exogenously specified. The joint distribution of households according to their per capita income and consumption expenditure was assumed to be log-normal in each period. However, the mean of the marginal distribution of logarithm of per capita income was allowed to vary over time with the growth of income. Other parameters, such as the variances, correlation coefficient, and the intercept of the linear regression of logarithm of per capita consumption on per capita income of the household, were assumed to remain constant at their estimated values from 1976 data. This meant that the mean of the conditional distribution of (the logarithm of) per capita household consumption varied linearly with the mean of logarithm of per capita household income. Thus, the relevant population of households falling within each of the ten expenditure classes as well as their mean per capita consumption expenditure could be determined for each year given aggregate consumer income for that year. The difference between income and consumption expenditure represents household savings.

Admittedly, the above distributional assumptions, including in particular the assumption that only the means of the logarithm of per capita household income (and consumption) vary over time, are strong. They imply that the concentration of the marginal distributions of logarithms of income and consumption do not change. A more satisfactory procedure would have been to specify an initial distribution of factor endowments and derive the changes in factor endowments from one period to the next, as well as the savings in each period from an intertemporal optimization procedure, given appropriate assumptions about expectations regarding the path of factor prices, including returns on assets. It goes without saying that implementing such a procedure is beyond the reach of modelers of developed countries with even more extensive data bases and econometric studies on savings, investment, and fertility behavior of households. Indeed modelers most often ignore distributional issues altogether by assuming that the society consists of a single household or alternatively avoiding dynamics by concentrating on static distributional effects. Given our interest in dynamics, our strong assumption has an operational justification that it enables us to derive the dynamic distributional effects in a relatively easy way. It is also consistent with econometric studies showing that a log normal distribution fits the data from the various rounds of the national sample survey on the distribution of households according to per capita private consumption expenditure.

Public consumption is assumed to be a constant proportion of GDP, and it is spent entirely on nonagricultural goods. The proportion of aggregate investment in GDP is exogenously specified. Income tax rates adjust to generate enough public savings (revenues minus consumption) so that, together with household savings and exogenously specified foreign capital inflow, they will equal aggregate investment. The share of agricultural investment in investment is a function of the relative price of agricultural goods. Agricultural investment influences the total gross cropped area as well as the irrigated portion of it. A detailed model of allocation of area among crops—based on a version of a Nerlovian adaptive expectations framework, choice of varieties to be cultivated (high yielding and traditional), and fertilizer intensity decisions that respond to relative prices—determines the vector of crop outputs. Capital is the only factor used in the production of the nonagricultural good. Capital stock in this sector is updated by net investment. Thus, the value of outputs of agriculture and nonagriculture together net of taxes and transfers determine the income available to consumers.

This brief description of the model is taken from Parikh, and Srinivasan 1989. The complete algebraic description of the model and its numerical version are available in Narayana, Parikh, and Srinivasan 1991. A more concise description is available in Narayana and Parikh 1987. It should be pointed out that the two major weaknesses of the model are the absence of a labor market and the extreme aggregation of all nonagricultural goods into one. By the absence of a labor market we mean, first, that labor is not formally treated as a factor of production in any of the ten sectors so that a demand function for labor (let alone for labor distinguished by age, sex, residence, and skill) cannot be derived from producer behavior, given the structure of wage rates, product prices, etc. Second, in the household utility function leisure does not enter nor does the value of labor endowment explicitly enter the household budget constraint. Thus, a labor supply function cannot be derived from household behavior. With both demand and supply functions absent, deriving an equilibrium wage rate for each period is ruled out. There is no capital or land market in the model so the only real choices of agricultural producers are the allocation of available land (irrigated and unirrigated) to crops (and varieties of crops), and the amount of fertilizers to use. Nonagricultural producers can choose the rate of capacity utilization. In short, only value added is endogenously derived in the model and not its allocation between factors. However, this does not preclude an analysis of distributional effects since the joint distribution of household income (which is obtained from value added) and consumption is specified directly. The major reason for not introducing an explicit labor market is the lack of satisfactory studies of labor supply and demand. After all, even in developed countries robust estimates of labor supply elasticities are scarce.

One could interpret the absence of an explicit labor market as implying that an infinitely elastic labor at some real wage is being assumed. But such an interpretation has no operational significance for most of the analysis except the simulations that involve rural works. In these scenarios, it is assumed that enough labor will find it attractive to be employed in rural works programs offering an exogenously set fixed real wage that is constant over a twenty-year period. It is impossible to say whether this is too strong an assumption without a well-specified labor market that realistically describes rural India. On the other hand, given the actual rural labor market environment, if indeed not enough labor will be forthcoming (that is, there will be an excess demand for labor at the offered wages), to that extent the scale of rural works programs could be reduced without affecting the extent of poverty alleviation. It is argued that because of the self-targeting nature of rural works employment, only those with relatively low reservation wages and capacity for physical work (e.g., women, children, and the elderly) will be attracted to the program, and to the extent that physical effort determines the capacity and durability of roads or irrigation canals constructed with their labor, the quality of such assets may suffer. But the complexity of the relationship between food energy intake and expenditure of energy in work effort precludes any firm conclusion. There are no carefully designed empirical studies available on which to base one's judgment on this issue.

The assumption that all goods are internationally traded precludes the analysis of the role of nontraded goods, particularly infrastructural goods in the development of the Indian economy. The model is better viewed as computing a sequence of temporary equilibria rather than a full-blown intertemporal equilibrium. In particular strong assumptions on preferences are needed to ensure intertemporal optimality of the household savings behavior incorporated in the model. The specification that the proportion of aggregate investment in GDP is a function only of time also violates the spirit of models of intertemporal equilibrium. Almost all applied general equilibrium models including ours ignore considerations of political economy. The assumption that government policy is set exogenously and agents respond to the policy as if they have no influence in its formulation is extreme. In fact, lobbies form and spend resources in getting policies favored by them enacted or to appropriate the benefits of policies in place. These considerations, which form the core of the literature on neoclassical political economy, are absent from our model. On the other hand, if the model is broadened to generate a politicoeconomic general equilibrium there will be no room for policy change by definition. Only a comparative static analysis is possible with respect to changes in those exogenous variables that determine both equilibrium policies and economic variables.

The Reference and Policy Scenarios

The reference scenario serves as a benchmark for comparing other scenarios in which one or more policies are changed from their reference specification. It should be kept in mind that the model is not a forecasting model—all the scenarios including the reference scenario are counterfactual simulations. Although, unlike many models of the genre, in our model values of most of the parameters are econometrically estimated, several were indeed exogenously specified. It is our contention that any alternative specification of values of these parameters will change both the reference and policy scenarios in a similar way so that the impact of policies expressed as changes relative to the reference scenario would be the same whichever set of parameter values were used. In a way, this is more an article of faith than an analytically or empirically established fact. It is convenient to have as the reference scenario one in which the relevant policy regimes essentially remain unchanged in the simulation period as compared to the presimulation period. The more important assumptions and policies in the reference scenario are:

(1) The public distribution system for urban areas: The quantity of food grains distributed in any year as a share of net output of food grains is a nonlinear function of the level and the change over the previous year of net output per capita and real nonagricultural income per capita subject to a ceiling of 135 kgs per urban resident. Historically a maximum of little over 150 kgs per urban resident was distributed in the severe drought year of 1966. The price subsidy on publicly distributed grain is 20 percent. The quantity of food grains purchased below market prices was in general related to output and the ratio of procurement price relative to expected open market prices.

(2) Quantitative restrictions on the net foreign trade of different agricultural commodities range from 5 percent to 15 percent of domestic supply (that is, production plus initial stocks).

(3) Foreign trade deficit is set at 1.5 percent of GDP.

(4) Domestic price policy interventions steer the domestic market prices gradually toward exogenously specified world prices, that is, gradual liberalization of markets is postulated.

(5) Total population grows by 2.26 percent per year from its value of 674 million in 1980 to 1,048 million in year 2000. The proportion of total urban population rises from 23 percent in 1950 to 31.5 percent in 2000.

(6) Aggregate (public plus private) investment as a proportion of GDP was assumed to be a monotone function of time with an asymptote of 0.45.

To address the issues raised above, the following sets of counterfactual policy scenarios are considered:

(a) Abolition of the PDS, that is, no distribution and no procurement

(Scenario DPO). The results are compared with the reference scenario to assess the impact of PDS.

(b) The terms-of-trade (tot) for agriculture is altered so that the relative price of nonagriculture falls to 0.7 times its values in the reference scenario. The desired tot is realized through changes in trade and is financed through two alternate means into different scenarios, through changes in tax rates (Scenario TT.7) or reduction in public investment (Scenario TT.7X).

(c) The price of fertilizer is raised by 30 percent. This abolishes government allocation for subsidy for fertilizer (Scenario NS). In another scenario, part of the amount saved by this is used for financing a rural works program and part for additional investment in irrigation (Scenario NS − RW20 − IR + 1).

Simulation Results

The welfare impact of alternative policies can be seen by comparing the distribution of population according to their equivalent expenditures (that is, the consumption expenditure needed to achieve with 1970 prices the same welfare level as the one achieved under the policy). Since the average equivalent expenditure within each class as well as the proportion of population in the class can vary among policy scenarios, for an overall comparison we adapt the approach of Willig and Bailey (1981). They show that, given a population of individuals ranked from 1 to n according to their equivalent expenditures, m_i^1 and m_i^2, in two distributions (i.e., m_i^j = the equivalent expenditure that a person i has in distribution j, $j = 1, 2$), the first distribution is preferred to the second according to any social welfare function that satisfies the Pareto principle, anonymity, and aversion to regressive transfer if and only if,

$$\sum_{i=1}^{k} m_i^1 > \sum_{i=1}^{k} m_i^2 \quad \text{for } k = 1, 2, \ldots, n.$$

It should be noted that person i (i.e., the one having the ith lowest equivalent expenditure) in distribution 1 need not be the same as person i in distribution 2. As the authors point out, the above inequality for $k = 1$ corresponds to a Rawlsian social welfare function, and for $k = n$ corresponds to the Hicksian compensation criterion. But for a general social welfare function, the inequality has to hold for all k to ensure dominance. Of course, the ranking is not independent of the base price vector p_0 used to calculate equivalent expenditure, and this serious limitation has to be kept in mind in interpreting the results.

TABLE 1. Impact of Abolition of the Procurement and Distribution Systems on Selected Macroeconomic Indicators

Variable (units)	Year	Absolute values —— Reference scenario REF	Percentage change over reference scenario —— No procurement, no distribution DPO
GDP total*	1980	530.0	0.00
	2000	1429.0	-0.07
GDP agriculture*	1980	220.0	0.00
	2000	354.0	0.00
GDP non-agriculture*	1980	310.0	0.00
	2000	1075.0	-0.09
Total investment*	1980	110.0	0.00
	2000	492.0	0.00
Tax rate (%)	1980	2.3	39.00
	2000	9.8	11.20
Price index of agriculture over price index of non-agriculture	1980	0.93	-0.15
	2000	0.89	0.46

(*continued*)

TABLE 1.—*Continued*

GDP per capita+	1980	786.0	0.00
	2000	1363.0	-0.07
Food energy Calorie intake (Kcal/person/day)	1980	2162.0	0.42
	2000	2569.0	0.45
Average equivalent income (AEI)++	1980	544.0	0.00
	2000	661.0	-0.18

* 10^9 rupees at 1970 prices.
+ number of rupees at 1970 prices
++ AEI: Income needed at 1970 prices to provide same utility as provided by current consumption at current prices.

Impact of Abolition of the Present Public Food Distribution System

By comparing the reference scenario REF with the scenario DPO in which both procurement and urban distribution of food grains are abolished, one can study the impact of removing the present procurement and distribution policy (see tables 1, 2, and 3). In DPO, with public investment unchanged, the net budgetary effect of the loss of procurement tax and the gain from not having to subsidize urban distribution results in a slight increase in the aggregate tax rate by 0.91 in the year 1980 and 1.15 in the year 2000. These appear small in the aggregate but, as a proportion of the tax rate in REF, these amount to a substantial 39 percent and 11 percent respectively. With total investment

TABLE 2. Distribution of Income and Food Energy Intake in the Reference Scenario (REF)

	Expenditure classes (Rs./person/year)				
	(1)	(2)	(3)	(4)	(5)
	<216	216-336	336-516	516-900	>900
Rural 1980					
Population	0.316	0.180	0.179	0.182	0.144
Equivalent income	129.0	266.0	407.0	635.0	1309.0
Calorie level	981.0	1896.0	2475.0	2491.0	3653.0
Urban 1980					
Population	0.019	0.079	0.187	0.340	0.375
Equivalent income	165.0	264.0	397.0	626.0	1322.0
Calorie level	1085.0	1556.0	1935.0	2332.0	3108.0
Rural 2000					
Population	0.205	0.159	0.189	0.216	0.231
Equivalent income	133.0	261.0	399.0	616.0	1227.0
Calorie level	1059.0	2019.0	2673.0	2796.0	3858.0
Urban 2000					
Population	0.004	0.032	0.125	0.331	0.508
Equivalent income	172.0	273.0	395.0	605.0	1224.0
Calorie level	1252.0	1742.0	2059.0	2375.0	3021.0

TABLE 3.   Distributional Impact of Removing Present Procurement and Distribution Policy (DPO Compared to REF)

	Percentage change over reference Scenario				
	Expenditure classes				
	(1)	(2)	(3)	(4)	(5)
Rural 1980					
Population	0.00	0.00	0.00	0.00	0.00
Equivalent income	1.32	1.58	1.57	1.32	0.63
Calorie level	1.33	1.42	1.21	1.00	0.38
Urban 1980					
Population	52.63	7.59	0.00	-2.35	-2.40
Equivalent income	-1.03	0.49	-0.25	-0.54	-0.48
Calorie level	-1.11	0.39	-0.21	-0.39	-0.26
Rural 2000					
Population	1.46	-0.63	-0.53	-0.46	0.00
Equivalent income	2.64	3.52	3.58	2.94	0.53
Calorie level	2.08	2.67	2.69	2.15	0.05
Urban 2000					
Population	75.00	15.63	3.20	-0.91	-1.77
Equivalent income	-1.51	-0.48	-1.06	-1.36	-2.00
Calorie level	-2.64	-1.09	-1.17	-1.18	-1.06

unchanged, it is not surprising that the growth of GDP and its components and the aggregate welfare indicators are virtually identical in the two scenarios. However, somewhat more significant distributional effects are seen. The rural classes benefit in DPO from the fact that they no longer have to bear the implicit procurement tax on their agricultural incomes. On the other hand, they have to pay slightly higher taxes on their nonagricultural incomes, the proportion of which in their total income increases over time. On balance, although there is a slight increase in the year 2000 in the proportion of the population in the poorest class compared to REF, the average energy intake and, more comprehensively, the average equivalent income of each class improves. The urban population loses on two counts in DPO: the withdrawal of public distribution on the one hand and the increase in tax rate on the other. Thus the distribution of urban population shifts to the left (toward lower real consumption expenditure classes) and the average energy intake and equivalent income of each urban class is lower in the year 2000 compared to REF.

Summarizing, the present procurement and distribution policy makes a net contribution to government revenue (of course, continuing procurement at below market prices and abolishing subsidized distribution will make a larger contribution) and transfers income from the rural to the urban population. The urban welfare is better and rural welfare worse than it would have been without such a policy.

Terms of Trade Policy

Often demands are made for better farm prices. Politicians in developing countries often find it expedient to support such demands. Yet the question is not always raised how an improvement in the real terms of trade for agriculture is to be realized: that it will call for a change in government stock and/or trade policies and that it will call for some resources is not fully appreciated. When these changes are accounted for the effects may be quite counterinitutive. In our scenarios, we have changed the real price of nonagriculture to 70 percent of its value in the reference scenario, and we use trade changes to realize the price targets. In scenario TT.7 the financing of needed operations is done through additional taxation, whereas in scenario TT.7X, the tax rates are kept fixed at the level of the reference scenario and public investment is adjusted.

Some of the important macro-economic indicators are shown in Table 4 for 1985 and 2000.

It is striking that as relative prices of agriculture are increased, as in scenarios TT.5 and TT.7, real GDP from agriculture as well as nonagriculture sectors increases relative to REF. This results mainly from the larger real investment made possible by the lower price of nonagriculture.

TABLE 4. Macroeconomic Impact of Changes in Agricultural Terms of Trade

	Scenario		
	REF	TT.7	TT.7X
	Absolute values	Ratio to reference run value	

1. Pag/Pna

1985	0.86	1.56	1.57
2000	0.74	1.65	1.66

2. GDP (10^9 Rs.1970)

1985	654.0	1.05	0.99
2000	1391.0	1.14	0.92

3. GDP agriculture (10^9 Rs.1970)

1985	247.0	1.05	1.03
2000	337.0	1.10	1.03

4. GDP non-agriculture (10^9 Rs.1970)

1985	407.0	1.04	0.96
2000	1054.0	1.16	0.88

TABLE 4.—*Continued*

5. Price index of non-agriculture			
(1970 = 1)			
1985	2.19	0.70	0.70
2000	2.61	0.70	0.70
6. Investment (10^9 Rs.1970)			
1980	110.0	1.18	0.85
1985	152.0	1.22	0.82
2000	465.0	1.25	0.82

The desired domestic prices in each of the policy scenarios are realized by imposing a suitable ad valorem tariff on the world prices. Thus, when the domestic relative prices are changed, in different scenarios, the government's tariff revenue changes for two reasons. First, when the domestic price of a commodity is increased (decreased), it leads to changes in production and consumption in an opposite direction so that net exports increase (decrease). Second, the difference between the world price and the domestic price, the implicit tariff, changes. When the government is unable to raise tax rates to bring about budget balance, then something else will have to adjust.

In the TT.7X scenario we have assumed that the level of public investment and hence total investment adjusts. In the TT.7 scenario when terms of trade changes are introduced in 1980, the government's tariff revenue falls by 10 percent of the targeted investment level compared to REF. In TT.7 this deficit is made good by raising the tax rate and the investment level is maintained. In the TT.7X case, on the other hand, investment is lower by 15 percent in 1980 and by 18 percent in 2000. Thus, the stimulating effect of the lower price of investment goods is more than offset by the loss in public investment leading to a lower real GDP in TT.7X relative to REF. While nonagricultural GDP falls relative to REF and by increasing amounts because of the shortfall in investment, agricultural GDP rises since the stimulating

effect of more favorable terms of trade more than offsets the negative investment effect. Of course, agricultural GDP rises by a smaller proportion relative
to REF in TT.7X compared to TT.7. Thus, if achieving improved terms of
trade for agriculture involves the use of a policy instrument that affects budget
balance adversely, and if higher levels of taxation are not feasible for political
or administrative reasons, growth will suffer.

Changes in agricultural terms of trade have significant effects on income
and consumption distribution in the economy. In Table 5 the effect on some
welfare indicators is presented. Though with higher relative prices of agriculture compared to REF, real GDP (valued at constant 1970 prices) increases,
the average equivalent incomes are lower. In TT.7, in which relative prices are
increased by about 50 percent, the fall in equivalent income is 10 percent in
1985 and 3 percent in 2000.

Several points have to be kept in mind in interpreting these results. First,
the trend in the national average equivalent incomes is the weighted average
of the trends of the average equivalent incomes of the ten rural and urban
expenditure classes, and the trends of classwise equivalent incomes may
move in different directions. Second, if the relative price in REF in the initial
years differs significantly from world prices in one direction, say, it is higher,
then reducing it through policy will reduce distortions provided the reduction
is not too much, while increasing it will increase distortions. Third, the
pricing policy in REF brings the domestic prices closer to the world prices so
that the degree of "price distortion" reduces over time. Thus, large changes in
the relative price of agriculture introduced in our various scenarios compared
to REF may introduce distortion in the later years by a significant amount.

Turning now to the effects on the welfare of different groups it is seen
that rural population gains and the income parity between rural and urban
incomes improve. The poorest rural class clearly gains when relative prices of
agricultural commodities increase. Thus in TT.7 there are 11 to 15 percent
fewer people in the poorest rural class (20 to 25 million persons), and the
equivalent income of this class is 7 to 12 percent higher.

The welfare of urban poor on the other hand is adversely affected by
higher agricultural prices. The equivalent income of the poorest class is 3
percent lower in TT.7 in 1985. Although the number of persons in this class
increases substantially (by 95 percent), the absolute numbers involved are
exceedingly small as a proportion of the urban population.

Welfare comparisons using the Bailey-Willig (B-W) criteria are summarized in Table 6. None of the scenarios leads to an improvement by the B-W
social welfare criterion for the total population.

In summary, the results indicate that none of the changes in the terms of
trade compared to REF through trade policy leads to an unambiguous

TABLE 5. Impact on Welfare Due to Changes in Agricultural Terms of Trade

	Scenario		
	REF	TT.7	TT.7X
	Absolute values	Ratio to reference run value	
1. Equivalent income (Rs./person)			
1985	575	0.90	0.97
2000	711	0.97	0.90
2. Energy intake/capita (Kcal/day)			
1985	2200	0.94	0.96
2000	2430	0.99	0.95
3. Rural/urban (Ratio) income parity			
1985	0.51	1.32	1.38
2000	0.48	1.22	1.36
4. Rural poorest*			
a. persons (Million)			
1985	172	0.89	0.91
2000	174	0.85	0.90

(*continued*)

TABLE 5.—*Continued*

b. equivalent income (Rs./person)			
1985	127	1.07	1.07
2000	125	1.12	1.11
5. Urban poorest*			
a. persons (Million)			
1985	3	1.94	2.42
2000	2	1.09	2.55
b. equivalent income (Rs./person)			
1985	167	0.97	0.98
2000	172	0.99	0.98

* Those with per capita consumption expenditure below what is equivalent to Rs.216 per person per year at 1970 prices.

improvement in all indicators. Two critical assumptions made in these scenarios may explain this outcome.

First, as pointed out earlier, domestic prices gradually shift toward world prices in REF. Increases in domestic prices of agriculture through trade policy lead to changes in tariff and tax rates that reduce government revenues. This, in turn, reduces investment. The growth reduction associated with the fall in investment may outweigh any favorable effect of the price change.

Second, although average agricultural income changes with time and across scenarios, by assumption, the variance in the rural agriculture income distribution does not change. One may interpret this loosely to mean that the shares of each factor including labor in agricultural output remain constant and that factor prices adjust fully to agricultural output prices. Thus, even landless agricultural laborers gain fully from increases in agricultural prices. Were this not the case, an increase in the relative price of agriculture could have perhaps adversely affected the rural poor.

**TABLE 6.   Social Welfare Comparison with Reference Scenario
for the Year 2000**

	TT.7	TT.7X
	Relative price of agriculture increased	Relative price of agriculture increased
	Tax adjusted	Investment adjusted
Rural population	Better off	Poor better off
		Rich indeterminate
Urban population	Worse off	Worse off
Total population	Poor better off	Poor better off
	Rich worse off	Rich worse off

Note: "Poor better off" in this table implies that the bottom 50% or more are better off and that the Bailey-Willig curve for the scenario is above the curve for the reference scenario for the poor.

Impact of Alternative Subsidy Policies

Budgetary allocation for subsidies on fertilizer and for PDS together amounted to Rs 56 billion in 1988–89, of which fertilizer accounted for Rs 36 billion. The total expenditure of the central government in 1988–89 was Rs 758 billion (revised estimate) and that of the states was Rs 542 billion (budget estimate). Thus, these subsidies account for roughly 7 percent of the central budget and 4 percent of the budget of the center and states together.

Government budgetary allocation corresponds to roughly 30 percent of the price of fertilizer. If farmers are charged a 30 percent higher price, government would have that much more budgetary resources to use to counteract some of the undesirable effects of a higher fertilizer price and the consequent increase in food prices. For example, rural works programs can be started to give the poor more income, or additional investment in irrigation can be made to stimulate higher agricultural production, or both.

In both the scenarios represented here, fertilizer price is raised by 30 percent. In scenario NS (No Subsidy), the resources saved are used for investment, whereas in scenario NS − RW20 − IR + 1, part of the resources released are used for financing a rural works program that provides wage income equivalent to 20 Kg of wheat per person per year to the rural poor (roughly 40 percent of the rural population) and part is used to create additional irrigation capacity of 1 million hectares per year. The policy changes are introduced in 1989, and results for 1990 and 2000 are compared with these in the reference scenario.

Impact of Removal of Fertilizer Subsidy by Raising Prices
Charged to Farmers
The fertilizer subsidy can be removed by either raising prices charged to farmers or lowering the retention price paid to producers or a combination of these policies. Here we remove the subsidy completely by raising the price charged to farmers by 30 percent.

Immediate consequences are twofold. First, farmers have to pay more for the fertilizer. Second, fertilizer use goes down as does food grains output. This is clearly brought out in Table 7. In 1990 fertilizer consumption falls by around 14 percent to 8.6 million tonnes from 10 million tonnes on the reference scenario. Food grains output falls from 161 million tonnes to 154.5 million tonnes, a reduction of 3.4 percent. Fertilizer consumption and food grains output continue to remain lower by these percentages through 2000.

Though agricultural output goes down, GDP agriculture measured at 1970 prices goes up compared to the reference run. This is because for the reference run GDP agriculture at 1970 prices is computed by imputing to fertilizer the unsubsidized price.

As the resources used for fertilizer subsidy are now used for additional investment, the growth rate of the GDP increases. The GDP in 2000 in this scenario is Rs 1280 billion (at 1970 prices), 1.4 percent higher than in the reference scenario. This higher GDP is, however, not adequate to compensate the poor for the welfare loss, see Table 8, due to loss in income of the agricultural population due to loss of fertilizer subsidy and lower food production. There is a general decline in welfare levels as indicated by the various welfare parameters, which persists in spite of the higher growth. Thus the equivalent income of the poorest rural class remains below the levels in the reference scenario throughout 1990 to 2000.

TABLE 7. Macroeconomic Development in Various Scenarios

	Reference Run(fert. subsidy (30%) continued)	NS (No fert. subsidy from 1989)	NS-RW20 -IR+1 (no subsidy fm 1989)
GDP 70 (10^9 1970 Rs)			
1990	746.01	746.23	747.28
2000	1262.93	1280.43	1296.40
GDP Agr* 70(")			
1990	247.47	247.69	248.74
2000	315.55	317.13	330.71
GDP Non-agr70(")			
1990	498.54	498.54	498.54
2000	947.38	963.30	965.70
Investment@(")			
1990	185.39	193.60	186.31
2000	416.72	435.62	435.58
Fertilizer subsidy (10^9 Current Price)			
1990	41.26	..	..
2000	52.83	..	..

(*continued*)

TABLE 7.—*Continued*

Fertilizer use(10^3N)

1990	10007.	8625.	8736.
2000	12874.	11160.	12277.

Wheat Production (10^6 tons)

1990	57.82	52.78	53.38
2000	82.18	76.67	84.03

Rice Production (10^6 tons)

1990	64.37	63.67	64.47
2000	85.84	85.74	94.25

Foodgrains (10^6 tons)

1990	161.03	154.45	155.74
2000	209.47	201.76	217.15

Total irrigated area (10^6 hectares)

1990	56.19	56.19	57.19
2000	77.8	79.24	90.38

GDPAgr* (10^6 current Rs.)

1990	535.04	545.99	547.51
2000	718.57	735.38	756.78

* GDP Agriculture excludes fertilizer subsidy which is however added to farm income.
** and associated P_2O_5 and K_2O
@ Excluding the investments for RWP and additional irrigation.

TABLE 8.   Welfare Impact

		Reference Run	NS	NS-RW20 IR+1
TOTAL POPULATION				
Energy intake	1990	2129	2101	2123
(Kcal/person/day)	2000	2307	2292	2322
Average equivalent	1990	516.7	509.4	513.3
income(Rs/person/ day	2000	580.3	578.0	585.1
RURAL POOREST CLASS				
Proportion of rural	1990	0.389	0.404	0.404
population	2000	0.307	0.320	0.312
Equivalent income	1990	120.2	118.8	124.5
	2000	124.7	123.5	129.4
URBAN POOREST CLASS				
Proportion of urban	1990	0.020	0.020	0.020
population	2000	0.010	0.009	0.009
Equivalent income	1990	172.7	172.7	172.7
	2000	172.5	172.6	172.6

It should be pointed out that in the model, fertilizer subsidy increases the incomes of all agricultural groups by the same proportion. Thus when the fertilizer subsidy is removed, the landless laborers who constitute the bulk of the poorest rural class suffer the same percentage decrease in their incomes as others. Thus the adverse impact on the welfare of the poorest rural class may be exaggerated. Yet one cannot say that removing fertilizer by increasing prices charged to the farmers is an unambiguously superior policy. Alternative to fertilizer subsidy is investment in irrigation and rural works.

The relevant results from the model simulation given in Table 7 show this to be superior to the reference scenario in terms of growth and welfare of the poor. They show higher GDP and also higher equivalent incomes for the rural poorest class from 1990 onward.

The increase in investment resulting from the withdrawal of fertilizer subsidy is more than the actual resource gains resulting from such withdrawal. This is because of the increases in GDP that accompany such scenarios. With a reduction in subsidy, fertilizer use goes down. In 1990 it goes down by about 13 percent for the subsidy withdrawal case. The resulting reduction in food grain production is 3.3 percent. However, in the long run, with increased income and irrigation availability, fertilizer use catches up and even exceeds that of the reference run level and so does food grains production.

On welfare grounds, NS − RW20 − IR + 1 strategy comes out as the best option tried. The aggregate indicators of welfare, average per capita income and average per capital energy intake, show this particular strategy to be superior both in the short run and long run. The same conclusion arises if one considers as criterion the status of the rural poorest class. For the urban poor, this option is superior to others only in the short run.

One could have tried many other combinations of fertilizer subsidy reduction and additional irrigation development. Some of those options may turn out to be superior to any of our scenarios. Yet the results presented here do indicate that one can find policies which are superior to the present policy of subsidizing fertilizer.

We can now summarize the various insights obtained and draw some conclusions.

(1) Fertilizer subsidy in the form of cheaper fertilizer for the farmer does increase the welfare of the poor.

(2) Though withdrawal of the fertilizer subsidy by increasing the prices charged to the farmers increases growth, the rural poor remain worse off even after 10 years of such growth. Thus such withdrawal without any other associated policy is not desirable.

(3) Even when irrigation targeting is not possible, withdrawal of the fertilizer subsidy, a modest rural works program and additional irri-

gation all together constitute an unambiguously superior policy combination to present policy. Withdrawing fertilizer subsidy investing in 1 million hectares of additional irrigation per year and a rural works program that effectively provides additional employment of 20 person days per year per family increases growth significantly and improves welfare of the poor.

Summary and Conclusions

Using an AGE model, we have examined some of the major agricultural policies followed by the Indian government to provide incentives to the farmers while at the same time guarding the food consumption levels of the poor. In particular, we have explored the policies of dual food markets involving public distribution system (PDS), terms of trade policy, and issues concerning subsidized inputs for agriculture. The simulation results provide some insights into the working of the Indian economy and lead to some policy conclusions.

Under the dual market policy, the government procures a part of cereal output at a price that is lower than the market price and distributes it at a subsidized price to urban consumers up to a fixed entitlement. It is obvious that the subsidized distribution benefits the urban consumers. The impact of the PDS on the rural consumers, the large majority of whom depend on agriculture, is not obvious and has been a subject of much debate among Indian economists (Bhagwati and Chakravarty 1969). This is because the PDS operations also affect the free market price and the net impact on farm income can be either way. The model results show that while the PDS operations increase the free market price, the increase is not sufficient to compensate the producers for the loss in income due to procurement at below market price. The PDS transfers income from the rural to the urban population. The urban welfare is better and the rural welfare worse than it would have been without such a policy.

Procurement of food grains at below market price is sometimes justified as an instrument to tax agricultural income on which, under the Indian constitution, the central government has no power to levy income tax. The simulation results show that the present PDS does make a net contribution to government revenue (of course, continuing procurement at below market price and abolishing subsidized distribution will make a larger contribution).

When the price of agricultural products relative to that of nonagriculture is increased, the welfare of the urban population, who are net purchasers of food, worsens. The rural poor, who are also net purchasers of food, however, are better off in scenarios that assume that higher agricultural prices lead to corresponding increases in wages of agricultural laborers. Thus, the income effect of higher agricultural prices more than compensates the rural poor for the higher prices they have to pay as consumers of agricultural products, even though they are net purchasers of food.

Higher agricultural prices do lead to higher growth of agricultural GDP. However, the total GDP goes down a bit. The higher growth of agriculture is obtained by diverting investment from nonagriculture to agriculture. Also, the reference scenario prices were closer to world prices, and improving terms of trade for agriculture increased distortion.

Our exploration of the consequences of subsidizing agricultural inputs such as fertilizer showed that the fertilizer subsidy increases the welfare of the rural poor, assuming once again that the fertilizer subsidy is distributed to all agricultural groups in the same proportion as agricultural income. When the amount spent on input subsidies is instead spent on additional investment, the economy grows faster. However, even after 10 years, the rural poor remain worse off than when fertilizer is subsidized.

While subsidizing agricultural inputs improves the welfare of the poor, it is not the best policy. Subsidizing investment in irrigation coupled with a modest rural works program leads to higher growth as well as improvement in the welfare of the rural poor. It is thus a pareto superior policy alternative to subsidizing fertilizer.

While the nature of some of these policy consequences could have been stipulated from theoretical considerations, their relative magnitudes and even their direction could not have been assessed without such a model. For agricultural price policy explorations an AGE model is a potent tool. From a methodological viewpoint, the policy issues explored through simulations show the importance in policy assessments of accounting for the general equilibrium feedbacks. Supply responses, the effect of food prices on consumer welfare, the importance of financing mechanism—all are seen to be important. Not to be underestimated is the discipline that an AGE model imposes. It forces one to pose the policy issues in a comprehensive context. One cannot fudge uncomfortable questions of who will bear the costs of populist giveaways.

Comment

Gary McMahon

In this chapter the author has chosen an ideal situation in which to use an applied general equilibrium (AGE) model. A complex pricing and distribution system exists in the middle of a sector that is heavily subsidized and lightly taxed. Moreover, this sector is in the middle of an economy with a number of structural features—especially the heavy reliance on administered pricing—that makes standard economic analysis very difficult. In addition, there is also the possibility of comparing the results with the AGE analysis of agricultural pricing policy in India undertaken previously by de Janvry and Subbarao (1986) (J-S hereafter).[1] Note, however, that in this earlier study the researchers used a comparative statics approach and not a sequence of temporary equilibria as in this chapter.

Perhaps the most difficult problem facing Parikh was to build a model able to give both satisfactory results and cope with the severe data limitations. While in his simulations he highlights the distributional implications of different policy scenarios, he is working with a model without labor markets or a distribution of factor endowments. The method he uses to get around these deficiencies is the standard in AGE models of India; that is, different income classes are assumed to have a fixed share claim on value added in the different sectors. This means that policy changes cannot affect income distribution via changes in the wage-rental ratio or unemployment, but only indirectly through changes in the proportion of value added generated by each sector. It is not clear how serious this assumption is for the results generated. For example, one would think that a policy which increases agricultural output would increase the demand for rural labor and raise the relative wage. However, given the potential for surplus labor in the Indian economy, this may not be the case. We would like to suggest that it may be interesting to run some

---

1. Note that Ratha (1987) also examines agricultural pricing policy in India with the use of an AGE model. However, he puts much less emphasis on distributional issues than the other authors, and the experiments he undertakes are not directly comparable.

simulations in which the value-added share of a particular class increases under certain conditions.

In the rest of this comment, we would like to look at each of the three main simulations in turn, comparing the results with J-S where warranted. In the first simulation the author abolishes the Indian procurement and distribution system. The main result is that the present system is at the expense of the rural classes, which is not surprising given that they do not have access to the lower priced grains and that they must pay the implicit tax on the distribution system. It is a bit more surprising, however, that all rural classes benefit from the removal of the scheme, but this may be due to the data problems discussed above. According to J-S (1986, 64), the poor rural classes are net consumers of food grains. This suggests that they would not benefit much from the removal of the implicit tax, toward which they pay little or nothing. Moreover, they do not have access to the distribution system. Consequently, the change in the market price of food grains generated by the abolition of the existing system has important consequences for their welfare. It would have been interesting to know what happened to the prices and quantities of the food grains in this case but no information is given. If the procurement price acts as a support price, its abolition should result in a decrease in the market price of grain—and vice-versa if it is an implicit tax. J-S (1986, 20) argue that in the 1980s it has acted as the former rather than the latter. J-S (1986, 64) also argue that the real conflict with regard to agricultural pricing policy in India is between net buyers and net sellers of food, not between the rural and urban classes. However, the present model is not capable of capturing this distinction.

In the second simulation Parikh reduces the terms-of-trade between non-agriculture and agriculture to 70 percent of its reference value. This is done by having implicit trade liberalization in the nonagricultural sector; that is, tariffs are reduced. When the tax shortfall is made up by increases in income taxes, real GDP rises in both the agricultural and nonagricultural sector. This result comes directly from the increase in real investment caused by the drop in nonagricultural prices. Note that in the absence of an urban labor market, the large reduction in protection has no effect on employment in urban areas. The model also does not allow for any change in rural-urban migration from the reference scenario despite a 32 percent improvement in the rural-urban income ratio toward the former.

When the tax shortfall in this simulation is made up by a reduction in public investment, real GDP falls. The contrasts between the two results is quite important as it shows the large differences that can occur when declines in tariff revenues cannot be met by increases in other taxes for either political or administrative reasons. In the 1980s most heavily indebted Latin American countries adjusted their fiscal deficits primarily by cutting back on public investment, as it was politically much easier. This policy has made prospects for future growth even more difficult than it otherwise would have been.

J-S (1986, 65) do a similar experiment (although in a static setting) when they move the terms of trade 10 percent in agriculture's favor. While they also get a net gain to this sector, in contrast to Parikh they find that the poor rural classes—small farmers and landless laborers—suffer as they are net consumers of food. The extra employment generated by the higher agriculture prices is not enough to offset the higher food prices. Note that Parikh does point out that if the shares of the different factors in his model were not more or less fixed, then poor rural classes could be losers in this policy scenario.

In the last simulation Parikh eliminates the 30 percent fertilizer subsidy that the producers receive. He clearly shows that due to the loss of the subsidy and the drop in food production both rural and urban poor would suffer from the policy unless it is balanced off with a complementary policy—such as using the savings for rural works and/or irrigation investment. It would have been interesting to see the results of a simulation that included the elimination of both the food procurement and subsidy program as well as the fertilizer subsidies, with the option of using the savings in irrigation or public investment. Note that J-S (1986, 87–91) ran an experiment similar to this one and found that increased investment in irrigation combined with food subsidies targeted at poor urban consumers was the optimal policy in the Indian context. (Also note that the Rao government in India reduced this subsidy by 40 percent in August, 1991, allowing for interesting comparisons in the near future.)

The author of this chapter has undertaken an ambitious research project on one of the most important matters confronting Indian policymakers. He clearly shows some of the important trade-offs that have to be faced in this complex situation. The major limitation of the model is the absence of a labor market. Given the available data it may be worthwhile in the future to include a stylized labor market to get some feel for the changes that might take place in this area. There is also a tendency to go straight to the final results in this chapter. In future simulations it would be helpful to the reader if the author spent some time analyzing the (likely) transmission mechanisms of the policy changes.

Comment

André Martens

Before making my comments on this chapter, I wish to acknowledge two things. First, I probably spent more time reading this chapter than I ever spent in India. This tells you how much firsthand information I have on the subcontinent. Second, when I was a graduate student of Jean Waelbroeck at the Université de Bruxelles, Dr. Parikh's work was already on my compulsory reading list. This explains why I always approach Dr. Parikh's contributions with an unusual amount of respect—unusual in relation to the aggressively critical approach that prevails, and rightly so, in North America.

This being said, let me do my job as a commentator to the best of my ability.

We have in front of us a very professional piece of work. The conceptualization in the model of the real sector of India's economy, with the emphasis on agriculture and agricultural technologies, is clear. The model's framework captures a complex system of food subsidies and is geared to address, among others, very relevant issues of income distribution. The effort of including econometric estimates for a subset of parameters singles out Dr. Parikh's undertaking when compared to most AGEs where guesstimates are more the rule. Finally, an effort is made to express simulation results in terms of overall welfare gains or losses in an unambiguous fashion with the help of a well-defined welfare index.

Let me now take one simulation at a time.

In the first simulation, where India's public distribution system is removed, farmers get better off and urbanites get worse off. This would not have been a surprise in Africa and possibly in Central America, where such distribution systems are much more rudimentary—in most cases, low consumer prices are immediately translated into lower producer prices. In India, the system is, as we said, much more complex, trying to protect some form of incentives for the farmers. As such, Dr. Parikh's result is of particular interest since it shows that, whatever the refinement of the food-subsidy system, the farmer always gets hurt.

In the second experiment, the internal terms of trade are exogenously made more favorable to the agricultural sector with various impacts on output, prices, and incomes. Suddenly, however, in one of the two variants of that simulation, the initial nonclassical closure of the Johansen type becomes a classical closure—the tax rates remain fixed and consequently investments are obliged to adjust to available savings. One would have wished to see in all and not only one experiment what would happen if such a change of closure would occur.

In the third experiment, fertilizer prices, which are initially government subsidized, are raised by 30 percent. The corresponding additional revenues are used by the authorities to finance, according to the author, investment *or* public rural works. Are we to understand that public rural works do not generate productive assets in India, and is the simulation not a little bit artificial, since removal of input subsidies is usually accompanied, in real life, by higher producer prices, which is not the case in the mentioned exercise?

Leaving the individual experiments, I have four brief comments that apply more or less to all three simulations and to the model itself.

First, the author states that for up to the 1980 period, that is, the model's validation period, most price and quantity variables were set at their observed levels, and the simulation shocks were absorbed by inventory accumulation or decumulation. The latter was then judged as plausible or not. Confronted with such a validation procedure, I have to admit that data on inventory changes must be much better in India (and this is an understatement) than anywhere in the world, Canada included. If not, how is plausibility defined in such a case?

Second, the model is concerned, as we said, with income distribution. However, each activity only generates total value added. Its allocation between factors of production is not endogenous to the model. This, in turn, is explained by the fact that there is neither a specification of the labor market— which, I agree, would be almost impossible given India's labor market's segmentation and the importance of seasonal employment—nor a direct link between the ownership of assets and income groups. I wonder if more effort could not be put in the specification of the latter link, as it has been done, even tentatively, elsewhere.

Third, the author talks about trade quotas. I thought that India was a net grain exporter. I wish to receive some clarification on that point.

Fourth, simulations are made until the year 2000, whereas the dynamization procedure is clearly of the ad hoc recursive type, and econometric estimates use 1950–51 to 1973–75 data. Should we not be a little less affirmative than the author when we look at the year 2000 results?

Part 2
Analysis of Stabilization Programs

CHAPTER 3

Macroeconomic Stabilization and Adjustment Policies in a General Equilibrium Model with Financial Markets: Turkey

Jeffrey D. Lewis

The theoretical basis for most CGE models is derived from Walrasian general equilibrium theory, with its assumption of complete price and wage flexibility. In developing economies, however, the extensive evidence of structural "imperfections" in markets, such as sticky prices, rigid wages, and regulated interest rates, suggests the need for some departure from the Walrasian paradigm. For modelers, serious questions emerge over the appropriate specification for their empirical models. Unfortunately, the solution technique often restricts the specification choice and prevents important questions from being addressed. This has been particularly true of efforts to model the "stabilization and structural adjustment" experienced by many developing countries. By its very definition, this adjustment process requires attention to both macroeconomic and financial phenomena (the stabilization component) as well as inducing changes in the real sectors of the economy (the structural adjustment component). Macromodels designed to look at the first problem failed to consider the structural issues, while traditional CGE models that were adequate on the real structural component could contribute little to the stabilization issue.

This chapter develops a computable general equilibrium (CGE) model that moves beyond the "real" focus of its predecessors with the incorporation of asset markets. Adding just two financial markets permits the modeling of important features of developing countries that govern response to both stabilization and structural adjustment policies. These features include the working

The model developed in this chapter has also been used to analyze the impact of liberalization in a financially repressed economy (see Lewis 1992a). I would like to thank Sherman Robinson and Shanta Devarajan for their comments, as well as feedback from participants at the Montréal Workshop on Applied General Equilibrium and Economic Development: Present Achievements and Future Trends (Montréal, January 1990), Centre de recherche et développement en économique (C.R.D.E.), Université de Montréal. The usual disclaimers apply.

capital financing needs of firms, the existence of segmented credit markets, and wide variations in the sectoral cost of borrowing. This financial CGE model is then used to analyze the implications of alternative composite adjustment policies. By controlling for differences in initial conditions and timing, this approach facilitates more careful consideration of the link between policies and performance.

A CGE Model with Financial Markets

The Real Sector

The real sector of the model resembles the class of CGE models that in recent years have been applied to issues of trade strategy, income distribution, and policy analysis in developing countries. Such models are characterized by their simulation of the operation of a market system in which prices, wages, and the exchange rate vary in order to equate supply and demand in the markets for goods, labor, and foreign exchange. Economic decision making is modeled as the outcome of decentralized optimizing by producers and consumers. A variety of substitution mechanisms are specified in these models, with substitution among labor types, between capital and labor, between imports and domestic goods, and between exports and domestic sales all occurring in response to variations in relative prices. Institutional rigidities and imperfect markets are captured by the exogenous imposition of features such as immobile sectoral capital stocks, labor market segmentation, and a fixed exchange rate, which together limit a neoclassical interpretation of the models but permit their more realistic application to developing countries.

Because thorough expositions of these real models are available, the treatment here will be brief.[1] The discussion will focus on model features that embody the linkages between real and financial sectors, such as working capital financing and segmented credit markets.

Production, Income, and Demand
The production structure used in the model is a series of nested Constant Elasticity of Substitution (CES) functions. Domestic output is a CES function of value added and intermediate inputs. Value added is in turn a CES aggregate of capital and labor inputs. The composite intermediate input is a fixed

---

1. For a comprehensive theoretical treatment of the current generation of CGE models, see Dervis, de Melo, and Robinson 1982. See Robinson 1989 for a recent review of CGE model applications to developing countries, and Robinson 1991 for a survey focused on CGE models incorporating financial markets. Dervis and Robinson (1978), Lewis and Urata (1984), and Lewis (1992b) provide alternative CGE-based analyses of Turkey. The model used in this chapter is presented in its entirety in Lewis (1992a), or a full listing can be obtained from the author.

coefficients aggregate of sectoral intermediate inputs. Capital in place is immobile. Total employment in each labor category can be set exogenously, so that the wage adjusts, or the (real) wage can be fixed with total employment endogenous.

The demand side is characterized by imperfect substitutability between domestic output and both exports and imports. Sectoral exports are assumed different from output sold domestically and are combined using a CET function to form domestic output. This treatment reflects explicit differences between exports and domestic goods (such as quality), as well as the existence of barriers preventing costless reallocation of output between the two markets (such as market penetration costs). Hence, the price of the good on domestic markets need not equal the domestic price of exports, which is determined by the world price, the exchange rate, and exogenous export subsidies. Producers maximize revenue from selling to the two markets, so that the ratio of exports to domestic sales is a function of their price ratio.

As with exports, sectoral imports and domestically produced goods are imperfect substitutes in both intermediate and final uses. Demanders of imports minimize the cost of acquiring a "composite" good (Q), defined as a CES aggregation of imports and domestic demand.[2] Substitution elasticities vary by sector, with lower elasticities reflecting greater differences between the domestic and imported good. Retaining the small country assumption, the supply of imports is assumed infinitely elastic at a price fixed by world market conditions. The domestic price of the imported good is determined by the world price times the exchange rate, plus any tariffs and import premia. The assumption of cost minimizing behavior by demanders implies that for each sector the desired ratio of imports to domestic goods is a function of their price ratio.

Four separate income recipients are distinguished in the model: firms, labor households, capitalist households, and the government. Each group receives income from a variety of sources and has explicit behavioral rules governing its savings and expenditure behavior.

Firms receive sales revenue, pay indirect taxes, and purchase intermediate inputs. From value added, they make payments to labor, retain earnings for investment, and pay the balance as dividends to capitalist households. Firms make interest payments on their borrowing from the banking sector to finance fixed and working capital investment, and also receive interest income on their net holdings of working capital balances in the banking system.

Labor households receive wage income, remittance income from abroad,

2. This characterization of imperfect substitutability was developed by Armington (1969). It has since become a standard feature in numerous applied models; see, for example, Dervis, de Melo, and Robinson 1982 and Dixon, Parmenter, Sutton, and Vincent 1982.

transfers from the government, and interest payments on deposits held in the banking system. They save a fixed fraction of this current income, which is added to their financial wealth; the remaining income is consumed. In periods of high inflation, incremental currency demand may exceed savings, in which case a "forced savings" mechanism is used to generate the needed (involuntary) savings.

Capitalist household income consists of net firm profits, interest income from their deposits held in the banking system, and any net profits of the banking sector. Reliance on premium rationing of imports to achieve foreign balance results in an income flow (as demanders of imports pay higher prices to obtain scarce imports) that accrues to capitalist households. Capitalists are taxed by the government and save at a rate (determined according to a logistic function) that depends on the real return available to funds deposited in the banking system. The remainder of their current income is consumed.

The government receives tax revenue from import tariffs, indirect (sales) taxes, and income taxes on capitalists; it spends money on export subsidies, transfers to labor households, goods and services, fixed investment, and interest on its share of foreign borrowing. The budget deficit, together with the increase in foreign reserves, determines the overall deficit that must be financed by the government through increases in borrowing or in the money supply.

Determining the remaining components of sectoral final demand is straightforward. Sectoral private consumption is determined through the expenditure decisions of labor and capitalist households according to fixed expenditure shares.[3] Government consumption is also allocated using fixed expenditure shares. Final demand for intermediate goods is the sum of the intermediate demands generated by each producing sector. Investment demand by sector of destination (described below) is a fixed-coefficients aggregate of various sectoral components, and is converted to final demand for investment goods using a capital coefficients matrix.

Investment Demand

Existing CGE models have focused on determining the sectoral *allocation* of investment, while relying on some simple macro "closure" rule to determine aggregate investment (e.g., setting investment equal to available savings). While possibly adequate for the smooth growth paths produced by medium-term, real-growth models, such a simple treatment limits these models' relevance to the problems of adjustment to external shocks, which are linked to the financial sector through channels such as differential access to subsidized credit, or government crowding out of private investment.

---

3. Households are thus assumed to have Cobb-Douglas utility functions.

In this model, the investment specification has been reformulated to address this range of issues. Demand for investment by firms is determined along neoclassical lines, but as with other neoclassical features of the model, imperfections and rigidities have been incorporated. The investment specification starts from the familiar first order condition requiring that the marginal revenue product of capital equal the cost of acquiring an additional unit:

$$PV_i \cdot \frac{\partial V_i}{\partial K_i} = PK_i \cdot \left(r + \delta_i - \frac{\partial PK_i}{\partial t} \right). \tag{1}$$

In the usual formulation, taken from Jorgenson 1963, this equation is solved to yield the "desired" capital stock that corresponds to the first order condition in equation 1, where PV and PK are the prices of the output and the capital stock, respectively, δ is the depreciation rate, and r represents the relevant real opportunity cost to the investor (typically, investing in an interest-bearing bond).

Several reservations prevent immediate use of this approach in developing countries.[4] First, the single opportunity cost is not easy to observe; underdeveloped financial markets in developing economies typically lack the long-term investment instruments that permit such long rates to emerge. Second, the capital gains term is less relevant to investors evaluating investment opportunities, since the absence of well-developed equity markets precludes capitalization of such gains. Finally, persistent differentials in capital productivity are observed, which imply divergent rates of return to investment in various sectors, and preclude measurement of a single rate of return.

In response to these reservations, the investment specification is instead based on a revised version of equation 1. The capital gains term is dropped, the (economywide) real opportunity cost is replaced by sectoral parameters (r_i) that reflect existing differentials in sectoral rates of return, and the price of the capital good is augmented by the sectoral real cost of borrowing ($I_i - PINF$), since these costs differ and will influence investment demand:

$$PV_i \cdot \frac{\partial V_i}{\partial K_i} = PK_i \cdot (1 + I_i - PINF) \cdot (r_i + \delta_t). \tag{2}$$

This modified first order condition is then solved for the desired sectoral capital stock. Sectoral investment demand each period is a function of: (1) the

---

4. Kwack (1983) uses this neoclassical formulation in a CGE model to examine the impact of tax policy changes in Korea, but his treatment requires the assumption that capital markets function perfectly and that statutory and actual tax rates are the same. Dervis (1975) presents a long-run model in which profit rates, including capital gains, are equalized across sectors.

ratio of desired to actual capital stock, with incomplete adjustment imposed to reflect adjustment lags, investor uncertainty, and pessimism about the future; and (2) any government "crowding out" of private investment.[5]

The Foreign Exchange Market

In the foreign exchange market, total import expenditures are constrained by the sum of export earnings and other net foreign exchange inflows. The model distinguishes four different sources of such inflows: (1) foreign remittances, which flow to labor households; (2) net foreign borrowing, which is split between foreign deposits held by the domestic banking system and direct inflows to the government; (3) interest payments on foreign borrowing; and (4) changes in official foreign exchange reserve holdings, which affect the monetary base. Remittance inflows and foreign borrowing are exogenous, reflecting the belief that, in countries with capital controls, the availability of external funds is limited by the willingness of foreign banks to lend, so that borrowing is neither a policy instrument of the government nor dependent on endogenous conditions.

The role of foreign reserve changes is linked to the functioning of the foreign exchange market. Equilibrium in the foreign exchange market is determined primarily by commodity (export and import) flows, rather than asset flows. No role for substitution between domestic and foreign assets is provided, which again is a realistic simplification for many semi-industrial countries with regulated capital accounts that prevent or limit cross-currency substitution.

Foreign exchange market equilibrium can be achieved via three alternative mechanisms. First, the exchange rate can adjust, so that the change in reserves is exogenous. Second, the exchange rate can be fixed (or, alternatively, set by policymakers according to a particular rule); in the absence of any mechanism to limit imports, the government (through the monetary authorities) must supply foreign exchange at the fixed rate, so that foreign exchange reserves vary endogenously. Finally, a premium rationing scheme for imports can be imposed, in which both the exchange rate and foreign reserve changes are fixed, and an endogenous import premium rate equilibrates supply and demand for foreign exchange by affecting the domestic price of imports. In this import rationing scheme, importers pay a premium

---

5. The desired capital stock includes both public and private components. Government investment is fixed exogenously. "Crowding out" refers to how private investment demand is determined. If public and private investment are perfect substitutes (no crowding out), private investment is equal to total desired investment minus government investment. If imperfect substitutes, each unit of government investment reduces private investment by more than one unit, so that direct crowding out of private investment occurs. The degree of crowding out can be varied parametrically.

over the official exchange rate to obtain the necessary foreign currency. This flexprice rationing scheme assumes the existence of a functioning secondary market for foreign exchange, either officially sanctioned or (as in the case of Turkey) an unofficial "parallel" market. Conceptually, the premium system is equivalent to a uniform import tariff sufficiently high to curtail imports as required; unlike a tariff, however, the government does not receive the premia income.[6]

The Financial Sector

In the trade literature, theoretical models concerning exchange rate determination and volatility emphasize issues of portfolio balance.[7] This literature assumes the existence and smooth operation of financial markets for a variety of assets, with asset market equilibrium determined through complex portfolio allocation processes taking into account both risk and return. Asset markets are often portrayed as clearing more rapidly than goods markets, with the presumption that returns to alternative assets will be equated on the margin after accounting for different risk factors.

In developing countries, however, financial markets generally are *less* developed than goods markets, making models constructed around assumptions of financial market efficiency less relevant.[8] The current model incorporates the important stylized features of financial markets in these countries by integrating the usual real CGE model with the macroeconomic and financial markets.[9] As in the real side of the model, special emphasis is placed on the various structural and institutional "stylized facts" that shape activity in these financial systems.

Introduction of financial assets opens the door to innumerable alternative model specifications. Our guiding principle has been to keep the model simple, while at the same time trying to capture the most important features of the financial system in semi-industrial countries.

---

6. See Dervis, de Melo, and Robinson 1982, chap. 9, for a discussion of other equilibrating mechanisms for the foreign exchange market used in empirical applications.

7. The seminal reference in the area of asset models is, of course, Tobin 1969. An early example of the incorporation of asset markets in the trade literature treatment can be found in the Mundell-Fleming model emphasizing the role of capital mobility. More recent examples include Dornbusch 1976 and Dornbusch and Fischer 1980.

8. The work on financial intermediation led by McKinnon (1973) and Shaw (1973), for example, deals primarily with the effects of inefficient, underdeveloped financial markets on resource allocation and growth.

9. There are, of course, numerous difficult theoretical problems associated with integrating macroeconomic phenomena and a microeconomic multisectoral framework. For a useful discussion of these issues, see Robinson and Tyson 1984 and Robinson 1991. For a similar effort to link real and financial markets, see Taylor and Rosensweig 1990.

Asset Markets

In standard CGE models, the only wealth in the closed real system is the capital stock, with savings channeled into the purchase of investment goods; a decision to save translates *directly* into capital investment, since no alternative store of wealth exists. In our model, this direct link has been replaced by behavioral rules that govern savings (or wealth accumulation) decisions for households. Introducing financial assets in addition to real capital assets means that savings no longer translates automatically into real capital investment. Instead, wealth is allocated according to behavioral rules specified for portfolio allocation.

The model includes two financial assets, currency and interest-bearing deposits or loans, that provide alternative assets to wealth holders. Each asset represents a new market for which supply and demand behavior must be specified. Moreover, the introduction of money with a fixed price of unity designates money as the numéraire in the model. In other words, prices and wages now have natural units, rather than being pure relative prices as in a Walrasian model.

An overview of the financial sector can be seen in the balance sheets in table 1. Four primary actors are identified: firms, households, the central bank, and a banking sector. Reflecting the frequent absence of equities markets in developing economies, no *financial* claims on the capital stock appear in the balance sheet. The actual capital stock is shown as an asset of households.

Firms: The Demand for Loanable Funds

In the model, firms demand loans for two distinct purposes. First, and most obviously, to finance the acquisition of new capital stock when its purchase price exceeds the firm's retained profits. Second, to finance a fraction of the advance purchases of working capital, defined as intermediate inputs and labor, needed in production:

$$WC_i = wc_i \cdot \left(\sum_k W_k \cdot L_{ik} + PN_i \cdot ND_i \right). \tag{3}$$

This second motive reflects the fact that a substantial portion of the credit available from capital markets is devoted not to financing capital accumulation but instead to financing the production process. Recent research has emphasized this mechanism in discussing the potential stagflationary or destabilizing effects of orthodox stabilization measures.[10]

---

10. See Bruno 1979 or Cavallo 1981 for theoretical treatments of this phenomenon. Van Wijnbergen (1982) and Taylor (1983) incorporate the cost of working capital finance in empirical models applied to less-developed countries.

TABLE 1.   Financial Balance Sheets

Government

Assets		*Liabilities*	
		Government debt	*(D)*

CentralBank

Assets		*Liabilities*	
Government debt	*(D)*	Currency	*(CS)*
Foreign reserves ($)	*(FR)*	Required reserves	*(RR)*
		Government borrowing	
		from abroad ($)	(FL)

Households

Assets		*Liabilities*	
Currency	*(CD)*	Private wealth	
Deposits in banks	*(TD)*		
Capital stock	*(K)*		

Firms

Assets		*Liabilities*	
Working capital deposits	*(WCD)*	Subsidized loans	*(LS)*
Working capital currency	*(WCC)*	Unsubsidized loans	*(LU)*

Banking Sector

Assets		*Liabilities*	
Subsidized loans	*(LS)*	Firm deposits	*(WCD)*
Unsubsidized loans	*(LU)*	Foreign deposits	*(FD)*
Required reserves	*(RR)*	Household time deposits	*(TD)*

Total demand for new loans or credit (CR) in the current period is the sum of the fixed investment demand (net of retained profits) and incremental working capital needs:

$$CR_i = (ZDP_i - RETP_i) + \Delta WC_i. \qquad (4)$$

Firms naturally will turn first to credit available from the government or from the banking system at below-market rates fixed by the government. While borrowers in certain preferred groups (e.g., exporters, agricultural producers, state enterprises) may have virtually unlimited access to credit at regulated (and highly subsidized) rates, other groups must obtain large portions of their credit needs from banks at competitive rates or from an unofficial "curb" market. Thus, access to credit at preferential rates represents an important subsidy controlled by government policymakers.[11]

In the model, this credit market segmentation is captured by making the borrowing rate (I) facing each sector an average of the subsidized (IS) and unsubsidized (IU) rates:

$$I_i = \gamma_i \cdot IS + (1 - \gamma_i) \cdot IU. \tag{5}$$

Here, γ is a government policy instrument representing the fraction of each sector's credit that is available at the subsidized rate. The total new demand for subsidized (LS) and unsubsidized (LU) loans can now be obtained by summing up the incremental credit needs for each sector, weighted by the fraction γ.

Note finally that total working capital balances appear as an *asset* of firms, divided between time deposits in the banking sector (WCD) and currency (WCC). Working capital balances represent advance payments for current production inputs. Since such payments by one firm are receipts of other firms or laborers (who in turn purchase output), the *aggregate* quantity of such advance payments must be held in some form as net balances by firms. The assumption here is that these balances are split between currency and bank deposits, so that half the aggregate is held as currency, and the other half as deposits.[12]

Households: Transactions Demand and Liquidity
Preference
Savings by both labor and capitalist households are increments to their financial wealth (FW), which is composed of currency and time deposits held in the

---

11. Van Wijnbergen (1983) provides a theoretical treatment of the short- and long-run impact of credit policy management in developing countries, using an open economy growth model.

12. See Taylor 1981, 473–75, for a discussion of this point. Note that this treatment implies that the demand for working capital is a *financial* demand, rather than a demand for a *physical* asset such as inventories of intermediate inputs. Taylor has working capital balances held entirely in the banking system; Buffie (1984) chooses to show net working capital balances as cash holdings of firms, rather than deposits.

banking system. The allocation mechanism chosen is a simple Keynesian money demand function. Nominal currency demand (*CD*) is the combination of transactions demand, which is positively related to nominal household income (*Y*), and liquidity preference, which responds negatively to increases in the nominal interest rate (*ID*):

$$CD_h = \lambda_h \cdot Y_h \cdot (1 + ID)^{-\eta} \qquad (6)$$

for h = capital, labor, where λ is the reciprocal of the velocity of money and η the interest elasticity of money demand. The demand for time deposits (*TD*) for both labor and capitalist households is the difference between financial wealth and currency demand.

The portfolio choice for private households in the model assumes a behavioral separability between the role of capitalists as *owners* of firms who borrow and invest and their role as *consumers* who save and allocate financial wealth. Such separability simplifies the model since it permits the portfolio allocation of capitalist households to be treated as a choice between currency and time deposits alone, excluding physical capital and borrowing. In many developing countries, the stock market and other markets for real assets are imperfect, so that this separability assumption reflects the fact that capitalists are "captive" owners of firms, with little systematic opportunity to convert equity into financial assets through financial markets.[13]

The Central Bank
The central bank finances the government debt and serves as banker to the foreign sector by managing the exchange rate and balance of payments. However, the ability of the central bank to carry out these tasks is limited by the underdeveloped financial markets. Instead, fiscal and balance of payments deficits are largely monetized, reflecting the central bank's limited capacity to sterilize reserve changes or control the composition of the monetary base in the absence of a private market for government debt instruments. The flow relationship governing the central bank's actions can be expressed from its balance sheet in table 1 as:

$$DEF + \Delta FR \cdot ER = \Delta CS + \Delta RR + \Delta FL \cdot ER \cdot shg. \qquad (7)$$

To finance the government deficit (*DEF*) or accommodate increases in foreign

---

13. See Buffie 1984 for a similar characterization of the nonsubstitutability of capital for other assets in an analytic model examining the effects of financial liberalization when the curb market is the marginal supplier of loanable funds.

reserves (ΔFR), the central bank must respond with increases in the supply of currency (ΔCS), required reserves in the banking system (ΔRR), or foreign borrowing (ΔFL). The absence of *domestic* borrowing on the right-hand side reflects the absence of instruments with which the government can borrow from the private sector.

However, aggregate foreign capital inflow (ΔFL) is exogenous to the model and the government share (shg) of this inflow is also fixed. Therefore, the only *direct* monetary control mechanism is manipulation of reserve requirements, which can have undesirable real effects through crowding out of private sector borrowing and forcing up interest rates. In practice, many governments rely on more direct controls over commercial bank lending, as will be discussed below; equation 7 thus will determine how large a change in currency is required to finance the deficit and foreign reserve changes.

Banking Sector

The banking sector has no behavioral role; it serves only as a financial intermediary to insure that demand for loanable funds equals supply and that interest payments are channeled from borrowers to savers.[14] Two separate conditions are imposed on the activity of the banking sector. First is the stock equilibrium underlying the balance sheet in table 1:

$$RR + LS + LU = FD + \sum_h TD_h + WCD, \tag{8}$$

where h = capital, labor, which requires that total assets equal total liabilities.

Required reserves are a fixed fraction of total deposits. Foreign deposits are a fixed fraction of the foreign capital inflow into the economy (the government receives the remaining amount). Foreign-denominated assets or liabilities in the domestic balance sheets requires a decision on how to value them when the exchange rate changes. The approach taken here is to value the *flow* changes (e.g., ΔFR and ΔFL) at the *current* exchange rate, and leave the value of the preexisting stocks unchanged. For developing countries, this approach is more realistic than revaluing the entire stock each year using the current exchange rate. Interest payments on foreign lending are based on an interest rate applied to the dollar loan value.

The second condition normally imposed on the banking sector is a budget constraint requiring that interest payments equal interest receipts—in other words, a zero profit condition. If the government pays no interest on required reserves (the normal practice in developing countries), this implies:

---

14. For an alternative specification that incorporates behavioral rules for the banking sector, see van Wijnbergen 1982.

$$YBAN = IS \cdot LS + IU \cdot LU - ID \cdot \left(\sum_h TD_h + WCD \right)$$

$$- iw \cdot (1 - shg) \cdot ER \cdot FL. \tag{9}$$

The negative items are interest payments to domestic households, firms, and foreign depositors, while the positive items are interest receipts from loans outstanding. *YBAN* is the net income of the banking sector, which will be nonzero only if government intervention in the banking system involves regulation of both deposit and lending rates. If the interest rate received by depositors (*ID*) is not controlled by the government, then flexible borrowing (*IU*) and deposit rates together insure that supply and demand for credit are equal (eq. 8) and that the banking sector has zero profits (eq. 9). If the deposit rate is fixed, as is often the case in financially repressed economies, interest receipts need not equal payments, in which case capitalist households receive the net profits from the banking sector, which may be negative.

Asset Market Equilibrium and the Price Level
The financial CGE model includes two asset markets: loanable funds (credit) and currency. Equilibrium in the credit market comes from the requirement that total assets equal total liabilities for the banking sector (eq. 8); moreover, this equation also assures that savings-investment closure is achieved, as it is merely a restatement of the requirement that savings sources equal investment uses.

With no government regulation of interest rates, movements in *real* deposit and lending rates are the primary channel to bring about equilibrium in the credit market.[15] Parallel changes in real deposit and average borrowing rates (upward or downward) can bring about stock equilibrium in the banking sector (or equivalently, savings-investment balance). The wedge between the borrowing and deposit rates will widen or narrow to bring banking profits to zero. However, one key feature of the "repressed" financial systems typical of developing countries is that the economy is constrained by the availability of savings: in other words, if more savings could be generated, it could be readily invested. This disequilibrium view of savings investment, in which the deposit rate is *fixed* by the government and investors are rationed in the quantity of investment they can undertake, is at odds with a neoclassical

---

15. In the discussion of equilibrating variables in this section and elsewhere, one important confusion should be avoided. The model is a large, nonlinear, simultaneous equation system. Identifying one variable as responsible for bringing about equilibrium in any market (or equation) is of course not strictly correct. The expository approach pursued here draws on the natural link between variables and equations that arise from consideration of the economic linkages involved.

formulation in which the deposit rate was *flexible* and served to equilibrate the savings supply and investment demand. This model incorporates features of a repressed financial sector: deposit rates are negative in real terms, the reserve requirements provide an important means of (forced) borrowing from the private sector, and preferred borrowers receive heavily subsidized credit from the banking sector. The deposit rate of interest is fixed by government regulation, so that it can no longer adjust to bring about savings-investment balance. This also implies that savings need not equal *desired* investment. Instead, investors are rationed in the proportion of desired fixed investment they can undertake. This rationing proportion adjusts as needed to bring *actual* investment down to the level of available savings.[16]

In the market for currency, equilibrium requires that currency supply equal demand. Changes in supply arise from monetization of fiscal deficits or foreign reserve changes (eq. 7). Currency demand for capitalist and labor households is determined in equation 6 as a function of nominal income and the nominal interest rate. The major adjustment mechanism is changes in the price level. To illustrate, consider what happens if currency supply is suddenly increased. A 10 percent rise in the supply of currency will initially cause prices to rise by around 10 percent as well. On the demand side, the price level increase will have two countervailing effects: transactions demand for currency will rise by around 10 percent (assuming real income is unchanged); however, this will be offset somewhat by the fact that a higher inflation rate *lowers* currency demand since the return to holding currency falls relative to time deposits.[17] To induce currency demanders to hold more currency, the price level must fall somewhat; the result is a convergent adjustment process for market equilibrium, with the final price increase less than the initial 10 percent increment in currency supply.

To link the price level to individual prices, composite output prices are normalized with the price level. Using composite good (or demand) prices together with base year composite demand weights implies that the appropriate index in the behavioral equations is a consumer price index.

---

16. The investment rationing mechanism used here is similar to the quantity import rationing scheme used in earlier CGE models focusing on the foreign exchange regime. See Lewis and Urata 1984 or Dervis, de Melo, and Robinson 1982 for further discussion of these rationing schemes.

17. The inflation rate is calculated as the annual percentage change in the price level. Since the price level for the previous period is fixed, movements in the current price level translate directly into movements in the inflation rate. Expectations about future inflation or other variables play no behavioral role in the model. The usual assumption of "rational" expectations is avoided, as it seems inappropriate to assume perfect foresight with regard to future markets in a model emphasizing imperfections in current markets.

Government Policy Instruments

The monetary authorities are limited in their policy options. Fluctuations in the government deficit and foreign reserves can be sizeable over a one year period; furthermore, the absence of government bonds or other financial instruments to facilitate borrowing from the private sector implies that such fluctuations are largely monetized. Sterilization of foreign reserve flows is difficult, and the money supply (currency and reserves) in this model is determined endogenously rather than as a policy instrument.[18] Reserve requirements provide a limited means of monetary management, although their usefulness as an instrument is limited since frequent changes are administratively costly and likely to encourage the growth of unregulated "curb" markets.

The credit market is a frequent target of government intervention, since regulation of interest rates and control over access to scarce, cheap credit comprise an off-budget means to subsidize favored groups within the economy. However, the allocational effects can be severe, as sectors or groups without preferential access are forced to compete for scarce funds at high marginal rates. This situation is often worsened by regulation of deposit rates, often leading to a negative real return to saving through the banking system and thus discouraging savings. These stylized features all are captured in this model, where the government, through regulation of the banking sector, can control a subsidized borrowing rate (*IS*), the deposit rate (*ID*), or both, as well as sectoral access to the subsidized funds (γ).

In the absence of an explicit optimizing framework, little can be said about the optimality of government policy packages. Strong potential for conflict between short-run stabilization and longer-run adjustment efforts exists in the model. For example, limiting access to subsidized loans may benefit short-run stabilization efforts by reducing the budget deficit, but may conflict with long-run efforts to restructure the economy through the use of investment incentives to potential exporters.

Adjustment to External Shocks

The base year data used in the model are representative of Turkey in 1978, although certain changes have been made so that the economy more closely resembles a "typical" semi-industrial country. Similarly, while the broad features of the external shocks in the dynamic period are derived from the analyses of Turkish performance in Dervis and Robinson 1982, Lewis and

---

18. See Taylor 1979 for further discussion of this view.

Urata 1984, and Lewis 1992b, certain aspects peculiar to Turkey have been replaced with a more representative treatment.

Regarding the model specification itself, commodity prices in all five sectors (primary goods, light industry, heavy industry, construction, and services) are flexible. In labor markets, real wages for the industrial and service sector labor categories are exogenous, so that aggregate employment of each type is variable. In keeping with the lack of evidence supporting wage rigidity in the agricultural sector in Turkey, the wage for agricultural labor varies in order to equate labor demand with the exogenous labor supply. In the foreign exchange market, foreign capital inflow is exogenous, the exchange rate is set according to a policy rule that "pegs" the price-level-deflated exchange rate but permits "real" devaluations as a policy instrument of the government, and balance between the supply of and demand for foreign exchange is brought about through movements in the import premium rate, which raises the domestic price of imported goods but leaves export prices unaffected.

In the financial sector, the government intervenes extensively in the credit markets. The government controls the interest rate on time deposits held in the banks, as well as the borrowing rate at which favored sectors can obtain credit to finance fixed and working capital investment. Differential access to subsidized credit leads to wide divergences in the sectoral cost of credit, while regulation of the deposit rate (leading to a negative real rate) lowers domestic savings and creates a situation in which investors are "rationed," with actual investment lower than desired investment at existing prices.[19]

Reference Run: No External Shocks

In order to assess the quantitative impact of different adjustment policy choices, it is necessary to have a yardstick with which to measure the various alternatives. This is achieved by using the model to generate a "reference solution" that provides a time path for the economy under favorable assumptions about exogenous variables and factors. This exercise produces a dynamic run that addresses the question: how would the Turkish economy have performed in 1978–83 in the absence of unfavorable external shocks or major policy reforms? The remainder of this section describes the broad outline of this counterfactual portrayal of the Turkish economy.

Regarding the external environment, the Reference Run assumes that remittances grow substantially in the early years, and then remain constant in real terms. Net capital inflow remains constant in nominal terms; since world

---

19. See Lewis 1992a for further discussion and analysis of the effect of investment rationing.

prices (both export and import) increase at an average rate of 7.5 percent, real foreign inflow falls. The nominal interest rate on foreign borrowing remains unchanged at 8 percent. Agricultural employment is constant throughout the period.[20] Institutional and contractual arrangements, together with government policies, combine to permit the real wages of industrial and service sector workers to grow at 2 percent annually, which is specified exogenously in the model. Sectoral rates of productivity growth for value added range from 1.5 percent (agriculture, services) to 2 percent (industry).[21]

Continuity of the government's basic policies is assumed. The exchange rate is controlled by the government and adjusted in order to offset the difference between domestic and world inflation. This policy maintains a constant price-level-deflated exchange rate, which implies that aggregate incentives to export or import substitute remain unchanged. Intervention in financial markets continues, and both the interest rate on time deposits and the subsidized borrowing rate are controlled by the monetary authorities. All government expenditure components are assumed to grow at 2 percent annually in real terms.

In this counterfactual portrayal of the 1978–83 period, inflation declines by about one-third (from 30 to 21 percent), with the largest drop (to 24 percent) occurring in 1979. The main cause for this decline is the steady fall in the government deficit, which drops from 10.7 percent of GDP in 1978 to 8.8 percent in 1983. Exports (in nominal dollar terms) grow at 11.8 percent, but the declining real value of the capital inflow and the increasing interest payments permit growth in dollar imports of only 9.1 percent. However, since import prices rise by 7.5 percent annually, real import growth is only 1.5 percent, significantly lower than the 4.4 percent growth rate of GDP. This increasing import scarcity is reflected in the import premium rate, which rises rapidly from 20–21 percent in 1978–80 to 48 percent in 1983.

GDP and employment growth decelerate over the period, reflecting the increasing import scarcity and resulting declines in labor absorption. On the financial side, the investment rationing apparent in 1978 is largely eliminated, as the ratio of actual to desired investment rises from 80 percent to 96 percent over the period. This reflects both an increase in savings, as the real deposit rate rises to near-positive levels, and a decrease in investment demand, due to higher borrowing rates and an increase in the cost of import-intensive capital goods.

---

20. Over the entire 1977–82 period, agricultural employment in Turkey changed by less than 1 percent.

21. This productivity increase affects the productivity of capital and labor in combining to produce value added. The productivity of value added and intermediate inputs in producing output is unchanged, so there are no exogenous changes in input-output coefficients.

Overall, the performance of the economy in the absence of external shocks is mixed. On the positive side, inflation and the deficit are reduced somewhat, and investment rationing almost disappears; on the negative side, the slow growth in real foreign exchange earnings means imports cannot keep pace with output, and foreign exchange rationing becomes quite pronounced by 1983. These results are in keeping with earlier analyses of Turkey by Lewis and Urata 1984 and Dervis and Robinson 1982, which conclude that although external events hastened the arrival of the foreign exchange crisis in Turkey, existing strains in the domestic economy would have led eventually to similar problems. Underlying this pessimism is the economy's legacy of inward-looking development, which fostered industrialization behind protective barriers and hindered the growth of efficient export industries. Continued growth requires imports, and since the Turkish economy in 1978 lacked the export base to earn the necessary foreign exchange to finance these import needs, growing foreign exchange scarcity was inevitable.

External Shocks with No Policy Changes: Experiment 1

The previous section presented a counterfactual portrayal of the Turkish economy, based on the assumption that no external shocks affected the economy in the late 1970s. In this section, the economy is adversely affected by external shocks, under the assumption of no changes in government policies. This scenario provides a benchmark against which the effects of positive policy changes can be contrasted in later sections. In a sense, the portrayal in this section, where external shocks occur and policies remain unchanged, and the portrayal in the previous section, where no shocks occurred, provide lower and upper bounds on the performance of the economy during the period. Subsequent sections address the question of how effective alternative policy choices are in improving the growth performance and in moving the economy back toward the no-shock growth path.

There are three external shocks that hit the economy in this experiment, and all subsequent experiments in this chapter. First, remittances grow at only a slow real rate in 1979–80 and remain constant in nominal terms after 1980. Second, the nominal interest rate on foreign loans rises from 8 percent in 1978 to 10 percent in 1979 and 12 percent in 1980 before dropping back down to 9 percent in 1982–83. Finally, the world price of heavy industry imports (which includes both petroleum and capital goods) rises 20 percent faster in 1979 and 1980 than in the Reference Run.[22]

Two other changes are imposed in this no-adjustment scenario. First,

---

22. The decline in demand for Turkish exports resulting from recession in the industrialized economies is not included in the composite shock analyzed in this chapter.

foreign reserves decline in 1979–80 and remain unchanged in 1981–83, rather than increasing steadily as in the Reference Run. Second, the government fails to devalue the exchange rate rapidly enough to offset the difference in external and internal inflation, so that a modest appreciation of the price-level-deflated exchange rate occurs in 1979–80.[23]

In macroeconomic terms, by every criterion, the economy is worse off than in the Reference Run. Inflation accelerates to over 65 percent by 1980 and remains high for the remainder of the period. The deficit increases substantially to over 14 percent of GDP in 1983. With real wages growing at 2 percent, industrial employment drops by 14 percent in the 1978–80 period, and service sector employment by 7 percent. Investment rationing worsens as the high negative real deposit rate discourages savings. The real appreciation of the exchange rate hampers export growth, and lower exports together with lower remittances and higher debt service payments imply that import capacity declines substantially. Consequently, the import premium necessary to ration imports surges to over 100 percent in Experiment 1. GDP growth averages only 1.5 percent over the entire period, with no growth in 1980.[24] Real imports decline by over 30 percent between 1978 and 1980.

Turning to the financial sector, table 2 compares the structure of the banking sector balance sheets in Experiment 1 and the Reference Run in 1980 and 1983. The asset structure is almost identical and reflects the specification of the segmented credit system. Since access to subsidized credit is specified as a percentage of each sector's total credit needs, changes in the split between subsidized and unsubsidized loans occur only because of changes in the sectoral composition of credit demand, which are quite small. On the liability side, however, more variation is evident. First, the sustained high inflation of Experiment 1 implies that the financial wealth of labor households is increasingly held as currency, not time deposits. In Experiment 1, by 1983, the labor households' share of deposits has dropped to zero from its initial value of 15

---

23. Both of these changes reflect typical performance under these circumstances. Few countries increased their foreign reserves when hit with external shocks such as those described here. In addition, exchange rate adjustments frequently failed to offset fully differences in inflation, due both to inadequate indexing rules and to attempts to insulate the domestic economy from the full inflationary impact of world price increases. The pattern of reserve changes is the same in all subsequent experiments in this chapter; the exchange rate pattern will be explicitly varied as a policy response in the next section.

24. The decline in GDP growth is probably understated here, since no change in productivity growth is assumed between the Reference Run and Experiment 1. Many specific country analyses, such as Lewis and Urata 1984 on Turkey or Robinson and Tyson 1985 on Yugoslavia, suggest that productivity growth declines or even becomes negative during periods of extensive disruption and adjustment. If Experiment 1 is run with no productivity growth assumed, annual GDP growth declines by an additional 2 percentage points (from 1.4 to −0.7 percent), thus increasing the disparity between the no-shock and shock scenarios.

percent. Second, the share of working capital balances in the banking system increases rapidly in Experiment 1, reflecting the increased demand by firms for credit to finance production in periods of high inflation. This increased working capital financing comes at the expense of fixed investment: in Experiment 1, nearly 70 percent of the total flow of new loans created in 1980–83 is used by firms to finance working capital, as compared to only about 25 percent in the Reference Run. Finally, the real size of the banking sector shrinks, as the failure to provide a reasonable return to depositors discourages financial deepening.

Table 3 shows the differences in the sources and uses of savings between the two experiments. The most notable change in the sources of savings is the decline in the share of capitalist savings, induced by the fall in the real deposit rate, and the correspondent increase in the share of government savings, which represents the government investment program. The size of the real government investment program is the same in the two experiments, but since

TABLE 2. Structure of the Banking System: Reference Run and Experiment 1

Variable	1978	Ref. Run 1980	1983	Exp. 1 1980	1983
Assets	(Percent composition)				
Subsidized loans	25.2	25.3	25.5	25.6	25.9
Unsubsidized loans	54.8	54.7	54.5	54.4	54.1
Required reserves	20.0	20.0	20.0	20.0	20.0
Total assets		100.0	100.0	100.0	100.0
Liabilities	(Percent composition)				
Capitalist deposits	60.1	59.6	60.0	54.4	41.5
Labor deposits	15.0	13.3	13.1	10.1	0.0
Firm working capital	15.5	16.9	17.2	23.8	43.8
Foreign deposits	9.3	10.1	9.8	11.7	14.7
Total liabilities		100.0	100.0	100.0	100.0
Other	(Percent composition)				
Total assets/nominal GDP	59.0	54.6	53.5	37.5	20.3

real GDP is lower in Experiment 1, the relative importance of the government rises. One cost of high inflation is apparent in the changing structure of the uses of savings: while the total savings/GDP ratio in 1983 is nearly equal in the two runs, the share of fixed investment in the total is nearly 15 percentage points lower in Experiment 1 than in the Reference Run, which translates into slower growth in the capital stock.

Policy Options and Macroeconomic Performance

We now turn to an assessment of the viability of alternative adjustment policy choices and of their impact on growth, inflation, and other macroeconomic targets of the government. The reference point is the performance of the

TABLE 3.   Sources and Uses of Savings: Reference Run and Experiment 1

		Ref. Run		Exp. 1	
Variable	1978	1980	1983	1980	1983
Sources	(Percent composition)				
Labor savings	10.5	11.1	11.4	11.3	11.0
Forced savings	0.0	0.0	0.0	0.0	2.1
Capitalist savings	21.0	23.6	25.5	16.5	16.6
Government savings	31.8	31.2	30.8	38.0	38.4
Retained profits	25.0	25.3	24.9	24.9	23.8
Foreign savings	11.7	8.8	7.4	9.3	8.2
Total sources	100.0	100.0	100.0	100.0	100.0
Uses	(Percent composition)				
Fixed investment	68.5	70.1	71.7	57.5	55.4
Government deficit	31.5	29.0	27.6	43.9	44.6
Reserve increases	0.0	0.9	0.7	-1.4	0.0
Total uses	100.0	100.0	100.0	100.0	100.0
Other	(Percent)				
Total savings/nominal GDP	34.0	33.0	31.9	31.0	31.4

Turkish economy in Experiment 1, when no explicit policy response to the changing external conditions was permitted. We now allow for three different policy interventions, each focused on a separate target variable. First, concerning external adjustment, the government changes its exchange rate policy, with the import premium rate the target. Second, to address the fiscal imbalance, real government expenditure (and its pattern) is changed, while the ratio of the deficit to GDP is the target. Third, existing financial repression is tackled through interest rate liberalization, with the extent of investment rationing as the target.

Rather than examining each policy separately, we focus instead on two different combinations of the responses: *moderate policy adjustment,* in which the government takes limited action in response to the external shocks, and *extensive policy adjustment,* in which the government takes more active reform measures for each policy. In addition to different adjustment policy packages, we also consider the importance of wage responsiveness in adjustment, by examining the role of labor market rigidities and real wage stickiness.

Table 4 summarizes the features of the experiment sequence. In the *moderate policy adjustment* experiments, the government devalues the exchange rate by 10 percent in real terms in 1979 and 1980, curtails the growth of all components of government expenditure (consumption, investment, and transfers), and liberalizes the financial sector by freeing the deposit rate from government control. In the *extensive policy adjustment* experiments, the government pursues more radical policy reforms, including a flexible exchange rate policy, cuts in the real government deficit through a balanced package of expenditure reduction, and near-elimination of financial sector regulation by freeing the deposit rate and forcing the real cost of credit to preferred borrowers to zero, rather than allowing them access to funds at negative real rates.

For the no-adjustment scenario (Experiment 1) and each of the two balanced paths, two labor market patterns are simulated in addition to the real wage growth of 2 percent used earlier: first, constant real wages over the entire 1978–83 period, and second, fixed annual employment levels from 1978–83, where the annual figures for both industrial and service sector labor are taken from the no-shock Reference Run. This second option, with real wages endogenous, permits consideration of the question of what real wage decline will keep employment growing at the rate it would have in the absence of any world shocks.

Table 5 summarizes the performance of the model economy for each of these experiments. Looking first at the no-adjustment runs, it is evident that the assumption of 2 percent growth in real wages is responsible for some of the poor performance associated with this scenario. When real wages are

TABLE 4.   Balanced Adjustment and Wage Rigidity Experiments

Experiment	*Description*
No Adjustment	
Experiment 1	No-adjustment scenario; real wages of industrial and service sector labor grow 2 percent annually.
Experiment 1B	Experiment 1 but with constant real wages for industrial and service sector labor.
Experiment 1C	Experiment 1 but with industrial and service sector employment fixed at annual levels from no-shock Reference Run. Real wages endogenous.
Moderate Policy Adjustment	
Experiment 2A	Exchange rate devalued 10 percent in real terms in 1979 and 1980; real government expenditure constant over period; interest rate on time deposits freed, investment rationing eliminated.
Experiment 2B	Experiment 2A but with constant real wages for industrial and service sector labor.
Experiment 2C	Experiment 2A but with industrial and service sector employment fixed at annual levels from no-shock Reference Run. Real wages endogenous.
Extensive Policy Adjustment	
Experiment 3A	Flexible exchange rate policy eliminates import rationing after 1978; real government expenditure reduced to achieve Reference Run deficit/GDP pattern; interest rate on time deposits freed, real subsidized borrowing rate set to zero.
Experiment 3B	Experiment 3A but with constant real wages for industrial and service sector labor.
Experiment 3C	Experiment 3A but with industrial and service sector employment fixed at annual levels from no-shock Reference Run. Real wages endogenous.

constant (Experiment 1B), GDP growth averages 2.2 percent over the period, which represents a decline in growth from the Reference Run that is only three-quarters the size of that witnessed in Experiment 1, where real wages grow at 2 percent. If aggregate nonagricultural employment follows the path of the Reference Run (Experiment 1C), GDP growth of 3.2 percent is attained. The one percentage point difference between growth in the Reference

TABLE 5. Balanced Policies, Wage Rigidities, and Growth

Experiment	Annual growth rate				Terminal 1983 value		
	GDP	Indus. labor	Serv. labor	Cap. stock	Infla-tion	Premium rate	Def/ GDP
Reference Run	4.3	2.2	1.9	4.4	20.7	48.4	8.8
Shocks, No Adjustment							
Experiment 1	1.4	-3.3	-1.7	2.4	69.5	105.7	14.0
Experiment 1B	2.2	-1.2	-0.1	2.6	57.5	121.6	12.9
Experiment 1C	3.2	2.2	1.9	3.1	43.4	156.3	11.4
Moderate Policy Adjustment							
Experiment 2A	2.4	-1.0	-1.3	3.3	29.5	68.6	10.2
Experiment 2B	3.2	1.2	0.3	3.5	21.4	82.7	9.1
Experiment 2C	3.8	2.2	1.9	3.7	17.1	95.7	8.4
Extensive Policy Adjustment							
Experiment 3A	3.4	0.8	0.1	3.9	16.4	0.0	8.8
Experiment 3B	4.2	3.1	2.0	4.0	15.5	0.0	8.8
Experiment 3C	4.1	2.2	1.9	4.0	16.0	0.0	8.8

Notes: Experiments are described in Table 4.
    GDP   = Growth rate in real GDP.
    Indus. labor   = Growth rate of industrial employment.
    Serv. labor   = Growth rate of service sector employment.
    Cap. stock   = Growth rate of real capital stock.
    Inflation   = Inflation rate, 1983.
    Premium rate = Import premium rate, 1983.
    Def/GDP   = Ratio of government deficit to GDP, 1983.

Run and in Experiment 1C is thus a measure of the cost of the shocks to the economy, holding employment constant. A major portion of this difference can in turn be traced to capital stock growth rates, which vary by more than a percentage point. The more rapid growth associated with lower real wages improves inflation and the deficit, but worsens the import premium rate; this reflects the fact that since the share of imports in GDP is substantially larger than the share of exports (10.1 versus 6.1 percent in 1978), more rapid growth leads to import demand rising more rapidly than export supply, so that import scarcity (and thus rationing) increases.

Turning to the other sections of the table, the importance of balanced policy response is seen in the features of Experiments 2A and 3A, which retain the 2 percent growth in real wages but combine elements of three different policy responses. The *moderate policy adjustment* sequence is perhaps more interesting, since it represents the most likely response for many developing countries: reform in many areas, but not to the degree necessary to eliminate fully the effects of traditional government interventions.[25] Economic performance with the moderate policy adjustments of Experiment 2A yields an encouraging picture: GDP growth averages 2.4 percent, inflation is only 30 percent in 1983 (the same as its 1978 value), the deficit is 10.2 percent of GDP, which is less than it was in 1978, and import rationing, while significant, is not much more severe in 1983 than it is in the Reference Run (an import premium rate of 68.6 percent versus 48.4). Industrial and service sector employment has fallen, although industrial employment in particular shows a marked improvement over the no-adjustment alternative of Experiment 1. If, in addition to these policy reforms, the annual real wage growth of 2 percent is replaced by constant real wages (Experiment 2B), the story improves even more: average GDP growth rises to 3.3 percent, inflation falls to only 21 percent, the deficit declines substantially, and nonagricultural employment grows, albeit modestly. The import premium worsens, but additional real devaluations in the latter part of the period could prevent this and further stimulate the economy.

The *extensive policy adjustment* experiments—where the government adopts sweeping exchange rate policy reforms, curtails expenditure, and deregulates financial markets—are the most optimistic. Even with growing real wages (Experiment 3A), employment grows, and the GDP growth rate of 3.4 percent is less than one percentage point lower than that in the Reference Run. If real wages are constant (Experiment 3B), the economy outperforms the Reference Run by most indicators: led by export growth of 9.2 percent, GDP growth is nearly the same as in the Reference Run, employment growth is more rapid, inflation is lower, and the deficit is the same (by assumption). In other words, if real wage growth can be curtailed, the activist policy reform measures discussed here can return the economy to its preshock growth trajectory, as measured by the Reference Run.[26]

---

25. This is especially the case as more countries become subject to broad reforms undertaken as part of the conditionality requirements of current IMF or World Bank lending assistance for stabilization or structural adjustment.

26. Experiment 3C, which uses the employment figures from the Reference Run, exhibits slower growth than Experiment 3B, and therefore is not discussed in the text. This lower growth is because employment growth in Experiment 3B, with constant real wages, is more rapid than that in the Reference Run.

Until now, the growth comparisons between the Reference Run and the various adjustment policy packages have focused on average growth over the entire 1978–83 period. Such comparisons, however, will tend to understate the stimulative effect of the policy reforms, since growth in the 1978–80 period will necessarily be worse in experiments where the economy is subject to the external shocks. Table 6 examines the growth of employment and GDP for various policy options, distinguishing between the 1978–80 period, when the shocks occurred, and the 1980–83 period, when external conditions had stabilized.[27]

Comparing the results for the two subperiods reveals that the adjustment policy options look even better. In the Reference Run, the increasing import scarcity and continued financial market regulation leads to a deceleration in employment and GDP growth in the second period. With no policy changes, there is an acceleration in GDP growth of 1.3–1.4 percentage points between the 1978–80 period, when the shocks occur, and the 1980–83 period (Experiments 1 and 1B). Policy changes are associated with two different effects. First, they drastically reduce the negative impact of the shocks in the years that they occur. This appears in the 1.4 percentage point increment in the GDP growth rate for 1978–80 with moderate policy adjustments compared to the no-adjustment case, and the 2.5 percentage increment in GDP growth in the extensive-adjustment scenarios. Second, they place the economy on a higher growth trajectory in the latter part of the period (1980–83), due to the reduction of the distortions and allocative inefficiencies associated with import rationing, continued high inflation due to large government deficits, and financial repression. With constant real wages, even the moderate policy adjustment option (Experiment 2B) results in more rapid GDP and employment growth than the Reference Run.

Finally, a concluding comment on real wages and the operation of labor markets. The results for Experiment 1C, where employment is fixed at levels derived from the Reference Run, indicate that a decline in real wages of 12–15 percent in the 1978–80 period is necessary to keep employment fixed. While declines of this magnitude were not uncommon in many developing countries during this period, this result focuses attention on the wage-determination mechanisms that operate in labor markets in these economies. From the perspective of growth alone, wage flexibility is advantageous. Fixity of real wages worsens the impact of the shock, and slows down recovery.[28] Indexation of wages, whereby current wages are determined based on lagged inflation rates, will tend to ameliorate the impact of the shock when inflation

---

27. Results for Experiments 1C, 2C, and 3C are not shown since employment is set exogenously; real wage behavior in these experiments is discussed below.

28. See Dewatripont and Robinson 1985 for a CGE model incorporating simultaneous rationing in product and labor markets where this conclusion does not hold.

TABLE 6. GDP and Employment Growth by Subperiod

	GDP		Indus. labor		Serv. labor	
Experiment	1978-80	1980-83	1978-80	1980-83	1978-80	1980-83
	(Annual percentage growth rates)					
Reference Run	4.6	4.1	2.7	1.9	1.8	1.5
Shocks, No Adjustment						
Experiment 1	0.7	2.0	-7.1	-0.4	-3.5	-0.5
Experiment 1B	1.3	2.7	-5.3	1.5	-2.0	1.3
Moderate Policy Adjustment						
Experiment 2A	2.1	2.7	-3.3	0.6	-2.9	-0.2
Experiment 2B	2.7	3.5	-1.2	2.9	-1.4	1.5
Extensive Policy Adjustment						
Experiment 3A	3.2	3.4	0.2	1.4	-1.8	1.4
Experiment 3B	4.0	4.3	2.3	3.7	0.0	3.4

Notes: Experiments are described in Table 4.
　　　GDP　　　　　= Growth rate in real GDP.
　　　Indus. labor　= Growth rate of industrial employment.
　　　Serv. labor　　= Growth rate of service sector employment.

is accelerating, but will hamper subsequent recovery when inflation begins to decelerate, and nominal wages (and thus real wages) remain higher.

Adjustment Policies and Structural Change

The discussion of adjustment in earlier sections of this chapter focused primarily on aspects of macroeconomic performance. In this final section, we turn to the sectoral implications of adjustment. First, we examine the structural changes that underlie the Reference Run and various adjustment alternatives and, second, we consider the efficacy of government policies designed to influence the sectoral pattern of response to the external shocks.

In the CGE model, sectoral supply and demand respond to changing price incentives, so that external shocks that affect the structure of relative prices will change the pattern of resource allocation and growth in the economy. Such structural changes, which are often labeled output and expenditure "switching," will occur even in the absence of any explicit government attempts to induce them, although government policy can either facilitate or hinder the adjustment.

Below, we examine the pattern of structural change in four experiments presented above: the Reference Run, where no external shocks occur; Experiment 1, where no policy changes occur in response to the external shocks; Experiment 2B, where moderate, balanced policy changes occur in response to the shocks; and Experiment 3B, where aggressive policy changes occur.[29]

In the Reference Run, where external conditions remain unchanged, the structure of GDP by expenditure category in 1983 shows only modest compositional differences from the structure in 1978. Labor consumption has risen (although relatively little in real terms) and capitalist consumption has fallen. Despite growing at 2 percent annually in real terms, the government's share in GDP has declined by nearly 2 percentage points, and the rise in foreign exchange scarcity evident in the rising premium rate is reflected in a decline in the importance of trade in GDP. Comparing the structure of GDP in 1983 for the four experiments, it is evident that substantial expenditure switching occurs in response to the external shocks. The most drastic changes appear in Experiment 1, as the share of private fixed investment drops from 13.0 to 5.3 percent. Labor consumption also drops, and the share of the government rises substantially, even though real government activity is growing at the same 2 percent rate as in the Reference Run. The decline in private investment is matched by a rise in the share of capitalist consumption.

The moderate adjustment of Experiment 2B, with its financial liberalization and elimination of investment rationing, facilitates a complete recovery of private investment. Since nonagricultural employment growth is still substantially lower than in the Reference Run, this policy package benefits labor far less, which recovers less than one-quarter of the ground lost relative to the Reference Run. The aggressive adjustment of Experiment 3B, which includes elimination of import rationing, yields a structure of GDP most like the Reference Run, with a moderate redistribution of consumption from capitalists to labor. This redistribution occurs as the flexible exchange rate eliminates the income to capitalists associated with the import premium, and rising private investment demand diverts income from consumption to savings.

Mirroring these shifts in patterns of aggregate final demand are changing

---

29. Recall that in the Reference Run and Experiment 1, industrial and service sector real wages grow at 2 percent annually, while in Experiments 2B and 3B, real wages are constant during the period.

patterns of production. The sector most affected by the shocks is construction, as is expected from the decline in investment demand noted above. It is interesting that, in general, GDP is less adversely affected by the shocks than output; this is because the external shocks raise the average price of intermediate inputs and thus lead to substitution of value added (composed of capital and labor) for more costly intermediate goods.

Table 7 summarizes the performance of aggregate and sectoral prices for the same four experiments. In the upper portion of the table, aggregate price indices are shown for 1983, relative to the aggregate price level in that year, which is defined as the weighted sum of consumer (or composite demand) prices.[30] Most notable, of course, is the movement in the import price index. The rising import premium that occurs in the Reference Run results in a 23 percent relative increase in this index, but this change is swamped when external shocks occur, as import prices nearly double when the premium rate climbs above 100 percent. Only with the complete liberalization of the exchange rate regime in Experiment 3B is any real reversal achieved; in this scenario, the flexible exchange rate leads to a much lower increase in the domestic cost of imports, as the real depreciation increases exports and alleviates the pressure on import demand apparent in the earlier experiments. The high import prices are directly responsible for the rise in the relative prices of capital and intermediate goods. Capital goods contain a large heavy industry component, which in turn is very import-intensive. The increase in import prices is sufficient to drive the relative price of capital goods nearly 10 percentage points higher in Experiment 2B than it is in the Reference Run, which in turn has a direct impact on investment demand.[31]

A similar, more modest, effect occurs with intermediate inputs, where the rise in the relative price is limited to around 4 percent. The small magnitude of this second effect is in fact surprising, given the prominence of intermediate input costs in the literature on the stagflationary effects of devaluation.[32] These models usually make the assumption that intermediate inputs are all imported, so that increases in import prices translate into equivalent

---

30. Recall that consumer prices (PQ) are a CES aggregate of import (PM) and domestic (PD) prices; sales prices (PX) are a CET aggregate of export (PE) and domestic prices on the demand side, and a CES aggregate of value added (PV) and intermediate good (PN) prices on the supply side. Finally, capital goods (PK) and intermediate goods (PN) prices are fixed coefficient aggregates of consumer prices, using the capital coefficient and input-output coefficient matrices for weights. All of the aggregate indices in the table equal 100 in 1978, the base year.

31. In some CGE models, this investment effect occurs because increasing the price of capital goods lowers the real value of a fixed nominal investment level; see, for example, Chenery, Lewis, de Melo, and Robinson 1986. In the current model, independent investment demand equations are specified with the cost of capital goods as an argument.

32. See Buffie 1984 for an example.

TABLE 7. Aggregate Prices and Sectoral Incentives, 1983

Variable		Ref.Run	Ex. 1	Ex. 2B	Ex. 3B
Aggregate price indices		(Ratio to 1983 price level)			
Consumer prices	(P)	100.0	100.0	100.0	100.0
Import prices	(PM)	123.1	190.3	197.8	165.2
Average sales	(PS)	98.1	92.5	83.8	90.9
Export prices	(PE)	103.7	92.0	105.9	143.6
Domestic prices	(PD)	98.0	92.5	92.0	94.5
Value added prices	(PV)	95.2	84.3	83.8	90.9
Capital goods	(PK)	97.9	106.0	107.2	102.5
Intermediate goods	(PN)	100.6	103.7	103.9	102.7

Note: Experiments are described in Table 4.

increases in input prices. The results noted here seem to suggest that once one moves beyond this simple assumption, and the multisectoral aspects of the story are considered, the importance of this channel is substantially diminished.

The relative price of value added represents the net return to domestic factors of production and directly influences the supply decisions of firms. While it declines in the Reference Run, the fall is even sharper when external shocks occur. In Experiment 3B, where aggregate GDP growth is as rapid as in the Reference Run, the aggregate price of value added remains 5 percent lower, thus providing an indication of the decline in the productivity of domestic factors that results from the external shocks.[33]

Policies to Induce Structural Adjustment

The structural changes outlined above reflect choices about policies, although economic *structure* was not explicitly a target. Frequently, however, policymakers try to influence this pattern and induce adjustment in particular directions, which may reinforce or run counter to underlying market forces.

In this section, we define a narrow set of structural adjustment objec-

---

33. This is similar to the effect derived by Bruno and Sachs (1982), in which an increase in the price of imported intermediate goods (the supply shock) reduces the return to domestic capital and labor.

tives, and examine the effect of government policies designed to achieve them. We consider how the government can increase exports from light industry, and increase domestic production in heavy industry, thereby reducing dependence on imports. Policies to encourage exports include subsidizing investment in the sector, and reducing the anti-export bias through increasing export subsidies and cuts in tariffs on imported intermediate goods. Import substitution is encouraged through investment incentives, since tariff protection is ruled out due to the desire to reduce input costs.

Table 8 summarizes the features of the experiments presented in this section. From the starting point of the moderate and extensive adjustment scenarios discussed earlier (Experiments 2B and 3B), three different experiments are considered. In the first, growth in the light and heavy industry sectors is encouraged by manipulating sectoral access to subsidized credit. Raising the proportion of credit available at subsidized rates to these sectors lowers investment costs, and more rapid capital stock growth occurs. In the second experiment, the government provides an export subsidy of 20 percent on light industry exports. In the third experiment, the export subsidy is supplemented by a reduction in the tariff on light industry imports from 45 to 25 percent, and on heavy industry imports from 35 to 25 percent.

Table 9 summarizes performance in the various investment experiments. In the heavy industry sector, the proportion of subsidized credit rises from 30 to 50 percent; in the light industry sector, the increase is from 20 to 40 percent.[34] Total and private fixed investment by sector in 1983 are shown relative to their values in the Reference Run in that year. The investment incentives appear most successful in the moderate adjustment case: private investment in the two target sectors is 7–8 percent higher in Experiment 2B-1, when the new access pattern is imposed after 1978. The effect is less important in the extensive adjustment experiment, with investment in the target sectors only around 2 percent higher when the new pattern of access is imposed. This poorer outcome occurs because, in the extensive adjustment case, the subsidized borrowing rate was tied to inflation so that the real rate is zero. This reduces the gap between the subsidized and unsubsidized rates from 20 percent in Experiment 2B to only 6 percent in Experiment 3B, which in turn lowers the value of the subsidy to new (or existing) recipients. The resulting higher efficiency lowers the government's ability to directly influence the pattern of investment.

Changed investment incentives has only a negligible effect on the struc-

---

34. The access of the primary goods and service sectors was reduced, with the result that the division of aggregate credit between subsidized and unsubsidized borrowing is unchanged. This permits focus on the compositional effects of the incentives.

TABLE 8. Investment and Trade Adjustment Experiments

Experiment	*Description*
	Moderate Policy Adjustment
Experiment 2B	Exchange rate devalued 10 percent in real terms in 1979 and 1980; real government expenditure constant over period; interest rate on time deposits freed, investment rationing eliminated. Constant real wages for non-agricultural labor.
Experiment 2B-1	Experiment 2B but with increased access to subsidized credit for light and heavy industry sectors, at expense of primary goods and services.
Experiment 2B-2	Experiment 2B but with 20 percent export subsidy on light industry exports.
Experiment 2B-3	Experiment 2B but with 20 percent export subsidy on light industry exports, and tariffs on light and heavy industry imports cut to 25 percent.
	Extensive Policy Adjustment
Experiment 3B	Flexible exchange rate policy eliminates import rationing after 1978; real government expenditure reduced to achieve Reference Run deficit/GDP pattern; interest rate on time deposits freed, real subsidized borrowing rate set to zero. Constant real wages for non-agricultural labor.
Experiment 3B-1	Experiment 3B but with increased access to subsidized credit for light and heavy industry sectors, at expense of primary goods and services.
Experiment 3B-2	Experiment 3B but with 20 percent export subsidy on light industry exports.
Experiment 3B-3	Experiment 3B but with 20 percent export subsidy on light industry exports, and tariffs on light and heavy industry imports cut to 25 percent.

ture of the capital stock, and almost no effect on the composition of output or exports. Sectoral interventions of this type are swamped by the financial liberalization and elimination of investment rationing.[35]

---

35. Although a greater effect could be achieved if the exogenous sectoral pattern of government investment were changed as well, the experiments leave this pattern unchanged to focus on the difficulty of influencing private investment. In most CGE models, the allocation of total fixed investment is exogenous, and substantial structural change can be brought about by imposing

TABLE 9.   Sectoral Access to Credit and Investment Growth

		No adjust.	Moderate adjust.		Extensive adjust.	
Variable	Ref.Run	Ex. 1	Ex.2B	Ex.2B-1	Ex.3B	Ex.3B-1
Total investment	(Index.	1983	Reference	Run value=100)		
Primary goods	100.0	65.3	86.5	83.6	98.1	97.1
Light industry	100.0	59.4	91.2	95.0	104.4	106.0
Heavy industry	100.0	56.4	92.5	96.1	99.8	101.3
Construction	100.0	30.5	85.7	86.7	97.1	97.1
Services	100.0	56.5	73.9	73.6	87.0	86.7
Total	100.0	57.3	80.7	81.1	92.6	92.7
Private investment	(Index.	1983	Reference	Run value=100)		
Primary goods	100.0	38.4	86.5	81.1	103.2	101.4
Light industry	100.0	34.7	92.9	99.0	111.2	113.8
Heavy industry	100.0	59.5	97.7	104.0	106.3	108.6
Construction	100.0	0.0	82.8	84.5	100.0	100.0
Services	100.0	33.1	69.5	69.1	86.8	86.3
Total	100.0	30.6	79.0	79.5	94.9	94.9
Other	(Index.	1983	Reference	Run value=100)		
Relative aggregate price of capital goods	100.0	108.3	109.5	109.1	104.7	102.4

Note: Experiments are described in Table 8.

The last line of table 9 shows the aggregate price of capital goods for each experiment relative to the Reference Run. In the no-adjustment experiment, relative capital goods prices are 8 percent higher than in the Reference Run. With moderate adjustment, this rises slightly to 9 percent. Only with the

---

sizeable changes in these shares, together with the assertion that the government pursues the policies "necessary" to bring them about. These experiments highlight the difficulties in undertaking those "necessary" policies.

elimination of the import premium in the extensive adjustment scenarios does the relative cost of capital goods drop back down. Behind this aggregate pattern is substantial sectoral deviation because of compositional differences in the capital stock. Capital goods used in the service sector are the most costly, reflecting the large import-intensive heavy industry (e.g., machinery) component. The industrial sectors have a larger construction component, which as a nontraded good, is less affected by rising import prices.

Turning to trade incentives, the success of sectoral interventions improves. Table 10 first presents growth rates of GDP, exports, and imports for

TABLE 10. Sectoral Trade Incentives and Growth

Variable	Moderate Adjustment			Extensive Adjustment		
	Ex. 2B	Ex.2B-2	Ex.2B-3	Ex. 3B	Ex.3B-2	Ex.3B-3
(Annual growth rate, 1978-83)						
GDP	3.2	3.4	3.5	4.2	4.3	4.4
Light industry output	3.0	4.0	3.8	4.7	5.8	6.0
Total exports	4.2	5.6	5.3	9.2	10.0	10.7
Light industry exports	5.1	8.3	8.1	10.2	13.2	14.0
Total imports	-5.8	-4.8	-5.0	-2.2	-1.7	-1.1
Light industry imports	-7.9	-6.4	-5.9	-3.8	-2.8	-0.4
Heavy industry imports	-5.6	-4.7	-4.8	-2.4	-1.9	-1.3
(Percent)						
Share of exports in gross output, light industry	9.7	10.9	10.8	11.6	12.8	13.2
Share of imports in domestic supply, heavy industry	34.3	35.1	34.9	36.8	37.3	37.9
(Index. 1978=100)						
Bias of trade regime, light industry	138.1	107.9	98.7	87.9	73.2	63.1
Bias of trade regime, heavy industry	194.5	182.1	187.6	120.6	120.7	111.6
Relative aggregate price of capital goods	107.2	105.8	106.3	102.7	101.6	100.9

Note: Experiments are described in Table 8.

the experiments. In both the moderate and extensive adjustment experiments with export subsidies only, GDP growth rises, as the growth rate of light industry exports increases by around 3 percentage points as a result of the export subsidy, which adds a percentage point to the growth rate of sectoral output. The tariff reduction has a mixed effect. With extensive policy adjustment, the tariff reduction further contributes to growth, as GDP and export growth both increase. With the moderate adjustment policies, however, the tariff reductions are ineffective, as export growth falls and GDP growth is unchanged. This differential response stems from the foreign exchange market. With extensive adjustment, the exchange rate is flexible; reductions in tariff rates lead to exchange rate depreciation, which stimulates exports and growth. With moderate adjustment, the exchange rate is pegged, and the import premium rate clears the market. Reducing tariffs raises import demand, but leaves the exchange rate unchanged, so that no export response occurs. To reduce import demand to available export earnings requires a higher premium rate. The only aggregate change is distributional, as government revenues are replaced with private premium income. The existence of import rationing thus makes it impossible to eliminate the trade bias. Since the premium increase is larger than the reduction in the tariff rate on heavy industry imports, the price of heavy industry imports increases, which further lowers growth. This is shown in the trade bias figure (defined as the ratio of the import to the export price), shown relative to its 1978 value. With extensive adjustment, the tariff reduction reduces the bias, indicating an increase in the incentive to export. With moderate adjustment, the reverse occurs for heavy industry imports.

Conclusion

In this chapter, we have carried out a series of dynamic experiments with the CGE model that focused on the economy's response to external shocks representative of those experienced by many semi-industrial countries in the late 1970s. Using the model, two comparative benchmarks were established: first, the economy's performance in the absence of any external shocks, and second, its performance when shocks occur, but no policy changes are made. These two experiments delimit reasonable upper and lower bounds from which to evaluate the effectiveness of alternative adjustment policies.

The inclusion of financial and macroeconomic considerations expanded the model's applicability to adjustment processes in developing countries. Different types of adjustment policies (external adjustment, fiscal restraint, and financial liberalization) were found to vary widely in their impact on different macroeconomic targets. Balanced strategies combining elements of all three policy types were in turn found to be more successful both at controlling the damage caused by the shocks as well as returning the economy to its no-shock growth trajectory. The role of wage rigidities was crucial, with lower real wage trajectories associated with more rapid growth; however, with active pursuit of other policy reforms, the decline in real wages required to prevent extensive growth in unemployment was reduced. Finally, the structural implications of adjustment were considered, and aspects of the macro environment were seen to play a large part in the ability of sectoral interventions to influence structural adjustment.

Comment

Eduardo Lora

Although the theoretical principles for modeling financial activities in a general equilibrium setting were first laid out more than two decades ago,[1] the financial sector is still a very unusual component of general equilibrium models that are applied to developing countries.[2] Compared to their real counterparts, financial submodels are still in a very experimental state, bearing little resemblance to the structure and behavior of the actual financial sectors of the economies under scrutiny.

This comment specifically questions the validity of the "stylizations" adopted by Lewis in order to incorporate the financial sector to his model for Turkey. The discussion that follows is entirely restricted to the financial submodel and its links with the real submodel, which in most respects is a fairly conventional one.

The Accounting Structure

As in most real and financial CGE, the private sector is sharply divided between a household subsector and a firm subsector with different roles.[3] While the former is the main holder of all financial assets, and does not receive any type of credits, the latter is the only recipient of all the credits to the private sector and only a very restricted holder of financial assets.[4] This way of defining the economic activities of each subsector severely restricts the behavior of the financial submodel. The reason is that by separating the roles of the two subsectors so sharply, the changes in the stock of (private domestic) liabilities of the financial sector are totally determined by the real side of the

---

1. That work was originally due to Tobin (1969). See also Tobin 1980.

2. Along with Taylor and Rosensweig (1984), Lewis (1985) was one of the first authors to develop a CGE model explicitly incorporating a full-fledged financial sector.

3. See, for instance, Taylor and Rosensweig 1984, and Bourguignon, Branson, and de Melo 1988.

4. The amount of financial assets held by the firms is supposed identical to their working capital needs.

model (that is, by the flow of savings and the working capital requirements of the firms). By the same token, the flow of credits to the private sector must necessarily match the level of private investment (net of internal financing by the firms) plus the variation in working capital requirements. Thus, both sides of the balance of the financial system with the private sector are restricted to reflect the behavior of real variables.[5] This is why, as Lewis himself points out, the balance of the banking sector "is merely a restatement of the requirement that saving sources equal investment sources," thus ruling out the existence of inside money.[6] What macro-accountancy requires is only that *net* changes in the financial position of the private sector are identically equal to private *net* saving (that is, saving minus investment).

Restricting the size of both sides of the financial balance between the private sector and the financial system, implicitly excluding inside money, has two main implications: 1) monetary and financial policies cannot affect the size but only the composition of credit and the private sector's portfolio, and 2) real investment cannot be restricted by the availability of credit. As we will see, this pervades the behavior of the whole financial submodel.

The Institutional Structure

The financial system is small and extremely underdeveloped in Turkey. The ratio of M2 to GNP is below 20 percent, the bond and stock markets are of negligible size, and there are no important financial institutions apart from the Central Bank and the deposit money banks (World Bank 1983). Lewis's model adequately reflects these features. However, the model contains a number of additional simplifications that are hardly tenable. One is the assumption that the whole of M1 is made up of currency issued by the Central Bank, ruling out demand deposits issued by the banks. This is a very gross simplification for Turkey, where the currency-to-demand deposits ratio is below 0.5 (it has fluctuated between 0.37 and 0.49 since 1982).[7] The implications of this oversimplification will become clear below. Lewis's model also tends to be excessively simple in its treatment of the Turkish selective credit system. The only policy parameters incorporated in the model are the shares of subsidized loans in the stock of credits by sector. By virtue of the accountancy structure discussed above, these parameters can affect the distribution but not the

---

5. For an alternative treatment, see Lora 1989.

6. This deficiency is also present in the models developed by Taylor and Rosensweig (1984) and by Bourguignon, Branson, and de Melo 1992.

7. These are end-of-period figures. The ratio has a strong seasonal pattern, with greater values in the first three quarters (around 0.6 or 0.7). Calculations based on *International Financial Statistics*, August 1989.

availability of the credit received by each sector. Since the only difference between the selective loans and the rest is their cost, the whole role of these parameters is to determine the (weighted average) active interest rate by sector. This sweeps away some of the most interesting topics of discussion in relation to the Turkish selective credit policy, namely, the alleged importance of the availability of credit in the supply of some specific sectors and the link between the selective credit system and the money aggregates (mainly through the rediscount window, also not included in the model).

As it is widely recognized, the combination of a selective credit system with controls to the active and passive interest rates has been a major source of financial distortions in Turkey. Presumably, the existence of a parallel or "curb" financial market is one of such distortions, which suggests itself as an interesting component of a financial general equilibrium model.[8] The same applies to the foreign exchange market, especially considering the importance given by Lewis to premium rationing as the main mechanism equilibrating that market.

Supply and Demand for Financial Assets

Given the accounting and institutional assumptions discussed above, the backbone of the financial submodel are the following equations:

$$B = CS + RR, \tag{1}$$

$$CD_h = k \cdot Y_h \cdot (1 + ID)^{-n}, \tag{2}$$

$$CD_f = (1 - swcb) \cdot WCB, \tag{3}$$

$$CS = CD_h + CD_f, \tag{4}$$

$$TD_h = FW - CD_h, \tag{5}$$

$$TD_f = swcb \cdot WCB, \tag{6}$$

$$TD = TD_h + TD_f, \tag{7}$$

$$RR = rrat \cdot TD. \tag{8}$$

---

8. The conclusions of a standard CGE model with financial transactions can be substantially altered by the inclusion of a curb market, as pointed out by Buffie (1984).

In (1) the money base (B) is by definition identical to the supply of currency (CS) plus required bank reserves (RR).[9] Since the rediscount window is not considered, the money base does not depend directly on the rest of the financial submodel.[10] Equation (2) is the demand for nominal currency by the household sector (CD_h), which is assumed homogeneous of degree one in nominal household income (Y_h)—and, hence, also in the price level $(PLEV)$ and real household income (X_h)—and inversely related to the rate of interest of time deposits (ID) through the parameter n.[11] Equation (3) is the demand for currency by the firms (CD_f), which is the proportion of working capital balances (WCB) not held in the banking sector $(1 - swcb)$. Equation (4) is the equilibrium condition for the money market. According to equation (5) the demand for time deposits by the household sector (TD_h) is a residual from the amount of private financial wealth (FW) and the corresponding demand for currency (CD_h), where the former can be taken as given for the financial submodel for the reasons discussed above. Equation (6) is the demand for time deposits by the firm sector (given by the share of working capital balances held in the banking sector, $swcb$), while equation (7) is the equilibrium condition for the market of time deposits. Lastly, equation (8) defines bank reserves as a proportion of time deposits, given the required reserve ratio $(rrat)$.

Some arguable points result from this system of equations. One is the way in which the amount of time deposits is implicitly determined (which follows from equations 1 and 3 through 8, independently of the demand for money function),

$$TD = (FW + WCB - B) / (1 - rrat), \qquad (9)$$

which exhibits a number of peculiarities. First, it shows that time deposits are the same irrespective of the arguments and parameters of the demand for money, in disagreement with the principles of construction of financial general equilibrium models (Tobin 1969 and 1980). Second, it shows an inverse

---

9. The concept of money base is not used by Lewis. However, from the balance sheet of the Central Bank (see table 1 of Lewis's article), it is immediate that

$B = D + FR - FL$,

where D is public debt, FR foreign reserves, and FL government external debt, all valued in local currency.

10. Though it may depend indirectly through the links between the real and the financial submodels.

11. The models consider two of these demands, one for the workers, one for the capitalists. This makes no difference for this discussion.

relationship between time deposits and the money base, which is difficult to justify. Third, it demonstrates that the reserve ratio (*rrat*)—the only monetary policy parameter—acts perversely on the amount of time deposits (that is, increasing them when the reserve requirement goes up), in spite of the fact that it is based on those deposits.

If working capital needs are expressed as a proportion b of nominal GDP ($WCB = b \cdot PLEV \cdot GDP$), and real household income as a proportion h of real GDP ($X_h = h \cdot GDP$), the system of equations (1) through (8) boils down to the following expression establishing the conditions of equilibrium of the financial submodel,

$$PLEV = [b - (rrat \cdot FW)]/GDP\{b - (1 - rrat)$$

$$\times (k \cdot h[1 + ID]^{-n} - swcb)\}. \qquad (10)$$

As figure 1 shows, this expression implies a direct relationship between the level of prices and the rate of interest (see the curve MM). This line is shifted upward when the money base goes up and downward when the stock of financial wealth or the level of real income are increased. It follows that, other things constant, the rate of interest is also positively related to the stock of financial wealth, another rather peculiar result, which is required by the model to crowd out the demand for currency in order to accommodate an

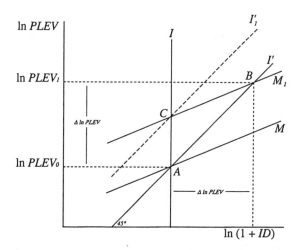

Fig. 1. Determination of the price level and the rate of interest in the complete model

increased amount of bank reserves within the money base when the amount of time deposits goes up.

The Level of Nominal Prices and the Rate of Inflation

In order to close the system in connection with the real submodel, another relationship between the level of prices and the rate of interest is required.[12] In this respect, Lewis endorses the classical view that the real rate of interest is a completely real phenomenon,[13] while the level of prices is a purely monetary phenomenon. In other words, he assumes that the rate of interest is the equilibrating variable in the saving-investment function, while the price level has the role of clearing up the money market. This type of dichotomy is usually associated with the assumption of money and price neutrality of all real variables. Except for the inclusion of interest earnings on time deposits as a determinant of incomes and consumption, this is also implied in the basic version of Lewis model.[14] Hence, leaving aside this effect, a vertical line (in the plane I,P) is the second relationship needed to close the system (II in figure 1). However, since the rate of return relevant for the equilibrium between saving and investment in the real submodel is the *real* rate of interest, this vertical line shifts sideward in response to changes in the rate of inflation. Since the rate of inflation corresponds to the change in the price level between two situations of (sequential) static equilibrium, this second relationship will be a straight line with unitary slope, as shown in the graphic (line $I'I'$). Provided that the slope of MM is less than one,[15] the system is now closed and will provide solution values for the level of nominal prices, the rate of inflation, and the nominal rate of interest. (Figure 1 shows the effects of an increase in the money base that shifts the MM curve upward: equilibrium goes from A to B.)

The whole argument is not entirely convincing, however, for one may question the purpose of modeling the financial sector of the economy when it is assumed that the real rate of interest is determined entirely by the real sector and neither the availability of credit nor the size of the portfolio may affect the saving-investment function.

---

12. As mentioned below, GDP and FW are determined jointly by the real submodel and the rate of interest.

13. This discussion assumes a unique interest rate. If there is an active and a passive interest rate, only the wedge between the two is a financial phenomenon.

14. Interest earnings on workers' time deposits is the only nominal variable entering the basic real submodel (in which the exchange rate and the wage rate are either flexible or fixed in real terms).

15. This condition implies that $n > 1$.

Investment Rationing and Crowding Out

The investment functions used by Lewis are adapted from Jorgenson (1963) in order to reflect the main limitations of capital markets in developing countries. The deduction is neat and convincing, expect for two elements that are introduced through the back door, namely crowding out and rationing. Both are added to the basic functions as exogenous coefficients arbitrarily chosen. Why public investment crowds out private capital expenditure is never known. Since the model already captures the effects of public expenditure on relative prices and credit costs, what is obviously lacking is its effect on the availability of credit. But, as we have seen, the accounting restrictions imposed to the model compel the flow of new credits to match the private sector net borrowing requirement. Therefore, the crowding-out coefficient is just a device to correct this deficiency of the model. The same applies to the introduction of a rationing coefficient in order to restrict desired investment to the availability of total saving when the rate of interest of credits is assumed fixed in nominal terms. This procedure is a simple way of determining the distribution of total investment by sector while sticking to a neoclassical closure of the model (that is, one in which investment is determined by saving). In terms of figure 1, if the situation of initial equilibrium (A) is upset by an expansion in the money base, rationing moves the $I'I'$ curve upward so that it crosses the point C, where the new equilibrium in the money market is consistent with the given nominal interest rate. However, in a model that includes both real and financial variables, this device is highly questionable because the financial system is the channel through which investment is equilibrated with saving in the real world.

Summary and Conclusions

As we have seen, "stylization" may be a perilous task in financial model building.[16] Its main unwanted consequences in the model developed by Lewis can be summarized as follows:

1) Monetary and financial policies (including the selective credit policies) affect neither the total supply of credit nor the size of the asset portfolio held by the private sector.
2) Real investment is never restricted by the availability of credit, not even when planned investment exceeds total savings. Rationing becomes an ad hoc method to equilibrate both.

---

16. The seminal article on this issue is Brainard and Tobin 1968.

3) The equilibrium in the market of time deposits is independent of the parameters and variables entering the demand for money function, but depends perversely on the supply of high-powered money and the reserve ratio.
4) Other things constant, equilibrium in the financial submodel implies that the nominal rate of interest is positively related to the stock of financial wealth.
5) The real rate of interest is not affected by the financial side of the model.

Comment

Nancy Benjamin

This investigation of structural adjustment shocks and policies in a model based on the Turkish economy contains a number of useful features. The model portrays the combined effects of foreign exchange rationing, endogenous investment decisions, a segmented financial market, and money. The role of money is mainly to show the inflationary consequences of monetizing certain deficits. What most affects saving and investment decisions are real income, real rates of return and credit rationing.

The "institutional rigidities" of the model are mainly incorporated by means of a few fixed prices. The nominal exchange rate is set exogenously while the quantity of foreign exchange is also fixed and rationed at a premium. The real wage is fixed for the manufacturing and services sectors. And the borrowing rate in one segment of the credit market is set exogenously. Results from the base run show that these constraints are binding. The contractionary shocks applied to the model increase the pressure on these fixed prices: foreign remittances grow more slowly while a major import price and the interest rate on foreign loans rise, and the rate of currency devaluation falls below the inflation rate.

The negative shocks are imposed as a package, and policy responses are also implemented in set combinations. To understand the role of structural adjustment policy in the chapter's experiments, we need to take stock of the way in which the policies proposed act to release the rigidities described above. The policy packages are used first to loosen binding constraints and then to release them completely. The exchange rate, cost of borrowing, and real wage rate are all made flexible so as to eliminate rationing. The result is that GDP always grows more with policy accompanying the negative shocks than without. Since CGE models often contain a mix of market imperfections, we cannot always predict that releasing a quota, fixed price, or tax will increase total output. But in this case, information from the reference run gives a fair indication that releasing the rigidities indicated will expand real growth.

Since GDP is always higher with adjustment policy than without, the portrait of adjustment that emerges here is not one of trade-offs between different segments of the economy. Possible trade-offs and reallocations are obscured by the growth dividend. On the basis of these results, it would be hard to justify giving such a country an adjustment loan.

The experiment results in this chapter provide useful information about the outcome of important adjustment scenarios. Most pointedly, the experiments show how distortions impinge on economic growth under conditions of negative shocks and indicate the value of removing them. But this does not explain why countries resist implementing IMF adjustment packages or currency devaluations. The field needs to address the question of adjustment in countries that cannot easily undo structural rigidities. Aside from releasing fixed prices, what else can governments do to cope with negative shocks?

CHAPTER 4

A Financial Computable General Equilibrium Model for the Analysis of Stabilization Programs

André Fargeix and Elisabeth Sadoulet

Building a Policy Laboratory for the Analysis of Stabilization

During the past fifteen years, the developing countries have been hit by a series of severe external shocks—deterioration in their terms of trade, high interest rates, appreciation of the U.S. dollar (in which most of their debt is denominated), and more recently a sharp reduction in the inflow of foreign capital. These shocks came for most countries after long periods of high growth based on relatively easy foreign borrowing, rapid debt accumulation, and the building up of important domestic imbalances. When it became clear, in 1982, that these shocks were not temporary in nature and that foreign financing would no longer be available in significant amounts, countries were forced into drastic adjustments of their economic policies. Yet, several years of adjustment experiences have led to mixed results at best: While many countries have successfully reduced their balance of payments disequilibrium, this has often been accomplished at the short-run cost of severe recession and deterioration in social welfare as well as through a sharp drop in public investment, compromising long-run recovery. The question is not whether these adjustments should have taken place or not, as there was indeed no choice for most countries, but whether the correct mix and intensity of instruments for adjustment has been chosen and whether alternative policy choices could have led to a less severe recession, a faster recovery, and/or lower social costs. To answer these questions we develop, in this chapter, a dynamic, multisectoral model with both real and financial sectors that allows us to assess the impact of the alternative instruments for stabilization.

The instruments that have been used to alleviate the balance of payments deficit include, among the most important, exchange rate devaluation, fiscal austerity, and restrictive monetary policies. They create effects on both real and monetary variables and on the role of the public sector. The way real and monetary phenomena interact and the way public expenditures affect growth and welfare are fundamental determinants of the effectiveness of these instruments for stabilization.

Exchange rate devaluation, an expenditure switching instrument, alters the relative prices of tradables to nontradables, leading to substitutions in consumption and production that will induce an increase in exports and a decrease in imports. The commonly acknowledged drawback of an exchange rate devaluation is an acceleration of domestic inflation, which may cancel the relative price change sought by devaluation, and the consequent need for further devaluation to reach an effective real devaluation. When the initial external imbalance comes, in particular, not so much from external terms of trade changes but from more structural domestic imbalances, such as domestic inflation and a large government deficit, explicit policies to curtail the level of expenditures are needed to complement the devaluation. Reductions in private expenditures are sought through restrictive credit policies, tightening of the money supply, and sometimes a tax increase. Reductions in public expenditures, that is, fiscal austerity, have included cuts in current expenditures (through reduction in government employment and real wages and cuts in subsidies and different welfare programs) as well as in public investment. Reduction of public expenditures is usually considered a high priority in the recommended adjustment policies. It is expected that this would reduce foreign borrowing directly if the deficit had been covered by direct loans to the government and indirectly through the release of funds for the domestic credit market if the government budget had been financed domestically. While usually fairly efficient in achieving this goal, fiscal policies have induced large short-term recessions, as the multiplier of public expenditures is large, and have had direct negative welfare effects induced by reduction in both employment and wages and in public welfare programs. In addition, reductions in public investment reduce productivity growth and hence the profitability and the level of private investment, undermining not only capital accumulation but also the productivity effects of new capital, and hence long-run growth. Monetary policies, by contrast, are thought to be most effective at reducing inflation, an essential prerequisite for successful devaluation, but may compromise long-term growth by raising interest rates and thus constraining investment. If inflation has a strong negative effect on investment and induces capital outflight, monetary instruments will be all the more essential for successful stabilization.

In complement to these demand side stabilization policies, many countries have implemented more structural policies such as credit reforms, liberalization of domestic and foreign trade markets, and some privatization. While the move toward such reforms has been precipitated by the pressing need to improve the efficiency of the economies in crisis, their rationale is not specifically linked to the resolution of the balance of payments problem. If beneficial to growth, their implementation should have been contemplated in any circumstance. For that reason, we will not include them in our analysis, despite the fact that they have been influential on the observed economic and welfare situation.

With such an intricate mix of policies, it is difficult to disentangle from historical analysis the contributions of any single stabilization instrument and to properly understand its specific growth and disaggregated welfare effects. The analysis of these policy packages is further complicated by the fact that the course of reforms rarely went smoothly, policies were introduced at different times, modified or interrupted during their course, while recurrent external shocks modified the conditions under which they applied. For these reasons, the methodology that we adopt is to build a model that will serve as a policy laboratory to analyze and compare the different instruments of stabilization policies and their impact on growth and welfare.

The characteristics of the model are dictated by the focus of our analysis. Our concern with both growth and poverty effects requires a multisectoral, multiclass approach characteristic of computable general equilibrium (CGE) models. Because stabilization programs involve financial phenomena, such as reduction of the rate of inflation and adjustment of interest rates, inclusion of a financial sector in the standard real-side CGE is necessary to allow experimentation with the policy instruments that affect these financial variables. Few CGE models with both real and financial components have been constructed. An early model built for South Korea by Adelman and Robinson 1978 introduced markets for loanable funds and for currency that clear for the equilibrium interest rate and the overall price level. In their specification, however, there is no effect of the overall price level on production and employment and no real balance effects. Therefore, inflation is essentially a monetary phenomenon without any major real effects. In Lewis's 1985 model for Turkey, the focus is on the importance of rigidities in the labor, product, and credit markets in determining the performance in adjustment to an external shock. The model, however, considers few policy instruments and cannot, in particular, distinguish between fiscal and monetary policies. Taylor and Rosensweig's 1984 model for Thailand, which has a more developed financial sector with detailed portfolio decisions by banks, firms, and households, addresses questions of exchange rate, fiscal, and monetary policies very similar to our own preoccupation. Their model is fundamentally Keynesian in spirit, and they can show that, with unemployment and fixed nominal wages, expansionist fiscal policies, even if financed by domestic borrowing, induce very strong growth. The income effect on savings can be so large as to dominate the government's borrowing effect, inducing an investment expansion (crowding in). Conversely, fiscal restraints can only have huge recessive effects. As for monetary contraction, it raises interest rates, reducing investment and national income. Inflation therefore has no detrimental effect on the real side of the economy, thus depreciating the potential role of monetary policies as instruments for stabilization. Finally, Bourguignon, Branson, and de Melo 1992 have further refined the specification of a financial CGE by introducing imperfect adjustment of wages to inflation, and expectations formation regarding inflation and devaluation. In contrast to the previous two studies, their model is dynamic, allowing for potentially interesting constrasts between the short- and long-term impacts of alternative policies.

All previous financial CGEs consequently underplay two mechanisms that we believe to be essential for the analysis of stabilization policies: The transmission between financial and real phenomena, with eventually important resulting growth and welfare effects; and the role of public investment and current expenditures as distinct from but complementary to, respectively, private investment and private income. We consequently include in our financial CGE model a number of features to capture these effects including the impact of the dynamics of inflation on wages, investment, and capital outflight; and the role of public expenditures on growth through public investment and on household welfare through current expenditures.

The model that we built is based on the economic structure of Ecuador. We rely on a complete set of structural data for the base year 1980 and on elasticities estimated for that country. It is, in that sense, a country model similar to the many CGEs built for specific countries. However, we do not use this model to analyze the particular situation of Ecuador but as a policy laboratory. In particular, our analysis differs from the more standard country model analyses on two counts. First, we do not calibrate the model to reproduce the historical path of the 1982–87 adjustment period. This procedure would require complete specification of the many shocks that have hit Ecuador, beside the balance of payments shock, which is our main concern, and to implement in the model the many other policy reforms adopted by Ecuador throughout the course of its adjustment program. Constructing a model to reflect many aspects of the Ecuadorian economy which are not the concern of our analysis, would imply tremendous costs. Instead, we calibrate the model on a smooth historical trend, extrapolated from the previous decade, that would have prevailed in the absence of shocks and with continuity of that period's policy choices. We then impose a foreign sector shock similar to that which affected Ecuador and look at the performance of alternative stabilization instruments in that context. The focus of the analysis also differs from the country case studies. We are less concerned with finding specific policy combinations for a specific country than with looking at structural variations that may represent alternative countries. In particular, the core of the analysis is a sensitivity analysis on the most crucial parameters of the financial sector, which allows identification of the structural features that strongly affect the performance of the different stabilization instruments.

In the remainder of the chapter, we first construct a CGE model with real and financial sides and present the corresponding data base. Then we use this model to perform dynamic simulations of different approaches to stabilization and assess their implications in terms of growth and income distribution. Finally, sensitivity analysis is performed to assess the impact of alternative economic structures on the solution of the model. The conclusion summarizes the main results.

The CGE Model: Real and Financial Sides

Financial Sector Overview

The present model integrates a neoclassical general equilibrium model into a complete macroeconomic framework. This framework is based on an IS-LM model of the economy where, for a given price level, the savings-investment imbalance is cleared by the interest rate. This IS-LM model determines the level of aggregate demand, while aggregate supply follows a neoclassical specification where supply depends inversely on the real wage. It is assumed, however, that nominal wages are "sticky" in the short run with the implication that the unemployment rate can differ from its natural rate. Wages adjust in the long run following an "inflation augmented" Phillips curve,

$$\frac{dw}{dt} = f(U) + \hat{\pi},$$

where U is the rate of unemployment and $\hat{\pi}$ the expected rate of inflation. The function f satisfies $f(\bar{U}) = 0$, where $\bar{U}$ is the natural rate of unemployment and takes positive values for $U < \bar{U}$ and negative values for $U > \bar{U}$. Complemented with an adaptative type of expectation formation, this macroeconomic model implies that both fiscal and monetary policies can have a short-run impact on economic activity and on employment. In a steady state with constant growth of money supply, agents will anticipate the correct rate of inflation, and the real wage will adjust to bring the unemployment rate back to its natural rate. (The Phillips curve implies that, with $\hat{\pi}$ equal to actual inflation, real wages will decrease if there is excess unemployment and increase if there is excess labor demand.) Consequently, the steady state level of economic activity is unaffected by growth of the money supply (see Sargent 1987, chap. 5 for a dynamic analysis of this type of model). Monetary policy can bring a permanent increase in the level of economic activity only with an infinitely accelerating growth of the money supply, with the consequence of an infinitely rising inflation.

The financial sector specification follows the approach of Tobin 1969, where households make decisions on consumption and savings, on one hand, and on the allocation of their accumulated savings (or wealth) between various assets, on the other hand. The present model extends that approach by allowing the existence of two domestic financial assets (money and interest-bearing accounts) and one foreign asset. These assets are considered imperfect substitutes because of their differential risks and degrees of liquidity, although the source of this imperfect substitutability is not explicitly modeled.

The various assets and liabilities held by the institutions of the economy can be summarized in the institutions' balance sheets (table 1). For each institution, the sum of assets is equal to the sum of liabilities. Although markets do not exist for all assets, all assets are assumed to have a price with which they can be valued, generally taken as their replacement cost during the current period. For instance, capital stock is valued at the current price of capital, stocks of commodities at the current price index, foreign exchange at the current exchange rate, and bonds at their face value. Consequently, each institution's "accumulated savings" includes the sum of all savings from the institution's current account accumulated over time as well as capital gains and losses on assets and liabilities.

Households can invest their wealth into capital (equity participation in firms) and three financial assets: money, interest-bearing time deposits, and foreign bonds, with the share of wealth allocated to each asset depending on their respective real yields. Money is further assumed to be held in constant proportion between currency and demand deposits. Households' domestic financial assets are deposited into commercial banks, which in turn lend all available funds on the domestic loan market. Firms borrow on both the domestic and international markets to finance their credit needs, with the share of each type of loan depending on the real interest rate on each loan. Assets held by firms are the stock of capital, inventories, and working capital. Working capital is held in money, with a constant currency-deposit ratio as for households. Consequently, their stock of credit need is the sum of their assets minus equity participation (from households) and accumulated retained earnings. As for the government, its assets consist of its stock of capital (accumulated public investment) and its equity participation in firms. These assets are covered by the government's accumulated savings and public borrowing. Borrowing comes from three sources (borrowing on the domestic market, foreign borrowing, and direct credit from the Central Bank), whose respective shares are considered policy variables.

The financial decisions of the households, firms, and government are reconciled through a financial system composed of the Central Bank and the

TABLE 1. Balance Sheet of the Institutions

Assets			Liabilities	
		Government		
Capital stock	PK_gK_g	Central Bank credit to government		DC_g
Equity held	EQ_g	Domestic borrowing		BD_g
Stocks	ST_g	Foreign borrowing		$ER\ BF_g$
		Accumulated savings		AS_g
		Central Bank		
Central Bank credit to government	DC_g	Currency		CU
Foreign currency reserves	$ER\ FF$	Required reserves		RR
Direct credit to private sector	DC_p	Accumulated savings		AS_{cb}
		Commercial Banks		
Required reserves	RR	Demand deposits		DD
Loans	BD	Time deposits		TD
		Accumulated savings		AS_b
		Firms		
Currency	CU_f	Domestic borrowing		BD_f
Demand deposits	DD_f	Foreign borrowing		$ER\ BF_f$
Stocks	ST_f	Accumulated savings		AS_f
Capital stock	$\Sigma_i\ PK_iK_i$	Equity		EQ_f
		Households		
Currency	CU_h	Accumulated savings		AS_h
Demand deposits	DD_h	(i.e., wealth WE_h)		
Time deposits	TD_h			
Foreign currency	$ER\ F_h$			
Equity	EQ_h			
		Rest of the World		
Foreign loans	$ER\ BF$	Foreign currency		$ER\ FF$
		Accumulated savings		AS_r

commercial banks. The financial system determines the supply of money and domestic loans in the economy. Money is composed of currency, CU, issued by the Central Bank and demand deposits, DD, in commercial banks. The Central Bank receives from the commercial banks the required reserve RR with a reserve requirement re on demand deposits. Assuming a constant currency-deposit ratio cu for all institutions holding money, the supply of currency and demand deposits can be summarized in the supply of money MS = $CU + DD = mm\ MB$, where

$$mm = \frac{cu + 1}{cu + re}$$

is the money multiplier and $MB = CU + RR$ the monetary base. The monetary base is equal to the Central Bank's assets net of capital gains (on foreign assets). The Central Bank's assets are foreign exchange reserves, direct credit to the government, and direct credit to the private sector. Credit to the private sector consists mainly of special, subsidized lines of credit aimed at encouraging some types of investment; it will be kept constant in real terms during the simulations.

Domestic loans are supplied in part by the Central Bank as described above and in part by the commercial banks. Commercial banks' availability of funds comes from the deposits of households and firms, from their own savings, and from direct equity participation from households. Domestic loans then will be the difference between these funds and the reserves that the commercial banks are required to hold in the form of deposits at the Central Bank. The amount of domestic loan thus depends on the reserve requirement ratio imposed by the Central Bank.

Most of the specific equations of the model described below combine in a very direct way this general approach with the traditional CGE modeling. Before turning to their detailed description, however, it is worth noting three particular features that have been introduced to capture the specific situation of developing countries and that were found to be critical in determining the outcome of the different instruments for stabilization. These are the influence of inflation on capital flight, the impact of inflation on investment, and the respective role of private and public investment in enhancing productivity growth.

Inflation and Capital Flight
Developing countries, and particularly Latin American countries, have suffered from extensive capital flight during the stabilization attempts of the 1980s. Following the standard portfolio model, the main determinant of the demand for foreign assets is the difference between the expected real rates of return on domestic and foreign assets. This differential is itself determined by expectations on domestic and foreign interest rates, domestic inflation, and devaluation. This is the basic relationship implemented in the overall portfolio allocation model between all four assets (money, domestic and foreign bonds, and equity). In this framework, if a flexible or crawling-peg exchange rate regime is adopted and the government is expected to pass all domestic inflation on to the exchange rate, and if the nominal interest rate reflects changes in domestic inflation, inflation itself has no direct impact on capital flight. Recent studies on capital flight and currency substitution (Khan and Ul Haque 1985, Dornbusch 1984, Cuddington 1987, Ize and Ortiz 1987, Keikar and Keikar 1989, Ramirez-Rojas 1985, Pastor 1990) have, however, pointed out the important role of the perceived relative risk in domestic and foreign assets.

And empirical analyses have in particular identified a significant positive impact of the size of the public deficit (as an indicator of the risk of default on government obligations or of an incentive for the government to tax domestic assets, either directly or through an inflation tax), political risk variables, inflation or expected inflation, and inflation uncertainty on capital flight. Inflation and inflation volatility are seen as sources of relative uncertainty in the real value of domestic assets as nominal interest rates may not adjust as completely and as rapidly as the exchange rate to inflationary pressure. As empirical evidence has also shown that inflation volatility rises with inflation (study by Logue and Willet, cited in Higham and Tomlison 1982), both variables can be represented by the level of inflation itself.

Inflation and Investment
An implication of the impact of inflation on capital flight is that inflation will have an indirect negative effect on investment because it reduces the domestic funds available for loans. There is also indication that inflation directly reduces the demand for investment. Inflation is perceived by agents as a signal of economic problems to come and thus of low future growth. This reduces the expected return on investment, which depends on the future demand for output. Dornbusch and Reynoso 1989 also argue that uncertainty about inflation and about the policy responses to accelerating inflation are a major source of distortions. With an uncertain future, the planning horizon of firms shrinks and, with the risk of controls and policy interventions to slow inflation, investment in productive assets becomes very risky. Resources are then allocated to exploit financial opportunities rather than to real investment. Taking again the inflation level as a proxy for the volatility of inflation, this behavior reinforces the direct negative impact of inflation on investment.

Impact of Private and Public Investment
The principal effect of investment in a five-year time period is not the mere increase in the stock of capital but the technological changes and productivity gains imbedded in the renewal of capital. A growing literature emphasizes the importance of public investment for productivity growth, especially in developing countries where the government has to provide so much of the basic infrastructure, electricity, and telecommunication. For instance, it is clear that the development of agriculture is very difficult without a basic system of roads necessary for the transportation of food to the cities.

This phenomenon is modeled with distinct and complementary productivity effects of both private and public investment in sectoral production functions. It is worth noting that most existing applied general equilibrium models implicitly assume this complementarity. Indeed, these real-side models do not take into account the source (in terms of institution) of investment. All private and public investments are aggregated into one account and then allocated toward sectors with constant shares. Here, on the contrary, the demand for investment as well as its financing are explicitly modeled for each institution.

Real Side of the Model

The equations of the model and a list of the variables are reported in table 2. The real side of the model follows the standard neoclassical specification of general equilibrium models (see Dervis, de Melo, and Robinson 1982). The specification of international trade allows for imperfect substitution between domestic goods and goods on the international market. Domestically produced goods X_i are allocated between exports E_i and goods sold on the domestic market D_i within a constant elasticity of transformation (CET) framework. Hence, the producer price PX_i is itself a CET function of the export price PE_i and of the price of goods sold on the domestic market PD_i (equation 4). D_i is then combined with imports M_i within a constant elasticity of substitution (CES) aggregation function to determine the total supply on the domestic market Q_i, whose price P_i is thus a CES function of PD_i and the import price PM_i (equation 2). Import and export prices (equations 1 and 3) are equal to the world price PW_i converted into domestic currency at the exchange rate ER and adjusted for import taxes tm_i, export taxes te_i, and indirect taxes td_i. A constant trade margin coefficient mg_i is also added to each transaction (hence included in the price), and the corresponding services will be added (see below) to the demand for the trade sector. Equations 5 to 7 compute a set of prices also used in the model: PN_i is the net price (or value-added price) received by the producer and is defined as the price of output from which the costs of intermediate inputs (a_{ji} is the input-output coefficient of input j in output i) and working capital are subtracted. As we shall see, the demand for working capital is assumed to be proportional to the nominal value of production so that the cost of working capital per unit of output is proportional to the nominal interest rate rd. The price of one unit of capital good used for investment in sector i, PK_i, is the average price of its components weighted by g_{ji}, the share of good j in the capital good of sector i. $PINDEX$ is an aggregate price index.

Sectoral gross output X_i^s is a CES function of the given capital stock K_i and labor (equation 8), while a Leontief technology is assumed for intermediate inputs and working capital. The demand for intermediate use of good j in the production of sector i, N_{ji}, is thus given by equation 9. Labor is divided in L imperfect substitute categories corresponding to different skills and aggregated in the production function with a Cobb-Douglas (CD) function. Sectoral labor demand by category L_{li}^d is derived from profit maximization by the firms

Price System

(1) $PM_i = \overline{PWM_i} \, ER \, (1 + tm_i + td_i + mg_i)$

(2) $P_i = CES\left(PD_i(1 + td_i + mg_i),\, PM_i\right)$

(3) $PE_i(1 + te_i + td_i + mg_i) = \overline{PWE_i} \, ER$

(4) $PX_i = CET\left(PD_i,\, PE_i\right)$

(5) $PN_i = PX_i - \sum_j a_{ji} P_j - k_i rd$

(6) $PK_i = \sum_j \gamma_{ji} P_j$

(7) $PINDEX = \sum_i \mu_i P_i$

Production

(8) $X_i^s = a_i \, CES\left(K_i,\, CD(L_{ii}^d)\right)$

(9) $N_{ji} = a_{ji} X_i^s$

Labor Market

(10) $L_{ii}^d = L_{ii}(PN_i, w)$

(11) $L_i^s = \bar{L}_i^s$

(12) $L_i = \sum_i L_{ii}^d$

Wage Determination

(13) $L_i = L_i^s$ full employment

(13) $w_i^t = \alpha \, w_i^{t-1} \left(\dfrac{PINDEX^t}{PINDEX^{t-1}}\right)^{\sigma_1} \left(\dfrac{PINDEX^{t-1}}{PINDEX^{t-2}}\right)^{1-\sigma_1} \left(\dfrac{U_i^{t-1}}{\bar{U}_i}\right)^{-e_2}$

partially indexed wage

(14) $U_i = L_i^s - L_i$

Institutions Income

(15) $KINC_i = (PN_i + k_i rd) \, X_i^s - \sum_l w_l \, L_{ii}^d$

(16) $Y_i = KINC_i - rd^{t-1} \, BD_i^{t-1} - ER \, rf^{t-1} \, BF_i^{t-1}$

(17) $Y_h = \sum_i \alpha_{hi} w_i L_i + \sum_i \alpha_{hi} dr_i Y_i + \alpha_{hb} dr_b Y_b + rd^{t-1} \, TD_h^{t-1}$

(18) $Y_g = \sum_i t_i Y_i + \sum_h t_h Y_h + \sum_i td_i(\overline{PWM_i}\, ER\, M_i + PE_i E_i + PD_i D_i^d)$

$+ \sum_i tm_i \, ER \, \overline{PWM_i} \, M_i + \sum_i te_i \, PE_i \, E_i - rd^{t-1} \, BD_g^{t-1} - ER \, rf^{t-1} \, BF_g^{t-1}$

(19) $Y_b = rd^{t-1}\left(\sum_i BD_i^{t-1} + BD_g^{t-1}\right) - rd^{t-1} \sum_h TD_h^{t-1}$

Product Demand

(20) $C_{hi} = LES\left((1 - t_h) Y_h - S_h,\, P\right)$

subject to the household budget constraint:

$S_h + \sum_i P_i C_{hi} = Y_h$

(21) $C_{gi} = gcons_i \, \overline{GCONS}$

(22) $Z_i = \sum_j \gamma_{ij} I_j + ginv_i \, \overline{GINV}$

(23) $N_i = \sum_j N_{ij}$

(24) $HOUSH_i = \dfrac{HOUSH_{0i}}{\sum_j P_j \, HOUSH_{0j}} \sum_h hous_h \, S_h$

(25) $DST_i = \dfrac{DST_{0i}}{\sum_j P_j \, DST_{0j}} \left(\sum_j \overline{\Delta ST}_j + \overline{\Delta ST}_g\right)$

(continued)

TABLE 2.—Continued

(26) $Q_i = \sum_h C_{hi} + C_{gi} + Z_i + N_i + DST_i + HOUSH_i$

(27) $Q_i = CES\left(D_i^d, M_i\right)$

(28) $\dfrac{M_i}{D_i^d} = CES^*\left(\dfrac{PM_i}{PD_i(1+td_i+mg_i)} \right)$

(29) $X_i^s = CET\left(D_i^s, E_i\right)$

(30) $\dfrac{E_i}{D_i^s} = CET^*\left(\dfrac{PE_i}{PD_i} \right)$

(31) $MG = \sum_i mg_i\left(\overline{PWM_i}\, ER\, M_i + PE_i\, E_i + PD_i\, D_i^d\right)$

(32) $D_i^s = D_i^d$ $i \neq$ trade sector
$D_i^s = D_i^d + \dfrac{MG}{P_i}$ $i =$ trade sector

Households' Capital Account

(33) $S_h = s_{0h}\left(\dfrac{ji_h}{1+\hat\pi} \right)^{\alpha_{Ah}} Y_h$

(34) $\dfrac{g_{1h}}{1-g_{1h}} = \phi_{1h}\left(\dfrac{jp}{jb_h} \right)^{\varepsilon_{1h}} (1+\hat\pi)^{-\varepsilon_{9h}}$

(35) $\dfrac{g_{2h}}{1-g_{2h}} = \phi_{2h}\left(\dfrac{1+rd}{(1+\overline{rf})(1+E\hat R)} \right)^{\varepsilon_{2h}} (1+\hat\pi)^{-\varepsilon_{10h}}$

(36) $jb_h = g_{2h}(1+rd) + (1-g_{2h})(1+\overline{rf})(1+E\hat R)$

(37) $jp = \left(1 + \dfrac{\sum_i KINC_i}{\sum_i PK_i K_i}(1+\hat\pi) \right)$

(38) ...

(39) $\log(H_h) = \alpha_{1h} + \alpha_{2h} \log(Y_h)$
$+ (1-\alpha_{2h}) \log(PINDEX) - \alpha_{3h} \log(ji_h)$

(40) $SK_h = (1-hous_h) S_h - \Delta H_h$

(41) $DEP_h = g_{1h} SK_h$

(42) $\Delta TD_h = g_{2h}(1-g_{1h}) SK_h$

(43) $ER\Delta F_h = (1-g_{2h})(1-g_{1h}) SK_h$

Firms' Capital Account

(44) $\dfrac{I_i}{K_i} = a_0 \left(\dfrac{KINC_i(1+\hat\pi)}{PK_i K_i(1+rd)} \right)^{\varepsilon_{5i}} (1+\hat\pi)^{-\varepsilon_{6i}}$

(45) $H_i = k_i PD_i X_i^s$

(46) $S_i = (1-t_i-dr_i) Y_i$

(47) $BREQ_i = PK_i I_i - S_i - \sum_h \beta_{ih} DEP_h - \beta_{ig} DEP_g + \Delta H_i + \overline{\Delta ST}_i$

(48) $\dfrac{g_{4i}}{1-g_{4i}} = \phi_{4i}\left(\dfrac{1+rd}{(1+\overline{rf})(1+E\hat R)} \right)^{-\varepsilon_{4i}}$

(49) $\Delta BD_i = g_{4i} BREQ_i$

(50) $ER\,\Delta BF_i = (1-g_{4i}) BREQ_i$

Government Capital Account

(51) $S_g = Y_g - \sum_i P_i C_{gi}$

(52) $BREQ_g = \sum_i PK_i\, ginv_i\, \overline{GINV} + \overline{\Delta ST}_g + \overline{DEP}_g - S_g$

(53) $\Delta DC_g = \omega_1 BREQ_g$

(54) $\Delta BD_g = \omega_2 BREQ_g$

(55) $ER\,\Delta BF_g = (1-\omega_1-\omega_2) BREQ_g$

Central Bank

PM_i	Import price in domestic currency
P_i	Price of composite good
PD_i	Price of domestically produced good for domestic market
PE_i	Export price in domestic currency
PX_i	Average producer price
PN_i	Net producer price
PK_i	Price of capital good for investment in sector i
$PINDEX$	Price index
a_i	Total factor productivity
K_i	Capital stock in sector i
X_i^a	Domestic production
N_{ji}	Use of input j in sector i
H_i	Working capital use in sector i
L_{li}^d	Demand of labor of category l in sector i
L_l^s	Supply of labor of category l
w_l	Wage of labor of category l
L_l	Employment of labor category l
U_l	Unemployment of labor category l
$KINC_i$	Capital income of firm i
Y_i	Income of firm i
Y_h	Income of household h
Y_g	Government revenues
Y_b	Banks' income
C_{hi}	Private consumption
C_{gi}	Government consumption
Z_i	Demand for good i for investment
N_i	Demand for intermediate input
$HOUSH_i$	Product demand for housing investment
DST_i	Change in stocks
Q_i	Domestic demand for composite good
M_i	Import
D_i^d	Domestic demand for domestically produced good
D_i^s	Supply of domestically produced good
E_i	Export
S_h	Savings of household h
MG	Trade margin revenues
rd	Nominal interest rate on time deposits and domestic loans
jb_h	Average yield on bonds for household h
jp	Yield on capital asset

(58) $MB = CU + RR$

(59) $RR = re\ DD$

Commercial Banks

(60) $S_b = (1 - t_b - dr_b)Y_b$

(61) $BD = \sum_h TD_h + DD - RR + AS_b$

(62) $AS_b = AS_b^{t-1} + S_b$

Asset Markets Equilibria

(63) $CU = cu\left(\sum_h H_h + \sum_i H_i\right)$

(64) $DD = (1-cu)\left(\sum_h H_h + \sum_i H_i\right)$

(65) $\sum_i \overline{PWE_i}E_i - \sum_i \overline{PWM_i}M_i - \sum_h \Delta F_h + \Delta BF_g + \sum_i \Delta BF_i = \Delta FF$

(66) $ER = \overline{ER}$ or $FF = \overline{FF}$

(67) $BD + DC_p = BD_g + \sum_i BD_i$

(68) $BF_r = BF_g + \sum_i BF_i$

Dynamic

(69) $\hat\pi = \sigma_3\left(\frac{PINDEX^t}{PINDEX^{t-1}} - 1\right) + (1-\sigma_3)\left(\frac{PINDEX^{t-1}}{PINDEX^{t-2}} - 1\right)$

(70) $E\hat R = \hat\pi$

(71) $a_i^t = a_i^{t-1}\ \alpha_i \left(\frac{GINV^{t-1}}{K_i^{t-1}}\right)^{\varepsilon_7}\left(\frac{I_i^{t-1}}{K_i^{t-1}}\right)^{\varepsilon_8}$

(72) $K_i^t = K_i^{t-1}(1 - dk_i) + I_i$

(continued)

TABLE 2.—Continued

Symbol	Definition
ji_h	Average yield on all assets for household h
H_h	Demand for money from household h
SK_h	Flow of savings allocated to investment assets (all assets except money)
g_{1h}	Share (in flows) of investment assets allocated to capital
g_{2h}	Share (in flows) of bonds allocated to domestic bonds (time deposits)
DEP_h	Household capital investment
TD_h	Time deposit of household h
F_h	Foreign bonds of household h
I_i	Investment of firm i
S_i	Retained earnings of firm i
$BREQ_i$	Borrowing requirement of firm i
g_{4i}	Share (in flows) of borrowing requirement financed by domestic borrowing
BD_i	Domestic borrowing from firm i
BF_i	Foreign borrowing from firm i
S_g	Government savings (− = deficit)
$BREQ_g$	Government borrowing requirement
DC_g	Domestic credit to government (from central bank)
BD_g	Government domestic borrowing
BF_g	Government foreign borrowing
MB	Monetary base
FF	Foreign currency reserve in central bank
AS_{cb}	Central bank net wealth (sum of capital gains on foreign reserves)
CU	Currency in circulation
RR	Required reserves
DD	Demand deposits in commercial banks
S_b	Retained earnings of commercial banks
BD	Total loan from commercial banks
AS_b	Commercial banks' net wealth (accumulated savings)
ER	Exchange rate
BF_r	Total foreign loans
$\hat{\pi}$	Expected inflation
$\hat{ER}$	Expected currency depreciation

Symbol	Definition
te_i, tm_i	Export and import taxes on good i
mg_i	Trade margin on good i
td_i	Indirect tax rate on good i
a_{ij}	Input-output coefficient
k_i	Working capital coefficient
γ_{ij}	Capital composition coefficient
μ_i	Weights in price index
t_i	Tax rate on profits in sector i
t_h	Tax rate on income of household h
dr_i, dr_b	Distributed profits for firm i and commercial banks
α_{hl}	Ownership share of household h in labor l
α_{hb}	Ownership share of household h in commercial banks
α_{hi}	Ownership share of household h in capital of sector i
$gcons_i$	Share of good i in government consumption
$ginv_i$	Flow of good i in government investment
$hous_h$	Share of household savings allocated to housing
$HOUSH_{0i}$	Share of good i in housing demand
DST_{0i}	Share of good i in change in stock
$\overline{\Delta ST}_i$, $\overline{\Delta ST}_g$	Change in stocks from firms and government
rf	Foreign interest rate
β_h	Sectoral share of household investment
DC_p	Direct credit from central bank to private sector
re	Reserve requirement ratio
cu	Currency/money ratio (same for households and firms)

Policy Variables

Symbol	Definition
$\overline{ER}$ or $\overline{FF}$	Exchange rate
$\overline{GCONS}$, $\overline{GINV}$	Government consumption and investment
$t's$	Taxes and tariff rates
ω_1, ω_2	Financing of deficit by central bank credit, domestic borrowing, or foreign borrowing
re	Reserve requirement

Functions

Symbol	Definition
CES	Constant elasticity of substitution function
CET	Constant elasticity of transformation function
CES*	Derived relation from cost minimization in a CES
CET*	Derived relation from revenue maximization in a CET
CD	Cobb-Douglas function

Exogenous Variables and Coefficients

Symbol	Definition
$\overline{PWM}_i$	World price of imported good i
$\overline{PWE}_i$	World price of exported good i

and depends on the net price of output and the vector of wages w (equation 10). Labor supply by category L_l^s is assumed to be given in the current period (equation 11). The labor market can be closed in two alternative ways: In the neoclassical closure (equation 13), the wage rate is perfectly flexible and adjusts to clear the labor market. In the Keynesian closure (equation 13'), the wage rate is given by an independent relation and unemployment appears. In both cases, realized employment in category l, L_l, is equal to the demand for labor (equation 12), and unemployment is defined by equation 14. In most simulations, the closure with partially adjusting wages will be used (see below under "dynamics" for a discussion of the wage adjustment mechanism).

Capital income by sector is given in equation 15 as sales revenues net of taxes, intermediate costs, and labor payments. A firm's net income Y_i (there is one firm by sector) is equal to its capital income from which interest on previous borrowing is deducted. The households derive their income from payments to labor services and other transfers. The households are divided into socioeconomic groups depending on their assets, education, and geographical location. Household h receives income (equation 17) from labor of each category l (in proportion α_{hl}, which is its ownership share in labor category l), distributed profit from each firm i and banks (in proportion α_{hi} and α_{hb}, which are its ownership shares in firm i and banks), and interest payments from its time deposit account. The government (equation 18) receives direct taxes on firms' profits and household incomes, import duties and export taxes, and pays interest on its borrowing from the previous year. Banks (equation 19) receive income from interest payments on government and firms' borrowing and pay interest on time deposits to households.

The demand for goods by households is given in equation 20. Households' consumption functions depend on their disposable income, savings, and the vector of prices. Saving behavior is described below in the capital account. The demand functions satisfy the household's budget constraint, which states that its income must equal the sum of its savings, tax payments, and consumption expenditures. A linear expenditure system (*LES*) is chosen as the functional form for the household consumption functions.

Government total demand for consumption (*GCONS*) and investment (*GINV*) are policy variables, but their sectoral allocation is given by fixed coefficients (in equations 21 and 22). Demand for goods for investment purposes also comes from the private sector. It is derived from sectoral investment demands through the matrix of coefficients γ_{ij} that gives the composition of investment goods in each sector. Total demand for investment is Z_i (equation 22). Demand of good i for intermediate use in equation 23 is the sum of the demands N_{ij} (from equation 9) from each sector j.

Equations 24 and 25 give the demand for goods for housing and changes in stocks. To simplify the model, it is assumed that nominal expenditures on these items (determined in the model's capital account) are allocated across goods with constant proportionality coefficients.

Total demand for goods Q_i (equation 26) is the sum of all demands described above. It is shared between imports and domestically produced goods according to a ratio that depends on their respective prices (equations 27 and 28), which determines the demand for domestically produced goods D_i^d. The supply of goods X_i^s is also allocated between goods sold for exports and goods sold domestically with a ratio depending on their respective prices (equations 29 and 30). Equation 31 defines the revenues from the trade margin, which is considered a demand for the trade sector output. The goods market is completed by equation 32, which imposes equilibrium between demand for and supply of domestic goods.

Financial Side of the Model

Although the balance sheets described above show the stocks of assets and liabilities, most behavioral equations are stated in flows rather than stocks in the formulation of the model. The only exceptions are the demand for money by households and firms. This formulation implies that previous period stocks of assets other than money are not renegotiated in the current period, the decision of allocation between assets corresponding only to the new savings of the period. This seems a reasonable assumption for a country that has a very underdeveloped stock market and financial sector. This restriction on portfolio reallocation, however, precludes the very large swings that would be produced by letting households and firms completely restructure their portfolios at each period and reduces the difference between monetary and fiscal policies with respect to their impact on the domestic interest rate. The description of the model in table 2, therefore, does not include the computation of the stock and value of the various "accumulated savings" mentioned in table 1, although this computation is done in the computer model to update assets for the following period.

Total households' savings (equation 33) respond with an elasticity α_{4h} to the average interest rate $jt/(1 + \hat{\pi})$ on all the assets they hold, with this interest rate being itself an outcome of the allocation decisions described below (equation 38). These savings are allocated between the different assets with a branching decision structure as follows: Money demand is given (equation 39) by a traditional money demand function, depending on real income (elasticity α_{2h}), the price level (elasticity 1), and the interest rate on all assets (elasticity α_{3h}). The residual from savings SK_h (from which a constant share $hous_h$ is spent on housing investment; equation 40) is allocated to productive investment DEP_h in proportion g_{1h} (equations 34 and 41). To limit the number of assets, DEP_h includes both equity participation in incorporated firms and direct investment from households in their own productive unit. The share g_1 depends on the return on capital $jp/(1 + \hat{\pi})$ and the average interest rate on financial assets $jb/(1 + \hat{\pi})$ (computed in equation 36). The return on capital (equation 37) is computed as the current period capital income divided by the value of productive capital stock. The remainder of a household's savings is then allocated between domestic assets (time deposits TD_h) and foreign assets F_h, with a share depending on their respective interest rates (equations 35, 42, and 43). The return on foreign assets takes into account the expected devaluation.

As explained above, households are also influenced by the expected level of inflation for their portfolio decisions. Because of liquidity and risk concerns, higher inflation will make them shift out of capital and domestic financial assets toward foreign assets. This effect is included in the model with the elasticity coefficients α_{9h} and α_{10h} and in the share equations 34 and 35.

Firms' investment and financing decisions are summarized in equations 44 to 50. From their income given in equation 16, firms pay profit taxes with a rate t_i fixed by government, distribute a fraction dr_i of their surplus (it is assumed that this fraction is exogenous, estimated from previous years), and keep S_i as savings (or retained earnings; equation 46). Firms require financing (equation 47) to cover their investment, changes in working capital, and changes in stocks. Changes in stocks are considered exogenous in the model and equal in real terms to their base year values. Working capital stock is assumed to be proportional to the nominal value of the firm's production (equation 45). Investment demand by sector depends on the rate of return to capital available in that sector relative to the cost of domestic borrowing rd, with an elasticity ϵ_{5i} (equation 44). As before, the return to capital is measured by the current period capital income (here in that sector) divided by the value of the sectoral stock of capital. As discussed above, investment demand also responds negatively to inflation with an elasticity ϵ_{6i}. Firms finance their holding of assets with their retained earnings, equity, and borrowing. Borrowing is divided between domestic and foreign borrowing with a share depending on their respective real costs (equation 48).

The government's capital expenditures consist of investment, change in stocks, and direct equity participation DEP_g (mostly transfers to public firms). Among these three variables, only investment is considered a policy variable. Equity participation is essentially financing of public firms and is taken as constant. Changes in stocks are also considered exogenous. Given the government savings (equation 51) and capital expenditures, equation 52 determines the government's borrowing requirement $BREQ_g$, which is met from three sources: direct credit from the Central Bank DC_g, borrowing on the domestic loan market BD_g, and foreign borrowing BF_g. The respective shares of borrowing met by these sources (ω_1, ω_2, and $1 - \omega_1 - \omega_2$) are instruments for the monetary policy of the government (equations 53 to 55).

The equations for the Central Bank and the commercial banks essentially restate the equality of their assets and liabilities from their balance sheets given in table 1. Equation 57 calculates the Central Bank's accumulated savings in terms of previous period value and current period capital gains on foreign assets. Equations 56 and 58 define the monetary base in its asset and liabilities forms. In equation 56, direct credit to the private sector DC_p is taken as exogenous. Given the direct credit to the government required by the government deficit financing policy and the foreign exchange reserve derived from the balance of payment equations, the only policy variable left to the Central Bank is the composition of the monetary base in terms of currency and demand deposits. By setting the reserve requirement, re, the Central Bank can implicitly control that composition (equation 59) and, therefore, the supply of money, as previously indicated. In the simulations, the money supply will often be used as the policy variable, implying that the Central Bank sets the reserve requirement necessary to reach the desired level of money supply.

Commercial banks' savings (equation 60) are defined in the same way as savings of the firms and are added to the previous period's accumulated savings to give the new stocks of savings (equation 62). Equation 61, which determines the availability of loans on the domestic market, is derived from the equality of assets and liabilities. The only assumed behavior for the commercial banks is to set the interest rate on loans and deposits such that there is equilibrium on the loan market. For simplicity, it is assumed that the commercial banks set the same interest rate on time deposits and domestic loans.

The remaining equations close the model by imposing equilibrium on all asset markets. Equilibrium on the money market is defined both in terms of currency and demand deposits. Households and firms are assumed to hold money allocated with constant proportions between currency (share cu) and demand deposit (share $[1 - cu]$); hence, the equilibrium conditions of equations 63 and 64. Equation 65 states that the excess supply of foreign exchange, resulting from current and capital account foreign exchange transactions, results in an equivalent increase in Central Bank reserves. With a fixed exchange rate, a change in reserves accommodates any excess supply or demand of foreign exchange. With a floating exchange rate, the Central Bank sets a given change in reserve (generally zero) and the exchange rate adjusts until excess supply or demand disappears (equation 66). Equations 67 and 68 show the equilibria on the domestic and foreign bond markets. In equation 68, BF_r is assumed to adjust to match the demand for foreign borrowing (infinitely elastic supply).

Expectations and Dynamics

As indicated in section 1, the formation of expectations is assumed to follow an adaptative framework. Equation 69 describes the specific equation for inflationary expectations. The expected next year's inflation $\hat{\pi}$ is a weighted average of this year's inflation and last year's inflation, with a weight σ_3 on the current year and $1 - \sigma_3$ on the previous year. As for expectations of devaluation, it is assumed that agents do not expect any real devaluation or revaluation so that expected devaluation is equal to expected inflation (equation 70).

The dynamic part of the model essentially consists in updating the exogenous variables (such as population, productivity gains, and international prices) and stocks of assets. Stocks of financial assets are computed, with beginning of period financial assets stocks equal to the stocks at the end of the previous period. Stocks of commodities in the firms are similarly updated. These are not reported in the table of equations, as they do not affect the rest of the model. For capital stocks, the new period's capital stock is the sum of last period's capital stock (net of depreciation) augmented by last period's investment (equation 72). The depreciation rate is constant over time but varies across sectors. Equation 71 relates total factor productivity growth in each sector i to the sectoral private investment in the sector and to public investment, both of them normalized by the sectoral capital stock. This expression supports both the differential role and the complementarity of public and private investment discussed above.

One important exception to this simple updating mechanism is in the wage adjustment mechanism. The adjustment equation 13' combines the Phillips curve type adjustment described above, with the change in wage negatively correlated with the rate of unemployment, and a partial adjustment mechanism. Rewriting equation 13' as follows,

$$
w_l^t = \alpha \, w_l^{t-1} \frac{PINDEX^{t-1}}{PINDEX^{t-2}} \left(\frac{PINDEX^t / PINDEX^{t-1}}{PINDEX^{t-1} / PINDEX^{t-2}} \right)^{\sigma_1} \left(\frac{U_l^{t-1}}{\bar{U}_l} \right)^{-\sigma_2} ,
$$

elucidates the underlying process of wage formation. Nominal wages are renegotiated at the beginning of each period with a "normal" increase (α) and full adjustment for last year's inflation (third term in the equation). Then, when actual inflation materializes during the period, only partial readjustment of the negotiated base is done to take into account the change in inflation rate from last year. This leads to a loss in real wage in periods of increasing inflation but an increase in real wage in periods of decreasing inflation. We will see that this lag in the wage adjustment process and related cost of labor has important consequences on the path of adjustment of the economy to external shocks that spur inflation and, symmetrically, on the effects of policies designed to control inflation. In the long run, when inflation is stabilized, the rate of unemployment comes back to its natural rate $\bar{U}_l$.

This completes the formal specification of the model. However, its behavior in response to an external shock, or to changes in policy, depends critically on the structural characteristics of the economy. This is imbedded both in the original distributional characteristics between sectors, between factors of production, and between households and in the parameter values used in the functional forms. The complete data base is described in the following section.

Data Base and Model Calibration

The data base for the model simulation consists in a complete set of values for the variables in the base year and in elasticity parameters.

The 1980 Social Accounting Matrix

The construction of the base year (1980) SAM (see Fargeix 1990 for a detailed description) is based on the updating of the 1975 SAM constructed by Kouwenaar 1988 for the real accounts and on original data collection for the capital accounts. A few key structural characteristics extracted from the SAM's flow accounts are given in table 3. Ecuador's economic structure is typical of a small, middle-income oil exporting country. Its GNP per capita places this country at the upper bound of the middle-income countries of the World Development Report classification. Its economy is fairly open to international trade, with imports representing 15.6 percent of domestic consumption and exports 27.4 percent of GDP. Exports are dominated by oil, while most of the imports are industrial goods. Benefiting from high oil prices in 1980, the balance of trade was almost in equilibrium. The balance of payments, however, was not, and its deficit amounted to 19.5 percent of export revenues, or 5.4 percent of GDP. Half of these foreign transfers were debt service payments.

Foreign borrowing in 1980 was, however, greater than this deficit by 60 percent. This covered the foreign asset accumulation of households and allowed for an increase in the foreign reserves of the Central Bank. The government accounted for 74 percent of foreign borrowing, and private firms for the remaining 26 percent. It is this public foreign borrowing that will be cut by 75 percent in the simulations of the debt crisis that follow.

The government occupies a large part in the economy. Its budget amounts to 30 percent of GDP. A particularity of Ecuador, and of many mineral exporters in general, is the importance of the revenues from these mineral exports in the government's budget. In Ecuador in 1980, 37 percent

TABLE 3. Structural Characteristics of the Ecuadorian Economy, 1980

<u>I. Macroeconomic Characteristics</u>

GDP per capita (US$)	1 406 US $	Balance of trade deficit/exports value	1,0 %
Population	7,65 millions	Balance of payments deficit/exports value	19,5 %
Imports/domestic demand	15,6 %	Balance of payments deficit/GDP	5,4 %
Exports/ GDP	27,4 %		

<u>II. Sectoral Characteristics</u>

	Agriculture	Oil	Industry	Util. Constr. Services	Administr.
Share in value-added	13,0	11,5	17,5	48,1	9,9
Share in exports	9,6	54,7	23,0	12,7	0,0
Share in imports	3,3	7,8	74,1	14,8	3,3

<u>III. Government Budget</u>

Share in Revenues			Share in Expenditures
Income taxes and transfers	28,2	Current expenditures	52,4
Indirect taxes and import tariffs	34,8	Transfer to rest of world (inc. debt service)	9,9
Oil revenues	37,0	Miscellaneous current account	9,9
Deficit	17,6	Investment	22,9
		Miscellaneous capital account	4,8

Financing of the deficit (percent)

Foreign borrowing	143
Domestic borrowing	-32
Credit from Central Bank	-11

<u>IV. Household Incomes</u>

	Class Income (U.S. dollars)	Labor Income Agric.	Unskilled nonagric.	Skilled nonagric.	Unincorporated Capital Income Agric.	Ind.	Other nonagric.	Other	Transfers from govt.	Benefits from Govt. Curr. Exp. (% of inc.)
Small farms	1 359	22,5	39,8	3,8	9,3	7,1	11,8	4,3	1,3	4,5
Medium farms	453	30,2	16,3	2,6	34,0	3,8	10,5	2,4	0,2	3,0
Large farms	524	22,5	9,0	4,0	46,2	2,3	13,5	2,1	0,4	3,0
Rural nonagric.	770	3,2	39,7	9,7	9,1	8,7	24,8	4,1	0,6	10,6
Urb. low educ.	2 836	1,4	44,5	8,8	2,7	11,7	19,8	7,3	3,8	9,6
Urb. med. educ.	2 220	0,5	32,8	29,8	0,7	6,4	14,9	9,6	5,3	9,1
Urb. high educ.	1 516	0,3	4,8	64,7	0,8	0,8	11,3	12,3	4,9	2,3
Rural	3 106	18,8	31,2	5,1	19,1	6,2	15,1	3,6	0,8	5,5
Urban	6 572	0,8	31,4	28,8	1,6	7,4	16,2	9,2	4,5	7,7
Total	9 678	6,6	31,3	21,2	7,2	7,0	15,9	7,4	3,3	7,0

<u>V. Income Per Capita</u>

	Population Share	Income per Capita (US$)	Relative to average	Utility* per Capita (US$)	Relative to average
Small farms	30,3	23	0,5	25	0,5
Medium farms	8,1	29	0,6	30	0,6
Large farms	5,0	55	1,1	56	1,0
Rural nonagric.	7,4	54	1,1	60	1,1
Urb. low educ.	32,5	46	0,9	50	0,9
Urb. med. educ.	12,5	93	1,8	101	1,9
Urb. high educ.	4,2	189	3,7	193	3,6
Rural	50,8	32	0,6	34	0,6
Urban	49,2	70	1,4	75	1,4
Total	7,7	51	1,0	54	1,0

* Utility is defined as the sum of net income including transfers plus the cost of imputed benefits from government social expenditures.

of the government's revenues came from oil. The rest came from income taxes and miscellaneous transfers (28 percent) and from commodity taxes (35 percent) in equal shares between taxation of domestic products and import tariffs. There were no export taxes. This direct link between oil exports and government revenues creates a particular problem in that a drop in the world price affects government resources dramatically, before any recession of the economy further decreases the other sources of revenues. But it also means that a devaluation, which revalorizes export revenues in domestic currency, will alleviate the government's budget deficit. Current expenditures on public services and public investment represent, respectively, 52 percent and 23 percent of the government's budget, the rest being transfers to the rest of the world (10 percent), for debt service in particular, and miscellaneous other transfers. Revenues cover only 85 percent of the expenditures. Foreign borrowing was, however, sufficiently large in this year that the government could actually put some money in the domestic credit market rather than borrow from it and reimburse Central Bank's credit rather than turn to this institution for money creation.

The level of disaggregation considered in the model includes nine sectors: two agricultural sectors (export agriculture and other agriculture), the oil sector, two industrial sectors (consumer goods, which include food processing, textiles, and leather; and producer and capital goods), and four mostly nontradable sectors (utilities; construction and transportation; trade; services; and the public sector). The relative importance of these sectors is close to the average values for the middle-income oil exporter countries, with 13 percent for agriculture, 17.5 percent for manufacturing, and 58 percent for the nontradable activities. Export revenues are dominated by oil exports (54.7 percent), followed by manufacturing (23 percent). These include processed agricultural products as well as the emerging shrimp exports, leaving a low share to raw agricultural exports.

For the social disaggregation, we consider three labor categories (unskilled, skilled, and agricultural labor), and seven household classes (small farmers, medium farmers, large farmers, and nonagricultural rural households; and three urban households by level of education). The total income of each class and its decomposition by source are reported in table 3. The poor have strikingly diversified sources of income. Small farmers earn 66 percent of their income from labor services (including labor on their own farm), with two-thirds originating in nonagricultural activities. All farm sizes obtain about 15 percent of their income from profits from nonagricultural activities. The urban poor also have diversified sources of income, with 34 percent of their income from profits in informal sector activities. This is an important feature since it implies that this urban group will be fairly well protected against wage repression policies. By contrast, the urban medium and rich households have high shares of their incomes coming from wages on the market for skilled nonagricultural labor. Profits earned by unincorporated capital and distributed profits from firms account for less than 20 percent of the upper-class income. The benefits from government social programs (health and education) are evaluated at their cost and attributed to each class in proportion to their participation rates. These numbers show the strong urban bias of social programs and the regressivity of their distribution in absolute per capita values.

The last section of table 3 characterizes the distribution of income per capita. Based on the distribution of population per class, income and utility per capita (with utility defined as income plus the cost of imputed benefits from government social programs) are computed. They show a moderate income inequality in rural areas with income and utility ratios of 1 to 2.5 and a higher urban inequality with ratios of 1 to 4. These measures of inequality across groups clearly depend on the level of aggregation considered, but the relatively low initial levels of inequality also reflect the fact that the oil and debt boom of the 1970s had benefited the rural and urban poor through extensive employment opportunities in construction and services and rising real wages. The ratio of 2.2 between average rural and urban incomes justifies the need to separate these two groups when looking at poverty issues.

Elasticities and Other Parameters

Elasticity parameters used in the simulations are reported in table 4. These parameters are as much as possible based on econometric estimates available for Ecuador. In particular, the consumption elasticities used were estimated by Kouwenaar. On the production side, however, his estimations give abnormally low levels of substitution between capital and labor, reflecting extreme short-term rigidities, and more generally accepted values are therefore chosen. Trade elasticities are chosen within the range estimated on more disaggregated data by the authors. Disaggregated estimation of the parameters for the financial side of the model is not feasible due to the lack of data. In particular, there is no time series available on household holdings of financial assets disaggregated by household groups. To limit the number of arbitrary parameter choices, all elasticity parameters are taken as constant across households and across firms. Econometric estimations were done at the aggregate level and compared with estimates found in the literature. The final choices reflect both econometric work and information from these other sources.

As for the other parameters, capital-output ratios and depreciation rates are taken from Kouwenaar. The estimation of the migration rate to urban areas

TABLE 4.   Elasticities and Parameters Used in the Model

I. Household Consumption Parameters

	Urban Households (level of education)			Rural Households (Farm size)			
	Low	Medium	High	Non agric	Small	Medium	Large
Ag exports	0,88	0,83	0,81	0,84	0,88	0,87	0,85
Other ag	0,77	0,73	0,71	0,84	0,88	0,87	0,85
Oil	0,78	0,74	0,72	0,98	1,03	1,02	1,00
Ind. consumer goods	0,71	0,67	0,66	0,81	0,85	0,85	0,83
Ind. producer goods	1,22	1,16	1,12	1,22	1,29	1,27	1,25
Util. Constr. Transp.	0,78	0,74	0,72	0,98	1,03	1,02	1,00
Trade	0,78	0,74	0,72	0,98	1,03	1,02	1,00
Services	1,23	1,17	1,13	1,07	1,13	1,11	1,10
Govt. services	0,99	1,00	1,01	1,01	0,99	1,01	1,03
Frish parameter	-4,00	-3,00	-2,00	-4,00	-4,00	-3,00	-2,00

II. Sectoral Parameters

	Ag exports	Other Ag	Oil	Industry cons.	Industry prod.	Util, const & services	Trade	Services	Govt. serv.
Capital-output ratio (initial)	0,94	1,77	0,53	0,32	0,50	0,94	0,60	1,50	0,00
Depreciation rate	0,02	0,06	0,01	0,09	0,17	0,09	0,14	0,05	0,08
Elasticity in import CES	0,60	0,80	0,80	0,90	0,80	0,60	0,80	0,60	0,90
Elasticity in export CET	0,80	0,60	0,90	0,90	0,60	0,80	0,95	0,95	0,95
Capital-labor in production	0,80	0,80	0,70	0,90	0,90	0,80	0,90	0,95	0,90

III. Household Financial Parameters
(identical for all households)

Savings elasticity	$\alpha 4$	2,00
Money demand function		
Income elasticity	$\alpha 2$	0,70
Interest elasticity	$\alpha 3$	0,70
Physical vs financial share allocation		
Interest rate elasticity	$\varepsilon 1$	4,00
Inflation elasticity	$\varepsilon 9$	4,00
Domestic vs foreign bonds allocation		
Interest rate elasticity	$\varepsilon 2$	6,00
Inflation elasticity	$\varepsilon 10$	3,00

IV. Sectoral Financial Parameters
(identical for all sectors)

Borrowing decision		
Dom. vs foreign borrowing	$\varepsilon 4$	2,00
Investment decision		
Interest rate elasticity	$\varepsilon 5$	1,00
Inflation elasticity	$\varepsilon 6$	1,50
Productivity of investment elasticities		
Public	$\varepsilon 7$	0,015
Private	$\varepsilon 8$	0,015

is based on census statistics that show an annual growth rate of population in the urban sector equal to 1.3 percent above that in the rural sector.

Base Run and Model Calibration

In conjunction with the available information reported above, parameters are finally chosen through calibration of the model. As discussed in the introduction, this Ecuadorian based model, which is used as a policy laboratory, has been calibrated through the generation of a steady-state economy when no foreign sector shocks occur. Trends closely reproduce those observed in the precrisis period in Ecuador, that is, where the annual growth rate was 3.4 percent in GDP, 1.5 percent in government expenditures, and 28 percent in

TABLE 5. Fiscal and Monetary Policies in Response to a Terms of Trade and Debt Crisis

Note: The three adjustment blocks (Exchange Rate Adjustment, Fiscal Adjustment, Monetary Adjustment) all fall under the heading "Terms of Trade and Debt Crisis." The BASE Values column additionally shows the figure "25" at the top of the column and again below the Private investment row.

	BASE Values	Base Run: No Shock				Exchange Rate Adjustment				Fiscal Adjustment				Monetary Adjustment			
	Year 1	Year 2	Year 3	Year 7	Last year growth	Year 2	Year 3	Year 7	Last year growth	Year 2	Year 3	Year 7	Last year growth	Year 2	Year 3	Year 7	Last year growth
GDP																	
Real GDP growth rate*	3,4%	3,4	3,1	2,6	2,6	-0,1	-1,9	1,0	1,0	-3,0	-0,5	1,5	1,5	-2,3	-0,2	1,3	1,3
Real GDP (millions US$)	10 758	3,4	6,6	18,8	2,6	-0,1	-1,9	0,5	1,0	-3,0	-3,5	3,4	1,5	-2,3	-2,5	3,5	1,3
Government deficit / GDP*	4,0%	3,9	3,8	3,8		7,1	8,5	9,9		3,4	4,0	3,7		8,4	9,3	9,2	
MONEY																	
Monetary base growth rate*	20%	21,5	23,9	36,8		111,9	94,7	51,5		35,4	51,5	42,9		121,5	78,1	35,7	
Money supply growth rate*	28%	30,0	30,0	30,0		40,0	40,0	40,0		40,0	40,0	40,0		25,0	25,0	25,0	
Inflation rate*	25%	26,2	26,5	27,2		46,7	45,6	39,5		48,3	41,7	38,6		32,4	25,9	24,0	
Real interest rate*	0%	-0,6	0,2	3,9		17,0	29,8	40,0		-4,8	5,1	6,8		32,1	42,4	43,6	
Private investment (millions US$)	1 678	2,8	5,2	13,1		-39,3	-46,8	-45,7		-28,7	-33,0	-26,0		-39,2	-40,1	-34,8	
BALANCE OF PAYMENTS																	
Exchange rate devaluation*	25%	25,0	25,1	25,3		75,3	41,9	39,0		81,1	38,5	37,8		54,3	23,5	23,5	
Exports (millions US$)	2 952	4,2	8,4	24,1		10,8	10,5	15,6		12,0	12,7	22,7		8,4	9,2	18,2	
Imports (millions US$)	2 981	3,6	7,0	20,9		-14,8	-16,6	-13,7		-16,2	-16,5	-9,6		-15,8	-15,6	-9,9	
Current account deficit / GDP*	4,9%	4,6	4,3	3,5		3,3	3,0	2,9		2,6	2,5	2,3		3,7	3,7	3,3	
Capital flight (millions US$)	196	8,9	16,0	34,8		-27,5	-27,2	-42,9		5,2	0,3	-6,6		-50,5	-57,6	-61,5	
EMPLOYMENT																	
Employment (1,000 persons)	1 593	0,3	0,4	0,7		2,5	-4,6	-3,7		0,0	-5,5	-1,4		-4,0	-6,9	-2,1	
Average real wage (US$)	3 600	4,4	8,9	26,7		-6,7	1,1	2,2		-8,9	-3,3	-1,1		0,0	4,4	4,4	
WELFARE																	
Per capita income (US$)																	
Rural small farmers	586	2,6	5,0	12,7	1,6	-0,9	-3,6	-6,9	-0,6	-3,0	-4,2	-2,6	0,2	-2,8	-4,0	-3,7	0,0
Rural medium farmers	731	2,5	4,6	10,7	1,2	1,2	-1,3	-7,3	-1,2	0,1	-0,2	0,4	-0,1	-1,2	-2,9	-4,3	-0,4
Rural large farmers	1 369	2,2	4,0	9,1	0,9	1,6	-1,2	-7,9	-1,3	0,7	0,1	0,1	-0,3	-1,1	-3,2	-5,0	-0,6
Rural nonagric. activities	1 360	2,4	4,5	11,8	1,5	-1,6	-5,2	-7,7	-0,3	-4,2	-6,7	-5,2	0,2	-3,8	-5,3	-4,4	0,1
Urban low education	1 141	1,2	2,2	4,7	0,4	-3,9	-8,1	-13,5	-1,3	-7,0	-10,3	-12,6	-0,8	-5,5	-7,7	-10,5	-0,9
Urban medium education	2 322	1,5	2,8	6,6	0,7	-5,2	-8,5	-13,5	-1,3	-9,5	-12,2	-14,4	-0,8	-6,1	-7,8	-10,7	-0,9
Urban high education	4 718	2,0	3,9	9,7	1,2	-6,0	-8,3	-13,4	-1,4	-12,2	-14,3	-17,0	-0,7	-6,0	-7,3	-10,7	-0,9
Per capita utility (US$)																	
Rural small farmers	613	2,5	4,8	12,2	1,5	-0,9	-3,4	-6,5	-0,5	-3,6	-4,8	-3,2	0,2	-2,6	-3,8	-3,4	0,0
Rural medium farmers	753	2,4	4,5	10,5	1,1	1,2	-1,2	-7,0	-1,1	-0,4	-0,7	-0,1	-0,1	-1,1	-2,8	-4,1	-0,4
Rural large farmers	1 410	2,1	3,9	8,8	0,9	1,6	-1,2	-7,6	-1,2	0,1	-0,4	-0,3	-0,3	-1,1	-3,0	-4,8	-0,5
Rural nonagric. activities	1 505	2,2	4,1	10,9	1,4	-1,4	-4,6	-6,7	-0,2	-5,5	-7,7	-6,2	0,2	-3,4	-4,8	-3,8	0,1
Urban low education	1 250	1,0	1,8	3,8	0,3	-3,7	-7,5	-12,8	-1,2	-8,0	-11,1	-13,4	-0,9	-5,1	-7,2	-10,1	-0,9
Urban medium education	2 533	1,3	2,4	5,6	0,6	-4,8	-7,9	-12,9	-1,2	-10,2	-12,8	-15,1	-0,8	-5,7	-7,3	-10,3	-0,9
Urban high education	4 826	2,0	3,7	9,4	1,1	-5,9	-8,1	-13,3	-1,4	-12,4	-14,4	-17,2	-0,7	-5,9	-7,2	-10,6	-0,9

* Results in level every year.
Results for Years 2 to 7 are in percent deviation from Year 1, except for rows marked with *.

money supply. These rates imply a rate of inflation of 25 percent. This is what is reported as the base run in table 5.

Simulations

The Policy Experiments

The foreign sector shock simulated here originates in a 40 percent reduction in the government's foreign borrowing and a 30 percent fall in the price of primary exports, oil in this case. In the model, variables are at their preshock levels in year 1 and the shock occurs in year 2. In table 5, we report the preshock values in year 1, the effects of the shock in years 2 and 3, and the values reached in the last year simulated, year 7. Since the growth rates in GDP and in per capita incomes or utilities in that last year are important in assessing future growth, they are also reported. The three policy responses available to the government in year 2 are the following.

Exchange Rate Adjustment
In this case, government's current expenditures and public investment continue to grow, as in the base run without shock, at an annual rate of 1.5 percent. All the macroeconomic adjustment to the foreign sector shock is expected to come from expenditure switching based on adjustment of the exchange rate. Devaluation occurs to save the necessary foreign exchange required by the foreign sector shock. Devaluation implies imported inflation, and the money supply is allowed, consequently, to increase by an exogenous 40 percent annually, compared to 27 percent in the preshock base run, in order to accommodate the rising demand for money.

Fiscal Adjustment
Public expenditures are reduced, in the shock year, in order to maintain the government deficit at the same level as before the shock. The cut affects current expenditures and public investment, which are both reduced by 18 percent relative to the level that they would have had without adjustment in year 2. Afterward, government expenditures are allowed to grow at the annual rate of 1.5 percent as in the base run. Money supply continues to grow by 40 percent annually.

Monetary Adjustment
To fight inflation that is fueled by devaluation and government domestic borrowing, the annual growth in money supply is reduced to 25 percent in all periods. Government expenditures continue to grow at 1.5 percent per year as in the case of exchange rate adjustment.

Simulation Results

The results obtained for the impact of the shock with exchange rate adjustment only and with implementation, in addition, of fiscal and monetary policies are given in table 5 and figure 1.

Exchange Rate Adjustment Only
Resisting the introduction of fiscal and monetary policies in spite of the foreign sector shock has two consequences that are commonly found with real CGE analysis: The loss of foreign exchange leads to a sharp devaluation of the exchange rate (75 percent in year 2) and to a fall in absorption, both of which are contractionary in GDP. The three additional phenomena that are captured by the financial CGE are the following:

1. The rising price of tradables, induced by exchange rate devaluation, creates inflation. Because wages are only partially indexed in a period of rising inflation, the level of real wages falls by 6.7 percent in year 2. This allows the quantity supplied in some of the more tradable sectors to increase and employment to increase temporarily. Overall, the short-run recession is, consequently, only minimal (−0.1 percent change in GDP relative to preshock). In period 3, however, the rate of inflation starts to decline and real wages overshoot. This occurs when the crisis induced by the foreign sector shock comes about full force. Employment falls by 4.6 percent and GDP by 1.9 percent. The partial wage adjustment mechanism, therefore, delays the recession, and the full negative effect of the crisis takes two years to materialize.
2. Falling foreign borrowing without reduction in expenditures increases the government deficit by 76.6 percent. By borrowing on the domestic

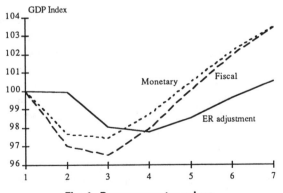

Fig. 1. Base parameter values

market, interest rates rise sharply and private investment is crowded out as it falls by 46.8 percent in year 3. It is this rise in interest rates that eventually will call upon implementation of fiscal policies.
3. Finally, inflation has a direct detrimental effect on investment. Indirectly, inflation could also have a negative effect on investment through increasing capital outflight and decreasing investable funds. In this case, this does not happen as the sharp rise in interest rates counteracts capital outflight.

Resorting to exchange rate adjustment only in response to the crisis thus has a low cost on economic growth in the very short run because of the lag in wage adjustment. In the medium run, however, it leads to a sharp increase in interest rates and inflation, resulting in a fall in economic growth. It is to counteract these negative effects on interest rates and inflation that fiscal and monetary policies are eventually introduced.

In terms of welfare effects, we see (table 5) that real exchange rate devaluation leads to terms of trade effects that benefit agricultural households but hurt urban households. In the short run, the main gainers are the large farmers. Over time, the small restoration of growth and the decline in the inflation rate lead to a fall in the real exchange rate, eroding the large farmers' real income gains, which become negative. In the short run, the main losers are the urban rich. This is due to the fact that real wages fall in year 2 and then employment falls in year 3 when wages recuperate, leading in all years to a decline in the wage bill. The urban poor, who are partially sheltered by the informal sector, suffer a lower decrease in real income. In the long run, however, the income levels of all classes tend to converge back to their initial levels, and the relative losses in per capita income are due only to differential population growth rates in the urban and rural areas.

Fiscal Adjustment
With a reduction in government expenditures, the levels of government deficit and borrowing decline, putting less pressure on the interest rate, which falls sharply relative to stabilization by exchange rate adjustment only. This allows private investment to increase relative to the exchange rate approach, and long-term growth is higher. This reduction in crowding out of private investment occurs through the loanable funds market. This long-term positive effect of fiscal policies will be all the more important if the productivity effect of private investment is large compared to that of public investment, an effect that we will detail later.

The long-term positive effect of fiscal policy is compromised by two negative short-term effects. The first is that fiscal austerity leads to a change in the composition of aggregate demand from government expenditures to private investment. Government expenditures were largely directed at labor intensive nontradables (public services and construction) while private investment has a high share of more capital intensive commodities and a high share of imported capital goods. The result is that it creates lower multiplier effects and reduces economic growth in the short run.

A second negative effect occurs specifically via monetary phenomena: Falling interest rates lower household savings and induce them to hold on to higher levels of currency. This form of hoarding creates a leakage that reduces aggregate demand and lowers economic growth. Displacement of one dollar of public expenditures is thus replaced by less than one dollar of private expenditures, deepening the short-run multiplier effect and the magnitude of the recession.

In terms of welfare, all households lose from the short-run recession induced by fiscal instruments compared to exchange rate adjustment only. By far, the main losers are the urban medium and rich classes since fiscal austerity reduces public sector employment, which is important to them. Urban poor and rural nonagricultural households, on the other hand, lose more from reductions in access to benefits that are included in the valuation of their utility. In the long run, however, fiscal austerity favors economic growth and lowers poverty relative to the exchange rate approach, particularly in the rural sector.

Monetary Adjustment
A quantitative comparison of fiscal and monetary adjustments in the CGE is not very meaningful. We have chosen to simulate a fiscal policy that cuts the fiscal deficit to its precrisis level and a monetary policy that restores a level of money growth close to its pre-crisis level. In both cases, some complementary exchange rate devaluation is needed to ensure that the balance of payments constraint, which is the only ultimate objective of the stabilization policies, is satisfied. It is clear that different levels of fiscal or monetary austerity would therefore displace the GDP curves represented in figure 1 and change the time at which these may cross each other. A comparison of the shape of these GDP curves, the achievements of these two approaches to stabilization on the intermediate objectives of public deficit and inflation, and the different ways by which they attain the external balance objective is, however, very revealing. This can already be seen in the present simulations and will be further explored in the sensitivity analysis.

As shown by figure 1, a monetary approach to stabilization induces a lower short-run recession but a lower level of long-run economic growth. In the short run, reduction in the money supply raises interest rates and lowers sharply private investment, which falls by 40 percent as in the case of exchange rate adjustment only. The fall in GDP is, however, less than with a fiscal adjustment since the level of government expenditures continues to increase, thus avoiding the negative short-run multiplier effect of fiscal policies. Also, in the short run, falling private investment has a low opportunity cost on productivity growth. Control of inflation has, however, long-term beneficial effects on investment.

Reduced inflation has a direct effect on investment since it increases the clarity of price signals and reduces risk. In addition, reduced inflation helps contain capital outflight to about 40 percent of the precrisis level, while a fiscal approach has no impact on capital outflight. Reduced capital outflight increases the availability of loanable funds and puts downward pressure on interest rates, favoring investment.

In terms of welfare, a monetary adjustment is more neutral on the distribution of income than a fiscal policy (table 5). Lower real exchange rate devaluation benefits less the large farmers and hurts less the urban consumers. Falling inflation also raises real wages which benefits both the rural poor and the urban classes. Finally, employment in public works projects and in government services is preserved, and this is of greatest benefit to the urban medium and high households.

In conclusion, the short-run cost of the crisis on economic growth is less with exchange rate adjustment than with monetary policies and less with monetary than with fiscal adjustment. Failing to adjust, although tempting in the short run, has a high opportunity cost in the long run as GDP growth remains sluggish. A fiscal approach has a highly negative short-run effect compared to a monetary approach. In the long run, however, the fiscal adjustment is superior for economic growth. Extended over a sufficient number of years, the trade-off between short- and long-run gains thus requires assessment of these different adjustment strategies in terms of alternative discount rates. In terms of welfare, a monetary approach distributes more equally the burden of stabilization while a fiscal approach shifts most of the cost to the urban households, skilled workers most particularly.

Sensitivity Analysis

With weak empirical validation for several parameters used in the model, it is important to see how the solutions obtained respond to different values given to a number of the model's key parameters. We do this by assessing how the optimum policy for growth, measured in different years and under alternative discount rates, is affected by a high or low impact of inflation on investment, a high or low impact of inflation on capital outflight, a rigid or flexible financial sector, and whether the formation of expectations on inflation responds to past inflation and, hence, to the ability of government to affect inflation. We give, in table 6, the ranking of policies for economic growth under these alternative parameter values.

TABLE 6.   Sensitivity Analysis (Ranking of Policies for Economic Growth)

Structural Features	Short Run Year 2	Discount Rates 30%	5%	Long Run Year 7
Reference parameters values	E > M > F	M > E > F	M > F > E	+M = +F > +E
Impact of inflation on investment				
Lower	E > M > F	E > F > M	+F > +E > M	+F > +M > +E
Higher	E > M > F	M > E > F	M > F > E	+M > +F > E
Impact of inflation on capital flight				
Lower	E > M > F	E > M > F	M > F > E	+F > +M > +E
Higher	E > M > F	M > E > F	M > F > E	+M > +F > +E
Rigidity of the financial sector				
More rigid	E > M > F	F > E > M	F > M > E	+F > M > E
More flexible	E > M > F	M > E > F	+M > E > F	+M > +F > +E
Constant expectations of inflation	E > M > F	E > F > M	F > E > M	+F > +E > M

E = Exchange rate adjustment
M = Monetary adjustment
F = Fiscal adjustment
+ = Positive GDP growth over base year

Impact of Inflation on Investment (fig. 2)

With the model's base parameter values, we have seen in figure 1 that fiscal policy is worse for GDP growth in the short run, but that it catches up with monetary policy in the last period, with a consequently higher long-run growth rate. The higher the elasticity of expected inflation on investment, the higher is the cost of letting inflation run away under either exchange rate adjustment or fiscal policy. The result is that the positive effect of a fiscal adjustment on investment is contradicted by high inflation. Except for the very short run, where the exchange rate adjustment option dominates, a monetary approach is thus most desirable when the impact of inflation on investment is high, while a fiscal policy is the most desirable when it is low.

Impact of Inflation on Capital Outflight (fig. 3)

Inflation increases capital outflight, which diminishes the supply of loanable funds. This raises the interest rate and lowers investment. As a result, the higher the effect of inflation on capital outflight, the more costly the neglect of inflation becomes. In this case, the dominance of monetary policies over fiscal policies is increased, even at low discount rates. If inflation has little effect on interest rates via capital outflight, then, to the contrary, the control of inflation is not as important and fiscal policies dominate in the long run. Even under this situation, the short-run cost of a fiscal over monetary adjustment leads to preference for a monetary approach when discount rates are high.

Role of Flexibility in the Financial System (fig. 4)

Greater flexibility in the financial system implies a higher response of savings

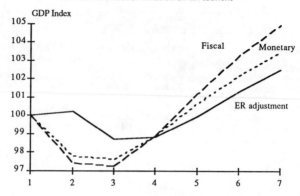

2a: Lower effect of inflation on investment

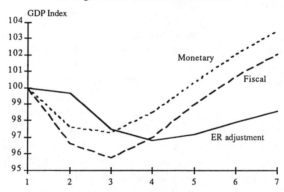

2b: Higher effect of inflation on investment

Fig. 2. Effect of inflation on investment

to interest rates and a greater substitutability in the allocation of assets between domestic and foreign bonds. This has a direct effect on the effectiveness
of monetary as opposed to fiscal policies in restoring economic growth. The
monetary approach to stabilization, in reducing the money supply, raises
interest rates. The positive side of the rise in interest rates is that it reduces
capital outflight and increases the flow of savings; the negative is that it deters
investment.

If the financial sector works well, the interest rate will not rise as much,
investment is preserved, and long-run growth is safeguarded. In this case a
monetary approach is best for growth, and even an exchange rate adjustment
approach is better than fiscal interventions. The converse holds under a shal-
low financial sector, and the fiscal approach to stabilization is best. This is
because, if the financial sector is not responsive to interest rates, resources

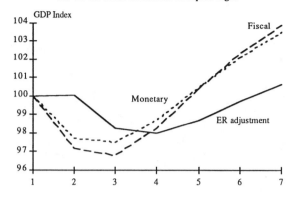

3a: Lower effect of inflation on capital flight

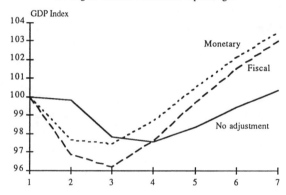

3b: Higher effect of inflation on capital flight

Fig. 3. Effect of inflation on capital outflight

need to be freed directly from use by government to lower interest rates. Thus, countries with well-developed financial institutions will not have to turn as intensely toward government resources in order to shelter private investment from the liquidity crisis.

Constant Expectations of Inflation
The formation of expectations on future inflation is key in portfolio allocation and investment decisions. If adjustment is not credible in breaking expectations of future inflation, monetary policy will be ineffective: capital outflight remains high, the rate of interest skyrockets, and investment is low. Implementation of a monetary policy provokes a recession without the benefits of reducing the rate of inflation. The result is that investment is lower than under exchange rate adjustment, and the economy does not recover from the crisis.

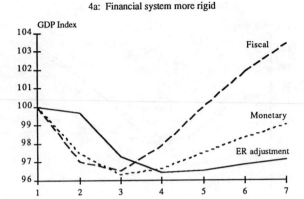

4a: Financial system more rigid

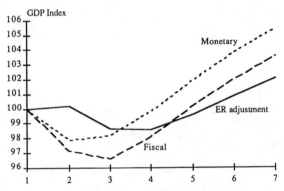

4b: Financial system more flexible

Fig. 4. Functioning of the financial system

In this case, with the formation of expectations out of control, a fiscal alternative is clearly superior. Making the control of inflation a credible component of stabilization policies is thus a key condition for success of a monetary approach. To a large extent, this is conditional on the degree of legitimacy that a government has been able to acquire in past experiences of crisis management and on its ability to communicate to the public the logic of its stabilization package.

Conclusion

In this paper, we have built a CGE model with a financial sector in order to analyze stabilization programs implemented in response to external debt crisis. The model differs from previous similar studies by several features that are essential in assessing the impact of the different instruments used in stabilization policies. First, we include the negative effects that inflation has on the economy, originating mainly in the uncertainty that it creates over the future development of the economic environment, thus inducing capital flight and discouraging productive investment. This specification allows us to capture the benefits that inflation control achieved by restrictive monetary policies can have on the economy in spite of the higher interest rates that they also induce. Second, we specify the complementary role of public and private investment in creating productivity gains. In doing so, we can assess the potential trade-off in fiscal policies, which, on the one hand, release the pressure on the interest rate and thus facilitate private investment, while, on the other hand, negatively affect growth by curtailing public investment. Third, we specify a mechanism of partial adjustment of wages to inflation by which real wages tend to fall when inflation accelerates and to rise when it decelerates. Finally, we measure the welfare effects of fiscal expenditures by computing for the different household classes a level of "utility," which is the sum of their real income and of the imputed benefits that they derive from access to public services.

The main results are the following: (1) Lack of adjustment beyond the use of a flexible exchange rate is tempting in the short term but has a long-term negative impact on growth; (2) All adjustments that include devaluation favor rural households over urban households and large farmers over small farmers; (3) Fiscal adjustment is necessary to protect private investment and enhance long-term growth but it has a very high short-run recessive impact and hits particularly hard the urban population; (4) The control of inflation by monetary policies is a necessary complement to fiscal policies in order to reduce capital flight and encourage investment; (5) Sensitivity analysis shows that monetary policy is less efficient the less responsive the financial market is and the less credible the ability of the government to control inflation. In both cases, fiscal adjustment tends to be a superior alternative; (6) On the other hand, monetary policies are more important the more responsive are capital flight and investment to inflation.

The optimal choice or mix of exchange rate, fiscal, and monetary policies for economic growth in the context of a foreign sector shock thus depends on structural features of the economy and on the discount rate used to weigh future years. In addition, choice of policy depends on the desired mix of growth and welfare objectives pursued by government. The model developed here allows us to capture some of the complex trade-offs implied by the choice of instruments for stabilization.

Comment

Lance Taylor

This chapter is an interesting application of the 1970s' vintage industrial economy macroanalysis to the case of Ecuador. I have little to say about the technicalities of the model, which are admirably described and deployed in the chapter. I am, however, perturbed by the spirit of the exercise.

The authors postulate either full employment of labor in equation 13 or an adjustment over time to full employment via a Phillips curve in equation 13'. Either way, a natural rate hypothesis is imposed, essentially determining the real wage from all the neoclassical marginal productivity apparatus built into the system. Moreover, with "traditional" money demand functions and a predetermined money supply, the price level will follow from the equation of exchange. Hence, in the natural rate equilibrium, there is no room for historical or institutional determination of money wages and prices.

The key question is whether this Friedmanite apparatus has anything to do with Ecuador. Postulating full employment in any run in a developing country seems risky. A predetermined money supply is something of a rare bird, and although Ecuador's inflation has historically not been fully up to Latin American standards, it must involve a fair degree of determination from the side of costs. If any of the authors' causal hypotheses are violated, the closure of the model would have to change and with it the degrees and directions of many of their results.

In running through their exercises, the authors do not seem to have paused to ask whether or not the causal structure they impose on their accounting has anything to do with the economy at hand. Unless they are willing to undertake a serious institutional justification of their closure, their results amount to clever manipulations of numbers without plausible policy use.

Comment

François Bourguignon

This chapter provides interesting new perspectives on the analysis of policies in an economywide CGE-type model with a financial sector. I have three sets of comments to make.

First, I am not fully convinced by some of the assumptions made in the model. Second, the whole simulation exercise seems to me a little too far from the actual experience of Ecuador. Third, I am not sure about how to interpret the main simulation results given in the chapter.

Modeling assumptions raise the following remarks.

—The assumption that inflation has a positive effect on capital flights and a negative one on investment seems rather ad hoc. Moreover, it largely conditions some important results reported in the last part of the chapter—e.g., those related to growth performances. In a crawling peg exchange rate regime, the monetary authority may well pass on all changes in domestic inflation instantaneously to the exchange rate, and domestic inflation may be perfectly reflected by changes in the nominal rate of interest. Under these conditions, an increase in the inflation rate would produce an increase in capital exports only inasmuch as it modifies future expectations. The assumption made in the model thus seems that a higher inflation rate results in an expected further acceleration of inflation. This may be debatable.

Concerning the effect of inflation on investment, on the other hand, the idea that higher rates imply more uncertainty and, therefore, less investment is also debatable. If they expect that the price of their own product and the cost of capital will follow the general rate of inflation, producers might not react to a change in the inflation rate. The uncertainty accompanying increasing inflation rates may be of second order.

—Modeling the effect of inflation should actually be made within the framework of the portfolio allocation model. Four assets should be distinguished: money, domestic and foreign bonds, and durables or producer goods (equity).

I am also concerned by the fact that portfolio reallocation mechanisms in the model take place only at the margin—except for money holdings—that is, on current savings rather than on the total wealth. This may severely limit the strength of the arbitrage between foreign and domestic interest rates, and also explain why monetary and fiscal policy appear to be rather efficient in the simulations.

—Capital gains are not accounted for in the model. The assumption that savings increase with the rate of interest may be a substitute for it. In any case, it would be of interest to put into evidence what the various policies may imply for the real wealth of domestic agents. This is certainly part of the distribution effects that one would like to investigate with this kind of model.

—The Phillips mechanism in the labor market is fine with me. However, the way it is specified may be considered as a strong assumption, and the fact that real wages fall in times of inflation may be considered as purely exogenous. On the other hand, if there is some temporary nominal rigidity on wages, why is not the same assumption made on prices, with quantity rather than price-clearing mechanisms? Presumably, the short-run effects of a shock or a policy measure would be different.

I turn now to the application of the model to Ecuador. In that perspective, the chapter is a little deceptive. It starts with a quick summary of the macroeconomic events in Ecuador, where it is shown that numerous policy measures have been actually used to stabilize the economy (import rationing, dual exchange rate systems, creation of new financial instruments, credit rationing). It would have been nice to see the effect of such policies analyzed with the model and compared with the efficiency of more orthodox policies. I know this would have required modifying substantially the whole model. However, a brief qualitative discussion of the likely effects of the actual policy decisions would have been useful.

I am not sure about the way the simulations reported in the chapter must be interpreted. In particular, the no-adjustment scenario is rather ambiguous. In fact, it truly corresponds to an adjustment of the balance of payments through a flexible exchange rate regime. Under these conditions, the only disequilibrium left is that of the government deficit. I am not sure this is the most important part of the adjustment packages observed in most developing countries, and the most relevant simulation to perform in the case of Ecuador. The only no-adjustment component in the no-adjustment scenario appears to be the expansionary monetary policy. But what is its objective? To generate inflation, by undoing what nominal devaluations are doing?

The comparison between the three policies (N, M, F) is difficult to interpret. The calibration of the fiscal and monetary policies through a common rate of growth seems questionable. If the objective is to stabilize the economy, both policies should be aimed at reducing the existing imbalances—here the budget deficit—in the same proportions, rather than at achieving the same rate of growth. True, the comparative efficiency of both policies may be analyzed in the present simulations by comparing the budget deficits they lead to. But this requires additional calculations by the reader—which, in fact, cannot be performed on the basis of the summary table of results given.

The sensitivity analysis performed on both simulations is certainly useful. However, I feel that, again, an explicit reference should be made to what the monetary and fiscal policies are supposed to achieve. For instance, by how much should public expenditures be further reduced in order to get the same rate of growth (or government deficit) when capital is more mobile or when the financial system is less flexible?

Part 3
Modeling Imperfect
Competition

CHAPTER 5

Tariffs and Export Subsidies when Domestic Markets Are Oligopolistic: Korea

Jaime de Melo and David Roland-Holst

New developments in the theory of international trade often suggest, implicitly or explicitly, that in imperfectly competitive markets there should be government intervention to achieve optimality. The most celebrated example in this new literature is the profit shifting argument developed by Brander and Spencer (1984). Another example is the argument developed by Krugman (1984), which shows that, under certain circumstances, protection can serve as an export promotion policy. On the other hand, in the trade and development literature, the imperfectly competitive nature of domestic markets has long been recognized but not formally analyzed. Notable exceptions are Balassa (1971) and Bergsman (1974) who recognized that the small size of domestic markets was a hindrance to the exploitation of scale economies and that restrictionist trade policies could lead to substantial monopolistic power by domestic firms. In a previous paper (de Melo and Roland-Holst 1990), we evaluated the Balassa suggestion that, in recognition of externalities, domestic "infant" industries should be granted an across-the-board temporary protection of approximately 10 percent.

In this chapter we explore more systematically how trade policy will be affected by differences in institutional characteristics governing the behavior of sectors with increasing returns to scale. The hallmark of our analysis is that in the typical semi-industrial developing economy, some sectors will have a constant returns to scale technology while others will have an increasing returns to scale technology. As the analytical and simulation results will show, this substantially complicates any assessment of trade and industrial policy.

This setting differs from the one usually treated in the literature on strategic trade policy. There, oligopolistic interactions occur in international

The research reported here is part of the research project "Industrial Efficiency and Trade Regimes," RPO 672–40, and the World Bank. The views expressed here are those of the authors and should not be attributed to their affiliated institutions.

191

markets so that trade policy affects the home country's terms-of-trade. However, the situation described above is more representative of industrial structure and market power for developing and semi-industrialized countries. The purpose of the chapter is then to reexamine the merits of protection, with and without neutrality of domestic and foreign sales incentives, where some sectors operate under increasing returns to scale (IRTS) and where in those sectors barriers to entry may allow firms to behave oligopolistically in the domestic market. In section 1, we derive analytically the welfare effects of trade policy reforms in the setting described above. The results generalize recent work of Dixit 1984 and Rodrik 1988 to the case where domestic output is sold on two markets (home and export) and to where trade policy may induce domestic firm market entry or exit. Because of intermediate linkages, the welfare effects of trade policy changes are not generally determinate in this multisectoral, general equilibrium setting. This motivates the empirical work in section 3 where we explore systematically the effects of tariffs and export subsidies on welfare with a CGE model of a representative semi-industrial country with increasing returns in selected manufacturing activities.

1. Welfare Effects of Tariffs and Export Subsidies

In this section, we derive the welfare effects of import and export policy (taking the form of tariffs and export subsidies) when domestic production takes place under IRTS and market conduct may be oligopolistic. We decompose the various channels by which trade policy affects welfare by treating two cases: 1) no firm entry/exit; 2) firm entry/exit to achieve an exogenously given "normal" profit rate. The case of no entry can be interpreted either as the short-run effects of trade policy or, in the long run, as trade policies combined with industrial policies that make entry sufficiently costly that firms can earn permanent rents (or above normal profits) from domestic sales. To derive analytical results that correspond to the numerical examples given later, we assume that sectoral domestic production is differentiated by destination of sales, that is, products sold on the domestic market and abroad are imperfect substitutes though they are produced by the same technology.[1] Besides allowing for the cross-hauling observed in even the most disaggregated trade statistics, this assumption reflects the widely held view that products for export are different from products sold on the internal market.

Notational conventions follow Dixit 1984. The economy has k tradeable sectors, each consisting of n_i identical firms ($i = 1, \ldots, k$) who produce

---

1. The same is also true of imports and domestic production for domestic use in the numerical application, but we omit this distinction from the analytics for convenience and without loss of generality.

output (z_i) for domestic use (y_i) and export (x_i). As in the numerical application below, the input and allocation decisions are separable. Hence the allocation decision, $z_i = F_i(x_i, y_i)$, only depends upon the relative prices in the producer's domestic and export markets for output.[2] Each identical firm has a representative cost function $c_i(x_i, y_i)$. Domestic and world prices are k-vectors p and P, respectively, as are ad valorem import tariffs t and export subsidies s. Sectoral domestic prices are an inverse function $p(q)$ of domestic demands $q_i = M_i + n_i y_i$, where imports M_i and domestic output are assumed to be perfect substitutes.[3]

To evaluate the welfare effect of import and export distortions, we consider all sectors simultaneously in a general equilibrium framework. In a situation where the government performs only lump-sum transfers and commodity preferences are represented by a single consumer, aggregate welfare can be decomposed into three components. The first of these is consumer surplus, defined over the k sectors as

$$g(q) = \int_0^q p(u)du - p(q)q. \tag{1}$$

This expression is the area under sectoral demand curves, netted of domestic sales revenues. The second component of domestic welfare is the sum across sectors of firm profits:

$$n'\pi = n'[\hat{p}y + \hat{P}(I + \hat{s})x - c(x,y)], \tag{2}$$

where a caret expands the vector in question into a diagonal matrix and a prime denotes a transpose. This expression accounts for revenues from domestic and export sales (which may be subsidized) and total cost. The third component of the domestic welfare function is tariff revenue net of export subsidy outlays, $[t'\hat{P}M - s'\hat{P}\hat{n}x]$. It reflects the direct change in domestic income due to imposing trade distortions at fixed world prices.

The overall domestic welfare function is then given by

$$W = g(q) + n'\pi + t'\hat{P}M - s'\hat{P}\hat{n}x$$

$$= g(q) + n'[\hat{p}y + \hat{P}x - c(x,y)] + t'\hat{P}M, \tag{3}$$

---

2. Imperfect substitutability in the allocation of sales implies that F_{xi}/F_{yi} varies along a convex transformation frontier. Lower case letters indicate variables.

3. By choice of units, the world price vectors for exports and imports are set equal. Purely nontraded goods are sectors for which $M_i = x_i = 0$.

indicating that export subsidies are a domestic transfer and only affect aggregate welfare indirectly.

No Firm Entry/Exit

This case corresponds to the contestable market pricing rule described below, where sunk costs are sufficiently low to make credible the threat of entry, thereby forcing incumbent firms to price at average costs. Alternatively, it can be viewed as a short-run equilibrium with profits and losses or a long-run equilibrium in which industrial policy sustains profits and losses. For the discussion here, the no entry case has the advantage of focusing on the issue of scale efficiency. Consider the comparative static expression

$$dW = t'\hat{P}dM + n'[(\hat{p} - c_y)dy + (\hat{P} - c_x)dx] + \pi dn, \tag{4}$$

obtained by total differentiation of expression 3. Assuming no firm entry then implies $dn = 0$. Expression 4 indicates how domestic welfare varies with imports and domestic output for domestic use and export. The first term indicates that welfare is an increasing function of imports when tariffs ($t = p - P$) are already present, that is, when the value of imports exceeds their marginal cost. The next two terms reflect the benefits to be realized by domestic firms whose marginal costs are below prices in domestic or export markets. Welfare can be increased if firms expand output while prices exceed marginal costs (c_y and c_x) in their respective product markets. This bears out the observations of Venables (1985), Horstmann and Markusen (1986), and Rodrik (1988) on the relationship between welfare and scale economies.

Since we are in a multisectoral general equilibrium setting, the marginal cost terms c_y and c_x are matrices. The off-diagonal elements represent the pecuniary externalities that sectors confer upon one another by changing their output. As will be shown in the numerical application below, expansion of IRTS sectors can shift down the cost curves of downstream sectors. In the case of economywide constant returns to scale (CRTS) and perfect competition, cost curves are flat and firms price at marginal cost, so the terms in brackets in expression 4 equal zero.

To further elucidate the role of tariffs and subsidies, assume that world prices are fixed at unity ($\hat{P} = I$), so $\hat{t} = I - \hat{p}$. Then, assuming $c_z = c_x = c_y$ and recalling that $q = M + \hat{n}y$, expression 4 can be rewritten as

$$dW = t'q_p \, (p_t dt + p_s ds) + n'(I - c_z) \, [z_p p_t dt + z_s ds]. \tag{5}$$

The first term reflects the tariffs' distortionary cost in consumption and will be negative if domestic demand is downward sloping. However, the next terms in brackets show that tariffs and export subsidies can be beneficial if the domestic firm's marginal costs for domestic and export goods are below world prices. Thus with no firm entry/exit, export subsidies are unambiguously beneficial and tariffs are beneficial if the efficiency gains from scale expansion exceed the distortionary costs of protection.[4]

Firm Entry/Exit

In the strategic trade policy literature, the assumption is that entry barriers are sufficient to make rent shifting a realistic possibility. This strong assumption is now under increasing attack (e.g., Harris 1989). In industrializing countries, the issue of entry barriers is even more complicated because of the cross-country diversity in industrial policies. The evidence seems to point toward two outcomes. In one of these, import quantity rationing regimes create strong barriers to entry from foreign competition, but profits under IRTS eventually induce some firm entry, eroding profits. The archetypal example here is the Latin American automobile industry. The other outcome is represented by East Asian examples, where protection in the domestic market is accompanied by subsidies to export sales and industrial policy prevents "excessive" market entry. Clearly, there is no easy way to model firm entry because of the interactions of trade and industrial policies, let alone "strategic" interactions between the government and firms. Hence we will consider two extremes: 1) entry-exit to sustain a zero profit rate; 2) entry/exit to sustain a fixed, nonzero profit rate whose level depends upon trade policy.

Before examining these two cases, it is useful to extend expression 5 to the case where $dn \neq 0$. The augmented expression is

$$dW = t'q_p dt + n'(I - c_z)(y_p dt + x_s ds) - n'(\hat{a} - c_z)\hat{z}\hat{n}^{-1}dn, \qquad (6)$$

where $a = \hat{z}^{-1}c(x,y)$ is a vector of sectoral average costs. The last term shows that, other things equal, wherever there are unexploited economies of scale, firm entry is detrimental to welfare. Since firm entry/exit depends upon profitability, it is useful to write down how the expression for firm profits depends on trade policy. Total differentiation of expression 2 gives

---

4. As before, the comparative static interpretation is complicated by general equilibrium interactions captured in the Jacobian terms q_p, y_p, x_s, c_y, and c_x. In the presence of resource constraints and intermediate linkages, supply and cost Jacobians are unlikely to be diagonal or even diagonal dominant. Unless very strong assumptions are made, one cannot hope to sign the individual terms in expression 5, and empirical estimation is recommended to assess the likely effects of trade policy on welfare.

$$dπ = [\hat{y} + (\hat{p} - c_y)y_p]dt + [\hat{x} + (I + \hat{s} - c_x)x_s]ds$$

$$- (\hat{a} - c_z)\hat{z}\hat{n}^{-1}dn. \tag{7}$$

Note that export subsidies and tariffs increase firm profitability unless there is firm entry to offset this positive effect on profits. If there is no firm entry and $dπ = 0$, as in the contestable market case discussed earlier starting from an initial equilibrium where $π = 0$, a subsidy to exports would lead firms to expand domestic sales, lowering domestic prices (that is, $dt = dp < 0$ is driven down by endogenous forces), and incurring losses until composite profits are zero.

2. Modeling Oligopolistic Domestic Markets

This section spells out the main assumptions describing the CGE model used to analyze trade policy in a setting with IRTS. We focus on the modeling of pricing rules in the domestic market since the remainder of the model is familiar from CGE simulation exercises in a CRTS setting.

In the numerical application, there is product differentiation between exports and domestic sales on the one hand, and between imports and domestically produced goods for domestic sale on the other. As in the discussion above, the country is small in international markets.[5] A Leontief technology is specified for intermediate technology. However, within sectors domestic and imported and domestic inputs are imperfect substitutes (as they are in final consumption). Consumption demand across sectors is described by an LES demand system with nonunitary income elasticities of demand. Finally, value added is produced by a CES technology for two primary factors of production, capital and labor (mobile across sectors), and there is a Leontief technology between aggregate value added and aggregate intermediates. All final demands arise from a representative consumer, who also receives net tax revenues as lump-sum transfer income.

We model imperfect competition by assuming that sectoral output is produced by n identical firms producing $z = F(x,y)$ for export and domestic markets, respectively. As in Harris 1984, fixed costs, $f(x,y)$, include fixed capital and labor costs (equal weight on each) and the variable cost component, $v(x,y)$, is subject to CRTS. Omitting sectoral subscripts, this gives the following definitions,

---

5. Table 1 gives the price elasticities of import demand and export supply for the corresponding CES and CET functional forms.

$$c(x,y) = f(x,y) + v(x,y),$$ (8)

$$a(x,y) = c(x,y)/z,$$ (9)

for total and average costs, respectively.

Under contestable market pricing (no firm entry), the unit price of composite domestic firm output is

$$p_z = G[p,(P + s)]$$ (10)

where $G (\bullet)$ denotes a CET cost function associated with the (primal) transformation function $F(x,y)$. Under contestable market pricing, we have

$$\bar{\pi} = [p_z - a(x,y)]z,$$ (11)

where the profit level, $\bar{\pi}$, will be specified exogenously.

To model oligopolistic behavior in domestic markets, we adopt the conjectural variation model, with $\Omega = \Delta z_{-j}/\Delta z_j$, for firm j, where Δz_{-j} denotes the change in aggregate output for the firm's sector, less its own output. Since all firms are assumed identical, these conjectures are assumed symmetric within sectors. Each firm then behaves as a monopolist in the domestic market, facing a downward sloping demand curve and equating marginal revenue with marginal costs on domestic sales.[6]

$$\frac{p - c_y}{c_y} = \frac{\tilde{\Omega}}{\pi\bar{\epsilon}},$$ (12)

where the perceived elasticity of market demand, $\bar{\epsilon}$, is given by an equation in the model.[7] Note that if one chose arbitrarily the number of firms in the industry and also had information on sectoral profit rates, the conjectural variation parameter, $\tilde{\Omega}$, would be determined residually (that is, calibrated). We normalize to $n = 1$ initially in all sectors and compute $\tilde{\Omega}$ for estimated profit rates.

---

6. We assume for this application that marginal costs $c_y = c_x$ for domestic and export production are equal.

7. This implies that the elasticity of demand is endogenous. Because $\bar{\epsilon}$ does not vary much for the functional forms used here, we do not discuss the effects of trade policy on the elasticity of demand as do Venables (1985) and Devarajan and Rodrik (1989a). For details on the magnitude of the procompetitive effects of trade liberalization in this type of model, see de Melo and Roland-Holst (1991).

It remains to set a rule governing firm entry. If we simply adopt the rule that $d\pi = 0$, firm entry/exit is governed by relation 8, or

$$\hat{n}^{-1}dn = -[(\hat{a} - c_z)]^{-1}\{[\hat{y} + (\hat{p} - c_y)y_p]dt + [\hat{x} + (I + \hat{s} - c_x)x_s]ds\}$$

$$= -\hat{\pi}_E^{-1}\{\pi_{Et}dt + \pi_{Es}ds\} = -\hat{\pi}_E^{-1}d\pi_E, \tag{13}$$

where π_E denotes efficiency or marginal cost–based profits.

3. Calibrated General Equilibrium Simulations with Tariffs and Subsidies

The earlier discussion suggests that trade policy in an economywide context of strong intersectoral linkages and IRTS is best evaluated by empirical means. This is so not only because of the sensitivity of the results to assumptions about pricing and entry behavior, but also because scale efficiency in IRTS sectors can be affected by policy-induced resource pulls. To isolate the mechanisms at work, we carry out illustrative simulations in which we calculate the welfare effects of individual (sectoral) trade policies. These simulations are carried out with a seven-sector CGE model calibrated to the Korean economy. All simulations are for departures from (hypothetical) free trade equilibrium obtained by solving the model after removing observed 1982 protection levels.[8]

The structure of the economy in the hypothetical free trade solution is described in table 1. Of the seven sectors, one is nontradeable. The data on sectoral structure indicates an open economy with high trade shares in GDP. Also, sectoral value-added ratios are quite low, indicating the strong interindustry linkages characteristic of a semi-industrial economy. The three sectors with IRTS (consumer goods, producer goods, and heavy industry) account for 42 percent of gross output, 73 percent of export sales, and 79 percent of import expenses. We have assumed a low and uniform cost-disadvantage ratio of 10 percent for the sector-by-sector comparisons in this section.[9]

Now consider two trade policy packages: 1) a 10 percent tariff on imports, which creates a home market bias; 2) a 10 percent import tariff, combined with a 10 percent export subsidy, which creates a second distortionary wedge but is intended to avoid bias. Both trade policy packages are introduced one sector at a time. Their welfare and efficiency effects are reported in

---

8. See table 1 for these protection levels, which are based on price comparisons.

9. The cost disadvantage ratio is the difference between average and marginal cost, divided by average cost, and gives an indication of unrealized scale economies.

TABLE 1.   Sectoral Features of the Semi-Industrial Economy

	Share in Gross Output[a]	Exports/ Output[a]	Imports/ Domestic Sales[a]	Elast. of Substit. in Production	Export Supply Elasticity[b]	Import Elasticity of Demand[b]	Nominal Tariff Rate[c]	Dom. Price Elasticity of Demand
	z	x/z	$M/(y+M)$	σ_p	σ_x	σ_M	t	ϵ
Primary	8.9	4.9	40.4	2.5	.75	1.8	59.7	---
Food proc.	9.6	2.5	6.5	1.5	1.5	2.5	18.4	---
Cons. goods	14.4	32.5	14.2	1.0	1.5	2.4	15.7	1.6
Prod. goods	20.1	16.6	19.2	.9	1.5	2.2	17.6	1.3
Heavy ind.	7.7	31.9	41.0	.9	1.5	1.9	28.3	1.4
Traded serv.	13.2	24.4	7.5	1.5	1.5	2.0	0.0	---
Nontrad serv.	26.1	---	---	0.9	---	.4	---	---

a)   Percent.
b)   Expenditure-compensated price elasticities. For imports (exports), expenditures (sales) on CES (CET) aggregate
     of domestic and import (export) goods held constant.
c)   Percent nominal tariff based on actual price comparisons.

Source: Young (1985) and de Melo and Roland-Holst (1991).

table 2. The welfare measure is the equivalent variation (EV), expressed as a share of free trade income. This EV measure captures the economywide effects of departures from free trade in the model, since it includes both the distortionary costs in consumption and the distortionary costs in production (including scale efficiency effects).[10] The second measure is the scale efficiency (SE) measure introduced by de Melo and Roland-Holst (1991). This is the output-

---

10. Strictly speaking, the true measure would be bounded between the equivalent and a compensating variation measure, but these proved to be virtually identical in our experiments.

**TABLE 2a.   Welfare and Scale Efficiency Effects,
Ten Percent Tariff**

	CRTS	Contestable		Cournot	
	EV	EV	SE	EV	SE
Primary	-5	-34	-29	-1	3
Food proc.	-1	-7	-6	6	7
Cons. good	-3	0	2	20	23
Prod. good	-5	-2	4	15	19
Heavy ind.	-3	-3	0	23	26
Trd. serv.	-1	-9	-8	8	9

weighted measure of average, economywide scale efficiency, essentially the change in the area between average and marginal cost curves, correcting for factor and input price changes, and corresponding to the last term in expression 6. Both measures are expressed here in basis points (hundredths of a percent) of initial (free trade) GDP.

Table 2 contrasts the effects of the two trade policy packages for three different assumptions about market structure and conduct: 1) CRTS and competitive pricing in all sectors; 2) Contestable market pricing with zero profits and IRTS in consumer goods, producer goods, and heavy industry; and 3) Oligopolistic competition with firm entry, zero profits, and IRTS in the same three sectors. Consider first the across-the-board CRTS case, reported in the first column of tables 2a and 2b. Three expected results stand out here. First, all entries are negative, indicating a welfare loss due to the usual distortionary production and consumption costs of a tax wedge. Second, the entries in table 2b are uniformly larger than their counterparts in 2a. This is because we have introduced a second wedge in 2b, where the sector specific import tariff and export subsidy are combined. Third, the welfare loss varies with the size of the base on which the wedge is applied. In the tariff case, the welfare loss is greatest for protection of the producer goods sector (a large share of imports in domestic sales). The same applies for the combined package, and it is the sectors with the highest share of exports in total production that have the highest welfare loss.

All this is familiar. Consider now the column of results for a contestable

TABLE 2b. Welfare and Scale Efficiency Effects, Ten Percent Tariff and Ten Percent Export Subsidy

	CRTS	Contestable		Cournot	
	EV	EV	SE	EV	SE
Primary	-5	-38	-32	2	7
Food proc.	-2	-9	-7	8	10
Cons. good	-17	16	40	-51	-40
Prod. good	-15	9	27	-49	-39
Heavy ind.	-12	1	19	-20	-12
Trd. serv.	-8	-49	-41	54	61

Notes: Values are expressed in basis points of initial GDP.
Results are for sector-by-sector protection, e.g., the figures in the rows report the aggregate effects of trade policy applied to that sector only.
CRTS = Constant Returns to Scale.
EV = $\{E[IU(p_1,w_1),p_1] - E[IU(p_0,w_0),p_0]\}/GDP_0$ for real consumption $E[]$ and income w_i, in hundredths of a percent.
SE = $[\ c(p_0,z_0) - c(p_0,z_1)]/GDP_0$, in hundredths of a percent.

market pricing rule in which all three sectors have relatively mild IRTS. Now protection of CRTS sectors will pull resources out of IRTS sectors. There are actually two additional costs of protecting sectors with CRTS. First, firms in IRTS sectors are forced up their average cost curves, resulting in lost scale efficiency. Second, since the sectors with IRTS have a relatively high share of intermediate sales in total sales (especially the producer goods sector), there will be a secondary cost resulting from higher intermediate costs for down-stream sectors purchasing inputs from these IRTS sectors.

For example, compare the results of protecting the primary sector under CRTS and under IRTS with contestable pricing. The welfare costs of protection are over seven times higher. Virtually all of the increased welfare cost comes from pulling resources out of the sectors with IRTS. For all CRTS sectors, protection is now more costly, with the extent of increased welfare loss depending on interindustry linkages that determine the sectors from which resources are pulled.

For the sectors with IRTS, the opposite forces are at work. Protection that results in a rightward shift of the demand curve for the representative firm allows the exploitation of economies of scale. Hence protection of sectors with IRTS raises the economywide average scale efficiency (a positive number in the SE column). Now avoidance of home market bias pays. Partial or complete equalization of incentives for domestic and export sales results in still greater scale efficiency gains. When this policy is applied on an individual basis, trade policy raises welfare.

The scale adjustments in IRTS sectors are disaggregated in table 3. A negative overall efficiency effect (SE) arises from tariff or tariff-subsidy protection of every CRTS sector in contestable markets. Indeed, the only scale expansion occurs when an IRTS sector is the direct beneficiary of protection. In each of these cases, the efficiency gains realized with fixed firm populations dominate the contractive losses of the other two IRTS sectors, and a positive aggregate SE at least partially offsets the purely distortionary costs of either form of protection. The greatest scale efficiency gains are enjoyed under the neutralist tariff-subsidy combination for IRTS sectors, and these lead to positive overall EV effects.

Note now that the same policies which yield the greatest benefits under contestable markets would lead to the greatest losses if market conduct were governed by Cournot criteria. The operational difference between the two specifications lies in their market entry/exit assumptions. The initial profit incentives created by a given trade policy are the same in both cases, but their ultimate effects differ because of scale adjustments. In the protected sector, rising (falling) profitability induces entry (exit). A tariff's effect on these IRTS sectors depends on their export and import shares (table 1) with the revaluation effect on export revenues counterbalanced against effective protection on sales of import substitutes. The entry/exit results are detailed in table 4, and these indicate (compare equation 11 above) slightly falling average profitability from most forms of tariff protection. To offset these losses, the remaining firms must expand output and realize new scale economies, hence scale efficiency gains in all cases of Cournot tariff protection. In the aggregate, these gains usually exceed their distortionary counterparts, suggesting that tariff protection in the presence of IRTS and Cournot competition is beneficial to the economy as a whole. This is especially so when IRTS sectors are the direct beneficiaries of the tariff. This result contrasts in sign and order of magnitude with tariff protection of IRTS under contestable markets.

The addition of an export subsidy offsets the revaluation effect of the tariff and unambiguously raises the profitability of the protected sector. Under

TABLE 3. Sectoral Scale Efficiency Gains

Tariff Alone	Contestable				Cournot			
	Cons.	Prod.	Heavy	Sum	Cons.	Prod.	Heavy	Sum
Primary	-8	-20	-1	-29	1	3	-1	3
Food proc.	-3	-2	-1	-6	4	2	1	7
Cons. good	7	-2	-3	2	13	6	4	23
Prod. good	-7	18	-7	4	9	3	7	19
Heavy ind.	-8	-1	9	0	11	6	9	26
Trade serv.	-3	-3	-2	-8	4	3	2	9

Tariff and Subsidy	Contestable				Cournot			
	Cons.	Prod.	Heavy	Sum	Cons.	Prod.	Heavy	Sum
Primary	-9	-21	-2	-32	3	5	-1	7
Food proc.	-4	-2	-1	-7	5	3	2	10
Cons. good	69	-11	-18	40	-77	22	15	-40
Prod. good	-16	53	-10	27	19	-70	12	-39
Heavy ind.	-25	1	43	19	20	14	-46	-12
Trade serv.	-15	-16	-10	-41	25	22	14	61

the constant average profit assumption, this has the effect predicted by expression 11, stimulating firm entry and sharply reducing returns to scale. The latter combine with distortionary costs to make neutralist protection highly unattractive for any IRTS sector. If Cournot conduct prevails in these sectors, however, then neutralist protection of the CRTS sectors can be beneficial, since it reduces profitability in the former, inducing exit and scale economies.

These results make it plain that an "optimal" trade policy should account for the existence of economies of scale and oligopolistic behavior. In the above simulations, with just a 10 percent tariff or combined tariff-subsidy on

TABLE 4.   Firm Entry and Demand Elasticities by Sector

Tariff Alone	Firm Entry[a]			Price Elasticity[b]		
	Cons.	Prod.	Heavy	Cons.	Prod.	Heavy
Primary	-2	-4	0	0	0	0
Food proc.	-2	-1	-1	0	0	0
Cons. good	-1	-1	-3	-1	0	0
Prod. good	-4	3	-6	0	-1	0
Heavy ind.	-4	-1	0	0	0	-12
Trade serv.	-2	-1	-2	4	3	2

Tariff and Subsidy	Firm Entry			Price Elasticity		
	Cons	Prod.	Heavy	Cons.	Prod.	Heavy
Primary	-2	-4	-1	0	0	0
Food proc.	-2	-1	-1	0	0	0
Cons. good	32	-6	-10	-2	0	0
Prod. good	-8	21	-10	0	-1	0
Heavy ind.	-8	-3	37	0	0	-1
Trade serv.	-8	-6	-10	0	0	0

a) Basis point change in sectoral firm population.
b) Basis point change in domestic elasticity of sectoral aggregate demand.

one sector, aggregate welfare can rise or fall by half a percentage point of real GDP, depending on the choice of the sector, its structure, and its behavior. General rules of thumb would thus seem unlikely to be the best choice unless information on market structure and conduct is very expensive to obtain.

The results in the right-hand columns of table 4 are the changes in the elasticity of domestic demand for the Cournot sectors. These results generally reveal the possibility for less competitive behavior when a firm is a direct beneficiary of protection and more competitive behavior otherwise, but the effects are generally negligible.

The assumption of zero fixed profits for these policy experiments is of course open to question.[11] Although the constant profits assumption helps clarify the roles of market structure and conduct in determining the effects of protection, it is unrealistic for at least three reasons. First, import protection often confers some degree of domestic monopoly power on domestic firms. Second, firms that are successful at influencing the trade policy process in their favor may also be effective at detering rate-of-return-related regulation. Last, expression 4 makes it apparent that the public itself may have an interest in advancing the profitability of IRTS sectors.

For these reasons, we now consider a case where firm profitability is allowed to rise with the level of protection. The profit rate is still exogenous, but for this example we let it rise from zero to the rate of the tariff or combined tariff-subsidy (10 percent), one sector at a time. The logic of this scenario is symmetric to that of the literature on "procompetitive" trade policies, which evaluate liberalization in the context of diluted market power.[12] Our results will support or reject the presumed procompetitive effects of trade liberalization, depending on the nature of domestic market conduct.

The results of protection under rising profits are given in table 5. In the Cournot case, the gains from protecting one IRTS sector with a 10 percent tariff can reach 4.9 percent of GDP. The direction of this result, which directly contradicts procompetitive intuition, is apparent from a restatement of expression 7 above as

$$\hat{n}^{-1}dn = [(\hat{a} - c_y)\hat{y} + (\hat{a} - c_x)\hat{x}]^{-1} [\{\pi_p dt + \pi_s ds\} - d\bar{\pi}]. \quad (14)$$

The rising average profit rate ($d\bar{\pi} > 0$) acts as a rising barrier in the domestic market and firms are induced to exit ($dn < 0$). This release of market share

---

11. We have run several series of alternative simulations with nonzero fixed and variable profits. The first reproduced those of tables 2–4 with a positive profit level of 10 percent in all sectors before and after protection. This altered the distortionary effects under CRTS, yielding benefits when tariffs and subsidies are applied to trade dependent sectors who are making profits under CRTS, but that is fully in accordance with expression 4, and the scale effects prevailing under contestable and Cournot IRTS conduct are qualitatively consistent with those obtained under zero profits. Thus the existence of fixed positive profits is important in itself, but it does not appear to alter the roles of market structure and conduct. Another set of simulations was run with a 20 percent cost disadvantage ratio, double that in these experiments, to see how increasing the degree of unrealized scale economies affected the above conclusions. These results do amplify the magnitude of all effects under IRTS, but qualitative differences were negligible.

12. See, e.g., Harris (1984) and Devarajan and Rodrik (1989).

TABLE 5.   Aggregate Effects with Rising Profits[a]
Effects in Basis Points of Initial Read GDP

Tariff Alone	CRTS EV	Contestable EV	SE	Cournot EV	SE	Firm Entry Cons.	Prod.	Heavy
Primary	-4	-14	-9	-32	-28	2	1	4
Food proc.	-4	0	5	-11	-7	0	1	2
Cons. good	-26	-86	-57	306	304	-47	3	2
Prod. good	-19	-85	-64	456	447	5	-44	1
Heavy ind.	-13	-47	-33	206	203	0	2	-48
Trd. serv.	-7	15	22	-75	-69	4	6	7

Tariff and Subsidy	CRTS EV	Contestable EV	SE	Cournot EV	SE	Firm Entry Cons.	Prod.	Heavy
Primary	-4	-16	-12	-28	-24	2	0	4
Food proc.	-4	-1	3	-9	-5	-1	1	2
Cons. good	-7	-39	-31	321	311	-30	0	-3
Prod. good	-7	-56	-48	473	458	1	-35	-2
Heavy ind.	-4	-23	-19	180	176	-3	0	-29
Tradr serv.	-2	-6	-4	-22	-20	0	2	2

Note: In these simulations, each sector (row) is given tariff or tariff-subsidy incentives of ten percent and allowed to increase average firm profits from zero to ten percent.

induces a dramatic expansion of per-firm output and scale efficiency. The opposite would occur under a contestable market scenario since incumbent firms move up their average cost curve, imposing scale efficiency losses on the economy. The contestable outcome is more consistent with procompetitive conclusions, but it requires a restraint on firm entry or exit that is difficult to justify.

As usual, protection of CRTS sectors is undesirable in most cases since it draws resources out of IRTS sectors. It is noteworthy in the rising profits case that tariff protection alone is actually more beneficial than combined tariffs and subsidies. This is so, here and in the fixed profits case as well, because enhanced export opportunities actually allow some of the firms that would otherwise exit to linger, diluting the average scale expansion in the protected sector. This effect is enough to reverse the overall welfare measures in the fixed profit cases, but it is overwhelmed by the general exodus when the domestic market barrier is raised from 0 to 10 percent. There may be a smaller increment, $d\bar{\pi}$, that would just equalize SE values between the tariff only and tariff-subsidy policies, but it would probably be too conservative an estimate of the monopoly power conferred by 10 percent nominal protection.

An interesting general implication of the rising profit results concerns the relationship between trade and industrial policy. It is apparent from our simulations that an industrial policy which grants increased domestic market power along with trade protection can dramatically increase the benefits (or reverse the losses) of implementing the latter alone.[13] This result appears consistent with the apparent success of some East Asian exporters, whose governments generally combine activism in trade and domestic industrial policy.

4. Conclusions

This paper seeks to clarify the roles of domestic market structure and conduct in determining the effects of trade policy. In a setting that allows for increasing returns to scale and oligopolistic behavior, we compare the effects of import tariffs and a more neutralist policy of equal import tariffs and export subsidies. The analytical results we report indicate that use of subsidies to neutralize biases between home and export sales can lead to benefits whether distortionary costs are present or not. This extends and generally sustains the conclusions obtained by others on tariff protection under increasing returns.

The degree of unrealized scale economies is not a sufficient statistic to predict the effects of either type of protection, however. Not surprisingly, we are able to show analytically that the specification of domestic market conduct, particularly in terms of firm entry/exit and barriers thereto, can amplify, attenuate, or completely reverse the effects of protection in increasing returns sectors. Apart from delineating the main forces at work in protection under increasing returns and oligopoly, the multisectoral analytical results are difficult to interpret directly. Therefore, the chapter closes with a set of numerical

---

13. In some LDCs, this fact may have implications for the efficient administration of revenue oriented tariff regimes.

simulations that illustrate the net effects of detailed interaction in a prototypical semi-industrial economy. These results highlight the sensitivity of welfare results to the industrial features of all sectors, not just those that are the target of protection.

Among other things, the numerical simulation results confirm the importance of market conduct assumptions for IRTS sectors. For example, protection of a sector with IRTS will be beneficial under Cournot behavior but detrimental under contestable market behavior. Tariff-subsidy protection of CRTS sectors in the presence of increasing returns sectors is generally detrimental under contestable behavior and beneficial under Cournot behavior, but, for low values of unrealized economies of scale, the potential costs in the former case usually exceed the benefits in the latter.

Results of simulations where protection confers domestic market power and allows for positive profits (because of barriers to entry) indicate dramatic gains from removing protection because it also eliminates profits (by eliminating barriers to entry). The distinction between protection that is biased in favor of the domestic market or more neutral protection via a tariff-cum-export subsidy trade policy is again important to the results, which depend on the specification of market conduct. Trade policy is most effective in IRTS sectors when pursued in combination with domestic industrial policies that encourage the realization of scale economies by preventing excessive entry.

When unrealized scale economies and oligopolistic behavior are present in an economy, trade protection can apparently yield costs or benefits greatly exceed traditional distortionary costs in magnitude. Which outcome prevails will depend on the country's circumstance. Thus, the most important conclusion to be drawn from these results is that a detailed understanding of market structure and conduct is essential in the design of trade policy.

Comment

Dominique Desruelle

In this chapter, de Melo and Roland-Holst analyze the impact of tariffs and export subsidies on an economy that features increasing returns to scale and oligopolistic behavior. They first reframe analytical results of Rodrik 1988 so as to bring out the importance of firm entry and exit on the welfare effects of trade policies. They then estimate the impact of sectoral-level tariffs and subsidies on a CGE model of the Korean economy.

The CGE model has the following structure: The economy is made of seven sectors, three of which exhibit increasing returns to scale (IRTS) at the firm level, and two countries, the home country—Korea—and the rest of the world. In each sector, there are three goods: a home good produced by domestic firms and sold domestically, an exported good produced by domestic and foreign firms and sold abroad, and an imported good produced by the foreign firms and sold in the home country. The economy is small with respect to the rest of the world; domestic firms take the prices of the exported and imported goods as given. In the three IRTS sectors, the domestic firms produce jointly the home and exported goods. This joint production is characterized by economies of scale and economies of scope; the production of one good, holding the production of the other fixed, may, however, exhibit diseconomies of scale. The domestic firms in the IRTS sectors have some monopoly power because only they produce the home goods, and the imports are imperfect substitutes for those. Two oligopolistic structures are considered: contestability and the conjectural variation model with free entry. There is a representative consumer whose preferences are those of society as well. This consumer pays production subsidies and receives tax revenues in a lump sum.

The authors derive various analytical expressions for the welfare effects of tariffs and trade subsidies. One expression—expression 4 in the text—shows that an increase in firm output in sectors where prices exceed marginal costs increases welfare if either the number of firms is held constant or the profit of each firm is zero. The first condition is satisfied when markets are contestable; the second condition is satisfied when entry is free and there are no sunk costs. This analytical result gives us the intuition behind the computational results presented in the second part of the chapter. Under contestability, prices are equal to average costs. Since average costs are higher than marginal costs in IRTS sectors, subsidization of IRTS sectors increases output and welfare; subsidization of the constant returns to scale sectors has opposite effects. In the conjectural variation model with free entry, subsidization of the IRTS sectors induces entry in these sectors, decreases firm output, and decreases welfare; subsidization of the CRTS sectors again has the opposite effects. Finally, when profits are allowed to rise with the level of protection, the welfare effects of tariffs and export subsidies may be the reverse of what they are with fixed profits. This is because an increase in profits translates into a decrease in output under contestability, which reduces welfare, and into less entry under the conjectural variation model, which increases welfare. Obviously, the importance of these latter effects depends on the speed at which profits rise with protection.

Two features of the numerical simulations dominate. First, the presence of IRTS and imperfect competition significantly increases the impact of tariffs and export subsidies. The welfare effect of these policies can be as much as seven times larger in this CGE model as in a benchmark CGE model where all sectors exhibit constant returns to scale. This result, which is in line with the findings of Harris (1984) and others on CGE models with imperfect competition, forcefully shows the importance of taking into account increasing returns to scale and imperfect competition. Second, the simulations are highly sensitive to the modelization of imperfect competition. This result conforms with the theoretical literature—see, e.g., Dixit 1984, Eaton and Grossman 1986. It implies that a trade policy analysis based on the outcome of any particular numerical simulation must be received with great caution.

I have two main criticisms to address to this CGE model. One regards the small country assumption and the other the use of conjectural variations. The small country assumption means that domestic firms take the prices of both exported and imported goods as exogenous. Exogenous export prices and increasing returns in the production of exported goods entail specialization in production. If a firm makes profits on its exports, it wants to increase production since this will decrease its average cost, leave its price unchanged, and strictly increase its profits. Therefore, in any equilibrium, only one such firm can exist. This is not appropriate for a CGE model that must simulate an economy that exports all types of goods. This difficulty is avoided in the present model at the cost of very specific assumptions regarding production. These are: 1) domestic firms produce two goods—a home good and an exported good; 2) foreign firms cannot produce the home good; 3) there are increasing returns to scale in the joint production of the domestic and exported good; and 4) the transformation frontier of the domestic and exported goods is convex, which implies that, holding the production of the domestic good constant, the production of the exported good eventually exhibits decreasing returns to scale. These assumptions are not satisfactory, for they imply that domestic firms can produce both the home and exported goods and can do so with economies of scope, whereas foreign firms cannot produce the home good at all. If they were able to do so, specialization in production at the sectoral level would again ensue. In short, an equilibrium with no specialization in production has been rescued at the cost of giving the home country an unreasonable technological advantage. Generically speaking, I do not believe that the problems caused by the combination of the small country assumption and increased returns in production can be eliminated. One is therefore left with the choice of explicitly modeling the rest of the world or at least introducing demand functions for the domestic country's exported goods.

Conjectural variations are often used in CGE models with imperfect competition. This practice, though understandable on practical grounds, is without theoretical basis. Since the work of Friedman 1971 and Abreu 1988 on repeated games, the pseudo-dynamic story that supports conjectural variations has been found wanting. More importantly for our purpose, oligopolistic firms that pursue collusive strategies may not react to changes in their environment, such as the introduction of taxes and subsidies, in a way predicted by a conjectural variation model. For instance, they may avoid any behavior that might look like a breach of collusion. Unfortunately, game theory does not provide a handy alternative to conjectural variations. Given that game theory cannot tell us how one equilibrium is selected among many possible equilibria, it cannot tell us how this selection varies with changes in the environment. A practical solution to this difficulty may be to introduce an arbitrary rule for choosing a collusive equilibrium among the set of all equilibria. One obvious such rule is to select the Cournot equilibrium; another to pick the most collusive, symmetric equilibrium. This would at least have the advantage of making the assumption regarding oligopolistic behavior explicit.

My final comments concern the policy implications of this work. Specifically, I wish to take issue with the authors' conclusion that trade policy can most effectively be pursued in combination with domestic industrial policies that encourage the realization of scale economies. First, it does not appear extravagant to believe that the cost of collecting the information needed to design a beneficial trade policy be of the order of a few percentage points of GNP. The needed information includes, for each industry, the production functions of existing firms or at least a measure of returns to scale, the market conduct, the existence and extent of barriers to entry and exit, the production function of potential entrants, the foreign demand for exports, the domestic demand for imports, the substitutability between domestic and foreign goods, the foreign ownership of domestic firms, the domestic ownership of foreign firms, and the extent of factor mobility between sectors of production. This seems nearly enough information to run a planned economy, and there is no doubt that that is quite costly. Furthermore, private agents have an incentive to report information untruthfully if they know to what use this information will be put. Under these conditions, the rule of thumb of free trade can very well be the best practical choice. Second, the authors come close to a call to establish national industrial "champions." As the authors point out, such policies seem to have helped East Asian exporters. They have also led to the establishment of many inefficient monopolies in all parts of the world. One is therefore tempted to conclude that the combination of trade and industrial policies is indeed potent, but that its result, large gains or large losses, depends upon one's ability to choose between winners and losers. Furthermore, given that these policies amount to creating monopolies and subsidizing them, they are very likely to aggravate wealth and income inequalities. If we are preoccupied with equity as well as efficiency, this combination of policies may lower social welfare even when they increase efficiency.

Comment

Ngo Van Long

Jaime de Melo and David Roland-Holst have presented us with a most interesting case study of the welfare effects of trade intervention for a small economy.

The distinguishing characteristic of their model is the exogeneity of the terms of trade. This allows the authors to abstract from the standard optimal tariff consideration, which is largely irrelevant for most semi-industrialized economies.

While the model is supposed to be a CGE model, there is a flavor of partial equilibrium analysis. Thus, in the theoretical part, the authors stay with the consumer surplus formulation and keep clear from the specification of direct or indirect utility functions. More importantly, the cost functions do not contain factor prices as arguments. Presumably, factor prices are kept constant, or are at best allowed to change in an indirect way, as the authors state that "the off-diagonal elements represent the pecuniary externalities that sectors confer on one another by changing their output."

The first major result of the chapter states that "with no firm entry/exit, export subsidies are unambiguously beneficial and tariffs are beneficial if the efficiency gains from scale expansion exceed the distortionary costs of protection." This conclusion was qualified by a preceding sentence that states the assumption that the marginal costs of producing the exported goods are below the world prices. It seems difficult to justify such an assumption, given that the country is the price taker in the world market. Second, it is assumed that the exportables are not consumed domestically. This may not apply to many products.

In the theoretical part of the chapter, it is assumed that imports and domestically produced goods for domestic sales are perfect substitutes. This simplifies the equations, but makes the results not quite compatible with the simulation part, where these two classes of goods are taken to be imperfect substitutes.

The authors adopt the conjectural variation model, and the conjectural variation parameter is determined residually. It is somewhat misleading to refer to this model as Cournot; I believe that normally the term *Cournot* implies a zero conjectural variation. However, in what follows, I shall keep the authors' wording.

Two types of market conduct are examined: contestable market and Cournot behavior with firm entry. It is rather surprising that, assuming Cournot behavior, a 10 percent import tariff, coupled with a 10 percent export subsidy on traded services (which account for 13.2 percent of gross output) results in a substantial increase in GNP (by half a percentage point). Apparently, this is brought about by reducing the profitability of firms in the increasing returns to scale sectors (consumer goods, producer goods, and heavy industry), causing exit and inducing scale economies.

Another surprising result is that protection of the increasing returns to scale sectors in the form of import tariffs will raise welfare (under the Cournot assumption), but welfare will be reduced if the tariffs are accompanied by export subsidies. This is explained in terms of the increase in the number of firms (see table 4), but the order of magnitude of such increases is bewildering.

Another set of simulation results is obtained under the assumption that the rate of profit of the protected sector rises with the tariff rate. One of the possible justifications for this assumption is that the rent seekers would want to make sure that their market power will not be diluted. While this argument seems convincing, the model does not offer a mechanism for the determination of the profit rate. Instead, it is assumed that the profit rate remains exogenous: it is allowed to rise from zero (the rate of tariff). This is a rather ad hoc way of dealing with a rising profit rate associated with rent-seeking behavior. Calculations show that there are significant welfare gains due to exit (both in the "tariff alone" case and the "tariff and subsidy" case). There is a conceptual difficulty here: if the rate of profit is zero, then exit can be explained, and it does not matter which firms exit. But with a positive profit rate, how would one induce a firm to exit?

A related criticism is the lack of any discussion of the social cost of rent seeking. If the government is ready to give tariff protection to industries, any scale efficiency gain may be more than offset by the loss of real resources used in contesting the potential rents created and assigned by the political process. While it is difficult directly to compute the costs of socially unproductive rent-seeking activities because the rent-seeking outlays are not observed, we can infer these from the value of rents assigned. Of course, to the extent that rent seekers are risk averse, not all rents are completely dissipated (see Long and Vousden 1987 for a discussion of rent dissipation in the context of contesting for a share of total rent). Procedures exist for inferring the cost of rent seeking from the observed value of the rent (see Hillman 1989). Considerations of the real resource cost of the quest for rents may render any protection socially wasteful.

In relation to the benefits obtained from having larger firms, and few of them, one should mention that the assumption that domestic firms produce homogeneous goods may result in an exaggeration of the benefit of rationalization, because it neglects the consumers' preference for diversity.

Other assumptions concerning the increasing returns to scale sectors could be relaxed. For example, in a wide range of manufacturing sectors in developing countries, a few firms tend to dominate and the possibility of collusion cannot be dismissed too lightly. Dynamic learning by doing effects could be allowed for, though the model would have to be modified substantially.

I now turn to the assumption of lump sum redistribution of the net proceeds of tariffs less subsidies. If the net proceeds are negative, the model implies lump sum taxes. In practice, lump sum taxes do not exist or are not feasible, and revenues must be raised by distorting taxes. The cost of public finance must therefore be taken into account.

The authors conclude by stating that the most important conclusion to be drawn from their results is that a detailed understanding of market structure and conduct is essential, not only to exploit gains protection can afford, but to avoid its pitfalls. To this we should add that a detailed understanding of how other countries react to the protective measure of the country in question is perhaps of equal importance.

CHAPTER 6

In the Cournot-Walras General Equilibrium Model, There May Be "More to Gain" by Changing the Numéraire than by Eliminating Imperfections: A Two-Good Economy Example

Victor Ginsburgh

It is well-known among theoreticians that in general equilibrium models with imperfect competition à la Cournot, price normalization matters: changing the numéraire has real effects. This is already discussed in Bronsard 1971, 102–3 and Gabszewicz and Vial 1972;[1] the issue is further taken up in Dierker and Grodal 1986, who construct an example of a two-good economy in which an equilibrium (in pure strategies) exists if, say, good 1 is chosen as numéraire, and fails to exist (even using mixed strategies) if the numéraire is good 2.[2] See also Hart 1985 on existence issues and Böhm 1990 on normalization.

Imperfect competition is now entering the field of applied general equilibrium. The avenue was opened by Harris 1984, followed by many others.[3] None of these discusses normalizations as if applied researchers considered

I am grateful to Camille Bronsard, Steve de Castro, Mathias Dewatripont, Jean Gabszewicz, Louis-André Gérard-Varet, Michiel Keyzer, Philippe Michel, T. N. Srinivasan, and Jean Waelbroeck for many interesting comments, and in some cases lively discussions. This chapter was initiated by a research project financed by Direction Générale 2 (DG 2) of the European Commission.

1. And even earlier than that, in a paper by Siamwalla and Schydlowsky, as was pointed out to me by L. Gevers.

2. Berthélémy and Bourguignon 1989 set up a three-region (North, South, and OPEC) model in which each region may be considered as having some monopoly power over the output of the commodity it produces; their algorithm, fails to find an equilibrium when each region acts as a monopolist. According to F. Bourguignon, this is not due to the computer algorithm which fails to find solutions, but to the nonexistence of such a solution.

3. See chapters 5 and 10 in this volume; Burniaux and Waelbroeck 1990; de Melo and Roland-Holst 1990; Devarajan and Rodrik 1989a, b). See also Smith and Venables 1988, 1989, on partial equilibrium effects on industry of the 1992 "internal market" in the European Community.

that the "numéraire does not matter" principle extended without any problem from competitive to noncompetitive equilibria.

In this note, we construct an example in which a simple change in the numéraire leads to "larger" welfare gains than going from an economy with consumption taxes to a tax-free economy. This may be a problem when one interprets the results obtained by applied noncompetitive general equilibrium models: indeed, these usually exhibit much larger welfare gains from trade liberalization than those obtained in similar experiments with competitive equilibrium models.

1. The Model

We consider the following two-good economy.[4] There are two monopolists; each of them produces one single good and uses the other one as an input; returns to scale are constant; the production possibility set Y_1 of producer 1 (who produces commodity 1) consists of production plans $(y_{11}, y_{12}) = (1, -\alpha_1)y_1$ with $y_1 \in [0, 1]$; likewise, Y_2, the production set of producer 2 (who produces commodity 2) consists of plans $(y_{21}, y_{22}) = (-\alpha_2, 1)y_2$, with $y_2 \in [0, 1]$. Each monopolist ($i = 1, 2$) takes the other's output and price as given and chooses his output level y_i in such a way that:

$$y_i \in \text{argmax } (p_i - \alpha_i p_j)y_i , \tag{1.1}$$

where $i = 1, 2$, and $i \neq j$.

There is one representative consumer whose utility function is:

$$u(x_1, x_2) = 4x_1 + 2x_2 - (2/3x_1^2) - (2/3x_2^2) - (1/2x_1x_2) \tag{1.2}$$

and whose endowment is $(0, 0)$; his income consists of the profits Π_1 and Π_2 of the the two producers. Ad valorem taxes at rates τ_1 and τ_2 may be levied on his consumption bundle (x_1, x_2); the total amount of taxes $T = \tau_1 p_1 x_1 + \tau_2 p_2 x_2$ is paid back to him under the form of a lump sum transfer; his budget constraint thus reads:

$$(1 + \tau_1)p_1x_1 + (1 + \tau_2)p_2x_2 = \Pi_1 + \Pi_2 + T. \tag{1.3}$$

Finally, the market equilibrium conditions are:

$$x_1 + \alpha_2 y_2 = y_1 , \tag{1.4}$$

---

4. The example consists of a modification of an example that was provided to me by L.-A. Gérard-Varet, who stimulated my interest in the subject.

and

$$x_2 + \alpha_1 y_1 = y_2. \tag{1.5}$$

2. Definition of the Cournot-Walras Equilibrium

The equilibrium prices (p_1, p_2), together with the consumption bundle (x_1, x_2) and the production levels y_1 and y_2, have to satisfy a certain number of conditions, which will be described now.

The consumer takes tax-ridden prices $(1 + \tau_i)p_i$ and income $\Pi_1 + \Pi_2 + T$ as given and chooses a consumption bundle (x_1, x_2) that maximizes his utility (1.2) subject to his budget constraint (1.3). To be an optimal consumption bundle, (x_1, x_2) has thus to satisfy the following marginal condition:

$$\frac{p_2(1 + \tau_2)}{p_1(1 + \tau_1)} = \frac{12 - 8x_2 - 3x_1}{24 - 8x_1 - 3x_2}. \tag{2.1}$$

Taking into account the two market equilibrium conditions (1.4) and (1.5), this leads to a system of three equations (1.4, 1.5, and 2.1) in four variables $(p_1, p_2, y_1,$ and $y_2)$ defining aggregate demands $y_i (p_1, p_2)$, $i = 1, 2$ or inverse demands $p_i (y_1, y_2)$, $i = 1, 2$.

Obviously, one of the four variables has to be fixed; this can be obtained, as in the pure Walrasian model, by normalizing prices. Since we deal with Cournot-behaving producers, we need inverse demands.

Normalizing first by setting $p_1 = 1$, the inverse demand system is given by:

$$p_1 = 1, \tag{2.2}$$

and

$$p_2 = \frac{1 + \tau_1}{1 + \tau_2} \cdot \frac{12 - (8 - 3\alpha_2)y_2 - (3 - 8\alpha_1)y_1}{24 - (8 - 3\alpha_1)y_1 - (3 - 8\alpha_2)y_2}. \tag{2.3}$$

It is then easy to express the two producers' profits in terms of (y_1, y_2) as:

$$\Pi_1(y_1, y_2) = \left[1 - \alpha_1 \frac{1 + \tau_1}{1 + \tau_2} \cdot \right.$$

$$\left. \frac{12 - (8 - 3\alpha_2)y_2 - (3 - 8\alpha_1)y_1}{24 - (8 - 3\alpha_1)y_1 - (3 - 8\alpha_2)y_2} \right] \cdot y_1, \tag{2.4}$$

and

$$\Pi_2(y_1, y_2) = \left[\frac{1 + \tau_1}{1 + \tau_2} \cdot \right.$$

$$\left. \frac{12 - (8 - 3\alpha_2)y_2 - (3 - 8\alpha_1)y_1}{24 - (8 - 3\alpha_1)y_1 - (3 - 8\alpha_2)y_2} - \alpha_2 \right] \cdot y_2. \qquad (2.5)$$

The Cournot-Nash behavior of producers is, as usual, defined by a pair $(\bar{y}_1, \bar{y}_2)$ such that

$$\Pi_1 (\bar{y}_1, \bar{y}_2) \geq \Pi_1 (L_1, \bar{y}_2), \qquad (2.6)$$

$$\Pi_2 (\bar{y}_1, \bar{y}_2) \geq \Pi_2 (\bar{y}_1, y_2), \qquad (2.7)$$

and

$$y_i \in [0, 1]. \qquad (2.8)$$

A Cournot-Walras equilibrium can now be defined as a pair of prices $(\bar{p}_1, \bar{p}_2)$ and a pair of production levels $(\bar{y}_1, \bar{y}_2)$ satisfying (2.2), (2.3), and (2.6) to (2.8). Alternatively, such an equilibrium is a pair of prices $(\bar{p}_1, \bar{p}_2)$, a pair of production levels $(\bar{y}_1, \bar{y}_2)$, and a pair of consumptions (n_1, n_2) satisfying (1.4), (1.5), (2.1) to (2.3), and (2.6) to (2.8).

Instead of setting $p_1 = 1$, we can also normalize by setting $p_2 = 1$ and, accordingly, define an equilibrium, which may or may not turn out to give the same values for prices, productions, and consumptions as the first one.

3. Equilibria of the Model

Let us consider first the equilibrium in which $\bar{p}_1 = 1$. We have to look for a solution of (2.4)–(2.6); the first order Kuhn-Tucker conditions have to be calculated, and the system of (in)equalities solved to find a Nash point. But it is easier to proceed as follows. Firm 1's decision is to compute y_1 such that

$$\bar{y}_1 \in \text{argmax}(1 - \alpha_1 p_2)y_1, \qquad y_1 \in [0, 1].$$

Observe that, as long as $(1 - \alpha_1 \bar{p}_2) > 0,$[5] the profit maximizing production schedule of monopolist 1 is $y_1 = 1$, no matter what the second monopolist decides. Let us thus assume this to be correct and set $\bar{y}_1 = 1$. The profit of the second monopolist is given by (2.5). Taking into account $\bar{p}_1 = 1$ and $\bar{y}_1 = 1$, it

---

5. This will become clear after p_2 is computed.

is easy to derive that the candidate Cournot-Nash solutions for the second monopolist are the roots of the following quadratic (in y_2) equation:

$$(1 + \tau_2)(16 + 3\alpha_1)[(1 + \tau_1)(9 + 8\alpha_1) - \alpha_2(1 + \tau_2)$$

$$\times (16 + 3\alpha_1)] + 2(1 + \tau_2)(16 + 3\alpha_1)[(1 + \tau_1)(3\alpha_2 - 8)$$

$$- \alpha_2(1 + \tau_2)(8\alpha_2 - 3)]y_2 + (1 + \tau_2)(8\alpha_2 - 3)[(1 + \tau_1)$$

$$\times (3\alpha_2 - 8) - \alpha_2(1 + \tau_2)(8\alpha_2 - 3)]y_2^2 = 0. \tag{3.1}$$

Setting $\alpha_1 = \alpha_2 = 0.1$, the roots of (3.1) are given by:

$$y_2 = \frac{251.02(1 + \tau_1) - 7.172(1 + \tau_2) \pm \eta}{33.88(1 + \tau_1) - 0.968(1 + \tau_2)} \tag{3.2}$$

with $\eta = \sqrt{52187(1 + \tau_1)^2 - 1491(1 + \tau_1)(1 + \tau_2)}$.

Assume now that $\tau_1 = 0.5$ and $\tau_2 = 0.25$; the profit maximizing solution for the second monopolist is $\bar{y}_2 = 0.5846$, with $\bar{p}_2 = 0.2942$; as can be checked, the pair $(\bar{y}_1, \bar{y}_2) = (1, 0.5846)$ is a Nash equilibrium.

In the absence of taxes ($\tau_1 = \tau_2 = 0$), a similar calculation shows that $\bar{y}_2 = 0.5679$ and, consequently, $\bar{p}_2 = 0.3606$. Again, the pair $(\bar{y}_1, \bar{y}_2) = (1, 0.5679)$ is a Nash equilibrium for the producers.

We now turn to the price normalization $\bar{p}_2 = 1$. Similar routine calculations lead to consider:

$$\bar{y}_2 \in \text{argmax}(1 - \alpha_2 p_1)y_2,$$

with $\bar{y}_2 = 1$ if $(1 - \alpha_2 \bar{p}_1) > 0$ and $\bar{y}_1$ is given by the roots of the following quadratic (in y_1) equation:

$$(1 + \tau_1)(4 + 3\alpha_2)[(1 + \tau_2)(21 + 8\alpha_2) - \alpha_1(1 + \tau_1)(4 + 3\alpha_2)]$$

$$+ 2(1 + \tau_1)(4 + 3\alpha_2)[(1 + \tau_2)(3\alpha_1 - 8) - \alpha_1(1 + \tau_1)$$

$$\times (8\alpha_1 - 3)]y_1 + (1 + \tau_1)(8\alpha_1 - 3)[(1 + \tau_2)(3\alpha_1 - 8)$$

$$- \alpha_1(1 + \tau_1)(8\alpha_1 - 3)]y_1^2 = 0. \tag{3.3}$$

As can be readily checked, (3.3) has only complex conjugate roots, so that the profit optimizing y_1 is on the boundary of $[0, 1]$, and will obviously be $\bar{y}_1 = 1$, whether consumption taxes are imposed or not. As before, setting $\alpha_1 = \alpha_2 =$

0.1, it is easy to calculate now that $\bar{p}_1 = 5.5952$ in the tax-ridden case ($\tau_1 = 0.5$, $\tau_2 = 0.25$), and $\bar{p}_1 = 6.7143$ in the absence of consumer taxes. In both cases, the pair ($\bar{y}_1$, $\bar{y}_2$) is a Nash equilibrium.

Table 1 gives an overview of the prices and the allocations. The results clearly show that normalization matters: the two normalizations result not only in different relative prices, but also in different allocations (compare column 1 with column 3 or column 2 with column 4).

Moreover, when the first normalization is used ($p_1 = 1$), welfare *decreases* when taxes are removed; when $p_2 = 1$, welfare remains constant. The first result is counterintuitive for those used to thinking in terms of competitive markets, where removing the price distortion created by taxes should *increase* welfare. Here, we are in a noncompetitive world in which we remove one imperfection (taxes), but keep the other one (noncompetitive producers); and as is known from second-best analysis, anything can happen in that context.

It also appears that a "good way" to increase consumer welfare in our

TABLE 1.   Results of the Two Normalizations

	$p_1 = 1$		$p_2 = 1$	
	with taxes	no taxes	yes taxes	no taxes
Prices				
p_1	1.0000	1.0000	5.5952	6.7143
p_2	0.2942	0.3606	1.0000	1.0000
Consumptions				
x_1	0.9415	0.9432	0.9000	0.9000
x_2	0.4846	0.4679	0.9000	0.9000
Productions				
y_1	1.0000	1.0000	1.0000	1.0000
y_2	0.5846	0.5679	1.0000	1.0000
Welfare	3.7598	3.7488	3.9150	3.9150

economy when there are consumer taxes is not to remove them, but to . . . change the normalization rule.

4. Concluding Comments

There are at least two important issues to which at least partial answers can be given. One is theoretical and concerns the consistency of the Cournot-Walras model; the second is empirical: does normalization matter in applied work?

Is the Cournot-Walras model proposed by Gabszewicz and Vial (and elaborated on by many others since, such as the survey by Hart 1985) theoretically consistent? This model can be considered as a direct extension of the Walrasian one in which each producer (firm) maximizes profits at given prices; here, producers also maximize profits, but have some power on prices. In the Walrasian case, what matters is the producing and consuming household whose activities can, since prices are given, be decentralized into pure consumer and pure producer activities (see Koopmans 1957). Firms do not, and cannot, fool consumers who own them, and profit maximization by firms "comes along" with utility maximization by consumers.[6] This can be easily seen by considering the Negishi 1960 format of a competitive equilibrium.[7]

This convenient decentralizing property does not hold in the Cournot-Walras model, in which, on their "own behalf," firms (indirectly) set prices, take some surplus away from consumers who own them, and prevent the economy from achieving a Pareto-optimal equilibrium. Why would consumers be stupid enough to fool themselves?

This has recently led Codognato and Gabszewicz 1990 to reconsider the Cournot-Walras model as one in which some consumers have market power in the sense that they *strategically* set the share of the initial endowment they will offer and withhold the remainder for themselves. This setup can be extended without difficulty to economies with producers, as long as every noncompetitive firm is owned by a unique consumer[8] who makes the selling decision, by maximizing his utility but *not* the firm's profit: at no point is the

---

6. This has been pointed out to me by Michiel Keyzer. See also Keyzer 1990.

7. This is best seen by considering the Negishi framework to define an equilibrium. Negishi shows that (under some assumptions that are almost identical to those needed for the Arrow-Debreu proof) there exist welfare weights $\alpha_i > 0$ such that the solution of the following mathematical program max $\Sigma_i \alpha_i u_i(x_i)$ subject to $\Sigma_i x_i \leq \Sigma_i \omega_i + \Sigma_j y_j$, $y_j \in Y_j, x_i \in X_i$ is an equilibrium. Profit maximization is implicitly obtained at every optimum (and thus at equilibrium), but does not appear explicitly in the formulation. In this program, $u_i(x_i)$, x_i and ω_i represent the utility function, the consumption plan, and the endowment of consumer i, X_i his consumption set, while y_j is the production plan of producer j and Y_j his production set.

8. Shared ownership can be taken care of by "aggregating" in some way those consumers who own the noncompetitive firm.

profit of a noncompetitive firm maximized. This is a theoretically satisfactory way of indirectly endowing firms with a utility maximizing behavior.[9] As a consequence, since profits of noncompetitive firms are not maximized, normalization will cease to matter.

One may think of avoiding the problem by normalizing prices *after* the first order conditions for profit maximization are taken and not *before* like is done in equations (2.4) and (2.5); this is unfortunately impossible here since, without further assumptions, prices cannot be solved, profits cannot be expressed in terms of quantities only, and one cannot compute a Cournot equilibrium.[10]

The second question that should be asked is whether normalization is a serious problem in *applied* Cournot-Walras models.

In the above example, producers who produce the two sole commodities traded in our economy are "big," and the power they have on prices is therefore large. In normalizing one of the prices, one indirectly constrains the choice set of the producer, and this can be seen as "more serious" than just normalizing. In applied models, no noncompetitive producer (or sector) will be as important, and it is likely that the effects of normalizing on his or other producers' prices will not be too large.

Also, in most applications, some sectors at least will be competitive, and the normalization can be made on the price of a bundle of the latter goods; this does not per se solve the normalization problem, but at least it will not affect the choice set of the noncompetitive producers. Moreover, as shown by Cripps and Myles 1988, this is the *only* normalization that does not affect the behavior of oligopolists.

For these two reasons, it may thus be that, in practice, the normalization issue is of no importance. This does not mean however that there is no problem: profit maximization (whether explicit or implicit in the Marshall-Lerner conditions) by oligopolistic producers cannot be part of the specification of the model; firms can optimize only through decisions made by consumers.

---

9. Endowing firms with a utility maximizing instead of a profit maximizing behavior is also suggested by Waelbroeck 1990.

10. See Keyzer 1990 on ways to achieve this, but in a framework that needs more assumptions on what is common knowledge to producers than the assumptions made in the Cournot-Walras model.

Comment

Jacques Robert

Attempts have been made to apply computable general equilibrium models to economies with imperfection competition à la Cournot. In these models, firms choose production plans; for each choice of quantities, a pure exchange economy is defined and a vector of Walrasian equilibrium prices determined. It is assumed that firms behave strategically when choosing their output and take explicitly into account the effect of their choices on prices. These applications suffer from two serious theoretical limitations. First, the existence of equilibria in Cournot-Walrasian games is not guaranteed, as shown by Roberts and Sonnenshein 1977 and Dierker and Grodal 1986. Second, the equilibrium allocation depends on the normalization rule. Ginsburgh's chapter deals with this latter issue.

Applied researchers may argue that these theoretical issues are not important in practice and need not be dealt with, at least on a first approximation. Indeed, if an empirical model can actually be computed numerically, one need not bother about the risk of the nonexistence of equilibrium. However, the second problem still remains. The objective of Ginsburgh's chapter is to convince applied researchers that they cannot assume away the normalization problem. He asks the following question: Is the evaluation of a proposed economic policy package invariant to the normalization rule, that is, to a specific choice of numéraire ? Using a judiciously constructed example, Ginsburgh shows that it is not the case. Hence, I can only agree with his verdict: applied researchers should take seriously the normalization problem when computing CGE models to economies with imperfect competition. In this comment, written as a note from a theorist to applied researchers, I try to clarify the theoretical underpinning behind this nonneutrality of the numéraire and suggest how this problem may be bypassed (at least from a theoretical perspective!).

The Cournot-Walrasian Game

In this section, I present the basic Cournot-Walrasian game and show why the normalization rule matters. I also simultaneously present the notations that will be used.

One can reinterpret the Cournot-Walrasian model as a three-stage game. In stage one, firms independently choose their production plans (input demands and output supplies). Given the firms' production plan y, the Walrasian auctioneer selects, in stage two, a price vector, $p = \{p_1, \ldots, p_m\}$, which specifies a price for all m goods in the economy. Formally, the strategy of the auctioneer in the game specifies a price vector, p, for every production plan y. The objective of the auctioneer is to find some price vector that would clear markets. In the last stage of the game, consumers trade their endowments, which include their share of firms' output.

We are looking for a subgame perfect equilibrium for the above game: that is, consumers trade optimally given their endowments and the price vector, the Walrasian auctioneer sets the market prices so as to clear the markets, given the firms' decisions; and firms select their production optimally. By moving first, firms strategically can take into account the effect of their production decisions on prices. Much like in a partial equilibrium Cournot model, firms set their quantities in order to manipulate the market-clearing prices.

It is implicitly assumed that firms seek to maximize nominal profits. This assumption is by no means innocuous and, as I will argue later, very debatable. Note that the nominal profits are homogeneous of degree 1 in prices, so that they directly depend on the absolute price level. If we allow the price normalization to depend arbitrarily on quantity choices, one can alter the firms' objective functions and incentives to produce in any arbitrary way. It turns out that a large set of allocations can be supported as a Cournot-Walrasian equilibrium in pure strategies.

Proposition 1: The production plan y^* can be supported as a subgame perfect equilibrium outcome of the Cournot-Walrasian game if there is a market-clearing price vector, p^*, for the production plan y^* such that all firms make strict positive profits when selling y^* at price p^*.

The proof of Proposition 1 proceeds by construction. We simply need to show that for all y^* satisfying the condition of Proposition 1 there exists a normalization rule that supports y^* as an equilibrium allocation.[1] Proposition 1

---

1. Let the price function $\hat{p}(\bullet)$ be such that $\hat{p}(y)$ clears the market, given production y. Since consumers' demands are homogeneous of degree 0 in prices and income, we are allowed to normalize any way we desire; so let us normalize $\hat{p}(\bullet)$ so that $\Sigma_k \hat{p}_k(w_k + \Sigma_j y_k) = 1$. By assumption, there exists some $\epsilon > 0$ so that $\Sigma_k \hat{p}_k y_{jk}^* > \epsilon$ for all firm j. Now, construct a pricing rule $p^*(\bullet)$, such that $p^*(y) = \hat{p}(y)$ for all $y \neq y^*$ and let $p^*(y^*) = \dfrac{\hat{p}(y^*)}{\epsilon}$. Since $\hat{p}(\bullet)$ is normalized so that the total value of all the goods traded in the economy is equal to one, no firm makes profits exceeding one whenever the production is not y^*. Hence, each firm j maximizes its nominal profits when producing y_j^*.

illustrates the magnitude of the normalization problem. A very large set of possible allocation can be supported as an equilibrium, provided we are free to chose any arbitrary normalization rule.[2]

The Cournot-Walrasian Model with Indirect Utility Maximization

There is something clearly wrong in the Cournot-Walrasian game presented in the previous section. Firms are assumed to maximize nominal profits without any regard to the objectives of their owners. This is odd. As Ginsburgh puts it: "Why would consumers be stupid enough to fool themselves ?" Firms are not independent identities with their own mind and preferences, they are instruments of individuals (consumers). Since individuals' preferences do not depend on the absolute level of prices but only the vector of final consumption, there is no reason why the normalization rule should matter.

It would seem only natural that the preferences of a firm reflect those of their owners. In particular, if every firm is owned by a unique consumer, it will seem natural to assume that firms choose their production plans in order to maximize the indirect utility of their owner.[3] Since the indirect utility functions are homogeneous of degree zero in prices and income, the normalization rule would not matter.

We think of a modified Cournot-Walrasian model as a model similar to the one presented in section 2 but where firms' preferences coincide with those of their owner. For now, I will not bother to specify how these preferences are aggregated when owners do not have the same preferences over what firms should produce; I simply explore the implications of the indirect utility maximization.

Consumer's Preference over Production Plans

Consider some individual i with some well-behaved indirect utility function. We characterize, here, i's preferences of the space of production plans. The exercise may help understand how and why indirect utility maximization differs from profit maximization. It is not important, here, whether i effectively controls the decision of any firm in the economy. What is first necessary is to specify consumer's preferences over the space of production plans.

Let $V_i(M_i, p)$ denote the indirect utility function of individual i. Let $w^i = \{w^i_1, \ldots, w^i_m\}$ represent individual i's initial endowment, and θ^i_j denote individual i's ownership share in firm j, where for all j: $\Sigma_i \theta^i_j = 1$. Let y_{jk}

---

2. Similar results can be found in Dierker and Grodal 1986, Gabszewicz and Vial 1972, and Böhm 1990.

3. This has been raised by Dierker and Grodal 1986 and Ginsburgh (this chapter).

denote the production by firm j of good k; note that y_{jk} can be negative if good k is an input in j's production. Individual i's virtual income is given by $M^i = \Sigma_k p_k(w_k^i + \Sigma_j \theta_j^i y_{yk})$, where $\Sigma_j \theta_j^i y_{jk}$ represents the share of the production of good k accruing to individual i through his ownership shares in the firms. Consumer i's preferred choice is determined by maximizing his indirect utility subject to the production constraints, and whereby assumption prices depend on y:

$$\max_{y} V_i\{M_i[y, p(y)], p(y)\} \text{ s.t. } F_j(y_j) \geq 0 \text{ for all firm } j. \tag{1}$$

The optimal production plan from the viewpoint of individual i specifies how much of each good k every firm j produces. Hence for every y_{jk}, we have the following first-order condition:

$$\frac{\partial V_i}{\partial M_i} \cdot \theta_j^i p_k + \frac{\partial V_i}{\partial M_i} \cdot \left[\sum_l \frac{\partial p_l}{\partial y_{jk}} \left(w_l^i + \sum_f \theta_f^i y_{fl} \right) \right]$$

$$+ \sum_l \frac{\partial V_i}{\partial p_l} \cdot \frac{\partial p_l}{\partial y_{jk}} + \lambda_j^i \cdot \frac{\partial F_j}{\partial y_{jk}} = 0, \tag{2}$$

where λ_j^i is individual i's Lagrange multiplier associated with firm j's production constraint. Let the vector x^i represent the final consumption of individual i, $x^i = \{x_1^i, \ldots x_m^i\}$, where x_k^i is the final consumption of good k by individual i; then, by Roy's identity, we have

$$-x_k^i = \frac{(\partial V_i/\partial p_k)}{(\partial V_i/\partial M_i)}.$$

So if we let

$$\delta_j^i = \frac{\lambda_j^i}{(\partial V_i/\partial M_i)},$$

we have the following for all firm j and good k and individual i:

$$\left(\theta_j^i p_k + \delta_j^i \cdot \frac{\partial F_j}{\partial y_{jk}} \right) + \left[\sum_l \frac{\partial p_l}{\partial y_{jk}} \left(w_l^i + \sum_f \theta_f^i y_{fl} - x_l^i \right) \right] = 0. \tag{3}$$

The above marginal condition has two components: the left-hand side bracket corresponds to the direct marginal effect of y_{jk}, j's production of good k, on firm j's profits; the bracket on the right corresponds to the marginal indirect effects of y_{jk} through prices on consumer's welfare. Note that a rational consumer will not only consider the effect of y_{jk} on the price of good k, but on all the other goods he trades. The consumer's preferences over the space of production plans depends on many parameters; they depend on his utility function (on his final consumption of each good), his initial endowment, and ownership shares. Ultimately, they depend on his position as a net trader in the market. If individual i is a net supplier of some good, he will seek to raise its price (if he can). Conversely, if he is a net demander of some good, he will want to decrease its market price. Stronger is his position as a net trader, greater are the incentives to distort prices.

Cournot vs. Competitive Behavior

We present here two simple general equilibrium models and show that the equilibrium of the modified Cournot-Walrasian game can, according to the parameters of the model, generate either the perfect competition or the Cournot outcome. In neither of these two examples does the aggregation of owners' preferences constitute a problem. In the first example, each firm has multiple owners, but they all share the same preferences over the possible production of the firm. In the second example, each firm is owned by a unique individual. In either case, we assume that the firm acts according to these preferences.

Proposition 2: If all consumers were perfectly identical, that is, with identical preferences, endowment, and ownership rights, then equilibrium outcome will correspond to the first-best, perfect competition allocation.

Proof of Proposition 2: The proof is intuitively straightforward. In an economy where all consumers are perfectly identical, there is no room for trade among them. Each individual will consume in equilibrium its own endowment and its share of firms output. Net trades are null for all individuals in the economy, so that no one finds it beneficial to distort prices one way or the other. Since $(w_l^i + \Sigma_f y_{fl} - x_l^i) = 0$ for all i and l, equation (3) can be rewritten as:

$$\theta_j^i p_k + \delta_j^i \cdot \frac{\partial F_j}{\partial y_{jk}} = 0, \quad \forall j \text{ and } k. \tag{4}$$

It follows that

$$\frac{\partial F_j / \partial y_{jk}}{p_k} = \frac{\partial F_j / \partial y_{jh}}{p_h}$$

for all goods k and h entering into j's production function. This corresponds to the profit maximization condition for firm j under perfect competition.

Q.E.D.

Now, consider the following economy. Each firm is owned by strictly one individual. Owners form a distinctive group of consumers in the economy. Every owner consumes only one good, labeled m, which is used as the numéraire. No firm produces good m, and owners hold no initial endowment (but their ownership rights). Other consumers detain no firm shares but hold initial endowments including that of good m.

Proposition 3: For the above economy, the equilibrium outcome (if it exists) will correspond to the Cournot allocation.

Proof of Proposition 3: Let i be the unique owner of firm j. Recall that by assumption, we have $w_l^i = 0$ for all l, $\theta_k^i = 0$ for all $k \neq j$, and $x_l^i = 0$ for all $l \neq m$. Finally, since m is the numéraire, $\partial p_m / \partial y_{jk} = 0$ for all k. Thus equation (3) can be rewritten as:

$$\theta_j^i \left[p_k + \sum_l \frac{\partial p_l}{\partial y_{jk}} y_{jl} \right] + \delta_j^i \cdot \frac{\partial F_j}{\partial y_{jk}} = 0. \tag{5}$$

It follows that for all goods k and h and firm j, we have:

$$\frac{\partial F_j / \partial y_{jk}}{p_k + \sum_l \dfrac{\partial p_l}{\partial y_{jk}} y_{jl}} = \frac{\partial F_j / \partial y_{jh}}{p_h + \sum_l \dfrac{\partial p_l}{\partial y_{jh}} y_{jl}}. \tag{6}$$

This corresponds to the profit maximization condition of firm j under Cournot competition.

Q.E.D.

As we can see from propositions 2 and 3, the magnitude of the market inefficiencies due to imperfect competition depends on the distribution of endowments and shares, and the preferences of owners. The model predicts that in an economy where shares are concentrated in the hands of few individuals, the economic inefficiencies due to imperfect competition are greater than in an economy where shares are more widely distributed. It is the heterogeneity among individuals that leads to market inefficiencies in the later example. Here, the trading positions of owners are extreme: they sell everything they produce and buy everything they consume. Thus the incentives are great for each owner to distort prices in order to exploit his or her position as a net supplier or net demander in the market.

Conclusion

I believe it is possible to resolve the normalization problem by having firms maximize the indirect utility function of their representative owners. The above discussion stresses new modeling issues. A correct modelization of the Cournot-Walrasian model would require one to specify the structure of ownership in the economy. This may facilitate the calibration of the model as the parameters of the structure of ownership introduce new degrees of freedom. But more importantly, new economic questions may be answered with such models. In the above theory, the ownership structure matters; hence one can try to measure the welfare implications of changes in the ownership structure.

Part 4
Modeling Intertemporal Trade-offs

CHAPTER 7

Investment, Expectations, and Dutch Disease: A Comparative Study (Bolivia, Cameroon, Indonesia)

Nancy Benjamin

"Dutch disease" describes the adjustment of a country spending foreign earnings from an export boom. The new spending drives up prices of nontraded goods relative to traded goods, which are held to world prices by competition from imports. This real exchange rate appreciation leads to contraction of the nonbooming export sector as production of nontraded goods and windfall exports becomes relatively more attractive.[1] The phenomenon was called "Dutch" because the experience of the Dutch exporting natural gas gave rise to its study. It was called "disease" because this structural transformation was considered to be unfavorable.

Van Wijnbergen (1985) addresses the perception that real appreciation and contraction of nonwindfall–traded goods are dangerous developments. He shows that with complete knowledge of the total amount of the windfall, thus knowledge of the value of all future current accounts, an increase in a country's lifetime foreign exchange earnings will naturally shift the economy's path in the direction of real appreciation and decline of traditional exports, regardless of the distribution over time of the windfall. With these "symptoms" cast as a natural and even necessary structural adjustment, any fear of "disease" has to be founded on some form of market failure.

If we consider the cases of countries who feel they have indeed suffered from adjustments to their foreign earnings windfalls, we may conclude that the assumption of perfect foresight of future foreign earnings is often inappropriate. The uncertainties over quantity and the price of booming export commodities make forecasting future current accounts difficult. During the oil boom, Mexico built up foreign debts it could not repay on schedule. Nigeria,

I am grateful to Jean Mercenier and Moustapha Nabli for their comments.
1. Corden (1982) surveys Dutch disease theory.

formerly a food exporter, became a food importer during high oil earnings, and continued to devote much foreign exchange to food imports long after oil prices fell. This indicates that one problem with adjustment to temporary export booms is that it is costly to change the sectoral structure of the capital stock when windfall earnings disappear. Investment may allocate capital according to short-term incentives, but it will have long-term repercussions if capital cannot be freely transferred across sectors. Nigeria, for example, has found it difficult to rebuild its food sector or to cultivate alternative export crops.

This chapter will consider Dutch disease in a framework where the only foresight of future foreign earnings is the expectation that current conditions will continue, where investment responds to short-term incentives, and where standing capital stock cannot be moved from its sector. We will examine the impact of a foreign earnings shock on the structure of the capital stock and consider how this would affect a country's ability to adjust to a reversal of export fortunes. The purpose is neither to find the model that best explains recent performance in any country nor to consider public expectations and public investment. Rather, the object is to explore what might happen in an economy driven by private decisions based on imperfect foresight.

Export booms will be simulated with computable general equilibrium (CGE) models for three different countries: Indonesia, Bolivia, and Cameroon. CGE models capture the relative price, structural, and general equilibrium effects inherent in Dutch disease. Using three countries allows us to examine these effects in economies with varying structures of intermediate and final demand. Each country is treated with three CGE models that differ in their rules about expectations formation. The different expectation rules allow the modeler to manipulate the extent to which the model's investors will respond to temporary price changes.

Since we are concerned about the evolution of the capital stock over time, experiments are run over five years. Model simulations include endogenous, forward-looking saving and investment decisions based on expectations about future profitability, but not based on perfect foresight. Producers form expectations about next year's sales from developments in the current period, but they do not know all future prices nor equilibrium output levels. Thus there is no guarantee their expectations will be realized. Savers, likewise, make guesses about the next year's price level. The loanable funds market is cleared by an equilibrium real interest rate, but the model includes no money nor monetary policy.

Summary descriptions of the models follow. A representative set of equations is listed in the appendix. The final section reports the results and conclusions of model experiments.

Models and Data

The first model is a standard developing country CGE model in the tradition of Dervis, de Melo, and Robinson (1982). It includes Cobb-Douglas production functions, Armington trade elasticities, and balance of payments adjustment through real exchange rate changes. Foreign capital inflow and the nominal exchange rate are fixed; domestic prices fluctuate against the fixed foreign price level, which is the numéraire of the model. This model is myopic because the level and structure of investment are determined only by current period outcomes. The level of investment stems from fixed or residual amounts of savings, and the sectoral allocation respects fixed base year shares. The model can be run forward over a number of years by updating the capital stock according to the last solution's investment pattern, updating the labor supply, and finding a new comparative static solution. This yields an investment stream where each year's investment is the result of myopic decisions. I call this the "no expectations" model.

The second model incorporates the forward-looking saving and investment behavior described in the first section.[2] However, expectations about sales growth are set exogenously, independent of the economic response to the expansionary shock. In this way, adjustment to the shock is isolated from (possibly erroneous) expectations that it will continue. Thus, agents in the model can be fooled by a continuous adjustment, but the shock may have less effect if expectations do not adjust. The purpose is to test the role of incorrect expectations by comparing the model outcome with those of different expectations regimes.

Given these rigid production targets, investment still responds dynamically. Projected output levels generate demand for new capital and loanable funds. This demand is equilibrated with the supply from savers through a flexible interest rate that becomes the expected price of next period's capital. Similarly, demand for next period's labor matches with an exogenous labor supply growth to determine the expected next period wage. The following summary equations show that to satisfy output targets, producers plan to employ next period the optimal combination of factors for the expected relative factor prices, and they invest accordingly. Production functions are CES.

$$K_2 = \left(\frac{\alpha}{(1 - \alpha)}\right)^\epsilon \left(\frac{W_2}{R_2}\right)^\epsilon \cdot L_2,$$

where investment $= K_2 - K_1 +$ depreciation.

---

2. A similar framework was used to study Dutch disease in Benjamin (forthcoming).

Similarly, households choose current consumption and saving based on income level, *Yd,* expected future price level, P_2 (consistent with projected factor prices), and the interest rate, R_2.[3]

Household savings $= Yd - P_1 C_1$,

where C_1 derives from:

$$\max Yd = C_1^\beta \, C_2^{1-\beta},$$

$$\text{st. } Yd = \frac{P_2 C_2}{1 + R_2} + P_1 C_1.$$

The third model also incorporates these forward-looking decisions, but output targets are based on changes in current sales from their value at the beginning of that period's solution. These targets could be based on any development in the current solution, but are never guaranteed to be realized. This "endogenous expectations" model and the "rigid expectations" model can both be run over time like the first model, by applying the labor supply growth rate and updating capital stock according to investments.

Such a sequence of solutions, even if forward looking, is clearly different from a dynamic model that finds optimal dynamic paths through the simultaneous solution of several periods. In these dynamic paths, investment in any one period is governed by the characteristics of the steady state. Agents are assumed to have perfect foresight, and each period's developments are an adjustment toward the steady state. The sequential solution method used here makes investment decisions a function of current economic developments and current expectations under imperfect foresight.

Even in most standard two-period, general equilibrium models, agents must know all prices for both periods. In the current model, producers have information on only two macroeconomic prices: the wage and the interest rate. This allows producers to infer their future value-added price but not their future selling price, nor any other sector's selling price. In the same way, households maximize utility with incomplete information about the future.

In this sense the model functions like a temporary equilibrium model

---

3. The household choice between present and future consumption is expressed with a Cobb-Douglas function. Experimentation with a generalized CES function showed that varying the substitution elasticity from less than one to greater than one yielded no difference in sign or pattern of results. Therefore, setting the elasticity to one, as in the Cobb-Douglas function, is not critical, but rather a choice from a noncritical range.

where agents adjust the distributions from which they take expected values of future prices according to changes in the current period. Perceptions of the second period serve to generate expectations that complete the first period solution. When producers actually enter the second period, they will behave the same as in earlier periods, but they could not have completely planned all decisions because they did not have all necessary information. They may find their expectations about variables endogenous to the current period are not realized.

The three economies tested in this framework are all oil or mineral exporters. They import mostly manufactures, capital goods and intermediate goods in particular. Cameroon has important cash crop exports. In the other two countries, food is tradable, with some sectoral export shares near 20 percent. Table 1 lists some significant summary statistics from the base data. All three data sets were developed for standard "myopic" CGE models used in planning exercises. These are the models used for the "no expectations" case. In all three model types the original parameters have been retained, though all exogenous updating (e.g., productivity growth) has been eliminated except for capital and labor. Comparative results were not sensitive to cross-country variation in parameters, though only the Indonesia and Bolivia models support experiments of the same design. Since the Cameroon sectoral data does not distinguish oil production as a separate sector, experiments with this model have a different structure, as is explained below.

Dutch Disease Simulations

The data sets for Indonesia and Bolivia distinguish the booming export sectors, oil and gas, so a foreign earnings shock can be imposed by raising the world price of these exports. For Bolivia, base year mineral exports total 10 million bolivianos while GDP is 100 million bolivianos. In model experiments the world price of these exports is maintained at double the base level. In Indonesia, oil exports are 13 trillion rupiahs while GDP is 92 trillion rupiahs. To test for Dutch disease effects, the world price for oil is kept 50 percent above the base value. In both models, there are no other major exporting sectors, but in each case there is one significant importing sector. These will indicate the results for import substitutes. The data for Cameroon aggregate oil production and sales with other intermediate goods. A foreign earnings windfall, then, cannot be introduced through the world price, but rather through an increase in foreign capital inflow, representing an increase in rents paid for the scarce resource. In experiments, the foreign inflow is increased by 100 million dollars, about two percent of the model's GDP, and is held at the new level for each year. While this clearly presents a different form

TABLE 1.

Indonesia

Population 1986	GDP/capita 1986	Number of sectors in the model	Model base year
166 mil.	$490	13	1984-85

Shares for aggregated sectors

	Agriculture	Oil/Mining	Industry	Services
Share in total prodn.	.17	.12	.28	.43
Exports/ output	.07	.63	.07	.04
Imports/ output	.03	.06	.35	.04

Bolivia

Population 1986	GDP/capita 1986	Number of sectors in the model	Model base year
6.6 mil.	$600	9	1985-86

Shares for aggregated sectors

	Agriculture	Oil/Mining	Industry	Services
Share in total prodn.	.18	.08	.16	.57
Exports/ output	.20	.72	.08	.04

TABLE 1.—*Continued*

Imports/				
output	.04	.04	.69	.04

Cameroon

Population 1986	GDP/capita 1986	Number of sectors in the model	Model base year
10.5 mil.	$910	11	1984-85

Shares for aggregated sectors

	Agriculture	Oil/Mining[4]	Industry	Services
Share in total prodn.	.19	.	.33	.48
Exports/ output	.23	.	.22	.07
Imports/ output	.02	.	.38	.08

Sources: World Development Report 1988. Devarajan and Lewis 1988. Huarachi and Beltran 1988. G. Djophant, Cameroon Ministry of Plan.

Note: Cameroon includes oil and mining in one of its industry sectors. The size and trade shares for industry in aggregate reflect this inclusion.

of experiment, it allows us to test the impact of new foreign earnings on a traditional export sector. Cameroon's cash crop exports provide a case in contrast to the other countries, whose exports are concentrated in the boom sectors.

To examine Dutch disease effects in the various investment environments described, we report results on growth of output and capital stock. Table 2 lists summary figures for five year simulations of all three models. In each case we use the percentage growth of capital or output from its base to its final level and report the difference in percentage growth points between the export boom results and the reference run (no shock). For example, with endogenous expectations the aggregate Bolivian capital stock grows 26 percent in the five year reference run. It grows 34 percent with the export windfall, or eight points more. The table entry is 8. Table 2 also gives results for the sector most at risk in each country—the main import substitute in Indonesia and Bolivia ("industry") and the traditional export in Cameroon. Clearly the sector experiencing the most change in each case is the construction sector. But concern over Dutch disease is not a matter of whether nontraded goods production grows—rather, whether nonbooming traded sectors contract.

The first point to note is that import competing sectors grow during the export boom, not only in absolute terms, but more than in the base case. The zero entries for Bolivia represent positive increases of less than one-half percent. Even in Cameroon import substitutes improved their growth rates by about one percent. The positive results for the two industry sectors derive from favorable trends in prices, demand, and aggregate investment, and from the relation between imports and domestic production.

With either form of increased foreign earnings, higher export prices or new injections of foreign exchange, the increase in domestic spending drives up domestic prices. Typically, net importers experience relatively less appreciation, due to foreign competition. The lower price sectors earn less value added, offer lower wages, and lose workers to higher price sectors. Since labor is the only mobile factor within the period, output growth follows the labor migration. The first year results for Indonesia replicate this typical pattern for prices, but output changes are biased against the small, nonboom exporting sectors, rather than against industry, which actually expands. After the first year, various forces are favorable to industry. The higher foreign earnings finance an investment boom that raises demand for industry as a supplier of capital goods. Starting in the second year, output and investment growth in the sector reinforce each other, and the relative price of industry improves significantly.

The pattern of price changes is an important development in this experiment. In Indonesia, almost all of the real appreciation occurs in the first period. Afterward, prices fluctuate as supply expansion catches up with new demand. The export boom revenues have less effect in this inflated economy

TABLE 2. Changes in Percentage Growth of Capital Stock and Output (in Italics) Due to Increased Foreign Earnings

		Indonesia	Bolivia	Cameroon
Endogenous investment	aggregate	10 *1*	8 *3*	3 *1*
Endogenous expectations	traditional traded good	3 *6*	1 *1*	-3 *-5*
Endogenous investment	aggregate	9 *2*	5 *2*	2 *0*
Exogenous expectations	traditional traded good	-6 *4*	0 *0*	1 *-5*
Exogenous investment	aggregate	4 *2*	12 *9*	2 *2*
Exogenous expectations	traditional traded good	4 *1*	10 *8*	5 *2*

with greatly expanded production capacity. Thus, unless the world oil price continually increases, the impact of the windfall will naturally decline. Sectors that enjoyed great price appreciation from the boom will see their price growth diminish. A few sectors, especially traded agriculture, show steady declines in price after the first year. (As will be seen in several cases, exports are especially vulnerable.) Meanwhile, industry's price, which benefits less from the initial windfall, rises along with the most dynamic component of final demand: investment. The potential for expansion of a tradable supplying investment goods was shown in a static framework with a fixed savings rate by Benjamin, Devarajan, and Weiner (1989). In the current study, the amount of investment expansion from any windfall is endogenous as investors compete with forward-looking consumers for new resources.

In the Indonesia experiment, the investment boom is especially large, in part for reasons traceable to the distribution of income. Great oil profits favor the wealthier households, which generate higher savings rates. Also, the oil sector begins the experiment receiving one-third of total investment. So when the world oil price rises, growth is promoted in the largest component of aggregate investment.

Finally, this new investment rapidly expands the oil export base and leads to a similar increase in imports (since the trade balance is fixed). The broadest avenue for imports is through the industry sector, but these imports obviously do not undermine domestic production to the point of contracting the sector. The elasticity of substitution between imports and home goods is low, only .4, so a jump in imports can even encourage domestic production.

While the discussion has focused on the main import substitute, we note here that all sectors show positive output and investment growth. This relies on the nature of the capital market. In a comparative static model, structural change is zero-sum—sectors grow at the expense of contraction in others. In a dynamic framework, this pattern can persist, especially if standing capital can be dismantled and supplied as investible resources to other sectors, or if all new investment is allocated to sectors with the highest rates of return. In the current model, expected returns in investing sectors do not have to be better than other sectors, they only have to be better than the market interest rate. Investors consider only the profitability of expanding capital stock in their own sector.

The role of expectations in this capital market can be seen by comparing results with the exogenous expectations model. The aggregate results are quite similar, but in the second case, industry's capital grows less under the Dutch disease shock. When the previously discussed improvements in industry's relative price take place and output expands, producers do not respond by increasing investment because their expectation of output growth is predetermined. Instead, the higher price finances an increase in employment, so that output grows more than in the base run but investment does not.

When both expectations and investment decisions are exogenous, the investment boom is smaller as output growth is not reinforced by accelerated investment demand. If model agents cannot bid for resources to bet on future economic expansion, the expansion will be limited. In this experiment, aggregate consumption posts a higher growth rate than investment—a reverse of the first two cases. Still, the overall expansion is enough to maintain the industry sector above its base run level.

Since the foreign earnings shock was shown in the first model to generate endogenous forces favorable to import substitutes, it is not surprising that the effects are diminished when these forces are restricted. Adding rigidities, though, does not help the sector suffering most from the shock. Without a direct subsidy, negative output trends for traded agriculture will persist in all three models, even the most rigid, which maintains the sector's capital stock but cannot retain its workers.

In Bolivia, it is the most rigid model that produces the greatest economic growth and the most positive outcome for the industry sector. Endogenously responsive investment generates forces much less mutually beneficial across sectors compared to Indonesia. The Bolivian mineral exports start out with a smaller share of total investment allocation. The world price increase causes the sector to bid strongly for loanable funds. This one-sector investment boom places proportionately more demand on construction services than in the other countries. Since construction is both the major nontraded good and the principle capital good, it receives an added measure of upward pressure. This extra price appreciation in construction raises the price of capital goods to all the nonboom sectors and discourages their expansion. Thus the concentration of the investment boom in one sector causes capital goods price appreciation that curtails growth in the others.

With fixed expected growth rates across sectors, investment in boom exports is held back, but the scarcity of construction services still arises from the supply side. When investment does not respond to new demand to expand the sector's capacity, the price appreciation is worse than before. Only forced investment shares achieve the economy's greater potential. Enforcing a balanced growth pattern yields a much lower construction price and, of the three models, allows the most increase in construction output. Since construction relies on itself for capital goods, the former demand from boom exports choked off its own growth. Of the three, the myopic model produces the greatest increase in output over base year values from a foreign earnings shock.

Cameroon also fares relatively well under the myopic model. In contrast to Bolivia, the main investment good is supplied by the capital goods sector where imports are eight times domestic production. In the reference run of the myopic model, cash crop exports increase steadily, which finances more imports as the economy grows. The higher exports require a lower price for cash crops, but output does not suffer as a consequence. Because the sector pays the lowest wage in relation to the market wage (because it has the lowest ω_i in equation 12, see the appendix), it is least affected by the rising market wage. So cash crops are able to hold onto their workers while capital allocation is guaranteed by the model specification. This pattern is not disturbed by the new foreign earnings inflow, which is used to finance an increase in imports, especially of capital goods, rather than a decrease in exports.

In the model with exogenous expected output growth, the output growth rates chosen (about 2.7 percent for all sectors in all three countries) lead to very high factor costs in the reference run. This is exacerbated by the new foreign capital inflow. The high interest rate inhibits the construction sector, which is one of the most capital intensive and therefore interest sensitive sectors. Overall the growth of production, trade, and prices is low compared to the other models. With such heavy demand for domestic nontraded productive factors, capital and labor, the model responds to a foreign earnings shock by cutting back on exports, which releases domestic resources, rather than by bringing in imports that only relieve selling prices. When investment decisions are fully endogenous, investment in cash crops cannot hold up under the negative price trend. Production contracts, as it does in the rigid expectations model, but now investment falls as well.

Conclusion

Classic Dutch disease structural adjustments, a variant of the transfer problem, are well known and carry with some inevitability across all types of modeling frameworks. If a country can make accurate forecasts of future current account balances and rely on a perfect international capital market to allow intertemporal smoothing of consumption, then there is no disease and no policy recommendation. However, in a developing country that is likely to face an unpredictable need to reduce its current account deficit and which cannot depend on the international capital market for all the help it needs, the question for the modeler becomes this: What is there in the detail of adjustment to foreign earnings fluctuations that can help the policymaker overcome these market imperfections?

Experimenting with the forward-looking models described here reveals some insights. First, given the Armington assumption, the observation that foreign capital inflow will be more harmful to net exporters than to import substitutes is robust across the different types of expectations formation in Indonesia. The endogenous expectations model reveals a plausible time pattern of relative price changes that is favorable to import substitutes during the adjustment period. One possible conclusion is that import substitution is likely to be a more successful strategy than export promotion. Vigorous import substitution policies are most often found in countries whose abundant resources preclude dropping wages low enough to compete as exporters in manufactures. The model results indicate, however, that import substitutes are promoted even without policy.

The favoring of importing over exporting sectors ironically does not hold in the myopic model for Cameroon, where the result was first observed. We may conclude that for both Cameroon and Bolivia, models with fixed investment shares forestall certain negative output trends and present an optimistic view of response to shocks that cause those trends. The Cameroon case also shows the importance of changes in factor prices and the responsiveness of different sectors to them. One hint to modelers is to determine base year capital stocks and investment allocations carefully, because results from a model with an endogenous interest rate may depend on the capital intensity of some sectors and whether they start out with abundant investible resources or have to bid them away.

The Bolivian case demonstrates one of the costly aspects of Dutch disease adjustment—pouring money through a bottleneck in the economy. This occurs when endogenous investment trends concentrate demand on construction services, causing more rapid price inflation. Such occurrences could contribute to arguments for economic diversification or centrally planned investment shares. The simple response is to find a way to supply more investment needs through imports. The models with different investment markets indicate that avoiding the bottleneck could be worth several percentage points in growth of total output.

. CGE models have always been useful for analyzing problems where the structure of the economy plays an important role in the outcome. This exercise with comparative Dutch disease experiments shows that the more adjustment issues involved—investment, expectations—the more structural features of the economy that become critical. Using different models for different countries provides some guideposts for predicting adjustment outcomes from structural features of the economy and its markets.

APPENDIX: MODEL SPECIFICATION

These equations represent the single period version of the myopic model. As in the Bolivia model, the equations only include one labor group and one household. The Cameroon model actually has three labor groups, and for Indonesia there are four labor groups and four households. The basic model structure, however, is the same for all three countries. Only labor and capital are updated between periods. In the forward-looking versions, the exogenous household saving rate and the exogenous investment allocations are replaced by the endogenous two-period decisions described in this chapter.

Imports

Imperfectly substitutable imports M_i and domestically produced goods D_i form the composite good X_i:

$$X_i = A_i^c [\delta_i M_i^{-\rho_i} + (1 - \delta_i) D_i^{-\rho_i}]^{-1/\rho_i} . \tag{1}$$

A_i^c and δ_i are constants and σ_i, the elasticity of substitution, is:

$$\sigma_i = 1/(1 + \rho_i) .$$

Consumers minimize the cost of obtaining the composite good

$$P_i X_i = PM_i M_i + PD_i D_i \tag{2}$$

subject to (1). This yields the demand function:

$$M_i/D_i = (PD_i/PM_i)^{\sigma_i} (\delta_i/(1 - \delta_i)^{\sigma_i} . \tag{3}$$

PD_i and PM_i are the prices of domestic and imported goods and P_i the price of the composite commodity. PM_i is linked to the world (dollar) price as follows:

$$PM_i = PW_i (1 + tm_i) ER , \tag{4}$$

where ER is the exchange rate and tm_i the tariff rate on imports in sector i.

Exports

Exporters face a constant elasticity world demand function:

$$E_i = E_{io}(\Pi_i/PE_i)^{\eta_i} , \tag{5}$$

where Π_i is a weighted average of world prices for good i.

Export supply is determined by a constant elasticity of transformation function between domestically consumed D_i and exported E_i goods:

$$XD_i = A_i^T[\gamma_i E_i^{\phi_i} + (1 - \gamma_i)D_i^{\phi_i}]^{1/\phi_i} , \tag{6}$$

where XD_i is gross output and A_i^T and γ_i are constants. The elasticity of transformation ψ_i is:

$$\psi_i = 1/(1 - \phi_i) .$$

Firms maximize revenue from a given level of output

$$PX_i XD_i = PE_i E_i + PD_i D_i \tag{7}$$

subject to (6). This yields the following allocation between domestic sales and exports:

$$E_i/D_i = (PE_i/PD_i)^{\psi_i} (\phi_i/(1 - \phi_i))^{\psi_i} . \tag{8}$$

The export price PE_i is defined by:

$$PWE_i = PE_i/ER , \tag{9}$$

where PWE_i is the dollar price of exports in sector i.

Domestic Supply of Goods and Demand for Labor

Domestic production is Cobb-Douglas with sector specific capital K_i which is fixed within the current period:

$$XD_i = A_i L_i^{\alpha_i} K_i^{1-\alpha_i} . \tag{10}$$

The unit value added price of sector i is:

$$PV_i = PX_i(1 - td_i) - \sum_j P_j a_{ji} , \tag{11}$$

where a_{ji} is the (j,i) input-output coefficient and td_i the indirect tax rate. Profit maximization yields:

$$\omega_i w = (\alpha_i PV_i XD_i) / L_i , \tag{12}$$

where w is the wage rate and ω_i is the proportion of sector i's wage to the average wage in the economy. Total labor supply is fixed, so labor market clearing requires:

$$\sum_i L_i = \bar{L} . \tag{13}$$

Intermediate Demand

Demand for intermediate inputs W_i is:

$$W_i = \sum_j a_{ij} X_j . \tag{14}$$

Consumer Demand

One representative household buys consumer goods according to fixed expenditure shares:

$$P_i C_i = \beta_i C^T , \tag{15}$$

where C_i is consumer demand for good i, C^T is total consumption and β_i the share spent on good i.

Total consumption is a fixed fraction of disposable income Y:

$$C^T = (1 - s)(1 - t) Y, \tag{16}$$

where s is the private savings rate, and t the income tax rate. Gross income is the sum of factor earnings less transfers to the government:

$$Y = \sum_i PV_i XD_i - \overline{YPFB}. \tag{17}$$

Government Demand

The government keeps fixed the level of expenditure on each commodity. Hence, government demand for commodity i is

$$G_i = \beta_i^G G, \tag{18}$$

where β_i^G is zero for all sectors except public administration, for which β_i^G is one.

Investment Demand

The level of investment demand is determined by the level of savings. The latter is the sum of private, public, and foreign savings:

$$S = S^P + S^G + F \cdot ER, \tag{19}$$

where

$$S^P = s(1 - t)Y,$$

and

$$S^G = tY + \sum_i tm_i PW_i M_i + \sum_i td_i PX_i XD_i + YPFB - \sum_i P_i G_i - INT,$$

where INT represents interest payments on foreign debt and F is the level of foreign savings. The composition of investment by sector of origin is given by:

$$Z_i = \sum_j h_{ij} H_j S / \sum_k P_k h_{kj}, \tag{20}$$

where h_{ij} is the (i,j) element of the capital coefficients matrix and H_j is the (exogenous) share of investment by sector of destination accruing to sector j.

Inventory demand is a fixed fraction of output:

$$ST_i = v_i XD_i \tag{21}$$

By Walras's Law, the current account deficit is equal to the level of foreign savings.

$$\sum_i PW_i M_i + \text{INT} = \sum_i PWE_i E_i + F. \tag{22}$$

Supply-Demand Equilibrium

The equilibrium condition for each sector is:

$$X_i = W_i + C_i + G_i + ST_i + Z_i. \tag{23}$$

All export demand is for the domestically produced good rather than for the composite commodity.

Comment

Gary McMahon

This very interesting chapter examines the phenomenon of Dutch disease in three different behavioral settings in three different countries. The study starts out by noting that an export boom can only end in disease if there is market failure, and then it proceeds to look at three different combinations of "market failures," moving from the case of no foresight to somewhat imperfect foresight. The most interesting result is that there is very little disease in any of the three scenarios for the three countries, although the amount does depend quite significantly on the expectations and investment allocation mechanisms. Part of the reason for this strong result is that the author follows the illness through its first five years. With the increased export earnings and possibilities for higher investment, the economy is no longer a zero-sum game with regard to investment allocation and growth. In this comment we will largely focus on the assumptions of the model, which may have led to this result as well as others that, if employed, would likely have strengthened it.

In general the Dutch disease only really becomes a problem after the windfall disappears. As the author notes: "This indicates that one problem with adjustment to temporary export booms is that it is costly to change the sectoral structure of the capital stock when windfall earnings disappear." However, in the simulations Benjamin increases the level of boom sector export earnings in the first year and then maintains them at this level (more or less) throughout the five years. It would have been interesting to continue the diagnosis for another five years without the windfall or, perhaps, to have two years of windfall and three years of normal earnings.

There is also no sensitivity analysis for some of the key elasticities. In the simulations the elasticity of substitution between home goods and imports is very low. This means that the import-competing sectors are not hit very hard by the appreciation of the currency. In the paper by Benjamin, Devarajan, and Weiner (1989, 88), they found that the effects of an export boom in Cameroon were quite different when the elasticities of substitution were assumed to be quite high versus very low. In fact, the Dutch disease was very mild in the latter case, while quite strong in the former.

253

On the other hand, there are at least two major assumptions that, if changed, would have made the effects of the disease even weaker than they were. In the model the trade balance is fixed; thus, any increase in exports is met by an increase in imports. The government is not allowed, for example, to put any money in foreign bonds, which would dampen the effect on the exchange rate. In fact, as noted by Benjamin, Devarajan, and Weiner (1989, 91), this is precisely what the government of Cameroon did, and subsequently it suffered little if at all from the disease. This result highlights the possibility that countries that have suffered from the illness did not really have a disease at all, but a self-inflicted wound. (See Gelb 1988 for an analysis of destructive policy responses to windfalls in a number of oil-producing countries.)

Second, the simulations assume full employment. Therefore, any expansion in production puts strong pressure on wages and prices. In the simulations this result comes out most strongly in the case of Bolivia, where a large part of the increase in demand ends up in the construction services sector, raising price substantially and reducing the increase in aggregate real investment. Given the large amount of open (or nearly open) unemployment that exists in Bolivia, it seems likely that, at least after a short adjustment period, the construction sector could expand substantially without significant pressure on prices to rise.

In sum, Benjamin has done a very good job of showing that the Dutch disease is probably more a malady of the mind than the body. With the qualifications made above, she demonstrates that, barring gross policy errors, there is really nothing much to fear from the illness. Implicitly she also demonstrates that in many cases there is more to be gained from the construction boom approach to positive export shocks (as emphasized in the work of Bevan, Collier, and Gunning 1990) than the Dutch disease analysis. The author should also be congratulated for her explanations of the transmission of the simulated policies to the key variables. In a few pages she makes it clear to the reader what is inside the black boxes that she is working with. However, a more thorough explanation of the manner in which firms and households formed expectations about the next period's wage and interest rate would also have been helpful in understanding the results.

CHAPTER 8

A General Equilibrium Analysis of the Effects of Carbon Emission Restrictions on Economic Growth in a Developing Country: Egypt

Charles R. Blitzer, Richard S. Eckaus, Supriya Lahiri, and Alexander Meeraus

The consequences of environmental damage spread beyond the sectors in which they originate and have repercussions beyond their immediate impact. The same is true of policies designed to deal with environmental traumas. Computable general equilibrium models are particularly appropriate for the analysis of such issues as they make it possible to trace both the consequences of environmental damage and the proposals to deal with these effects.

This chapter is intended as a demonstration of the potential uses of a multisectoral, intertemporal, programming model embodying significant non-linearities in production and consumption to analyze the effects of environmental policies. The particular application chosen to illustrate the approach is an analysis of the effects on economic growth of the regulation of carbon emissions. Other applications to the analysis of environmental issues could be treated analogously.

The model used was not originally designed for the present purpose and the setting of the model is rather special.[1] For these reasons, the numerical results should be interpreted as illustrative, rather than definitive, with respect to the relationships involved. Nonetheless, the results have some characteristics that, we will claim, have general validity.[2]

As a by-product of the particular application, the methodology represents

The views expressed here are the authors' responsibility and do not necessarily reflect the views of the Center for Energy Policy Research, the University of Lowell, the Massachusetts Institute of Technology, or the World Bank. The project in which the original model was developed was sponsored by an MIT subcontract with MetaSystems of Cambridge, Massachusetts, contracting with the Organization for Energy Policy, the Government of Egypt, and financed by the U.S. Agency for International Development.

1. For a description of the original model, see Blitzer et al. 1989.
2. See, for example, Romer 1986.

a means of incorporating external economies in computable general equilibrium models. This may be of particular interest now as some types of externalities play an important role in the growth theories that have appeared in recent years.

The particular type of emission that will be analyzed is that of carbon generated by the use of petroleum and natural gas fuels. This leaves out other sources of carbon emission, other sources of greenhouse effects and other types of pollutants. The focus should not be interpreted as a judgment on the dangers, actual or incipient, of a greenhouse effect, on which no position is taken here.

Energy, the Environment, and the Economy

Many, though by no means all, of the assaults on the environment are associated directly or indirectly with the use of energy sources of various types. The creation of acid rain is traced to the burning of high sulfur coals in thermoelectric facilities. The generation of urban smog is related to automobile emissions of methane, nitrous oxides, sulfur dioxide, and particulates from gasoline and diesel fuels. Plastic trash, ground water pollution from leaking underground storage facilities and oil spills—all can be related directly or indirectly to fossil fuel inputs. The argument that there is a global warming danger is related mainly to the generation of carbon dioxide, methane, and nitrous oxide from the burning of all types of fossil fuels.[3]

These obvious relations have led to many simplistic proposals for reducing the use of fossil fuels. They are simplistic, not because they are not good-hearted and not necessarily because they have an incorrect association of direct causes and effects, but because they do not have a correct assessment, if any, of indirect causes and effects and the overall costs and benefits. Assessing causes and effects is, of course, difficult. In part the difficulties are due to inadequate understanding of the science involved in the physical and chemical interactions in the environment. Part of the difficulties are due to lack of adequate data to project the spatial distribution of physical and chemical consequences of processes that may be well understood.

Part of the difficulties is in the lack of adequate methods for evaluating the overall economic effects of environmental change and environmental policies, including in the evaluations the reactions that will take place throughout the economy to particular kinds of changes and policies that may be confined to only a few sectors. These latter issues are the province of the economist, and the profession should react to the challenge.

The reactions, so far, with a few important exceptions, have been rather

---

3. For a survey of some policy issues, see Lave 1988.

limited in their sophistication. They have relied on simple extrapolations of pollutants in relation to fuel inputs or on econometric estimates of energy demands and on extrapolations using energy/gross national product ratios. Input-output models have been used in which there is no possibility of substitution of inputs by producers or of commodity purchases by consumers, both in reaction to changes in relative costs.

One major exception, as might be expected, is in the modeling of the greenhouse effect associated with Alan Manne.[4] Manne (1989) also focuses on the trade-off between reduction in the generation of pollutants and the overall performance of the economy. In estimating the costs of a carbon emissions limit, a growth model is used in conjunction with a process analysis model for the energy sector. The integrated model, called ETA-MACRO, simulates a market economy through a dynamic nonlinear optimization process. The model is intertemporal in nature, and alternative carbon emission scenarios are evaluated in terms of their impact on present and future levels of consumption for the United States.

The methodology is extremely useful in tracing the complex energy economy and environmental interactions over time. Its major limitation is its highly aggregative nature. Outside of the energy sector, all of the nonenergy sectors are treated as a single aggregate. The model is not intended to capture the interactions between the different sectors of the economy as they affect energy supply and usage or sectoral adjustments to emission constraints. These are potentially significant since emission rates differ among the various types of inputs and outputs; overall emissions are therefore sensitive to changes in the sectoral pattern of growth. Thus the environmental and macro-consequences of alternative pollution abatement strategies cannot be evaluated adequately within the above framework.

Another major exception to the rule of simple approaches is the sophisticated analysis in Jorgenson and Wilcoxen 1989. It is designed to estimate the trade-off between pollution abatement and economic growth in the United States. The characteristics of the model will be summarized very briefly here as a means of contrasting it with the model that we will present.

The strengths of the Jorgenson-Wilcoxen study are in its careful and detailed econometric modeling of the production and consumption processes for each of the 35 commodity groups into which the economy is disaggregated. The costs of pollution abatement are also calculated carefully. In these respects the analysis appears to be the most advanced available.

The intertemporal results are calculated from steady state solutions of the model. In the base case pollution controls are in effect. Then, in order to determine the overall economic effects of environmental restrictions, the

---

4. See Manne and Richels 1989.

growth path of the U.S. economy is simulated in the absence of regulatory measures. This step is taken by first estimating pollution abatement cost shares. These costs are then subtracted from production costs in the base case and economic growth in the model is simulated again. This gives a comparison of growth performance with and without pollution abatement costs.

There are, however, some features of the model that are not well-suited to its purposes. One of those is the assumption that capital is fully mobile among sectors. That is certainly not a realistic characterization of the economy except in the very long term. However, it is necessary for the way in which economic growth is realized in the model, through the calculation of steady state growth and a transition toward that path.

An Economywide and Intertemporal Environmental Model with Substitution Possibilities

The model to be presented below, however, is in the same spirit as Manne's approach. Focusing on a single country and demonstrating a general methodology, it is more elaborate in a number of respects than would have been warranted in Manne's first environmental modeling research. In contrast with Manne's approach, our framework proposes a more disaggregated multisectoral model to evaluate the consequences of alternative pollution control strategies.

The basic structure of the model is well-known from previous work by the authors and many others. The complete mathematical structure of the model is presented in an appendix, and only those features that are particularly important for its present application will be described here. It is a multisector, intertemporal optimizing model with some distinguishing features. The model was originally constructed for the analysis of energy policy in Egypt. It was adapted to the analysis of environmental issues since it is relatively detailed with respect to the sources and uses of energy, which, as noted above, is one of the primary sources of environmental offense.

For many purposes of environmental analysis, a country-based analysis is the correct one. With some exceptions (such as the Montreal agreement on the control of fluorocarbon emissions and regulation of the quality of the Rhine river) environmental policies are now national, rather than international. Economic policies, with only a few exceptions, are also national rather than international. For large countries, national analysis is often appropriate, with important qualifications for border areas.

Nonetheless, some apologies are required for respecting national boundaries that are, for environmental purposes, often quite artificial. First, the local effects of some kinds of environmental pollution are the most important, and averaging over a larger area is misleading. Second, transnational effects may be not be confined only to border areas. With these apologies, a national model will be presented but with the belief that the methodology can be generalized and extended.

The model has a 25-year time-horizon, divided into five periods of five years each. This somewhat artificial pacing makes it possible to avoid a more detailed formulation of year-by-year interactions and dynamic processes, while still generating a close temporal approximation of growth conditions. Results are reported for five, evenly spaced years.

The economy is divided into ten sectors, six of which are nonenergy sectors: agriculture, manufacturing, construction, transportation, services, and noncompeting imports. There are four energy sectors: crude oil, natural gas, petroleum products, and electricity.

The economic variables determined by the model are investment, capital capacity, and production by each sector, household consumption by sector, energy demand and supply, imports and exports, and relative prices, all calculated for five evenly spaced periods that are also five years apart.

As noted, the model focuses only on the generation of carbon emissions due to fuel use, although the methods are completely adaptable to other types of emissions associated with the use of any input or to the output of particular goods with specific technologies. The carbon emissions are calculated for each sector, as well as in total, for each period.

As an optimizing model, it maximizes an objective or welfare function that is the discounted sum of aggregate consumer utility over the model's horizon. The utility of the representative consumer in each time period is a weighted logarithmic sum over all goods of the difference between its consumption of each type of good and a parametrically fixed consumption level. Individual utility is multiplied by the projected population to obtain aggregate utility. This formulation is identical to simulating the market behavior of a representative consumer modeled as a linear expenditure system. It should be noted, in the present context, that environmental conditions do not enter the consumer's utility function directly. However, the consumer's choice of goods in the consumption basket will depend on relative prices and income levels, which are determined within the model, and those can be expected to be affected by environmental policies.

The usual material balance constraints, which require that the aggregate uses of output can be no greater than the aggregate availabilities, apply in each period. Availabilities depend on domestic production and imports, where the latter is feasible.

One of the most significant features of the model for the purposes of assessing the environmental impacts of economic activity is that, in general, production of each good can be carried out by alternative technologies, or "activities," with different input patterns. The total output of each sector is the sum of the production from each of the technologies. Thus, there is the possibility of substitution among inputs in production processes. The substitution takes place endogenously, in response to the relative prices of inputs and outputs, which are also determined endogenously. This is important for the analysis of environmental policies that either directly or indirectly affect the cost of inputs.

The potential alternative requirements for production in each sector are, with one exception, specified exogenously, as if they were taken from engineering specifications. The exception is in the demand for fuels, where, in effect, the BTU requirements per unit of output are specified, but the requirements can be met by using either natural gas or petroleum. Here, again, the choice will be made endogenously, depending on relative prices and any constraints that affect those prices.

Only three primary energy sources are distinguished: hydropower, crude oil, and natural gas.[5] Production of each is constrained by availability. Crude oil is produced from petroleum reserves, and the creation and use of these and natural gas reserves is modeled to reflect the fact that the level of reserves is a function of the rate as well as the quantity of use of the resources and outputs to producers and consumers.

Production also requires labor inputs, whose unit requirements are also specified exogenously, but differently, for each technology or activity in each sector. There is an overall constraint on labor availability and, separately, a labor constraint in the agricultural sector intended to reflect limited rural-urban labor mobility and the tightness of the rural labor market over the past decade or so.

As is customary in such models, and different from the Jorgenson-Wilcoxen model, capital is specific to each sector; here, it is specific as well to the particular technology that it embodies. Capital formation in each period in each sector requires that investment be undertaken in the previous period. Depreciation rates are specified exogenously for the capital stock used by each technology in each period.

Foreign trade is confined to the tradable goods sectors: agriculture, manufacturing, transportation, other services, crude oil, and petroleum products. As an approximate way of recognizing limited flexibility in the response of exports and imports to changes in relative prices, the rate of change of each of these is constrained, although within wide bounds.

The overall balance of payments constraint, which limits imports to what

---

5. It should be recalled that the purpose in presenting the model is primarily methodological. The omission of coal as a primary energy source would, of course, be quite wrong for most countries, although correct in the case of Egypt.

can be paid for from exports and foreign exchange resources, must also be met. Foreign borrowing is allowed, within moving upper bounds.

The problems of establishing initial and terminal conditions in a model of this sort are well known. Here, they are largely finessed. The sectoral levels of investment in the initial period are constrained not to be greater than those actually achieved in 1987. The sectoral levels of investment in the terminal period are determined by the condition that they be adequate to sustain an exogenously specified rate of growth of output in the sector in the postterminal period. The terminal conditions, in particular, create some anomalies in the final periods of the model's time horizon. Since that horizon is relatively long, these have only modest effects on the intermediate years, for which results are reported.

With this description of the basic model in place it is possible now to turn to the features that deal with the environment, which can in fact be described quickly. The quantity of carbon, V, that is generated by the use of a particular fuel, i, in a technology, k, in a particular sector, j, in period, t, is V_{ikjt}. So the total amount of carbon generated by the use of a particular fuel in the sector is obtained by summing over all technologies:

$$V_{ijt} = \sum_k V_{ikjt}.$$

In addition carbon emissions are generated directly by consumption. The carbon emitted by a use of a fuel, i, in consumption, V_{ict} is related to consumption of that fuel, C_{it}, by a coefficient v_{ict}:

$$V_{ict} = v_{ict} C_{it}.$$

The total amount of carbon generated by the use of the particular fuel in all sectors and in consumption is:

$$V_{it} = \sum_j V_{ijt} + V_{ict}.$$

The generation of carbon is related to the use of the particular fuel in the sector by a coefficient, v_{kijt}. That is,

$$V_{kijt} = v_{kijt} V_{kjt},$$

where the V_{ik}'s are understood to refer only to the fuel inputs.

The simple relationships are the conventional ones used in projecting the generation of environmental agents. Now, however, that generation is a matter of endogenous determination in a complete model. So calculation of the generation of environmental agents is completely consistent with the calculation of the other features of the model, including its growth path.

Although the issues analyzed here are the consequences of carbon emissions constraints for economic growth, the model can be turned to other questions, for example, the environmental consequences of an increase in the efficiency of energy use in consumption. With modest modification of the consumer's utility function to make some types of consumer durables complementary with specific fuels, the implications of *requiring* the use of a particular fuel could be investigated.

In studying the trade-off between the generation of carbon emissions and overall economic performance, two alternative forms of quantitative restrictions will be analyzed. The first is a constraint on the generation of carbon emissions by the use of a particular fuel, i, in particular sectors, j. The constraint would be of the form:

$$V_{ijkt} \leq \bar{V}_{ijkt}.$$

It will be recalled that capital is committed to a particular technology in a particular sector. So it is quite possible that an "old" technology will continue to be used in a sector because its capital has not depreciated, while a new technology with different capital is being adopted. This constraint, therefore, makes it possible to investigate the consequences of essentially banning particular technologies.

The second type of restriction is a constraint on the total amount of the particular agent generated by a particular sector. This would take the form:

$$V_{it} \leq \bar{V}_{it}.$$

This discriminatory regulation of particular sectors is also a kind of environmental regulation that is frequently discussed. It may have a certain rationale in that there may be differences among sectors in the degree to which regulations can be enforced effectively.

The third type of restriction is a constraint on the total amount of the particular agent generated by two or more sectors. It would take the form:

$$\sum_i V_{it} \leq \bar{V}_i.$$

This type of restriction can be used to reflect the idea of "bubble" regulation. It is, essentially, regulating the total output of an environmental agent by a complex of industries so as to permit the individual industries to choose, themselves, the most efficient means of meeting the overall target.

Each of these types of restrictions can be applied with greater severity, to investigate the trade-offs between reduction in the generation of carbon emissions and overall economic performance.

Alternative Perspectives in the Use of the Model

An optimizing model has some advantages and disadvantages in the kind of application to which it is put here. In the analysis of the application of a particular policy to an economy, questions are always asked as to the assumptions made about the character of the adjustment to the policy. Is the adjustment an efficient one or do individuals and firms adapt ineffectively? In this model, the adjustment is optimal, in terms of the maximization of the objective function. Moreover, it is done with perfect foresight over the model's time-horizon. The implicit assumption is that agents in the economy act efficiently to maximize their welfare with perfect foresight. A single solution of the model provides, therefore, what must be regarded as an optimistic projection of what can be achieved in terms of the maximand, given the endowments, opportunities, and constraints that are represented in its framework.

As is customary in such modeling, a particular solution is of less interest than the comparisons among solutions, which provide insights into problems and opportunities. In the application reported here, the comparison will be between economic outcomes with and without carbon emission controls. In both cases the solution is one that is dynamically efficient with respect to the objective function. Therefore, it is less clear, in this case, that the results with respect to the effects of emission constraints should be interpreted as "optimistic," since the basis for the comparison is also an optimal result.

There are alternatives to the structure presented above for building preferences for lower emissions into a model of the sort presented. Emissions could be introduced into the objective function being maximized with a negative sign, or reductions in emissions could be put into the objective function with a positive sign. Solutions could then be found with different weights on the emissions variables in the objective function and the consequences traced out, just as we will trace out the consequences of different levels of constraints.

We believe that this approach would provide less insight than the direct application of emission constraints. That is partly because policy is often discussed in just these terms: constraining emissions. Then the question is asked: what is the cost? That question can be answered directly from the results of this type of model.

The first consideration will be the coverage of the constraints. The objective is usually stated in terms of the reduction of total emissions. However, the debate often quickly turns to reducing emissions from particular sources or particular types of activities, e.g. emissions from thermal-electric generating plants or emissions from automobiles. In the model to be presented, both types of constraints will be imposed, in separate sets of solutions: first, a constraint on total emissions; second, constraints on emissions by each sector.

The different types of constraints correspond to the analogous differences between emission constraints on individual plants and an emission constraint on a "bubble" covering a set of plants. The latter approach has been advocated and applied by environmental agencies in some instances to other types of emissions.

The next issue is the base to which emission reductions are related. The approach that receives the most publicity is the stipulation of reductions in absolute amounts of emissions (or equivalently, as percentages of a fixed base level of emissions). For example, goals are often articulated in terms of a reduction of emissions to a fraction of what they were in some base year.

Even without actually solving the model we know what the general nature of the results must be, if additional restrictions in the form of lower emissions are imposed. If the constraints are binding, and it is expected that they will be, economic performance measured in terms of the objective function and the related output and income levels will suffer. Only on the assumption that there are costless ways of adjusting to the constraints could the results be different. While it is often argued that increases in efficiency in the use of various fuels would reduce emissions, very few people believe that this would be costless.

It is plausible that advanced countries should think of adjustments and sacrifices, if necessary, in their material living standards in order to gain the benefits, which are hard to quantify but which may be important, of lower absolute levels of emissions. It is just as plausible that developing countries, which are not close to the levels of living in industrialized countries, would resist a goal formulated in terms of absolute reductions in emissions.

If developing countries are going to be involved in the debate over reduction in carbon emissions, a more plausible basis for comparison is a reduction in emissions *relative to what they would have been if the country had been following a growth path that was not constrained by emissions reduction.* This is the objective that is investigated here. It is, of course, different from targets related to the absolute levels of emissions at some original point in time.

Data Base and Parameterization

Data requirements of economywide general equilibrium models of this nature are quite rigorous since they require an extensive set of estimated parameters and exogenous projections.[6] The data needs can be classified into four broad categories: technological relationships, behavioral relationships, miscellaneous exogenous or predetermined variables, and initial conditions. The estimation of these relationships and parameters is described in Blitzer et al. 1989. However, since substitution among energy inputs in production and consumption has a central role in this model, the methods used to provide the necessary data will be described briefly.

The principal source of primary data on the interindustry structure of the Egyptian economy is a 37-sector transactions matrix for 1983/84 obtained from CAPMAS.[7] The 37-sector matrix is aggregated into a 10-sector classification, adjusted and updated to represent our base year transactions matrix of 1986/87. This transaction matrix provided much of the data for the implementation of the model.

The model is formulated to use one or more technologies to produce each good or service. The specific number of alternatives depends on sectoral characteristics. The alternative production technologies, k, are divided in two categories. The first, encompasses the implicit technologies implied by the transactions matrix in 1986/87. The second category of technologies are the alternatives to the initial technology. In general, the alternatives allow for substitution between fuels, electricity, labor, and capital. The alternative technologies were derived using a small program that has as inputs: (1) the initial technology; (2) the own-price elasticity of energy for the sector; and (3) the sectoral elasticities of substitution between labor and capital, labor and energy, capital and energy, and electricity and fuels. The model takes the unit demand for fuels as fixed for each technology, but this demand can be met by using either natural gas or petroleum products. At the same time, there are limits placed on the degree to which natural gas and petroleum products can be substituted for each other.

The methodology used in determining the parameters of the utility function in the maximand is based on a linear expenditure system of equations. The parameters of that function were first estimated econometrically and then adjusted for consistency with the model's base year. The complete system of consumer demand functions has $(2n - 1)$ independent parameters: $n - 1$ β_i's and n γ_i's. Since these equations are highly interrelated, a complete systems approach was used to econometrically estimate the parameters. The database for estimating these parameters was constructed by pooling cross-section family budget data that was available for two time periods, 1974/75 and 1980/81. Maximum likelihood estimates of the entire system were derived using the procedure of "seemingly unrelated regression."

---

6. See Blitzer et al. 1989.
7. Central Agency for Public Mobilization and Statistics (CAPMAS).

Model Results on the Effects of Restraining
Carbon Emissions

There are a number of potential uses of the model; only a few will be exemplified here. Perhaps the most important and most obvious is that mentioned above, analysis of the trade-offs between emission restrictions and economic performance. The effect of emissions restrictions will be tested in the two ways indicated: (1) as a global constraint on total emissions from the use of fuel inputs, and (2) as constraints on emissions by each sector. The effects of the emissions restrictions will always be calculated as comparisons to model solutions without emissions constraints.

The global constraints on total emissions that are applied in alternative solutions are presented in table 1, as percentages of the total emissions generated in each period in the unconstrained emissions solution. As will be noticed the emission limits are, in a general sense, increasingly restrictive, over time and in successive solutions.

When similar constraints were applied on a sector by sector basis, the solution often became infeasible. The infeasibility was located in the emissions constraint in the services sector. That sector uses relatively little fuel in any case, and when fuel usage was constrained by emissions limitations in the proportions corresponding to the G4 and G5 cases, the model simply could not find a feasible solution, that is, could not meet other economic constraints. That occurred in part because the substitution possibilities among fuels and other inputs in the sector were quite limited.

To continue the investigation, the emissions constraints on the service

TABLE 1. Constraints on Total Carbon
Emissions as Percentages of Total
Emissions in Unconstrained Solution

	1987	1992	1997	2002	2007	2012
G1	100	0.95	0.90	0.85	0.80	0.70
G2	100	0.95	0.85	0.70	0.70	0.65
G3	100	0.90	0.80	0.65	0.65	0.65
G4	100	0.90	0.80	0.65	0.60	0.55
G5	100	0.85	0.75	0.60	0.55	0.45

sector were then lifted, and the limitations were applied only to the other sectors. Table 2 summarizes the sectoral emissions constraints that were applied. There is an immediate and important lesson from this first result, which is also immediately obvious to an economist: sectoral emissions constraints, if not applied with care, may create serious difficulties for an economy. The flexibility in inputs within the sector and the demands for its outputs may not be sufficient to absorb the constraints without widespread repercussions.

Figure 1 presents the time paths of real GDP in the alternative solutions corresponding to table 1, with constraints on aggregate emissions. Notice that the successive 5 percent reductions in total emissions in each period are accommodated in the G1 solution without substantial effect on the economy that is being simulated. If 10 or 15 percent reductions are called for in the first period and later periods, as in the other solutions, the effect on GDP is quite substantial.

It is interesting to note that, although the emissions constraints in G3 and G4 are the same for the first three periods after the base year, GDP levels are lower in the G4 solutions because the simulated economy begins to adjust to the prospect of tighter restrictions in the last two periods of the model's time-horizon. The effects of the global constraints on emissions are shown in another way in figure 2, which summarizes the results from all of the five solutions. It indicates the percentage reductions in total carbon emissions, summed over the period from 1987 to 2002, versus the reduction in average annual growth rate over that period. The individual points on the chart represent each one of the five solutions. The picture may be a little misleading, since, as figure 1 indicates, the effects are not uniformly distributed over the model's time horizon.

TABLE 2. Sectoral Constraints on Carbon Emissions as Percentages of Sectoral Emissions in Unconstrained Solution

	1987	1992	1997	2002	2007	2012
S1	100	0.95	0.85	0.70	0.70	0.65
S2*	100	0.95	0.90	0.85	0.80	0.70
S3*	100	0.90	0.80	0.65	0.65	0.65

* Emissions in the Services sector are not constrained.

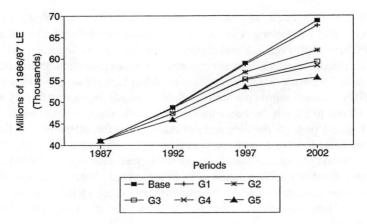

Fig. 1. Time path of GDP under alternative global constraints

Overall, there is an indication of an increase in the relative sacrifice in growth required to achieve increases in relative emissions reductions. This, again, is not a surprising result for economists. The difference between the G3 and G4 solution shows the effects of the impact of required relative reductions in emissions in the years beyond 2002. This is shown in table 3, which also presents elasticities of the changes in growth rates with respect to changes in carbon emissions. It is clear that the elasticities become relatively high and, in particular, are substantially larger in the G2 solution than in the G1 solution,

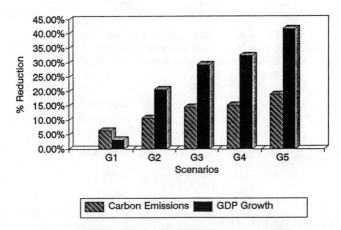

Fig. 2. Carbon emissions and GDP growth under alternative global constraints

TABLE 3. Carbon Emissions versus GDP Growth under Global Carbon Constraints (Thousands of Tons)

	Base Case	G1	G2	G3	G4	G5
Total carbon emissions*	75518	70779	67483	64607	64087	61259
Percent change in carbon		-6.28	-10.64	-14.45	-15.14	-18.88
Aggregate GDP growth	3.51	3.40	2.79	2.48	2.37	2.05
Percent change in GDP growth		-3.15	-20.62	-29.32	-32.44	-41.72
Elasticity		0.502	1.938	2.029	2.143	2.209

* This is a total for the years 1987, 1992, 2002 and, therefore, should only be regarded as an index for all the years in this period of time.

although the carbon emission restrictions in the former are only 5 and 10 percent higher, in specific years.

Figure 3 shows the growth paths of total private consumption that are associated with the alternative sets of global emissions constraints. It may be somewhat puzzling that the time path associated with the G1 set of constraints leads to a higher level of consumption in 2002 than if there were no emissions constraints at all, as represented by the base case. The 1992 levels of consumption in the G1 case, however, are significantly lower than for the base case. In effect, in the G1 case the optimization process found it desirable to depress consumption relatively in the near term and increase it in later years. The discounted value of the associated utility is, of course, higher in the base case.

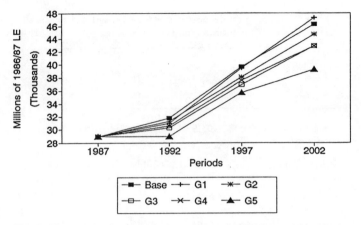

Fig. 3. Time path of private consumption under alternative global constraints

Figure 4 displays the relative welfare losses associated with each of the solutions as compared to the base solution without emissions constraints. Welfare is measured in terms of the objective function being maximized. It demonstrates differently the differential economic response to different degrees of restrictiveness. But even the most modest change tested creates almost a 1 percent loss in welfare, which is not modest in a poor country. Unfortunately we cannot know directly the welfare gain from the reduction in emissions.

The impact of the emissions restrictions differs substantially across sec-

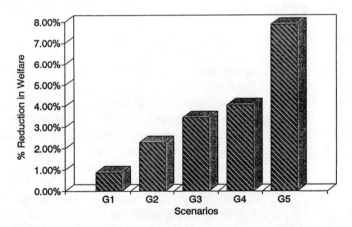

Fig. 4. Percent reduction in welfare under alternative global constraints

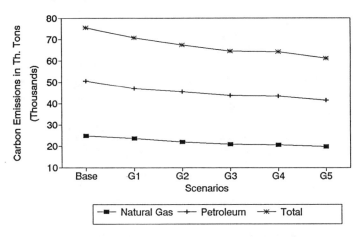

Fig. 5. Sources of carbon emissions under alternative global constraints

tors. The optimization process, which simulates profit-maximizing behavior by firms, is, of course, quite clever. There is a complete elimination of petroleum refining because that, itself, generates emissions. However, there is an increase in the production and export of crude petroleum, the proceeds of which are used to pay for the import of petroleum products. This provides a way for the economy to "export" its carbon emissions.

In general, there is a substitution of natural gas for petroleum products in both production and consumption. This is reflected in figure 5, which shows the changes in the relative importance of petroleum products and natural gas

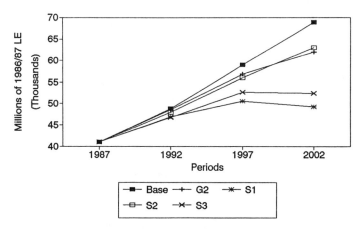

Fig. 6. Time path of GDP under alternative constraints

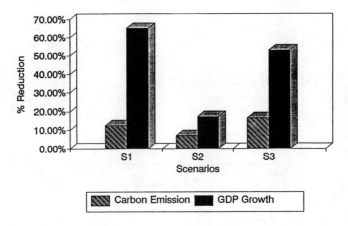

Fig. 7. Carbon emissions and GDP growth under alternative sectoral constraints

as a source of carbon emissions. The changes are modest, however, because of the rather severe limits imposed on substitution in most sectors.

There is also a movement toward the use of more capital intensive processes in all sectors where that is possible. That is one of the sources of the growth slowdown, since the capital intensity of production has to increase.

Turning to the analysis of the effects of emissions constraints when they are applied on a sectoral basis, figure 6 presents the time paths of GDP generated by the solutions to the base case, without emissions constraints, and

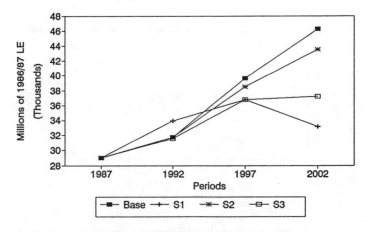

Fig. 8. Time path of private consumption under alternative sectoral constraints

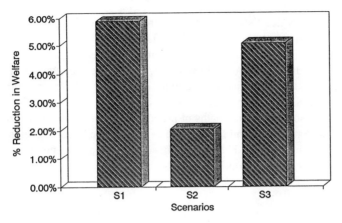

Fig. 9. Percent reduction in welfare under alternative sectoral constraints

the solutions with the constraints S1, S2, and S3 as stipulated in table 2. It is clear that the overall performance is more and more limited as the constraints become more restrictive. That is the case even though, in the cases of the S2 and S3 constraints, the service sector is not constrained.

Figure 6 also includes the time path of GDP for the solution with the global constraint, G2, with overall percentage reductions exactly the same as the percentage reductions that are applied sector by sector in the S1 case. It is clear that application of global constraints, which is sometimes called "bubble

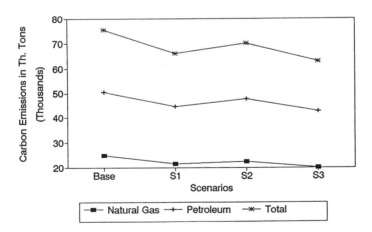

Fig. 10. Sources of carbon emissions under alternative sectoral constraints

regulation," provides the system with more flexibility. That is exploited to generate a significantly better overall level of performance.

The overall results in reducing carbon emissions for the three sets of sectoral constraints are shown in figure 7. The percent reductions in GDP growth that result from satisfying the required reductions in carbon emissions in the S2 and S3 cases are clearly quite substantial.

Figure 8 shows the time paths of private consumption under the alternative sectoral constraints, and figure 9 shows the welfare losses, again in terms of the specific maximand. The changes in sources of carbon emissions in this set of solutions are shown in figure 10.

Conclusions

The primary purpose of this chapter is methodological: to demonstrate the usefulness of a particular approach to analyzing a central issue of environmental quality and the trade-offs between improving that quality and economic growth. While there may be objections to the particular substantive results, those do not detract from the methodological point.

The substantive results are, in a general sense, not surprising: When additional binding constraints are added to a maximization problem, the value of the objective function is reduced. However, two specific aspects of these results are so striking that they clearly deserve more substantive research. The first of these is the nonlinearity in the trade-off between reduction in carbon emissions and economic growth. The second is the striking difference in the economic burden imposed by global and sectoral constraints on carbon emissions, with the latter being much more onerous.

APPENDIX: THE MODEL (DEFINITIONS OF VARIABLES AND PARAMETERS ARE GIVEN AT THE END OF THE MODEL)

Accounting Identities

$$X_{i,t} + M_{i,t} = Z_{i,t} + C_{i,t} + \bar{G}_{i,t} + I_{i,t} + E_{i,t} \tag{1}$$

$$X_{it} = \sum_{k} X_{i,k,t} \tag{2}$$

$$Z_{i,t} = \sum_{j} \sum_{k} a_{i,j,k} X_{j,k,t} \tag{3}$$

$$\sum_{i} P_{i,t}^{e} E_{i,t} + \bar{W}_{t} + \bar{T}_{t} + B_{t} = \sum_{i} P_{i,t}^{m} M_{i,t} + i_{t} D_{t} + \overline{FP}_{t} \tag{4}$$

Technology and Production Constraints

$$a_{\text{gas},j,k} + a_{\text{pet},j,k} = a_{\text{fuel},j,k} \tag{5}$$

$$a_{\text{gas},j,k} \leq s_{j,k} \, a_{\text{fuel},j,k} \tag{6}$$

$$\sum_i \sum_k l_{i,k} X_{i,k,t} \leq \bar{L}_t \tag{7}$$

$$\sum_k l_{\text{agr},k} X_{\text{agr},k,t} \leq \bar{L}_{\text{agr},t} \tag{8}$$

$$X_{i,k,t} \leq K_{i,k,t} \tag{9}$$

$$q_i \, X_{i,t} \leq a_i \, R_{i,t} \tag{10}$$

Balance of Payments and Trade Constraints

$$B_t \leq \bar{B}_t \tag{11}$$

$$M_{i,t} \geq (1 - m_i) \, M_{i,t-1} \tag{12}$$

$$E_{i,t} \leq (1 + e_i) \, E_{i,t-1} \tag{13}$$

Dynamic Linkages

$$K_{i,k,t+1} = K_{i,k,t}(1 - d_{i,k}) + f_{i,k} \, \Delta K_{i,k,t} \tag{14}$$

$$R_{i,t+1} = R_{i,t} + \overline{\Delta R}_{i,t+1} - 2.5(X_{i,t+1} + X_{i,t}) \, q_i \tag{15}$$

$$D_{t+1} = D_t + 2.5(B_{t+1} + B_t) \tag{16}$$

Investment Demand

$$I_{i,t} = \sum_j \sum_k I_{i,j,k,t} \tag{17}$$

$$I_{i,j,k,t} = b_{i,j,k} \, \text{ICOR}_{j,k,t} \, \Delta K_{j,k,t+1} \tag{18}$$

$$\sum_i I_{i,1987} \leq \bar{I}_{1987} \tag{19}$$

$$\sum_k K_{i,k,2017} \geq (1 + \bar{g}_i) \sum_k K_{i,k,2012} \tag{20}$$

Carbon Emissions

$$V_{ijt} = \sum_k V_{ikjt} \tag{21}$$

$$V_{it} = \sum_j V_{ijt} \tag{22}$$

$$V_{ict} = v_{ict} C_{it} \tag{23}$$

$$V_{kijt} = v_{kijt} X_{kjt} \tag{24}$$

$$V_{ijkt} \leq \bar{V}_{ijkt} \tag{25}$$

$$V_{it} \leq \bar{V}_{it} \tag{26}$$

$$\sum_i (V_{it} + V_{ict}) \leq \bar{V}_t \tag{27}$$

Objective Function

$$W = \sum_t \left(\frac{1}{1 + \rho}\right)^t N_t U(C_t) \tag{28}$$

$$U(C_t) = \sum_i \beta_i \log\left(\frac{C_{i,t}}{\bar{N}_t} - \gamma_i\right) \tag{29}$$

Definitions of Parameters and Exogenous Variables

a_i	Maximum annual rate of depletion of hydrocarbon resource i (oil or natural gas)
$a_{i,j,k}$	Input of good i per unit of production of good j using technology k
$a_{\text{fuel},j,k}$	Input fuel per unit of production of good j using technology k
$a_{\text{gas},j,k}$	Input of natural gas per unit of production of good j using technology k
$a_{\text{pet},j,k}$	Input of petroleum products per unit of production of good j using technology k
$b_{i,j,k}$	Proportion of capital good i in the capital required to produce good i using technology k
$d_{i,k}$	Five-year rate of depreciation of capital for production of good i using technology k
e_i	Maximum rate of increase of exports of good i between two periods
i_t	Interest rate of foreign debt in year t
g_i	Minimal post-terminal growth rate for sector i

$f_{i,k}$	Capacity conversion factor for capital producing good i using technology k
$\text{ICOR}_{i,k}$	Incremental capital-output ratio for production of good i using technology k
$l_{i,k}$	Demand for labor per unit of production of good i using technology k
$l_{\text{agr},k}$	Demand for labor per unit of agricultural production using technology k
m_i	Maximum rate of fall of imports of good i between two periods
q_i	Conversion factor for hydrocarbon resource i (oil or natural gas)
$s_{j,k}$	Maximum share of natural gas in meeting fuel demand of producing good j using technology k
β_i	Elasticity parameter for consumption good i
γ_i	Intercept parameter for consumption good i
ρ	Utility discount rate between periods
$\bar{B}_t$	Maximum net foreign borrowing in year t
$\bar{G}_{i,t}$	Public consumption of good i in year t
I_{1987}	Aggregate investment in 1987
$\bar{L}_t$	Total supply of labor in year t
$\bar{L}_{\text{agr},t}$	Supply of agricultural labor in year t
$\bar{N}_t$	Population in year t
$\overline{\Delta R}_{i,t+1}$	Discoveries of resource i (oil or natural gas) between year t and year $t+1$
$\bar{T}_t$	Other foreign exchange transfers in year t
$\overline{FP}_t$	Foreign firms' profit remittances in year t
$\bar{W}_t$	Workers' remittances in year t
$p_{i,t}^e$	World price of exports at good i in year t
$p_{i,t}^m$	World price of imports at good i in year t
$\bar{V}_t$	Maximum amount of carbon that may be generated in period t
$\bar{V}_{it}$	Maximum amount of carbon that may be generated by sector j in period t
$\bar{V}_{ikjt}$	Maximum amount of carbon that may be generated by the use of a particular fuel i, using technology k, in sector j, in period t

Definitions of Endogenous Variables

B_t	Net foreign borrowing in year t
$C_{i,t}$	Private consumption of good i in year t
D_t	Foreign debt in year t
$E_{i,t}$	Exports of good i in year t
$I_{i,t}$	Investment demand for good i in year t
$I_{i,j,k,t}$	Demand for investment good i by sector j, technology k, in year t
$K_{i,k,t}$	Installed capacity in year t to produce good i using technology k
$\Delta K_{i,k,t}$	New capacity to produce good i using technology k, first available in year t
$M_{i,t}$	Imports of good i in year t

$P_{i,t}$ Shadow price of good i in year t

$R_{i,t}$ Reserves of hydrocarbon i (oil or natural gas) in year t

$U(C_t)$ Utility of per capita consumption in year t

W Total discounted utility; the maximand

$X_{i,t}$ Gross domestic output of good i in year t

$X_{i,k,t}$ Gross output of good i, produced using technology k, in year t

$Z_{i,t}$ Intermediate deliveries of good i in year t

V_{it} Total amount of carbon generated by the use of a particular fuel i, in period t

V_{ijt} Total amount of carbon generated by the use of a particular fuel i, in sector j, in period t

V_{ikjt} Amount of carbon generated by the use of a fuel i, using technology k, in sector j, in period t

V_{ict} Amount of carbon generated by the use of a particular fuel i, in consumption, in period t

v_{ikjt} Quantity of carbon emission *per unit* use of particular fuel i, using technology k, in sector j, in period t

v_{ict} Quantity of carbon emission per unit use of a fuel i, in consumption, in period t

Comment

Shantayanan Devarajan

This chapter is a useful contribution to the nascent literature on the economic effects of carbon emission restrictions. The authors choose a dynamic, general equilibrium model, so that technological substitution possibilities can be incorporated. Their intertemporal optimizing model gives the "best case" scenario for the response of a developing country to carbon-gas restrictions.

While the choice of a dynamic, general equilibrium model is appropriate for the question at hand, and the authors' assumptions about fixed, sector-specific capital in the short run are realistic in most developing countries, some of the other modeling choices are somewhat problematic:

1. Foreign Trade: The model has several pure tradable goods sectors. To avoid full specialization, the authors restrict the rate of change of exports and imports within bounds. Since there exist several other, less ad hoc ways of circumventing the specialization problem (the Armington approach is but one example), I wonder why this route was chosen.
2. Capital Flows: The economy is allowed to borrow abroad "within bounds." There appears to be no intertemporal budget constraint. This is a serious problem in a dynamic model because there will always be an incentive for the economy to accumulate huge amounts of foreign debt (since repayment is not included).
3. Objective Function: The maximand is the discounted sum of the individual utilities in each period. This implies a particular value for the intertemporal elasticity of substitution. Since many results in dynamic models depend on this elasticity's being greater or less than one, the authors should at least point out the special nature of their objective function.
4. Terminal Conditions: The terminal condition is that the economy has adequate investment to sustain an exogenously specified rate of growth in the postterminal period. This has two drawbacks. First, it leads to aberrant behavior in the final periods under different experi-

279

ments. Second, it does not allow the economy to reach a new steady-state growth rate under the different policy, so that effects on growth rates are not discernible.

Perhaps most significantly, the model used is more of a nonlinear programming model than an applied general equilibrium model. Since there is only one representative consumer, the shadow prices of the model can be interpreted as market prices of a decentralized equilibrium. However, the programming nature of the model makes it impossible to ask questions about market-based instruments for carbon-gas reductions. For example, carbon taxes are currently the most actively debated policy for reducing greenhouse gases. The present model cannot shed any light on this question because taxes are endogenous to the model. Furthermore, the effects of these taxes on, say, public revenues cannot be captured, because that would involve bringing in another agent (the government) thereby losing the symmetry between shadow and market prices.

These caveats notwithstanding, the model yields results that are both empirically interesting and intuitively reasonable. The welfare loss from most carbon-restricting schemes is about one percent of welfare. The authors find this "not modest," although it is not that different from the gains calculated from trade liberalization in developing countries (and those *are* considered modest). The one counterintuitive result they obtain—that under one restriction scenario (G1), consumption is higher in the terminal year than in the base case—is probably due to their terminal conditions. (The model finds it necessary to squeeze consumption before the terminal period to build up investment to reach the postterminal targets.) Finally, in presenting the effects of constraints on emissions, the authors display the reductions in total carbon emissions, whereas the discounted sum of these emissions would have been more appropriate.

By using an energy-planning model to look at carbon-emission restrictions, the authors of this chapter have picked the right tool from a technological point of view. Yet, this same tool restricts the set of economic questions they can ask with the model, such as those about taxes and subsidies. The next step, therefore, is to incorporate the best elements of both approaches—the detailed energy technology of the planning model with the Walrasian, market-based system of AGE models—to develop a truly useful environmental policy model.

CHAPTER 9

Structural Adjustment and Growth in a Highly Indebted Market Economy: Brazil

Jean Mercenier and
Maria da Conceiçao Sampaïo de Souza

By 1990, the risk of a general collapse of the world's financial system due to the debt crisis had been considerably reduced. This was achieved, however, with considerable cost for most developing countries, and there is no reason to believe that their painful adjustments are over. This is particularly true for the Latin American countries, where the recent macroeconomic performances have been quite poor, compared to those of their East-Asian counterparts. (See Sachs 1985, 1989, for a well-documented comparative study.) It is now apparent that the recovery will be long and painful, involving considerable resource reallocations, especially in economies that have pursued during the past decades strong import–substitution oriented policies.

The severity of the crisis called for emergency measures: macroeconomic stabilization packages of the 1980s mainly aimed at generating large trade surpluses in a very short time. In doing so, they have been quite successful: the IMF's "highly indebted countries" taken as a whole managed to reduce their current account deficit from 50.6 to 10.5 billion U.S. dollars between 1982 and 1988. This performance was, however, achieved entirely through drastic reductions in investment and through import restrictions. The question now is how to move from the present situation to what Edwards (1989) calls "phase 2" of the adjustment process, that is, to a structural

We are grateful to Marie-Claude Martin for her help at an early stage of this work and to Alex Meeraus for kindly providing the GAMS/MINOS software that has proved so powerful a tool. We also wish to thank Steve de Castro, Victor Ginsburgh, Petr Hanel, Michiel Keyser, Pierre Lasserre, Philippe Michel, André Sapir, Lance Taylor, Jean Waelbroeck, and Randy Wigle for comments, discussions, and encouragements, as well as participants at the Montréal Workshop on *Applied General Equilibrium and Economic Development: Present Achievements and Future Trends* (Montréal, January 1990). The first author acknowledges financial support from the Université de Montréal (grant CAFIR) and from the SSHRC of Canada; the second author acknowledges financial support from the CNPQ of Brazil.

adjustment characterized by outward-oriented growth through more efficient resource allocations. Trade liberalization and low government intervention are the two policies forcefully put forward by some authors as the best ones to achieve these goals. Balassa et al. (1986), for example, strongly advocate the complete elimination of quantitative restrictions (QRs) and a reduction of all import tariffs to a uniform rate of 15 percent to 20 percent. Although some trade liberalization is no doubt needed in Latin American countries, there is little reason to believe that a recovery based on complete trade liberalization and low government intervention is desirable when the economy suffers from major imbalances; there is certainly no evidence to suggest that it is the best response to the present situation. There are two major reasons for that.

One reason is that there exists labor market imperfections. In most Latin American countries, institutional arrangements inherited from the past limit, to some extent, the flexibility of real wages. Although a first-best policy would be to reduce these rigidities, this may not be politically feasible. Thus, a lowering of tariffs may bring high unemployment rates in the short run as physical capital is reallocated among sectors; see Edwards (1988). Rapid trade liberalization may therefore not be politically credible. Producers will delay their adjustment decisions expecting reversal in the government's policies; these expectations may well turn out to be self-fulfilling.

A second reason is that beyond the claimed objective of shielding domestic firms from international competition, tariffs often represent an important source of revenues for governments in most developing countries. Thus, a drastic reduction of tariff protection will have important fiscal effects, if the administrative apparatus is too limited to compensate for this loss otherwise. These revenue-raising arguments for tariffs have long been neglected in both the theoretical and policy-oriented literature. Only recently have the works of Heady and Mitra 1987 and Dahl, Devarajan, and van Wijnbergen 1989 highlighted the importance of the trade-off that may exist between trade liberalization through tariff reduction and fiscal objectives. This literature raises the question of whether eliminating tariff barriers is particularly appropriate when a reduction of fiscal deficits is imperative. On the other hand, if one assumes that the government has the ability to raise taxes to compensate for the loss of tariff proceeds, say through lump-sum taxation, one may ask whether there is no better use of these new fiscal resources than the lowering of the domestic price of foreign goods. Indeed, in the present context where there is an urgent need for an export-led growth recovery, the Bhagwati-Johnson principle of targeting (see Dixit 1985) would suggest that these new fiscal resources be allocated directly to the most competitive export-oriented sectors in the form of export or investment subsidies, rather than used to subsidize imports.

Our objective in this chapter is to show that rapid trade liberalization may not be the most appropriate strategy in Latin American countries today. Our interest will focus on the Brazilian case. Brazil is no exception to the Latin American syndrome. But it is particularly interesting since it has some distinctive features that Cardoso and Fishlow (1989, 81) summarize as follows:

> First, a long tradition of inflation, and hence explicit indexing of wages, rents, financial assets, and the exchange rate, introduce special problems of adjustment to the sequence of balance of payments shocks since 1973. Second, Brazil is a continental economy, with limited reliance on trade. Export performance, although much improved relative to earlier periods, has remained somewhat erratic; the internal market has exercised much greater appeal. . . . Third, there is an imperative for rapid economic growth, which on the whole has been satisfied. In the postwar period, Brazil's trend rate of expansion of over 6 percent is one of the highest for developing countries. That standard is a constant source of pressure upon policy makers, whether under military or civilian government. Recession is not a permissible option. In combination, these three characteristics define very narrow limits for economic policy.

Standard CGE models do not provide an appropriate framework for dealing with these problems. They are static, or at best incorporate naive dynamic features in the form of a sequence of static one-period solutions. This ad hoc treatment of intertemporal trade-offs and of decision making result in solutions that are dynamically inefficient and often unstable. In other words, CGE models only take into account intersectoral and interclass resource shifts, but ignore their intertemporal reallocation through investment and consumption/savings decisions. This is unacceptable if one wants to focus on structural adjustment in highly indebted economies.

In recent years, multisector intertemporal general equilibrium models have been developed to remedy the above-mentioned deficiency of CGEs. Among others, see Blitzer and Eckaus 1986, Erlich, Ginsburgh, and Van der Heyden 1987, Kharas and Shishido 1987, Lipton and Sachs 1983, and Manne and Preckel 1985. Most of these studies, however, are based on a planning viewpoint, as though there was a single decision maker maximizing an economywide objective function subject to technical and behavioral constraints. (Erlich et al. 1987 and Lipton and Sachs 1983 are among the rare exceptions.) Although this is an appropriate method for calculations of economic efficiency in the absence of market imperfections (see Abel and Blanchard 1983 and d'Autume and Michel 1987), it is inappropriate for either analyzing equity issues among socioeconomic groups, or for dealing with market imperfections resulting from wage rigidities or price controls (which have been periodically used in the past by Brazilian policymakers).

In this chapter we develop a decentralized, multisector, intertemporal general equilibrium model of Brazil. Investment and saving decisions based on model-consistent expectations are made independently by firms and households to maximize the sum of discounted profits or instantaneous utilities, subject to intertemporal constraints. Although adjustment costs make capital sector-specific, asset markets ensure an efficient intertemporal, international, and intersectoral allocation of resources. The framework is designed to embed various degrees of short-term market imperfections such as price and wage rigidities into a long-run steady state characterized by market clearing. It is a strict intertemporal generalization of CGE models in the sense that none of the features characteristic of the CGE approach have been sacrificed. Our computable intertemporal general equilibrium model (CIGE), therefore, bridges the gap between recent developments of the macroliterature based on microfoundations (see Blanchard and Fischer 1989), the optimal growth literature (see Romer 1989), and the CGE literature.

The chapter is organized as follows. In the next section the structure of the CIGE model is laid down. Then, the calibration procedure, data, and parameter values are discussed. The next section compares alternative growth strategies and suggests that the rapid trade liberalization option is not the first-best strategy in the present context. Finally, the chapter closes with a short conclusion.

The Model

The Exogenous Environment and the Dynamic Setting

Any assumption concerning the country's exogenous environment will be arbitrary to some extent. However, given that in our counterfactual experiments we shall be interested only in deviations with respect to a reference path, these assumptions will be harmless to some extent. Calibration of the model to a specific base year data set will evidently call for specific amendments to the exogenous setting; these will be introduced in the next section.

The model we consider is that of a growing economy embedded in a world evolving along a balanced growth path. Along this path, foreign undiscounted prices are constant, hence providing a natural choice for the numéraire. Accordingly, all price symbols in the equations will refer to undiscounted prices. (In computing terms of trade between two goods at different dates, one therefore has to multiply the ratio of prices by the relevant discount factor.) Initial prices are set to unity. The country's population growth rate, denoted n hereafter, is constant. We assume for notational convenience that the world economy grows at the same rate, so that all variables in the model may be expressed in domestic per capita terms. In writing the model, we assume no exogenous technical progress.

Built in the model is the property that the economy should ultimately converge to a growth path that, in per capita terms, will be stationary. Clearly, the time-horizon must be chosen large enough for the system to spontaneously reach its steady state, yet keeping the dimension of the nonlinear fixed point problem numerically tractable. We make the following time aggregation assumptions: the intertemporal price system is determined by solving the model for 25 fully endogenous periods, distant from each other by a four-year interval. For the years in-between, flows are extrapolated linearly—see figure 1—so that stocks may be accumulated annually. To make this clear, we detail the treatment of the budget constraint of households, as an illustration.

Consider the discounted sum of yearly saving flows over a time-horizon of $N + 1$ years starting at year t. We define from now on N as the number of years separating two endogenous periods (hereafter referred to as periods as opposed to years). We have:

$$S_t + \psi S_{t+1} + \cdots + \psi^N S_{t+N}, \qquad \psi = \left[\frac{1}{1 + r} \right],$$

where r is the market interest rate (assumed here constant for notational convenience only), S_t and S_{t+N} are the annual saving flows of the two successive periods endogenously determined by the dynamically aggregated model. We approximate intermediate annual savings by linear extrapolation:

$$S_{t+i} = S_t + \frac{i}{N} (S_{t+N} - S_t) \qquad 1 \le i \le N.$$

Substituting these into the previous sum and rearranging, we get:

$$\alpha_1 S_t + \alpha_2 S_{t+N} + \psi^N S_{t+N},$$

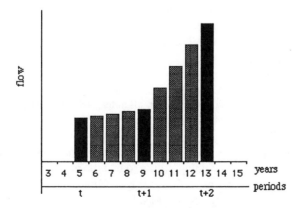

Fig. 1. Time aggregation procedure

where

$$\alpha_1 = \frac{1}{N} \sum_{i=1}^{N} (N - i + 1)\psi^{i-1},$$

and

$$\alpha_2 = \frac{1}{N} \sum_{i=1}^{N-1} i\,\psi^i.$$

Using these expressions and assuming stationarity of the economy, we obtain the following approximation to the intertemporal budget constraint:

$$\sum_{s=1}^{\infty} \psi^{s-1} S_s \approx \sum_{t=1}^{T-1} \beta_t(\alpha_1 S_t + \alpha_2 S_{t+1}) + \frac{\beta_T}{1 - \psi^N}(\alpha_1 + \alpha_2)S_T,$$

where $\beta_1 = 1$, $\beta_t = \beta_{t-1}\,\psi^N$, for $t > 1$. In this expression, as in the rest of the chapter, the time indices s and t refer respectively to years and periods. Also, in the rest of the paper, we shall write the right-hand side (RHS) expression more compactly as follows:

$$\sum_{t=1}^{\infty} \beta_t \Phi(L;N) S_t,$$

where $\Phi(L;N)$ is a first-order polynomial in the lead operator L. More generally, allowing for r_t to be nonconstant makes this polynomial a function of $t;$ we recognize this by writing $\Phi(L,t;N)$.

The Behavior of Firms

We assume that within a specific sector, all enterprises may be aggregated into a representative firm. We describe the behavior of the representative producer of sector i.

Assume that the firm has no outstanding debt and that it finances all its investment spending by retaining profits so that the number of equities issued by the private sector remains unchanged. By a suitable choice of unit, we may define the rate of return on the asset as:

$$r_{ai} = \frac{div_i}{V_i} + \frac{\Delta V_i}{V_i}, \tag{1}$$

where div and V denote, respectively, dividend payments and the market value of the firm, $\Delta V = V_{s+1} - V_s$ is the expected (annual) capital gain on the firm's equity. Assuming that agents rule out Ponzi schemes in forming their expectations, that is, imposing the following terminal condition:

$$\lim_{t \to \infty} R_{ai,t} V_{i,t} = o,$$

$$R_{ai,t} = R_{ai,t-1} \left[\frac{1}{1 + r_{ai,t-1} - n} \right]^N, \qquad R_{ai,1} = 1,$$

the difference equation 1 may be solved forward to yield:

$$V_{i,1} = \sum_{t=1}^{\infty} R_{ai,t} \, div_{i,t},$$

an expression that defines the market value of the asset (at period one) in terms of expected future revenues. The entrepreneur seeks to maximize the present value of future dividend payments to shareholders, which we shall now detail.

The sector produces a single perishable good using capital and labor and intermediate inputs. Primary factors are substitutable and combined using CES technologies. Public infrastructure has positive externalities on the sector's output so that the value added is generated by the following function:

$$y_i = [\alpha_{Li} L_i^{-\rho} + \alpha_{Ki} K_i^{-\rho}]^{-1/\rho} K_g^{\nu},$$

where K_g is a measure of the country's infrastructure development, independent of the firm's decisions, and $\nu > o$ is an externality parameter.

Intermediate goods enter the production process as complements. Imported goods are present in the intermediate inputs, which are defined as an aggregate of domestic and foreign goods, hereafter referred to as the composite good. The firm sells output at unit price p_x inclusive of taxes (at rates τ_x, net of subsidies), and pays its input flows of labor service and intermediate goods at prices w and p_c; all prices are independent of the individual enterprise's behavior. The following equations define the sector's total output, respectively at current and constant prices, the ratio of which defines the domestic price index p_x:

$$p_{xi} X_i = \left(p_{xi} \tau_{xi} + \sum_j p_{cj} a_{j,i} \right) X_i + p_{yi}(y_i - a_i)$$

$$X_i = \left(\tau_{xi} + \sum_j a_{j,i} \right) X_i + (y_i - a_i),$$

where τ_{xi} are base year rates, y_i is real value added, and a_i are indirect costs associated with investments, as detailed below.

New equipment becomes productive with a one-year lag. Its amount is determined endogenously once every period, with depreciation at exponential rate. For the years in-between, investment and scrapping flows are extrapolated linearly; this makes the capital stock at period $t + 1$ a function of investment decisions at periods t and $t + 1$:

$$K_{i,t+1} = \Delta_{1,i} I_{ki,t+1} + \Delta_{2,i} I_{ki,t} + \Delta_{3,i} K_{i,t}, \qquad K_{i,1} \text{ given,}$$

where the $\Delta_{j,i}$'s are parameters, related to sector i's constant annual depreciation rate and the number of years between periods:

$$\Delta_{j,i} = \Delta_j(\delta_i + n;N), \qquad j = 1,2,3.$$

Capital accumulation induces costs to firms other than the market price of machines. These take the form of disruption in production while new equipment is installed (Lucas 1976). The firm's total investment spending is therefore:

$$p_{ki} I_{ki} + p_{yi} a_i,$$

where a_i denotes installation costs—also referred to as adjustment costs—which are assumed of the following form:

$$a_i = \phi \frac{I_{ki}^2}{K_i},$$

where ϕ is a positive constant.

The structure of investment goods in terms of sectoral origin is fixed, and the sector specific unit price of equipment is a linear function of composite good prices:

$$p_{ki} = \sum_j \kappa_{j,i} p_{cj}.$$

We now have all the ingredients to define dividends:

$$div_i = p_{yi}(y_i - a_i) - w\,L_i - p_{ki}\,I_{ki},$$

and to restate the firm's intertemporal decision problem more rigorously as follows: choose the optimal investment and employment strategies, that is, choose the sequences $\{I_{ki,t}, L_{i,t}\}_{t=1,\ldots,\infty}$ that will maximize the present value of all future dividend payments to shareholders, taking into account expected future prices $\{p_{yi,t}, p_{ki,t}, w_t, r_{ai,t}\}_{t=1,\ldots,\infty}$ and the capital accumulation constraint. Formally:

$$\max_{I_{ki,t}, L_{i,t}} \sum_{t=1}^{\infty} R_{ai,t}[p_{yi,t}(y_{i,t} - a_{i,t}) - w_t L_{i,t} - p_{ki,t} I_{ki,t}]$$

such that

$$K_{i,t+1} = \Delta_{1,i}\,I_{ki,t+1} + \Delta_{2,i}\,I_{ki,t} + \Delta_{3,i}\,K_{i,t}, \qquad K_{i,1} \text{ given.}$$

There is one such problem for each representative firm, from which a sector-specific investment function is derived. Because of the presence of adjustment costs on capital, marginal products differ across sectors, resulting in unequal although optimal rates of investments. Observe that our formulation assumes that labor is perfectly mobile across sectors. It also assumes that firms never face any quantity constraints. As Blanchard and Sachs 1982 and Mercenier 1989 have shown, introducing quantity rationing in a general equilibrium framework with perfect foresight and intertemporal optimizing behaviors generates interesting short-term dynamics because of regime switches. In this chapter, however, our focus is on structural adjustment and growth rather than on short-term macroeconomic dynamics, and we therefore neglect these features.

The Behavior of the Representative Household

Households earn wages and receive dividends from firms, as well as interest payments on their portfolio of government and foreign bonds. After paying taxes on their labor earnings, they allocate their income flows between consumption and saving. They choose the composition of their consumption bundle in terms of the composite goods and share their savings between firms' equities, government bonds, and foreign assets. A completely general intertemporal utility function would imply that all these choices be made simultaneously. By assuming separability, we make the households' decision problem decomposable.

Savings Decisions
We assume a constant-elasticity-of-intertemporal-substitution utility function:

$$\sum_{t=1}^{\infty} \beta_t \frac{C_t^{1-\sigma}}{1-\sigma}, \qquad \beta_t = \beta_{t-1} \left(\frac{1}{1+\rho} \right)^N, \qquad \beta_1 = 1, \tag{2}$$

where ρ is the subjective discount rate, C is aggregate consumption, and σ is the inverse of the elasticity of time substitution in consumption. Denote by D the current price after-tax income of domestic households; flow savings is the demand for new bonds (remember, we assume that the number of equities remains constant); the wealth constraint can therefore be written as:

$$\Delta B = (r - n)B + D - p_{con} C, \qquad \lim_{t \to \infty} R_t B_t = o,$$

where p_{con} is the consumption price index and R_t is the rate at which a bond at time t may be traded for a bond at period one:

$$R_t = R_{t-1} \left(\frac{1}{1+r_{t-1}-n} \right)^N, \qquad R_1 = 1.$$

Forward integration of the difference equation yields an equivalent, more familiar expression for the households' intertemporal budget constraint:

$$\sum_{t=1}^{\infty} R_t \Phi(L, t; N) \{ p_{con,t} C_t \} = \sum_{t=1}^{\infty} R_t \Phi(L, t; N) D_t + B_1, \tag{3}$$

where B_1 stands for the households' initial stock of bond holding. The consumer is assumed to make model-consistent expectations of the term structure of future interest rates as well as of the complete stream of future earnings, net of taxes. The intertemporal decision problem of the rational consumer is, therefore, to choose a sequence of aggregate consumption $\{C_t\}_{t=1,\dots,\infty}$ that maximizes (2) subject to constraint (3). Solving this decision problem yields the time path of aggregate consumption and of the stock of bonds held by households.

The Consumption Basket
At each period, the optimal consumption basket results from maximization of a CES instantaneous utility under the constraint that

$$\sum_{i} p_{ci} c_i = p_{con} C,$$

where c_i are demands for the composite good i.

Portfolio Choices
Agents view domestic shares, government bonds, and foreign assets as near substitutes. Furthermore, given the time scale of the model, financial capital is sufficiently mobile to ensure that, along any perfect foresight path, speculators are indifferent between alternative portfolios. Rates of returns on different assets are continuously equalized:

$$r_{ai,t} = r_t = r_t^*,$$

where r^* is the exogenous yield on foreign bonds (a constant sector-specific premium will be added to r_{ai} during calibration, see below). For this reason, our assumption concerning the financial structure of the firms is harmless. Financing schemes are equivalent: they differ in terms of institutional arrangements, but any mix of financing through debt, new equity and retained earnings will lead to the same optimal path of capital accumulation (see Abel and Blanchard 1983). Consequently, the composition of portfolios only matters at the time of unexpected shocks when extraordinary capital gains realized on domestic shares imply symmetric losses on foreign assets and vice versa. Due to the lack of reliable data on the composition of domestic portfolios, we assume that at base year, domestic households own all claims on the domestic capital stock (they therefore receive all dividends from domestic firms), possess government bonds B_g on which they receive interest, and have accumulated a foreign debt B_f on which they pay interest. It might be worth observing that the previous arbitrage condition does *not* imply that domestic real interest rates are exogenously fixed, but only that they are fixed *in terms of the numéraire*. Note also that equalizing the domestic interest rate to the exogenous foreign rate imposes a restriction on the household's discount rate:

$$\rho = r_T^* - n.$$

Indeed, a bounded solution to the infinitely lived consumer problem requires that the interest rate and discount rate be equal (see Blanchard and Fischer 1989).

Given the information on the structure of the domestic portfolios, we may now detail the composition of after-tax income D:

$$D = (r - n)B + \sum_i [(1 - \tau_w)wL_i + div_i] + Tr. \tag{4}$$

D is the sum of interest on bond holdings ($B = B_g + B_f$), after-tax wages, dividends, and government transfers (Tr). We shall focus our attention on the future borrowing behavior of the government and assume for simplicity that

$B_{g1} = o$ (as in most CGE models, the behavior of the government is so extremely simplified that this is relatively minor; see below).

Government Behavior

The government receives taxes on wage earnings (τ_w), domestic production (τ_{xi}), and imports (τ_{mi}); subsidizes exports $(\tau_{ei} > o)$; supports welfare programs to the benefit of households (Tr); and consumes (G) and pays interest on its debt. The government also carries infrastructure programs. For conceptual ease, we assume that the deficit arising from noncapital operations are financed through short-term bonds while long-term bonds are issued to cover public investments. The supply of new short-term bonds is defined as:

$$\Delta B_{gs} = (r - n)B_{gs} + p_g G + Tr - \sum_i (\tau_w w L_i + \tau_{xi} p_{xi} X_i$$
$$+ \tau_{mi} m_i + \tau_{ei} p_{xi} e_i),$$

where

$$p_g = \sum_i \gamma_i p_{xi}, \sum_i \gamma_i = 1, \gamma_i \geq o,$$

τ_{mi} is the initial tariff rate (recall that the world price of the foreign good equals one), and Tr is assumed proportional to government consumption at current prices. Note that government consumption addresses exclusively to domestic goods. By integration, we obtain the alternative intertemporal constraint (assuming $B_{gs1} = o$):

$$\sum_{t=1}^{\infty} R_t \Phi(L, t; N)(p_{gt} G_t + Tr_t)$$

$$= \sum_{t=1}^{\infty} R_t \Phi(L, t; N) \sum_i (\tau_w w_t L_{i,t} + \tau_{xi} p_{xi,t} X_{i,t} + \tau_{mi} m_{i,t} + \tau_{ei} p_{xi,t} e_{i,t}).$$

To avoid the difficulties that would result from modeling the government as an intertemporal optimizing agent (see Kydland and Prescott 1977, Calvo 1978, Cohen and Michel 1988), we need simplifying assumptions concerning public consumption and saving. We assume that the first period government consumption is fixed in real terms, with public deficit (saving) residually determined. During the four periods that follow, we impose a geometrically declining profile to (undiscounted) government savings (deficits) and determine G residually; public budget balances thereafter. The intertemporal budget constraint therefore determines the level of the second period deficit (saving). Formally (denoting S_g public savings):

$$S_{gt} = \lambda^{t-2} S_{g2}, \quad 2 \leq t \leq 5,$$

$$S_{gt} = 0 \quad 5 < t.$$

Public spending on infrastructure programs has been of considerable importance in Brazil. Here again, we need some reasonable exogenous assumptions. We assume that I_{kg} represents a geometrically declining proportion of GDP during the first five periods; during the second part of the horizon, they are determined so as to maintain the public capital constant (that is, determined by depreciation):

$$p_{kgt} I_{kgt} = \left[\frac{1}{(1+\eta)}\right]^{t-1} \frac{I_{kg1}}{\sum\limits_i y_{i,1}} \sum_i p_{yi,t} y_{i,t}, \quad 1 \leq t \leq 5 \quad \text{and} \quad \eta > o$$

$$I_{kgt} = (\delta_g + n) K_{gt} \quad 5 < t,$$

where p_{kg}, I_{kg} denote, respectively, the unit cost and volume of government investment, and δ_g the associated depreciation rate. I_{kg} has a fixed structure in terms of sectoral origin:

$$p_{kgt} = \sum_j \kappa_{j,g} p_{cj,t},$$

and η is chosen so that the time profile of K_g is approximately smoothly concave:

$$K_{gt+1} = \Delta_{1,g} I_{kgt+1} + \Delta_{2,g} I_{kgt} + \Delta_{3,g} K_{gt}, \quad K_{g1} \text{ given}.$$

Long-term bonds are supplied to cover public investment spending:

$$\Delta B_{gt} = (r - n) B_{gt} + p_{kg} I_{kg}.$$

Note that our assumptions concerning government investment decisions ensure that $\lim\limits_{t \to \infty} R_t B_{glt} = o$.

The Foreign Behavior

The foreign intertemporal budget constraint imposes that the present value of the home country's trade surpluses compensate for its initial indebtedness:

$$B_{f1} = \sum_{t=1}^{\infty} R_t^* \Phi(L,t;N) \sum_i [(1 + \tau_{ei})p_{xi,t}e_{i,t} - m_{i,t}]$$

with

$$R_t^* = R_{t-1}^* \left(\frac{1}{1 + r_{t-1}^* - n} \right)^N, \qquad R_1^* = 1.$$

At each period, the demand for additional domestic bonds by foreigners can therefore be written as:

$$\Delta B_f = (r^* - n)B_f + \sum_i m_i - \sum_i [(1 + \tau_{ei})p_{xi}e_i, \qquad B_{f1} \text{ given.}$$

The country's exports depend exclusively on competitiveness:

$$e_i = \epsilon_i \left(\frac{1}{(1 + \tau_{ei})p_{xi}} \right)^{\eta_i}, \qquad \epsilon_i, \eta_i > 0.$$

Import Behavior

Domestically produced goods and foreign goods are assumed imperfect substitutes. They are aggregated into a composite good using a CES function. Minimizing costs, we obtain:

$$m_i = \pi_{mi} \left(\frac{p_{ci}}{1 + \tau_{mi}} \right)^{\theta_i} d_{ci},$$

and

$$d_{xi} = \pi_{xi} \left(\frac{p_{ci}}{p_{xi}} \right)^{\theta_i} d_{ci},$$

where π_{mi} and π_{xi} are parameters. The first equation defines sectoral import demands; the second determines the share of d_{ci} that addresses domestic production. The price of the composite good is defined by the following CES dual expression:

$$p_{ci}^{1-\theta_i} + \pi_{mi}(1 + \tau_{mi})^{1-\theta_i} \pi_{xi}(1 + p_{xi})^{1-\theta_i}.$$

From the description of firm, household, and government behavior, we know that total demand for the composite mix is

$$d_{ci} = c_i + \sum_j \kappa_{i,j} I_{kj} + \kappa_{jg} I_{kg} + \sum_j a_{i,j} X_j.$$

Equilibrium Conditions

There are three types of markets in the model: one for each domestically produced good, one for labor, and one for financial assets.

Flexible prices ensure that markets for goods always balance:

$$X_{i,t} = d_{xi,t} + \gamma_i G_t + e_{i,t}.$$

This equilibrium condition determines value-added prices $p_{yi,t}$. The model is written in per capita terms so that the labor market equilibrium requires that

$$\sum_i L_{i,t} = 1,$$

which determines the wage rate. In some simulations, however, in order to mimic both institutional factors (legal indexation schemes) and trade union influence, we assume that during the first two periods, workers tend to resist purchasing power erosion caused by policy changes. We model this by imposing a lower bound to the real wage (defined in terms of the consumer price index) in the following way:

$$\frac{w_t}{p_{cont}} \geq \frac{w_t^o}{p_{cont}^o}, \qquad t = 1, 2,$$

where in this expression, the symbol ^{o} refers to the baseline simulation. The temporary market equilibrium condition then becomes:

$$u_t = 1 - \sum_i L_{i,t}, \qquad t = 1, 2,$$

where u_t stands for unemployment. Asset market equilibrium is ensured by Walras's law.

Solving the model implies searching for a complete set of prices and/or quantities $\{p_{yi,t}, w_t, u_t\}_{t=1,\ldots\infty}$ such that the market equilibrium conditions are satisfied at all t, with all agents satisfying their respective intertemporal budget constraint. It might be worth calling attention to the fact that the economy is distorted by the presence of various taxes and subsidies. This, together with the incorporation of externalities in the model and the fact that the foreign agent is not endowed with an intertemporal maximizing behavior, prevents the equilibrium solution from coinciding with the optimal (efficient) time path of the economy.

Calibration Procedure, Data, and Parameter Values

Dynamic Calibration

We now turn to the discussion of how we generate a reference solution to which alternative runs will be compared. A reference solution is an intertemporal equilibrium (that is, a complete time path for all variables) that replicates the base year data set. Static general equilibrium calibration procedures are standard by now, and we only sketch the more subtle dynamic calibration.

Initial (first period) prices are set to unity; for the sake of argument, we assume that there is only one production sector and abstract from details to write the base year resource-balance equation in the following general terms:

$$Y(K,L) = C + I + G + (E - M).$$

Given our assumption that new equipment becomes productive with a one-year lag, the left-hand side (LHS) of this equality is fixed by factor endowments. Government consumption G is exogenous by assumption, and both E and M depend on current variables only, so that standard calibration techniques may be applied to the external sector. The difficulty, of course, comes from the fact that C and I result from optimal intertemporal decisions, and therefore depend *implicitly* on the complete time path of *all* variables. Intertemporal calibration therefore implies searching for an exogenous *future* environment such that *present* optimal decisions of firms and households coincide with the actual decisions as measured by the base year data set. Clearly, there are numerous procedures that may be devised to achieve this objective, but in any case we shall need as many "instruments" as targets. Obviously, too, the choice of these "instruments" will exert *some* influence on the results, although working in percentage-deviation form should take care of most biases.

Consider investments first. From the firm's intertemporal decision problem, we know that at all t, the optimal investment rate is uniquely determined as a function of the intertemporal shadow price of capital; see, e.g., Hayashi

1982. We write the expression of the shadow price of capital in continuous time as this is more familiar:

$$\lambda_o = \int_o^\infty P_{yt} \left(\frac{\partial y_t}{\partial K_t} - \frac{\partial a_t}{\partial K_t} \right) e^{-\int_o^t (r_s + \delta + n)\,ds}\, dt \,,$$

where δ denotes constant depreciation rate. What we are looking for is a way to equalize λ_o to a predetermined value implied by the base year data on I, and the adjustment-cost function, that is, such that $\lambda_o = \lambda(I_o, \phi)$. We achieve this by adding a constant term ξ to r_s and searching for the (unique) value of ξ that will realize the desired equality. In the multisector case, we search for a vector of parameters ξ_i such that:

$$\lambda(I_{i,o}, \phi_i) = \int_o^\infty P_{yi,t} \left(\frac{\partial y_{i,t}}{\partial K_{i,t}} - \frac{\partial a_{i,t}}{\partial K_{i,t}} \right) e^{-\int_o^t (r_s + \xi_i + \delta_i + n)\,ds}\, dt \,.$$

What makes this procedure attractive is that by introducing this coefficient we capture altogether sector-specific technological progress and risk premia, as well as errors made on the exogenous foreign environment. Observe that stability imposes the following restriction on ξ_i:

$$r_s + \xi_i + \delta_i + n > 0.$$

We next turn to private consumption. In order to replicate base year household savings, we relax our arbitrary assumption of a world economy evolving along a balanced growth path on the whole time-horizon. More specifically, we shall modify the short-term behavior of foreign demand for the home good as follows:

$$e_i = \epsilon_i (1 + \zeta)^{(1/t)-1} \left(\frac{1}{(1 + \tau_{ei}) P_{xi}} \right)^{\eta_i}, \qquad \epsilon_i, \eta_i > 0,$$

and search for the appropriate value of the calibration parameter ζ. Note that ζ is identical for all sectors. Observe also that this formulation respects the assumption of long-term stationarity (in per capita terms) of the foreign economy.

Data and Parameter Values

The model is calibrated on 1980 data. Choosing a base year is always delicate. Our choice of 1980 is motivated by the facts that 1980 is the year for which the latest input-output tables are available (thus taking into account the structural impact of the high energy prices of the late 1970s), and that it may be considered to precede the major adjustments due to the high interest rates and the slowing down of world economic growth of the early 1980s. It is, however, to a certain degree atypical because of the extraordinary expansionary government policies that led to an unsustainable boom during that year (see Bacha 1986 and Cardoso and Fishlow 1989).

The model distinguishes six sectors of production activity: agriculture and mining, metallurgy and mechanics, food and beverages, textiles, other manufacturings, and services. Table 1 summarizes the structure of the Brazilian economy in the early 1980s.

Important parameter values are presented in table 2. Most of these have been computed from more disaggregate data found in Brazilian empirical studies. The only exceptions are the elasticities of intertemporal substitution in consumption ($1/\sigma$), the substitution parameter of the instantaneous utility of consumers, and the externality coefficient of public infrastructure, for which no convincing empirical evidence has been found for Brazil. The values of the first two parameters have therefore been chosen within a range

TABLE 1. Structural Characteristics of the Brazilian Economy

	Agriculture and mining	Metallurgy and mechanics	Food and beverage	Textiles	Other manufacturings	Services	As share of GDP
Private consumption	.090	.095	.201	.068	.129	.417	.643
Government consumption	.0	.0	.0	.0	.0	1.0	.108
Investments	.114	.064	.024	.005	.090	.703	.251
Exports	.119	.246	.325	.042	.160	.108	.122
Imports	.404	.254	.022	.003	.190	.127	.124
Value added	.147	.133	.074	.035	.153	.458	1.000
Employment	.350	.045	.020	.023	.050	.512	

Debt / GDP :   .250

Government current deficit / GDP :   −.037

provided by other works in the econometric literature, the last one being more an educated guess than anything else. However, our qualitative results prove fairly robust to reasonable changes of this coefficient.

Concerning the initial tariff rates, we note from table 2 that they are rather low, at least lower than one would expect. As is well known, Brazilian nominal tariffs have a considerable amount of water in them. In contrast, true

TABLE 2. Values of Key Elasticities and Parameters

	Agriculture and mining	Metallurgy and mechanics	Food and beverage	Textiles	Other manufac- turings	Services
Capital - labor ratio	2.86	1.81	2.46	2.32	1.90	2.33
Depreciation rate (δ)	.06	.06	.04	.04	.06	.06
Adjustment cost (ϕ)	3.	3.	3.	3.	3.	3.
Substitution elasticity between (K,L)	1.1	1.073	1.09	.545	1.119	1.2
Import price elasticity	.11	1.85	1.85	1.85	1.85	.46
Substitution elasticity between (m,x)	1.15	3.06	2.89	2.86	3.00	1.47
Export price elasticity (η)	.31	2.82	2.82	2.82	2.82	.20
Output tax rate (net of subsidies τ_x)	−.073	.066	.121	.052	.097	.018
Import tariff rate (τ_m)	.212	.186	.725	.860	.330	.0
Export subsidy rate (τ_e)	.039	.253	.109	.260	.160	.0
Investment subsidy rate	.0	.0	.0	.0	.0	.0

Discount rate (ρ):   .05

Elasticity of intertemporal substitution ($1/\sigma$):   1.2

Elasticity of substitution between consumption goods: 0.8

Externality parameter of public infrastructure in production function (ν):   .05

Population growth rate (n):   .025

Number of time periods (T):   25

Number of years per period (N):   4

protection (that is, the ratio of tariff proceeds to imports) only provides a strongly downward biased estimate of tariff protection. The tariff rates we use are averages of the two rates. Clearly, these tariff rates account for a fraction only of Brazilian trade protection: of major importance are the nontariff barriers (NTBs) such as quota restrictions. As is well known, these are extremely difficult to measure and one usually has to rely in a very crude way on some equivalence between quotas and tariffs. This would very roughly lead to a doubling of the rates presented in table 2. However, in absence of reliable published data, we use the nonadjusted tariff rates.

External Shocks and Alternative Growth Strategies

Trade liberalization is one strategy for promoting export-led growth. Low tariff barriers reduce the price of intermediate goods, hence improving external competitiveness. Maybe more importantly, significant reductions of the domestic cost of capital goods will stimulate new investments in the most outward-oriented sectors, speeding up the structural adjustment process. The instrument behind this trade-liberalization–based strategy is import subsidizing in the sense that the difference between the initial domestic price of imports and the tariff-free price has to be financed somehow. If we exclude for sociopolitical reasons massive firing of civil servants as a feasible "source of revenue," trade liberalization implies a difficult trade-off between alternative allocations of fiscal resources. In that perspective, one may ask whether import subsidizing is the most appropriate choice. The Bhagwati-Johnson principle of targeting would suggest that, given the nature of the adverse foreign shocks of the early 1980s, a policy based on export or investment subsidies directed toward the most competitive outward-oriented sectors would lead to a more rapid recovery, at least if wages are flexible. The trade-off gets even more complex if one assumes that real wages resist to downward pressures in the short run. In this case, import subsidizing, by acting on the cost-of-living index, reduces domestic labor costs and improves the economy's competitiveness. We use our CIGE framework to evaluate these policy trade-offs.

Description of the Experiments

We simulate the changes in the world environment of the early 1980s by submitting our economy to two unexpected exogenous shocks: a rise of foreign interest rates, and a downward shift of world demand for exports. The assumed exogenous time profiles are reported in table 3. (In order to avoid end-of-period effects, we make a rather modest assumption concerning the interest rate; making this more realistic will not affect our qualitative conclu-

TABLE 3. External Shocks; Assumed Time Profile

	$t = 1$	$t = 2$	$t = 3$	$t = 4$	$t = 5$	$t = 6$
Interest rate	+ 50%	+ 24%	+ 12 %	+ 6 %	+ 4 %	2%
World demand	− 15%	− 15%	−10.5%	−6.5%	−4.5%	−2%

sions.) We perform these shocks with the two alternative labor market assumptions. Unemployment unambiguously results from these two shocks when real wages are assumed rigid downwards. These two simulations (with flexible versus rigid real wages) provide the description of the economy that policymakers faced in the early 1980s. We then perform the following four policy experiments using this background.

Import Subsidizing Financed by Lump-Sum Taxation
This is the standard assumption: tariff rates are changed from the initial sector specific rate τ_{mi} to a uniform rate of 15 percent. Lump-sum taxation of households compensates for the loss of government tariff proceeds due to trade liberalization; equation (4) is then modified as follows:

$$D = (r - n)B + \sum_i [(1 - \tau_w)wL + div + Tr + (\tau_m^1 - \tau_m)m_i]. \quad (4')$$

Import Subsidizing Financed by Reducing
Public Investments
In this scenario, we again implement a trade liberalization policy, but in this case households are not taxed to compensate for the loss of government revenues. Instead, we assume that import subsidies are financed by reducing public investments. Formally, we modify the public investment equation as follows:

$$p_{kgt}I_{kgt} + \sum_i (\tau_{mi}^1 - \tau_{mi})m_{i,t}$$

$$= \left(\frac{1}{(1 + \eta)}\right)^{t-1} \frac{I_{kg,1}}{\sum_i y_{i,1}} \sum_i p_{yi,t}y_{i,t}, \quad 1 \le t \le 5, \eta > o$$

$$I_{kgt} + \frac{1}{p_{kgt}} \sum_i (\tau_{mi}^1 - \tau_{mi})m_{i,t} = (\delta_g + n)K_{gt} \quad 5 < t .$$

Recall that public infrastructure has positive externalities on firms, which ensures an important feedback of the policy on the whole economy.

Export Subsidizing Financed by Lump-Sum Taxation
In this scenario, tariffs are maintained at their initial level. However, households are taxed in lump-sum fashion *as if* they were changed so that the equation (4') still applies. The new fiscal resources $- \sum_i (\tau_{mi}^1 - \tau_{mi}) m_{it}$ are used to increase export subsidies to the four manufacturing industries, which are the sectors with the highest export-price elasticities. Sector-specific export-subsidy rates are endogenously determined as follows:

$$\tau_{ej}^1 p_{xj,t} e_{j,t} = \left(- \sum_i (\tau_{mi}^1 - \tau_{mi}) m_{i,t} + \sum_j \tau_{ej} p_{xj,t} e_{j,t} \right) \frac{\tau_{ej} e_{j,1}}{\sum_j \tau_{ej} e_{j,1}} .$$

Here j refers to the manufacturing sectors and i to all six sectors. The LHS of this expression is the total flow of export subsidies allocated to sector j. The RHS allocates the total amount of resources granted to the manufacturing sector in the form of export subsidies, in proportion to the base year allocation.

Investment Subsidizing Financed by Lump-Sum Taxation
The last policy we consider also assumes that tariffs remain unchanged even though households transfer to the government resources in amount $- \sum_i (\tau_{mi}^1 - \tau_{mi}) m_i$. In this case, consider the fact that the major consequence of the adverse foreign shocks has been a sharp increase in the cost of capital. The government decides to use this new revenue to subsidize investments in the four manufacturing sectors. The rate of subsidy is assumed identical for the four sectors and is endogenously determined so that:

$$\tau_{kt} \sum_j p_{kj,t} I_{kj,t} = - \sum_i (\tau_{mi}^1 - \tau_{mi}) m_{i,t}.$$

Here again, j refers to the subset of manufacturing sectors while i refers to all sectors of activity. (Observe that initial investment subsidies are null.)

Evaluation of the Competing Growth Strategies

Flexible Wages
The simulation results obtained when assuming clearing labor markets are summarized in table 4. These are percentage deviations with respect to the base case. The first column—referred to as column (0)—describes the cumulative response of the economy to the two exogenous shocks. The four

TABLE 4. Growth Strategies Compared, Flexible Wages (% Deviations W.R. to Base Case)

Periods	(0)	(1)	(2)	(3)	(4)
			Intertemporal utility		
	−.18	−.47	−1.07	−.07	.63
			Felicity (undiscounted)		
1	−.8	−1.1	−1.0	−.8	−.9
2	−.6	−.9	−.8	−.6	−.4
3	−.4	−.6	−.7	−.4	.0
4	−.2	−.5	−.7	−.2	.4
5	−.1	−.4	−.8	−.1	.6
10	−.0	−.3	−1.2	.1	1.0
25	.0	−.3	−1.4	.2	1.2
			Aggregate private consumption		
1	−4.8	−6.4	−5.6	−4.9	−5.3
2	−3.7	−5.3	−4.9	−3.8	−2.5
3	−2.2	−3.8	−4.0	−2.1	.3
4	−1.4	−3.0	−4.1	−1.1	2.2
5	−.9	−2.6	−4.7	−.4	3.5
10	−.2	−1.9	−7.0	.8	6.3
25	−.0	−1.8	−7.8	1.1	7.2
			Terms of Trade		
1	−13.1	−18.0	−19.5	−15.6	−9.2
2	−7.3	−12.6	−14.2	−11.3	−5.2
3	−3.3	−8.9	−10.0	−7.9	−2.5
4	−1.3	−7.0	−7.3	−6.0	−1.6
5	−.4	−6.1	−5.5	−5.1	−1.5
10	.3	−5.4	−1.7	−4.0	−2.8
25	.2	−5.4	−.8	−3.8	−3.6
			GDP		
1	−.7	−.5	−1.3	−.1	.4
2	−1.5	−1.3	−3.2	−.6	1.5
3	−1.4	−1.2	−4.5	−.3	3.0
4	−1.2	−1.1	−5.7	.1	4.4
5	−1.0	−.8	−6.8	.4	5.5
10	−.4	−.1	−9.3	1.4	8.4
25	−.2	.1	−10.0	1.7	9.4
			Investment-GDP ratio (current prices)		
1	−8.0	−7.6	−11.1	−6.6	1.9
2	−.9	−1.0	−5.6	−.1	5.8
3	.2	.2	−5.0	.6	5.5
4	.4	.5	−4.9	.6	5.0
5	.5	.5	−4.8	.5	4.5
10	.1	.1	−4.4	.1	3.1
25	−.1	−.2	−3.9	−.2	2.4

following columns (columns 1 to 4) report on our policy experiments; the ordering of the columns follows the description of the competing policies in the previous subsection. (Note that these are percentage deviations with respect to the base case and *not* with respect to the first column.) In order to help the reader get a better feeling for the background environment, we first describe in some detail the adjustment behavior induced by the two exogenous shocks, and then comment more briefly on the other simulations.

Higher interest rates increase the cost of capital; this, together with poor export perspectives, reduces expected future profitability. The initial capital stock therefore exceeds its optimal level and firms drastically revise their investment plans downward: on impact, real private investment drops by 5 to 50 percent depending on the sector (-4.6 percent in metallurgy/mechanics; -51 percent in textiles). Production capacities are fixed during the first period so that output depends only on labor costs. The contraction of final demand induces a sharp decline of domestic prices and of wages: a reduction of 16.7 percent of w is necessary to maintain the labor market in equilibrium. The consequence is a reallocation of labor in favor of primary and industrial sectors: labor shifts away from services (-5.6 percent). This short-term improvement of the manufacturing sectors' competitiveness—terms of trade decline on impact by some 13.1 percent—stimulates external demand, which, together with the contraction of the demand for imports, results in a temporary improvement of the foreign trade balance. Simultaneously, households expect future consumption prices to rise because of low investment rates and reduced production capacities, and they shift forward their consumption plans; the intertemporal price substitution effect is not sufficient, however, to offset the negative wealth effect, and current real consumption drops by some 4.8 percent. The general equilibrium impact effect of the two exogenous shocks on felicity is a near to 1 percent contraction.

At period 2 (four years later), firms have already reduced their production capacities by approximately 2 percent, but the capital stock still exceeds its optimal level; the contraction of capital will continue in most sectors for more than ten years (in the metallurgy industries, capital declines during five consecutive periods). As one expects, rates of capital accumulation overshoot their reference-path level, as firms rebuild their production capacities. The convergence of aggregate consumption (and instantaneous utility) to its steady state level is monotonic. Observe that the economy's new long-run equilibrium is not identical to the base case steady state. The new steady state is characterized by a balanced current account but positive trade balance, improved terms of trade and lower private consumption levels. (Our assumptions on public investments also help to explain the dependence of the steady state on the transition dynamic path of the economy.) Figure 2 summarizes graphically the time profile of major aggregate variables.

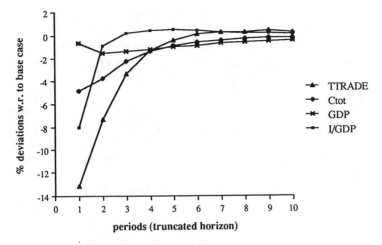

Fig. 2. Effects of adverse foreign shocks

Now that we have a better understanding of the background in which we perform our experiments, we turn to the welfare evaluation of our alternative growth-oriented policy options. Our first scenario is trade liberalization with tariff rates reduced to a uniform 15 percent across sectors *cum* lump-sum taxation of households. Comparing column (0) and (1) of the table, we see that the standard strategy does not provide a significant stimulus to growth. GDP is less than 0.2 percent superior on average during the first twenty years; the long-term effect of the policy is a mere 0.3 percent level increase of aggregate value added (a figure that masks large differences between sectors). However, the trade liberalization strategy also involves an important deterioration of the terms of trade: approximately 5.6 percent on average. As a result, the country's (undiscounted) welfare unambiguously deteriorates by some 0.3 percent on the whole time-horizon.

Public infrastructure plays an important role in the growth process, as column (2) illustrates: subsidizing imports by reducing public infrastructure programs is clearly harmful. Needless to say, the evaluation of a 1.4 percent loss in long-term (undiscounted) welfare resulting from the policy depends largely on the value of the externality parameter ν, which is extremely speculative. The welfare deterioration is, however, sufficiently important to suggest that the same qualitative conclusion will hold for a relatively large range of values.

In contrast to the two previous scenarios, a selective export-promotion strategy does provide some—although quite modest—impetus on growth. Comparing column (3) and column (0), we see that the policy has a positive impact on GDP on the whole time-horizon, ranging from a 0.6 percent increase on impact to 1.7 percent in the long run. The policy also involves a further deterioration of the terms of trade (by 3.7 percent on average during the first three periods, by 4 percent in the steady state). The resulting effect on felicity through time ranges between 0 percent and 0.2 percent in undiscounted terms.

Among the four competing strategies, the only one that has a significant impact on growth is the one that subsidizes investments in the most outward-oriented sectors. On impact, the investment to GDP ratio increases by almost 10 percent due to the policy action. The consequence is rapid capital accumulation in the manufacturing sectors, soon to be followed by expansion of capacities in the two other sectors (agriculture/mining and services, which do not benefit from investment subsidies). GDP expands unambiguously. Actually, aggregate value-added remains *above* the base case GDP on the whole time-horizon, while the country experiences an almost continuous deterioration of its terms of trade. The resulting effect on (undiscounted) instantaneous utility is an almost 0.4 percent improvement (that is, a 2.2 percent increase in real aggregate private consumption) on average during the first 20 years. At the risk of being overly repetitive, let us stress once again that because of the presence of various taxes/subsidies and of externalities in the production functions, the intertemporal market equilibrium will *not*, in general, coincide with the optimal time-path of the economy. (Rigorously speaking, a solution of our model is not a competitive equilibrium given that the foreign agent is not endowed with intertemporal utility maximization.) Consequently, there is nothing puzzling from a theoretical point of view in the fact that a government action may improve on the market economy's efficiency. That the strategy presently explored be welfare improving should in fact be no surprise to us: from our previous discussion of the dynamic adjustments induced by the two adverse external shocks, we know that the major force that pushes the economy deep into depression is the contraction of production capacities due to high investment costs. It seems therefore obvious that the best strategy should be the one that acts directly on the relevant margin: that is exactly what the Bhagwati-Johnson principle of targeting tells us. Figure 3 illustrates the time path of major aggregate variables.

Downward Rigid Wages
We now make the extreme assumption that during the first two periods, the purchasing power of wages is strictly maintained at the level that would have been realized in absence of external shocks; see the description of the labor market in section 2. The results are reported in table 5.

The dynamic response of the economy to the two adverse shocks (column 0) is not qualitatively different when short-term labor market imperfections are taken into account. The adjustment process is considerably more

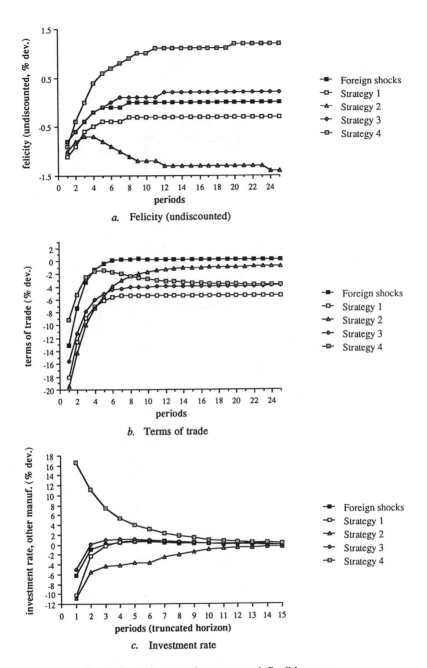

a. Felicity (undiscounted)

b. Terms of trade

c. Investment rate

Fig. 3. Growth strategies compared, flexible wages

TABLE 5. Growth Strategies Compared, Rigid Wages (% Deviations W.R. to Base Case)

Periods	(0)	(1)	(2)	(3)	(4)
			Intertemporal utility		
	−.31	−.59	−1.27	−.19	.60
			Felicity (undiscounted)		
1	−1.1	−1.4	−1.3	−1.1	−1.1
2	−1.0	−1.2	−1.3	−.9	−.5
3	−.6	−.8	−1.0	−.5	.0
4	−.4	−.7	−.9	−.3	.3
5	−.3	−.6	−1.0	−.2	.5
10	−.1	−.4	−1.3	.1	1.0
25	−.1	−.4	−1.5	.1	1.1
			Aggregate private consumption		
1	−6.4	−7.9	−7.7	−6.4	−6.4
2	−5.7	−7.1	−7.8	−5.5	−2.9
3	−3.4	−4.9	−5.7	−3.2	.0
4	−2.4	−3.9	−5.6	−2.0	1.9
5	−1.8	−3.4	−5.9	−1.2	3.3
10	−.6	−2.3	−7.8	.4	6.2
25	−.3	−2.1	−8.4	.8	7.1
			Terms of Trade		
1	−12.7	−17.7	−19.2	−15.1	−8.8
2	−6.2	−11.7	−12.8	−10.4	−5.0
3	−2.4	−8.1	−8.9	−7.2	−2.3
4	−.6	−6.4	−6.5	−5.5	−1.4
5	.2	−5.6	−4.8	−4.6	−1.4
10	.5	−5.3	−1.5	−3.9	−2.8
25	.2	−5.4	−.8	−3.8	−3.6
			GDP		
1	−3.4	−3.2	−4.6	−2.8	−1.6
2	−5.3	−4.7	−8.7	−3.9	1.0
3	−2.8	−2.5	−6.5	−1.6	2.6
4	−2.4	−2.1	−7.3	−.9	4.1
5	−2.0	−1.7	−8.2	−.4	5.3
10	−.9	−.6	−10.0	1.0	8.3
25	−.6	−.2	−10.6	1.4	9.3
			Investment-GDP ratio (current prices)		
1	−12.0	−11.5	−16.2	−10.5	−.7
2	−3.3	−3.1	−9.4	−2.0	6.0
3	.9	.8	−4.1	1.2	5.6
4	.9	.9	−4.4	1.0	5.1
5	.7	.8	−4.5	.8	4.5
10	.1	.1	−4.5	.1	3.1
25	−.2	−.3	−4.2	−.2	2.4
			Unemployment rate (%)		
1	6.9	6.7	8.7	6.8	4.8
2	6.6	5.7	9.7	5.3	0.0

painful, however. The contraction of GDP is approximately four times larger during the first two periods. The unemployment rate jumps to 6.9 percent during the first year and only very slightly declines (to 6.6 percent) during the four years that follow. The short-term deterioration of the terms of trade is more modest, while the welfare cost of the labor market imperfection amounts to some 0.4 percent (in undiscounted terms) during the two first periods.

Looking at columns (1) to (4), we see that our previous policy conclu-

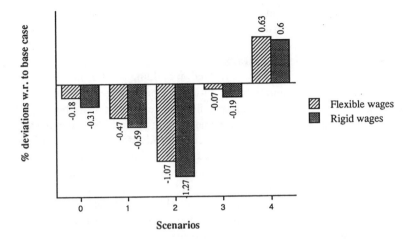

Fig. 4. Intertempral welfare effects of alternative growth strategies

sions are robust with respect to the labor market assumptions. The contrast between the four strategies is in fact more apparent and unambiguous: the only one that significantly speeds up the recovery is the one based on investment subsidies directed toward performing outward-oriented industries. Figure 4 summarizes the intertemporal welfare effects of the four policies, when wages are flexible versus rigid downward.

Conclusions

Applied general equilibrium analysis is primarily devoted to quantitative evaluations of alternative policies aiming at resource reallocations among sectors and social classes. Structural adjustment, however, takes time. This is even more true if one wishes to incorporate realistic features such as market imperfections and rigidities in the behavioral description of the economy. Yet, CGE models are static. Most of the rare intertemporal multisector models that can be found in the literature adopt a centralized viewpoint, which makes them equally inappropriate for the analysis of redistributive issues or policy evaluations in distorted economies with short-term imperfections.

In this chapter, we have built a computable intertemporal general equilibrium (CIGE) model, which is a strict generalization of the multisector market economy described in standard CGE models. The coherence between individual decisions is ensured by a vector of present and future prices and/or quantities that have to be determined simultaneously so that all budget constraints and market equilibrium conditions, present and future, are satisfied. Solving this model is, therefore, not an easy task; modern algorithms such as

MINOS (Murtagh and Saunders 1987), however, make this possible, as this chapter proves. The numerical problem could be further simplified by adopting time aggregation assumptions along the lines suggested by Manne 1988 and Mercenier and Michel 1991a,b.

One of the major difficulties involved in building a CIGE model lies, as one can expect, in the calibration: the initial intertemporal general equilibrium should be built so as to replicate a specific base year data set. In the chapter, we describe a calibration procedure that is both reasonable and powerful.

The model has been used to study structural adjustment issues in a highly indebted market economy facing the external adverse shocks of the early 1980s. We have shown that, contrary to a widespread opinion based largely on theoretical welfare arguments or more on political considerations (such as rent seeking—the importance of which is undeniable), rapid trade liberalization does not provide an impetus to recovery and growth in Brazil. Moreover, it has been shown that other strategies may be devised to speed up the structural adjustment and growth. More specifically, the following four alternative strategies have been compared: trade liberalization financed by lump-sum taxation of households, trade liberalization financed by reducing public investments, export-subsidizing financed by lump-sum taxation, and selective investment-subsidizing financed by lump-sum taxation. Our results show that in the world environment of the early 1980s, rapid recovery in Brazil would require a strategy based on investment subsidies directed toward the most competitive outward-oriented industries, rather than drastic tariff reduction. The suggestion is not that reducing trade distortions is undesirable, but rather that it may not be the most appropriate strategy in the present circumstances, whether wages are assumed flexible or not.

Comment

Lance Taylor

This chapter draws on the 1980s tradition of setting up Ramsey optimal saving/investment models to describe macroeconomic developments over time. I am sympathetic to the policy conclusions and impressed by the technical sophistication of the work, but must say that I find that the model has remarkably little to do with Brazil.

At the most abstract level, it is fair to ask whether the future of any economy in this world can be modeled in terms of perfect foresight or rational expectations with probability distributions applied to all future events. Ramsey (whom Wittgenstein considered a "bourgeois" thinker) believed so, but Keynes emphatically disagreed. In Brazil, how dynamic rationality can be imputed to Delfim Netto and the Generals is a mystery to me. After all, these are the people who gave us the debt crisis and the disaster of the Amazon.

At a more applied level, the authors fail to address a series of questions: how is Brazil distributionally overconstrained; how is its fiscal position compromised by external debt; how is inflation determined from cost pressures; and how does it generate immense deadweight losses from financial manipulation? All these problems are much more directly relevant to the nation than computation of model-consistent expectations in some sort of never-never land. I wish that the authors had applied their considerable ingenuity not to exercises in computation but to the problems confronting the Brazil of the world in which we live.

With much less fanfare, some sort of simple multigap formulation would fit the economy better than the complicated set of equations that the authors need so many pages to describe. As with much work in the CGE tradition, the authors seem to have devoted too much effort to their machinery and too little to trying to think through the most parsimonious description of the economy at hand.

Comment

Michiel Keyzer

Improving the capability to deal with intertemporal efficiency and dynamic welfare maximization in AGE-models is, in my view, the major challenge to the current AGE practice. I also think that it is now widely accepted that to deal appropriately with these matters, one needs to take an infinite horizon view, as the authors do. Their model bases itself on what is called infinite horizon optimal control. It seems to me that there still are many unresolved problems in this area, which I would like to classify into three groups: first, the specification of the infinite horizon model itself; second, an empirical elaboration of the model that goes beyond calibration for some base year; and third, the approximation of the infinite horizon model by one with a finite horizon, which can subsequently be solved numerically. I will make a few remarks on each of these problems in relation to the chapter presented.

Specification

In my view, the paper theoretically follows ideas such as those in Auerbach and Kotlikoff 1987 except that it does not distinguish overlapping generations. In that sense, it is closer to the model by Lipton and Sachs 1983. I would like to express my comments on specification in the form of questions.

(a) Why is there no substitution in intermediate demand in such a long-run model?

(b) Why is there no natural resource depletion or natural rate of resource regeneration? It seems to me that for a country like Brazil, a three-factor model with labor, capital goods, and land (forest) would be appropriate. Clearly, when labor and produced capital goods are the only factors, a balanced growth can be achieved equal to population growth, but would the author argue that population is the long-run constraint on growth in Brazil?

(c) I am particularly worried by the additive intertemporal utility of the representative household. This forces one to assume that the rate of

313

discount be set equal to an exogenous variable, the time preference parameter. Why not follow Stokey and Lucas 1989 and use recursive nonlinear utility instead?

Let me leave it at that with respect to specification and briefly turn to comments on the empirical elaboration of the model.

Empirical Elaboration

I would claim that the empirical status of a perfect foresight model is unclear. The world is permanently subject to unforeseen shocks. Therefore, I would argue that from an empirical point of view, one should work with recursive dynamics with time consistency of the planning behavior as a requirement rather than perfect foresight. This means that agents, when fed with perfect signals, should not need to revise their plans. Perfect foresight then becomes a limiting case that may or may not lead to a steady state but which by itself cannot be calibrated. All it says is that, if there are no further unforeseen developments and the agents know that, the outcome of some policy change would be what is shown. Therefore, I do not think that the calibration of such a scenario to base year outcomes is meaningful. The additive structure of intertemporal utility in fact makes meaningful parameter setting impossible, as one has to adjust eternally fixed time preference to a fluctuating interest rate.

Approximation

The chapter approximates an infinite horizon by twenty-five periods of four years each, forcing transition to the steady state path. The model is similar to the one by Lipton and Sachs, and that model is known to possess a turnpike property, as it can be cast in the format of the Cass model. Moreover, we know that there exists only one value of initial prices for the Cass-model. But the model in the chapter is different because it has heterogeneous capital. This may create two kinds of problems:

—The infinite horizon version may possess a turnpike property without saddlepoint instability, so that the initial values cannot be derived uniquely from the first-order conditions. Ryan and Bean 1989 show that this problem is generic.
—It may not possess such a turnpike property so that no convergence to the steady state occurs. But even if it possesses both the turnpike property and the saddlepoint instability, finite horizon approximation is no trivial matter. The authors may have tested sensitivity of the

outcomes to a change in the year of truncation. Still, even when little appears to change under a shift in this horizon, this does not prove that the approximation is all right. We are not interested in the difference between two possibly inadequate approximations but only in the difference of the approximating model with the true infinite horizon one.

To be practical, I would suggest in this model to test for saddlepoint instability by looking at the eigenvalues in the steady state. There should never be more negative eigenvalues than there are capital goods. To test for the turnpike property rather than extending the horizon, I would introduce "reasonable" variations in the valuation of final stocks. If there are little changes under such variations, there might not be any turnpike property, but still the path over these first hundred years is well-defined. (I do not know beforehand what the reasonable means are here. Maybe a maximum import price can be used as an upper bound.)

Finally, some remarks on model outcomes:

—I would expect that the assumption on quadratic adjustment costs would heavily affect the export promotion result, and, unfortunately, from an econometric point of view such adjustment cost models have not performed very well.

—The wage rigidity scenario is interesting because it shows an area where a long-term view may be particularly useful. Still, income distribution consequences should be looked at in this case as well as the difficulty of giving lump-sum transfers instead of, say, minimum wage to avoid poverty. Otherwise, clearly, wage rigidities perform no social function whatsoever and are purely harmful, as is found in the run.

To conclude, I would argue that I fully agree with the authors that intertemporal efficiency and dynamic welfare considerations do enrich AGE-modeling. However, I feel that the state of the art has not yet progressed sufficiently to allow operational policy debate on the basis of outcomes from these models.

CHAPTER 10

North-South-OPEC Trade Relations in an Intertemporal Applied General Equilibrium Model

Jean-Claude Berthélémy and François Bourguignon

Introducing an exhaustible resource like oil and allowing for departures from perfect competition in an applied general equilibrium setting raises formidable difficulties.

Because oil reserves are known to be limited, both producers and consumers must base their current decisions on expectations about future prices and/or supplies that must necessarily be forward-looking. This requires the whole model to be authentically dynamic, with each agent optimizing intertemporally on the basis of some forward-looking expectation rule. There have been only a few attempts, to date, at building such dynamic general equilibrium models—see, for instance, Auerbach and Kotlikoff 1987, Goulder and Eichengreen 1989, Mercenier and Sampaïo this volume[1]—but they often are extremely aggregated or focus mostly on steady state equilibria. On the contrary, the model at hand requires taking a disaggregated point of view—since oil is traded for and enters the production of other products—and no steady state of growth may exist in the presence of an exhaustible resource.

The experience of the 1970s has shown that there could be durable departures from perfect competition in markets as strategic as oil. Even though they cannot be expected to be permanent, this raises the question of how to handle imperfect competition and monopoly behavior in an applied general equilibrium model. Various authors have introduced imperfect competition in general equilibrium models, but this is generally done in an ad hoc way through exogenous markup on costs.[2] In the problem at hand, however,

---

We wish to thank conference participants at the Montréal Workshop on Applied General Equilibrium and Economic Development: Present Achievements and Future Trends (Montréal, January 1990) for useful comments.

1. See also the short survey included in S. Robinson 1989.

2. A more rigorous treatment is given in Harris 1985—see also Smith and Venables 1988—although the concept of monopolistic or oligopolistic equilibrium used there is still a partial one in the sense that imperfect competitors ignore the fact that their decisions affect prices in markets that they do not control directly.

there should be more than that. Monopolist oil producers, for instance, must be aware of the fact that their pricing policy will affect the evolution of the whole world economy. It thus would make little sense to use a *partial* approach to monopoly pricing, and "full monopolistic equilibria" must be investigated. It is well known that no general theorem of existence is available for these models in the theoretical literature—see J. Friedman 1982. This does not preclude, however, trying to design numerical algorithms that would identify situations where no monopolistic competition exists and would find the equilibrium (or one of the equilibria) in the opposite case.

The present chapter explores these various generalizations of standard applied general equilibrium modeling on the basis of a simple intertemporal model where the world economy consists of three zones (North, South, and OPEC), four commodities, and a financial asset. Each zone may enjoy monopoly power on a specific commodity market, but all of them produce and consume a 'standard' good that is traded competitively. The international capital market is also assumed to be fully competitive. At each point of time, the demand and supply of each zone results from an intertemporal optimization based on future price, or demand expectations.

The structure of this model bears much resemblance with that developed a few years ago by Manne and Preckel (1985).[3] However, the focus is rather different since our aim is to investigate monopolistic rather than competitive dynamic equilibria. This implies in particular substantial differences in some specifications—most noticeably the endogeneity in our own model of oil production.

The first section of this chapter presents the competitive perfect foresight model, insisting on the importance of the transversality conditions exogenously imposed to each agent. As it is numerically impossible to work in infinite time, competitive perfect foresight equilibria are, not surprisingly, strongly sensitive to these conditions. The terminal condition imposed to OPEC, in particular, plays a crucial role, although turnpike phenomena are readily apparent, even with a relatively short time-horizon. This is illustrated in sections 3 and 4, where the empirical calibration of the model and simple comparative dynamics experiments are briefly presented.

Full monopolistic equilibria of the world economy are investigated in the final section of this chapter. Such an equilibrium is shown to exist for the equipment good produced by the North, but not for the raw materials exported by the South or oil exported by OPEC. With exogenous terminal conditions and relatively little technical substitutability, intertemporal general equilibrium indirect effects arising from an increase in the price of these commodities prove not to be strong enough to temper the absolute monopoly power each

---

3. The present model was developed independently and approximately at the same time. The perfect competition version of the present model was published (in French) in 1984.

group of countries may enjoy on its own market. This result also denies the existence, under the same conditions, of more sophisticated dynamic game equilibria, where all countries would simultaneously try to exercise their monopoly power, along the lines of Chiarella 1980, Ulph and Folie 1980, or Ulph and Ulph 1982. We show, however, that monopolistic and more sophisticated imperfect competition equilibria do exist when monopoly power is restricted to some finite subperiod and this is common knowledge.

Analytical Structure of the Competitive Perfect Foresight Model

The world economy comprises three countries (North, South, and OPEC), and four commodities: a standard consumption good produced and consumed by all countries, a technological good produced by North, oil produced by OPEC, and other raw materials produced by South. Each country behaves as a single economic agent seeking to maximize some intertemporal objective under various technical and financial constraints. The competitive perfect foresight strategy of agent i may be expressed under the following general form:

$$\max_{x_i, k_i} V_i = \sum_{t=1}^{T} D_i^t U(x_{it}^t, k_i^t, p^t) + \bar{U}(k_i^{T+1}, p^{T+1}) \tag{1}$$

subject to

$$k_i^{t+1} - k_i^t \leq f_i(x_i^t, k_i^t, p^t),$$

for $t = 1, 2, \ldots, T$, with k_i^1 given, and $k_i^t \geq 0$, $x_i^t \geq 0$. In that program, k is a vector of state (stock) variables (productive capital installed in each productive sector, oil reserves, financial assets), x is a vector of control (flow) variables (production, final, and intermediate demand of the various commodities in the model), p is the price vector, and $f(\bullet)$ stands for the various technical and financial constraints to production and growth. The symbol T denotes the time-horizon and t is the time index. The first component of the objective function (V_i) is the discounted (at factor D^t) flow of utility derived from economic activities at period t (consumption, for instance). The second component is the utility of the terminal stocks, k^{T+1}, but it may also depend on the exogenous evolution of prices after the time-horizon summarized here by the vector p^{T+1}.

Two alternative specifications of the terminal objective $\bar{U}$ will be used in what follows. According to the first one, the flow of utility beyond the horizon T depends only on the total assets of the country, the various assets being valued at the exogenous prices p^{T+1}. More precisely, it is assumed that from time $T + 1$ to infinity, everything is as if each country were behaving as a rentier, maximizing the discounted flow of consumption utility it may obtain from its initial wealth, at an exogenous rate of interest. In the second specification, the terminal stock variables (physical capital, oil reserves, financial assets) are fixed at some exogenous levels $\bar{k}$, as in standard finite time optimal growth models.

As an example of the general formulation above, let us spell out the particular specification selected for South ($i = s$). The stock variables in this case are:

$$k_s = (k_{s1}, k_{s2}, A_s),$$

where k_{s1} and k_{s2} are, respectively, the capital stocks (per capita) in the production of the consumption good and exported raw materials, and A is the (net) financial asset holding. The flow variables are:

$$x_s = (c_{s1}, x_{s2}, e_{s1}, e_{s2}, b_{s1}, b_{s2}, i_s, \ell_{s1}, \alpha_{s1}),$$

where c_{s1} is (final) consumption, x_{s2} the exports of raw materials, e_{sj} and b_{sj} the intermediate consumption of oil and raw materials in the consumption ($j = 1$) and the raw material ($j = 2$) sectors, i_s the volume of investment, ℓ_{s1} the share of labor employed in the consumption sector, and α_{s1} the share of that sector in current investment expenditures (the last two shares for the raw material sector being respectively $1 - \ell_{s1}$ and $1 - \alpha_{s1}$). The objective function is:

$$V_s = \sum_{t=1}^{T} D_s^t U_s(c_{s1}^t) + \bar{U}_s(k_{s1}^{T+1}, k_{s2}^{T+1}, A_s^{T+1}, p^{T+1}),$$

and the accumulation constraints are:

$$f_s^1(\bullet) = -k_{s1}(\delta_{s1} + n) + \alpha_{s1} i_s,$$

$$f_s^2(\bullet) = -k_{s2}(\delta_{s2} + n) + (1 - \alpha_{s1}) i_s,$$

$$f_s^3(\bullet) = A_s(r - n) + p_2 F_s^2(k_{s2}, 1 - \ell_{s1}, b_{s2}, e_{s2}) - p_e(e_{s1} + e_{s2})$$

$$- p_i i_s + p_1[F_s^1(k_{s1}, \ell_{s1}, b_{s1}, e_{s1}) - c_{s1}]$$

$$- p_b(b_{s1} + b_{s2}),$$

where δ_{sj} and p_j are, respectively, the depreciation rates and the prices in the consumption and raw material sectors, n is the rate of demographic growth, r the rate of interest, p_e the price of oil, p_b the price of imported intermediate products, and p_i the price of investment goods. Functions $F_s^1(\bullet)$ and $F_s^2(\bullet)$ are the production functions in the two productive sectors of South. Thus, $F_s^1(\bullet) - c_{1s}$ is the (net) volume of exports of consumption goods, whereas F^2 is the volume of raw material exports. Finally, $f_s^3(\bullet)$ corresponds to the per capita accumulation of financial assets (interest payments on the initial asset plus the nonfactor trade balance).

The specifications for North is analogous, the production of raw materials being replaced by that of the technological good. For OPEC, the production of raw material is replaced by the extraction of oil with an additional constraint standing for the depletion of reserves.

The general solution of program (1) for each zone may be written as:

$$\tilde{x}_i^t(k_i^1, p^1, p^2, \ldots, p^T, p^{T+1}).$$

From these functions, we may derive the growth path of the corresponding economy by simple integration:

$$\bar{k}_i^{t+1} - \bar{k}_i^t = f_i(\tilde{x}_i^t, \bar{k}_i^t, p^t).$$

We may also derive the vector of net demands of zone i to the rest of the world:

$$X_i^t(k_i^1, p^1, p^2, \ldots, p^T, p^{T+1}).$$

These functions are obtained from simple transformations of the control variables x_i^t. In the case of South, for instance, the net demand—that is, imports—of the consumption good is:

$$X_{s1}^t = \tilde{c}_{s1}^t - F_s^1(\bar{k}_{s1}^t, \bar{\ell}_{s1}^t, \bar{b}_{s1}^t, \bar{e}_{s1}^t),$$

and the net demand for financial assets (capital outflows) is simply $f_s^3(\bullet)$.

An algorithm being available[4] to solve numerically program (1), it is possible, using the utility functions V_i and the accumulation functions $f_i(\bullet)$ to associate to each matrix of initial stocks, k_i^1, each matrix of prices $p^1, p^2, \ldots,$ p^T, and each vector of terminal prices p^{T+1} (or each matrix of terminal

---

4. The solution algorithm for these programs is presented in our earlier work (Berthélémy and Bourguignon 1984).

stocks), a matrix of net demand functions for each zone i, each good j in the model (including the financial asset), and each point t of time:

$$X_{ij}^t(k_i^1, p^1, p^2, \ldots, p^T, p^{T+1}).$$

The intertemporal competitive perfect foresight equilibrium of the economy is defined by the set of prices such that the sum of net demands X_{ij}^t across the three zones is equal to zero for each good and at each point of time. In other words, everything is as if all agents, at each point of time, were anticipating perfectly all future prices and were considering those prices as given. It is well known that this is equivalent to assuming that there are future markets at all dates and for all goods, and that each agent is a price taker on these markets. The whole intertemporal model thus is equivalent to a simple static Walrasian model and the set of equilibrium prices is such that:

$$\sum_{i=1}^{3} X_{ij}^t(k_i^1, p^1, p^2, \ldots, p^T, p^{T+1}) = 0, \qquad \forall j, \forall t. \tag{E}$$

If there are J goods (including the financial asset) and T periods, there are $J \times T$ markets and an equal number of individual prices. However, these markets are not independent. If the markets for all goods are at equilibrium at each point of time, accounting identities for all zones ensure that the market for the financial asset will be at equilibrium. Only $(J - 1) \times T$ equations in the preceding system are independent and some good must be chosen as the numéraire. In what follows, we shall assume that this role is assigned to the financial asset, or equivalently that the nominal rate of interest is arbitrary.[5]

A simple *tâtonnement* algorithm proved sufficient, and computationally cheaper than other algorithms, to solve the model. However, several difficulties arose in our first experiments in connection with the assumptions made for the initial and the terminal periods.

It seemed reasonable to postulate some rigidity in the supply behavior of goods in the short run, due for instance to some factor immobility. In order not to preclude the existence of an equilibrium during the initial period, this production rigidity has been associated with some downward price rigidity. On all markets for goods, the equilibrium may thus be of two types: (1) full capacity production at a price level greater or equal to some prespecified minimum level; and (2) proportional rationing of all net suppliers[6] of a given

---

5. Of course, the real rate of interest is endogenous and is determined by the evolution of commodity prices.

6. In other words, rationing occurs in world markets and not in the domestic markets implicit in each zone's optimal growth program (1).

good at the minimum price level. Of course, perfect competition implies that the rationing coefficient is considered as exogenous in the optimization program of each zone.

As mentioned before, two functional forms have been used for the terminal utility function of each zone. Under the rentier assumption, the objective function is:

$$V_i = \sum_{t=1}^{T} D_i^t U_i(c_i^t) + V_i(W_i^{T+1}), \tag{2}$$

with

$$W_i^{T+1} = \sum_i p_j^{T+1} k_j^{T+1},$$

and

$$V_i(W_i^{T+1}) = \max_{c_t} \sum_{t=T+1}^{\infty} D_i^t U_i(c_t),$$

$$\text{subject to} \quad \sum_{t=T+1}^{\infty} p_c^{T+1} c_t (1 + r)^{T-1} = W_i^{T+1}$$

where W_i^{T+1} is the final asset holding, r the rate of interest (taken to be constant), p_c the price of the consumption good, and U_i the current utility of consumption. The terminal utility function thus depends on a vector of terminal prices that should be determined by market equilibria beyond the horizon T.[7]

Calibration of the Model and Base Run

Empirically, the above model relies on three sets of parameters and structural data:

—a typology of international markets representing the salient features of North-South-OPEC trade relations;

---

7. In Auerbach and Kotlikoff 1987, these prices correspond to the steady state equilibrium of the economy. Because of limited oil reserves, there does not exist a steady state in the present model.

—the technical characteristics of the production of the various goods in the model for each zone;
—the parameters of the objective functions for the three zones.

Our stylized representation of the world economy relies on four aggregate goods. Each zone is producing two goods: a "standard" good produced everywhere, and a specific good that it is the unique supplier of in the world economy. The specific good produced by North (good 1) consists of technologically sophisticated products used as equipment and intermediate components; we shall call it the "technological" good. The specific good produced by OPEC (good 2) is oil, whereas that of South (good 3) is made up of raw materials (excluding oil) and some primary agricultural products. As mentioned above, the last good (good 4) is "standard" in the sense that it is simultaneously produced by the three zones. It is the only final consumption good in the model, but it may also be used for investment.

Reasonable orders of magnitude for the (net) international flows of the preceding aggregate goods at the beginning of the 1980s are given in table 1. They have been obtained through rough aggregations in standard international trade statistics. In accordance with the assumptions made on the zone-specificity of goods 1, 2, and 3, North is a net exporter of good 1, OPEC of

TABLE 1. Net Trade and Capital Flows in the World Economy (1980)[a]
1980 US Dollar Per Inhabitant of North

Good	North	South	OPEC
1. Technological good	-400	390	90
2. Oil	260	70	-330
3. Raw materials.	150	-180	30
4. Standard good	60	-170	110
Total (Net Capital inflows)	-10	110	-100

a) Exports are counted positively. All figures are expressed in 1980 US Dollar per inhabitant of North. This reference is convenient because North population is assumed to be stationary. To obtain per capita figures in the other zones, the above figures must be multiplied by .33 for South and .2 for OPEC.

good 2, and South of good 3. Concerning the "standard" good (good 4), the aggregation procedure led to South being the unique net exporter. The total row in table 1 corresponds to net international capital flows (gross of interest payments). As of the beginning of the 1980s, OPEC was the main supplier of capital and South the main borrower.

We now come to the optimal growth models of each zone. As seen in the preceding section, they are essentially defined by production functions, which together with accounting identities define the accumulation functions $f(\bullet)$, and by the objective functions V. Functional forms are the same across the three zones, but, of course, they are defined on different combinations of goods and do not exhibit the same elasticities.

In general, production functions involve four productive factors: labor, capital, and two imported intermediate products. Capital is made up of the technological good (good 1) and the standard good (good 4) combined in fixed proportions. Production functions are nested CES. With four factors X, Y, Z, and S, they write:

$$F(X, Y, Z, S) = G_3\{X, G_2[Y, G_1(Z, S)]\} \cdot (1 + g)^t,$$

where g is an exogenous coefficient of (neutral) technical progress and each function G_i is a CES function defined on two factors with a substitution elasticity equal to σ_i and constant returns to scale, except, in some cases, at the highest level $G_3(\bullet)$. In all functions, the productive factors enter sequentially by decreasing order of substitutability. Capital and labor always enter at the first level $[G_1(\bullet)]$ with an elasticity of substitution equal to unity (Cobb-Douglas). Oil enters at the highest level, $G_3(\bullet)$. Raw materials and/or the technological good enter at the intermediate level $[G_2(\bullet)]$. The corresponding elasticities of substitution, the overall coefficient of return to scale, and the rate of technical progress used in the simulations are reported in table 2.[8]

The current utility function in each zone depends only on consumption, which consists of good 4. The standard isoelastic function form is used:

$$U(c_t) = \frac{1}{\gamma} c_t^\gamma.$$

The value of γ has been set to 0.5 for all three zones.

The preceding current utility function also defines the terminal utility function when the latter is defined on the value of terminal physical and

---

8. By convention, output is netted out of intermediate consumption when corresponding to the same commodity. This explains why the production functions are defined with four factors and three levels, as well as the missing substitution elasticities in table 2.

TABLE 2. Calibration Parameters and Initial Values for the Three Zones

Zone	North		South		OPEC	
Sector	1 (Technological)	4 (Standard)	3 (Raw Materials)	4 (Standard)	2 (Oil)	4 (Standard)
Substitution elasticities [a]:						
- Capital labor	(1) 1.0	(1) 1.0	(1) 1.0	(1) 1.0	-	(1) 1.0
- Technological good	-		-	(2) 0.5	-	(2) 0.5
- Oil	(3) 0.2	(3) 0.2	(2) 0.2	(3) 0.2	-	-
- Raw materials	(2) 0.5	(2) 0.5	-	-	-	(3) 0.5
Returns to scale	0.9	1.0	0.8	1.0	0.4	1.0
Technical progress (Annual rate, %)	2.18	2.18	1.5	1.3	0.0	1.1
Output [b]	1,740	8,090	181	2,413	317	498
Intermediate consumption [b]						
- Technological good	-	-	-	178	-	24
- Oil	48	208	5	63	-	-
- Raw materials	29	119	-	-	-	34
Initial capital stock [b]	4,595	22,220	425	5,550	285	1,470
Initial allocation of labor[b]	1.16	0.84	0.2	2.8	0.0	0.5
Initial population	1		3		.5	
Population Growth Rates (%)	0		2		0.5	

a) See the definition of nested CES production functions in the text. Figures in brackets indicate the nesting order.
b) 1980 Dollars per North inhabitant. Multiply by .33 to get per capita figures for South, and by 2 for OPEC.

financial assets (including oil reserves in the case of OPEC) as in (2) above, rather than in terms of exogenous terminal stocks. However, a problem arises when production functions exhibit decreasing returns to scale, a natural assumption for some goods in the model—e.g., raw materials exported by South. This is because decreasing returns to scale logically correspond to the presence of an implicit fixed factor of production, which should enter into the calculation of the total wealth of a zone. To take care of that problem, an additional term, R^{T+1}, has been introduced in the terminal wealth valuation that may be interpreted as the value of the fixed factors implicit in the decreasing returns to scale assumptions. The wealth valuation formula thus becomes:

$$W^{T+1} = \sum_j p_j^{T+1} k_j^{T+1} + R^{T+1}.$$

The value selected for these exogenous corrective terms are those that make the levels of consumption per capita in the calibration run of the model consistent with those actually observed in the three zones (whereas consumption growth is calibrated through the time discount rates D_i).

Base Run and Some Simulations in the Competitive Perfect Foresight Model

Base Run

The above model was run over five unit periods of three years each.[9] The values of the exogenous variables and growth rates, the parameters of the behavioral functions in the models, and the initial values of the endogenous variables—summarized in table 2—were chosen so as to yield a relatively stable evolution of the world economy where the structure of international markets and the price system remain approximately constant over time, except of course for oil. However, the base run summarized in table 3 raises several remarks.

Global output per capita grows at an average annual rate of 3 percent, but its structure changes substantially over time. First, one may observe a strong substitution of oil—the output of which grows only at .8 percent—by other productive factors. This phenomenon is explained partly by the neutral exogenous technical progress in nonoil production—which is responsible for a little less than two-thirds of global growth—and partly by a truly economic substitution due to the strong increase in the relative price of oil, itself related to the real rate of interest, in accordance with the well-known Hotelling model for exhaustible resources.[10] Unlike the Hotelling model, however, the real price of oil rises at a rate below the real rate of interest—both being defined in relation with the price of the standard consumption good, which is practically

---

9. This seemed a convenient way of reducing the weight of terminal conditions while maintaining computation in reasonable bounds. A posteriori, however, it appeared that running the competitive perfect foresight model on 15 or 20 periods would not have been computationally very expensive.

10. See, for instance, Dasgupta and Heal 1980.

TABLE 3a. Base Run Results,
World Markets

Product	Period	Price	Capacity utilization rate [b]	Net trade flows			
				North	South	OPEC	Total
1. Technological	1	1.000	0.904	-469.0	383.1	85.8	-0.1
	2	0.997		-520.9	427.5	93.2	-0.1
	3	0.996		-580.9	476.4	104.4	-0.1
	4	0.994		-644.0	527.9	116.0	-0.1
	5	0.992		-712.3	589.4	122.8	-0.1
2. Oil	1	1.000	0.989	248.3	67.9	-336.2	-0.1
	2	1.122		254.5	72.3	-326.9	-0.1
	3	1.296		258.0	76.3	-334.3	-0.0
	4	1.502		261.3	80.5	-341.8	-0.1
	5	1.745		264.3	84.8	-349.2	-0.1
3. Raw materials	1	1.000	0.976	147.0	-180.2	33.3	-0.1
	2	0.998		157.3	-194.3	36.9	-0.1
	3	0.996		167.4	-208.4	40.9	-0.1
	4	0.993		178.1	-223.4	45.2	-0.1
	5	0.990		189.3	-239.5	50.1	-0.1
4. Standard	1	1.000	0.987	54.9	-169.6	114.6	-0.1
	2	1.002		96.3	-215.4	119.0	-0.1
	3	1.002		116.2	-249.0	132.5	-0.3
	4	1.002		146.0	-292.1	146.0	-0.1
	5	1.002		179.1	-331.6	152.2	-0.2
5. Financial asset	1	0.06[a]	-	-18.8	101.2	-82.6	-0.2
	2	0.06		19.7	97.6	-117.7	-0.4
	3	0.06		39.3	116.2	-155.9	-0.4
	4	0.06		75.3	131.1	-206.9	-0.4
	5	0.06		121.3	163.6	-285.5	-0.6

a) The interest rate is exogenous since the financial asset is taken to be the numeraire.
b) By assumption, supply rationing occurs only during the first period.
c) In 1980 US Dollars per North inhabitant.

constant.[11] This comes from the exogenous "long-run" price of oil, which enters the definition of OPEC, terminal wealth, and from the fix-price assumption made for the initial period. As may be seen in table 3, the world economy, including the oil sector in OPEC, initially works at less than full

---

11. This being the result of our calibration assumptions.

TABLE 3b.   Base Run Results,
Growth Performances by Zone

	North			South			OPEC		
	Period 1	Period 5	Annual rate of growth	Period 1	Period 5	Annual rate of growth	Period 1	Period 5	Annual rate of growth
Production									
1. Technological good	1,701	2,516	3,31	-	-		-	-	-
2. Oil	-	-	-	-	-		316	349	0.83
3. Raw materials	-	-	-	180	239	2.39	-	-	-
4. Standard good	8,088	11,772	3,17	2,404	3,849	4.00	496	793	4.00
Consumption	7,322	10,749	3,25	1,925	3,028	3.85	517	814	3.85
Physical capital[b]	26,670	41,851	3,04	5,975	10,438	3.79	1,755	3,007	3.65
Financial asset [b]	-50	-666	(c)	-50	-3,473	(c)	+100	+4,139	(c)

a) All figures in 1980 US Dollars per North inhabitant.
b) The second figure corresponds to the planning horizon (period 6).
c) The rate of growth is meaningless for that variable.

capacity. Had some price flexibility been allowed for the first period, the initial equilibrium price of oil would have been lower, and, given its exogenous long-run price, its rate of growth would have been higher throughout the period. The presence of terminal conditions, as well as variable extraction costs, explain some additional departures from the Hotelling rule.

Some substitution seems also to occur with the raw materials exported by South, the volume of which grows at an annual rate of 2.4 percent. However, this phenomenon is only apparent and essentially results from the differences in the rates of neutral exogenous technical progress between the three zones. Indeed, the price of raw materials relative to that of nonoil products is hardly modified over the simulation period.

Finally, notice that after correcting for demographic growth, the growth of the world economy over the simulated period is assumed to benefit North more than the other zones. The growth of production and consumption per capita is a little above 3 percent in the former, whereas it is a little less than 2 percent in South and OPEC.

To check further the consistency of the calibration assumptions, we now investigate the results of a few illustrative simulations.

North-South Transfers

There is a voluminous literature on the effects of North-South transfers.[12] However, there are few truly dynamic disaggregated models dealing with that issue. Models of the present type might contribute, empirically, to fill part of this gap.

In the simulation reported in the first column of table 4, it is assumed that, at each period, North transfers to South some fixed percentage of its GDP. To magnify the effects of the transfer, this percentage is set at the artificially high level of 3 percent. However, as the international capital market is assumed to be perfectly competitive, it is simpler to consider that transfers are fully equivalent to a unique initial transfer of financial assets between North and South, amounting to approximately U.S. $10,000 per North inhabitant.

The first effect of this transfer is a "wealth effect" on consumption. With no change in consumption with respect to the base run, the initial transfer would result in a higher terminal wealth for South, and a lower wealth for North. Optimality conditions thus imply that, with no change in prices, consumption should increase in the former and decrease in the latter by a discounted amount roughly equal to the initial asset transfer.

If both changes were approximately the same in absolute value, not much would happen since the market for the standard good would remain in equilibrium. On the contrary, if the increase in South consumption were much higher than the decrease in North, prices would be modified on the market for the standard good, inducing changes in production decisions, and subsequent modifications of consumption decisions.

As may be seen in table 4, the latter effects prove to be rather moderate. The initial asset transfer produces opposite changes of consumption between North and South. However, total consumption falls a little, which brings about a slight drop in world production and prices.

This result may seem somewhat counterintuitive since one would expect a priori that the positive change in South consumption would be larger than the negative change in North consumption. The explanation lies in the very structure of the model, and, in particular, in the fact that it is specified in finite time. In infinite time, changes in discounted optimal consumption should be equal to initial asset transfers. If the optimal growth rate of consumption is larger in South than in North, one should then observe an initial drop followed, after some time, by an increase in total consumption, and the opposite modification in the time profile of prices, which would imply an increase in the real rate of interest. Given the time-horizon in the model, the second stage

---

12. See, for instance, the survey by Eaton 1989.

TABLE 4. Effects of North-South Transfers and Accelerated Technical Progress in South

	Percentage deviations from base run [a]	
	North-South transfer	Accelerated technical progress in South
Average annual world output:		
1. Technological good	-0.21	0.09
2. Oil	-0.40	0.06
3. Raw materials	-0.29	1.04
4. Standard good	-0.32	0.02
Average annual consumption level:		
- North	-2.05	0.0
- South	5.81	0.05
- OPEC	0.0	0.06
Final financial asset		
(US$ per North inhabitant):		
- North	-20,950	74
- South	20,090	-90
- OPEC	-140	13
Objective function:		
- North	-0,94	0.03
- South	2.95	0.02
- OPEC	0.0	0.04
Price of raw materials:		
- Period 1	0.0	0.0
- Period 2	0.0	-1.0
- Period 3	0.0	-1.9
- Period 4	0.0	-3.0
- Period 5	0.0	-3.9

a) The precision limit of the equilibrium search algorithm is .02%. Figures close to that value are reported as 0%.

of this process is not observed in the simulation and the discounted balance of consumption effects is negative. As a matter of fact, the limited variation of financial assets over the planning period show that, indeed, a small part of the initial asset transfer has been made "effective," that is, transformed into consumption. [13]

Another important explanation of this result is that the capital market is assumed to be perfectly competitive. If some rationing on South borrowing in the base run were realistically introduced, the effect of a transfer from North would clearly be modified. The initial impact on consumption, production, and prices would then be larger and unambiguously positive.

Technical Progress in the South

The structure of the model implies a strong interdependence of economic growth rates across the three zones. The growth of South, for instance, depends on the availability of the technological good produced by North, which, in turn, depends on raw materials exported by South. A way of accelerating growth in South, independently from capital accumulation, would be to increase its rate of exogenous technical progress.

In the present simulation—reported in the second column of table 4—this rate is raised annually by .3 percentage point in the production of exported raw materials. However, the overall effect of that change on the world economy and on South is practically negligible. On average, world output and consumption in the three zones increase by less than .1 percent.

The explanation of that result is relatively simple. The initial increase in productivity leads South to reallocate its factors of production in favor of exported raw materials and to raise its level of consumption. At the initial level of prices, an excess supply of raw materials and an excess demand for the standard good develop. The price of the former tends to fall relatively to the latter, transferring part of the initial gain by South to the other zones. Somehow, South's productivity gain is confiscated by competitive market mechanisms. As a matter of fact, it may be seen in table 4 that, in terms of the objective functions, South ultimately benefits relatively less than the two other zones from that exogenous gain.

Oil Shock

The base run has been calibrated so as to yield a continuous increase in the price of oil. This was obtained with an exogenous initial level of oil reserves

---

13. Of course, this is the reason why it would be desirable to extend substantially the planning horizon in the model.

TABLE 5. Effects of an Oil Shock

	Deviations from base run (%)		
Average annual world output:			
1. Technological good	-1.0	of which first period:	-5.0
2. Oil	-0.5		-1.0
3. Raw materials	-2.1		-1.3
4. Standard good	-0.5		-1.2
Average annual consumption level:			
- North	-0.4		
- South	-0.4		
- OPEC	-1.5		
Final financial asset:			
- North	-1.9		
- South	-5.0		
- OPEC	-8.0		
Objective function:			
- North	-0.2		
- South	-0.2		
- OPEC	-1.7		
Price of oil:			
Period 1	6.0		
Period 2	10.9		
Period 3	14.4		
Period 4	12.9		
Period 5	11.9		

and a (partly) exogenous terminal price of oil. Of course, the price of oil will change in a totally different way if we introduce unexpected changes in reserves—that is, discoveries—or in the terminal price. To get some insight on the possible effects of such changes, we simulate here a 20 percent reduction of known reserves—for instance, some new fields prove less rich than expected—in the initial period, accompanied by a 12 percent increase in the terminal price of oil.[14]

---

14. This elasticity is consistent with the elasticity of oil demand in the base run.

The resulting increase of oil prices throughout the period has a moderate negative impact on the world economy. Other things equal, terminal wealth falls in North and South and consumption declines. Also, real returns on physical capital fall with negative effects on production. These phenomena are reinforced by OPEC, because the less than unity elasticity of the terminal price of oil with respect to reserves implies that the final wealth of OPEC also declines.

The result—see table 5—is a fall in world production, particularly pronounced during the initial period, where capacity utilization rather than prices adjust. Because the recession bears relatively more on investment than other goods, North is initially the most affected zone. Later on, North and South compensate the rise in relative oil prices by modifying production techniques. This partly offsets the initial drop in the demand for the technological good. Over the rest of the period, the drop in world output is rather moderate since it amounts, on average, to only .5 percent for the consumption good, .3 percent for the technological good, and 2.5 percent for oil.

Exploring Monopolistic Equilibria

According to the preceding simulation, what may be considered as a major shock on the oil market proves in fact to have rather moderate effects in the world economy, when its effects are perfectly anticipated and all markets are competitive. The results of that simulation have certainly little to do with the actual shocks witnessed by the world economy during the 1970s, which partly resulted from the cartelization of oil producers. We investigate in this section the existence of such monopolistic equilibria in the world economy and, where they exist, differences with the competitive equilibria analyzed above. Although similar in spirit, the way imperfect competition is modeled in what follows differs substantially from what is done in now conventional references such as Harris (1984) or Smith and Venables (1988).

The concept of monopolistic equilibrium used in what follows is in the tradition of oligopoly, or monopolistic competition theory. Assume that a zone exploits the monopoly power it enjoys on the market for its specific good by setting the price of the good and supplying whatever quantity is demanded by the market at that price. In setting its price, the monopolistic zone must take into account not only that the demand on the market it controls will change, as in the standard textbook model, but also that the (net) demand and prices on other markets, known to work in a competitive manner, will change. So, even though OPEC is faced with a demand for oil that is little elastic when all other prices are given, it might refrain from pushing oil prices too high because it would perfectly anticipate that induced price changes in the competitive markets may offset its gain from doing so.

Formally, let $V[p_0 Q_0(p_0, \bar{p}), \bar{p}]$ be the indirect utility obtained by a given zone when it sets the price of its specific good to p_0, the demand for that good being then Q_0, and the price of other goods being $\bar{p}$. The function V is increasing with respect to its first argument, increasing with respect to the components of $\bar{p}$, which correspond to goods for which the zone is a net (competitive) exporter and decreasing with respect to the others. Partial monopoly equilibrium would simply consist of the maximization of export receipts for the specified good, that is $p_0 \cdot Q(p_0, \bar{p})$, with $\bar{p}$ given. The "full monopoly" equilibrium concept accounts in addition for the fact that, through competition in other markets, any change in p_0 will produce changes in $\bar{p}$. The condition for full monopoly equilibrium thus writes as:

$$V_1 Q(1 - \epsilon) + \left(V_1 \frac{\partial Q_0}{\partial \bar{p}} + \frac{\partial V}{\partial \bar{p}} \right) \frac{\partial \bar{p}}{\partial p_0} = 0, \tag{4}$$

where ϵ is the "partial" price elasticity of the demand for the specific good, and V_1 is the marginal utility of export receipts. There are two corrective terms in comparison with the standard partial equilibrium condition—which corresponds to the first term—both depending on the reaction of competitive prices $\bar{p}$ to the monopoly prices p_0. Under these conditions, an inelastic partial demand for the specific good—that is, $\epsilon < 1$—does not necessarily rule out the existence of an equilibrium, since the sum of the corrective terms may be negative and larger than the first term. It is precisely that point that we investigate in what follows.

The algorithm used for the search of monopolistic equilibria involves several modifications of the original one. The general organization of the algorithm is described in figure 1. We first start from a given vector of prices for the specific good produced by the monopoly, p_0, and we look for a "fix-p_0" competitive equilibrium of the world economy. This equilibrium is defined by a set of prices, $\bar{p}$, for the goods exchanged on competitive markets and by a vector of "shadow-prices," μ, for the market controlled by the monopoly. These shadow-prices correspond to the prices that would induce the monopoly to produce the quantity of the specific good actually demanded at the fix-price p_0, and prices $\bar{p}$ for the other goods, if the monopoly were in fact a price taker on its own market. They also correspond to the multipliers associated with the additional constraint:

$$x_0^t \geq X_1^t(p_0, \bar{p}),$$

which must be included in the optimal growth program (1) of the monopolistic zone. In that constraint, x_0^t stands for the production of the specific good at period t, whereas X_1^t represents the demand for that good by the other zones.

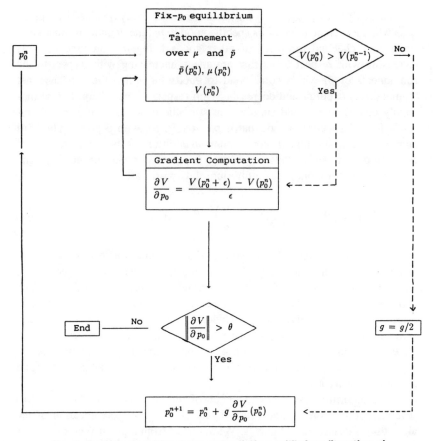

Fig. 1. Search algorithm for monopolistic equilibrium (iteration n)

The search for the fix-p_0 equilibrium values $\bar{p}$ and μ can be done by a simple transformation of the original algorithm. The set of prices ($\bar{p}$, μ) is allowed to vary proportionally to the excess demand on each market until equilibrium obtains on all markets. The only difference with the original algorithm is that changes in the (shadow) prices μ now imply no change in the actual price received by the monopoly and paid by the other zones for the specific good.

Once the equilibrium has been found for a given vector of fix-p_0, the gradient of the monopoly's objective function is computed numerically by repeating the exercise for fix-price vectors p_0 arbitrarily close to the initial one. The search for the optimal fix-price p_0 then goes on according to a simple gradient algorithm. As this procedure is necessarily convergent, an equilibrium will be said to be nonexistent if there is still no sign of decline in the norm of the gradient after considerable changes in the fix-prices p_0.

Implementing this procedure required modifying the terminal conditions imposed on each zone. Clearly, it would not make sense to relate, as we did before, the terminal prices of assets, p_k^{T+1}, to those obtained in the preceding period, p_k^T. Knowing that rule, North and OPEC, in a monopoly situation, would simply set the prices p_k^T to infinity.[15] On the other hand, choosing terminal prices in a totally arbitrary way is not satisfactory either. We thus switched to quantitative terminal restrictions of the type $p_j^{T+1} = \bar{k}_j$, for all stock variables j (including oil for OPEC and the financial asset for all zones) in the three zones, the values selected for the $\bar{k}_j$ being those obtained with the base run in the competitive case. Basically, this is equivalent to choose exogenous rates of accumulation for the three zones, and to restrict monopoly power to the time profile of that accumulation.

The Monopolistic Equilibrium of North

The procedure described above converged successfully in the case of North exercising its monopoly power on the market for the technological good. As may be seen from the results reported in table 6, there indeed are strong changes in the time profile of world growth over the period of analysis. The price of the technological good, relative to that of the consumption good, increases by 50 percent, this figure being a little smaller for the first period due to the initial existence of idle capacities, and substantially larger in the last period, probably because of a horizon effect. However, the impact of that rise on the structure of international trade differs very much across periods.

The optimal strategy of North may be summarized as follows. By increasing the price of the technological good, it initially reduces the investments made by South and OPEC. However, because these two zones must meet the terminal quantitative conditions on their capital stock, their investments rise again—compared to the base run—at the end of the period. The reason why North does not increase its price further by then is that this would produce a jump in the price of the standard good. Indeed, since this good is combined with the technological good in the definition of the capital stock of all zones, the strong capital accumulation at the end of the period would increase the relative price of consumption. Also, because the marginal propensity to consume is larger in North than in the other zones, any transfer of real income from the latter to the former necessarily increases the relative price of the consumption good and reduces the size of the initial transfer. To prevent that evolution, it is thus optimal for North to invest massively in the production of the standard good and to drastically modify its production structure. By doing so, it becomes self-sufficient in that good and is less

---

15. This would not be the case for South, since its specific good does not enter the definition of terminal assets.

**TABLE 6. North Monopoly Equilibrium
(Percentage Deviations from Base Run)**

	Period 1	Period 2	Period 3	Period 4	Period 5
Prices:					
1. Technological good	46.9	58.1	56.0	55.2	67.6
2. Oil	0.0	-3.3	-3.8	-5.3	-3.0
3. Raw materials	0.0	4.2	3.8	2.0	0.1
4. Standard good	5.4	8.1	6.5	4.7	4.8
North trade flows:					
Exports of technological good	-11.1	-75.9	-26.9	3.7	19.4
Imports of oil	0.0	0.0	0.1	0.1	0.0
Imports of raw materials	0.0	0.1	0.0	0.0	0.0
Imports of the standard good	2.2	8.0	0.2	-3.0	-3.1
Output of the technological good	2.8	21.5	6.8	-7.8	-18.7
Output of the standard good (North)	1.4	-5.0	3.0	6.5	5.1
Investment (North)	8.1	57.8	19.6	-12.3	-33.5

affected by a rise in its price. As may be seen from table 6, North eventually becomes a net exporter of the standard good toward the end of the period and contributes to a drop in the price of the consumption good.

The reason why North strategy looks somewhat complex in this simulation is probably the relatively short length of the planning period. In particular, the fact that North becomes a net exporter of the consumption good toward the end of the period may simply be a horizon effect. Under these conditions, the main effects of North exercising its monopoly power appear to be a fall in the volume of international trade and a drastic slowdown in the growth of South and OPEC. These results confirm the intuition.[16]

Monopolistic Equilibria in the Case of South and OPEC.

The same algorithm applied to South and OPEC failed to converge after a considerable number of iterations and implausible increases in the price of the

---

16. Note that the monopolistic price increase of North's specific product is in fact equivalent to an optimal tariff that would reduce the volume of trade. In that sense, the present exercise may be seen as a dynamic version of the game-theoretical view at tariffs and protection; see McMillan 1988, for instance.

specific goods. We are thus led to conclude that no full monopolistic equilibrium exists in the case of these two zones.

This result is not really surprising. Given the assumption made in the production functions of little substitutability between raw materials and oil, on one hand, and capital-labor combinations, on the other, the (partial) marginal revenue of both zones is certainly strongly positive, so that the two corrective terms in condition (4) are not sufficient to yield finite optimal prices.[17] In comparison, there was more flexibility in the case of North because of the possibility for South and OPEC to arbitrage intertemporally about investment expenditures. In the present case, the assumption of fixed elasticities of substitution between all productive factors seems indeed unreasonable when relative prices are allowed to become increasingly large. However, we have not tried to repeat the exercise with different specifications of the production functions. Nor have we attempted to determine the level of (constant) substitution elasticities beyond which well-defined monopolistic equilibria would exist for South and OPEC. Concerning indirect general equilibrium effects, it may also be stressed that the differences in consumption propensities, which was an offsetting factor of North's monopoly power, plays in the wrong direction in the case of OPEC. Any transfer of real income through higher prices of raw materials and oil reduces the total demand for consumption and increases the size of the transfer.

If no equilibrium exists when South and OPEC are assumed to exercise their monopoly power throughout the period of analysis, things are different when monopolistic equilibria are restricted to some subperiods and all agents (including OPEC) are aware of it. Table 7 shows an example of such an equilibrium. It is assumed and correctly anticipated here that OPEC countries will form a cartel in period 2, but the oil market will become competitive again from period 3 on.[18] The fact that oil consumers may react to a price increase in period 2 by postponing their purchases to a period where oil prices will be lower thanks to reestablished competition, obviously raises the elasticity of the demand for oil during that period. An equilibrium is then shown to exist.

The evolution of equilibrium prices in table 7 is simple to understand. Because of the underutilization of capacities, not much happens in period 1. In period 2, the OPEC cartel raises its prices, which lowers oil consumption.

---

17. Given that our solution algorithm necessarily improves the objective function, which is the indirect utility of the monopoly zone, at each iteration the problem encountered here is one of degenerate solution at infinity rather than nonexistence. Note also that we did not investigate the consequences of changing the numéraire on the existence of an equilibrium, although it is known that, with competitive imperfections, price normalization matters—see Gabzewicz and Vial 1972.

18. It would have been better to assume the cartel active in period 1. However, results for that period are affected by the fact that the world economy does not work at full capacity.

TABLE 7. Equilibrium Prices with OPEC in Monopoly Situation in Period 2

	Period 1	Period 2	Period 3	Period 4	Period 5
Prices:					
1. Technological good	-1.0	0.8	0.1	-0.1	-0.4
2. Oil	-1.2	158.7	-23.9	-23.9	-24.7
3. Raw materials	-0.2	0.5	0.2	0.0	-0.2
4. Standard good	-0.1	0.2	0.0	0.0	0.2

However, as there is a fixed terminal constraint on oil reserves, OPEC must increase its rate of extraction in subsequent periods. As a consequence, competitive oil prices fall. The price of other goods is little affected—as a matter of fact, oil imports represent a small share of GDP in North and South (see table 2). This implies that the production effects of changes in oil prices and the actual overall transfer from North and South to OPEC are limited. On the other hand, as this transfer tends to reduce total consumption and since the production of the standard good is itself reduced in period 2, only a very small change in the price of the consumption good is required to equilibrate the market.

Conclusion

In this chapter, we have investigated extensions of an applied general equilibrium model of world trade to a dynamic competitive perfect foresight framework, and then to imperfect competition. Given the presence of exhaustible resources in the model and the nonexistence of steady states, the perfect foresight competitive equilibrium proves to be quite sensitive to exogenous terminal conditions. However, this may be partly due to the rather moderate length of the planning horizon selected in the model. Ex post, it appears that much longer periods might have been analyzed with a consequent drop in the weight of transversality conditions. The search for full monopolistic equilibria also suggests that this kind of model may also be used to investigate various types of strategic equilibria. The fact that no monopoly equilibrium did exist for South and OPEC prevented us to investigate dynamic equilibria of the Nash or Stackleberg (open-loop) type. However, our last experiments shows that this would indeed be possible with alternative specification where imperfect competition would be restricted to some subperiod as in the two-period framework used by Erlich et al. (1987).

Comment

Victor Ginsburgh

The chapter by Berthélémy and Bourguignon goes exactly in the two directions that I think applied general equilibrium models should be going: dynamics and imperfect competition.[1] My comments will thus cover the two
issues. However, before going into more technical details, I would like to
stress why I think that the two issues are closely linked and why imperfect
competition hardly goes without perfect foresight dynamics.

On the one hand, perfect competition is clearly a *long-term* concept:
nobody believes that between 1990 and 1992, market forces will be powerful
enough to bring, say the Canadian economy into a state where prices will
clear all markets (including the labor market), where competition in industry
will be such that every Canadian firm will take prices as given, where every
consumer will be exactly on his budget constraint, and where the Canadian
trade balance with the rest of the world will be in equilibrium.

On the other hand, model builders have started to represent, within the
static general equilibrium framework, all kinds of *market imperfections,* like
downward real wage rigidities, trade balance disequilibria, and, more recently, after the way had been paved by Harris 1984, oligopolistic industries
and increasing returns to scale (under the form of fixed costs). These are more
or less short-term imperfections; indeed, as recent experience has shown, real
wages can be made relatively flexible over the medium run; positive profits
provide a good incentive for new firms to enter the market; and no country
(and no consumer) can afford running trade (or budget) deficits for too long.

The consequence is that static applied general equilibrium models are
used to represent short-run "stylized facts" and are simultaneously asked to
give answers to structural and long-term questions such as: does it pay to
lower tariffs; how can one solve the unemployment problem in rural areas;
and would better irrigation lead to large enough crops and eventually to food
self-sufficiency? And it is becoming more and more unclear whether such

---

1. See Ginsburgh and Mercenier 1988.

models deal with the short run, the medium run or the long run, or the three together. Modelers seem, in my opinion, to ask too much from their static models. And so-called recursively dynamic models, based on static expectations, are no good answer.

A structure that seems more consistent, without being technically too demanding, is the one used in Erlich, Ginsburgh, and Van der Heyden 1987. They build a two-period intertemporal model in which the first period may be affected by market imperfections, while the (long-run) second period is a purely Walrasian world. The imperfect short or medium run is thus embedded into a long run where perfect competition is the rule. Agents "are aware" of this since they have perfect knowledge of the future: they live, so to speak, under the long-run threat of market forces that they have to take into account in making their medium-run decisions. This also avoids the "two versions" presentation that some modelers, like Harris 1984 or Smith and Venables 1989 use in their imperfectly competitive market structure models: there is a "short-run" version in which the number of firms in each industry is fixed, and a "long-run" version where there is entry or exit until profits per firm drop to zero. This is easily taken into account in the two-period structure suggested above.

I now turn to technical questions that were more directly prompted by the Berthélémy and Bourguignon (BB) chapter.

Dynamics

An applied model builder has the choice between two sorts of dynamics: (a) the life of each agent is finite but the number of agents is infinite, since each agent who gets old and dies is replaced by a young agent; this is the *overlapping generations* model, the applied version of which was introduced and intensively used by Auerbach and Kotlikoff (1987) and Summers (1981);[2] or (b) the number of agents is finite but each of them is infinitely lived. The computational complexity of overlapping generations models has, until now, forced modelers to keep them small. Typically, there will be one or two sectors (firms),[3] one representative consumer, and a rather unsophisticated government. Likewise, the complexity of infinite horizon models has, with a few exceptions,[4] prompted model builders to truncate the horizon.[5]

---

2. See Auerbach and Kotlikoff 1987 and the references to earlier work contained in their book.

3. See Davis, Whalley, and Hamilton 1989 and Ginsburgh and Sneessens 1989 for two-sector models.

4. See among others Mercenier and Sampaïo de Souza 1989.

5. A good survey of such methods is given by Grinold 1983.

BB have worked with two such truncations. Their intertemporal utility function for a specific agent is:

$$\sum_{t=1}^{T} \delta_t u(c_t) + \phi(p_{T+1} k_{T+1}).$$

The first term is the discounted sum (at rate δ_t) of utilities u of consumption flows c_t, while the second term represents the discounted utility flows between $t = T + 1$ and $t = \infty$, consistent with terminal capital stocks k_{T+1} and prices p_{T+1}. In one of the truncations k_{T+1} is exogenous, in the second one it is p_{T+1}. But rather than choosing arbitrary prices, BB set $p_{T+1} = p_T$, where p_T is the endogenous price vector in period T.[6]

There are two problems with intertemporal utility functions. The first is the choice of the discount factors δ_t, the second one is the terminal truncation.

Let me write the intertemporal problem faced by a consumer (country) as:

$$\max \sum_{t=1}^{T} \delta_t u(c_t) + \phi(p_{T+1} k_{T+1}),$$

subject to the intertemporal budget constraint:

$$\sum_{t=1}^{T} (p_t c_t + s_t) = \sum_{t=1}^{T} r_t,$$

where r_t and s_t, respectively, represent income and savings in period t. Forget for some time the terminal conditions issue. It is obvious that a specific sequence of discount factors δ_t will generate a specific sequence of savings s_t and vice versa: choosing a sequence of s_t's (or a sequence of savings rates $\sigma_t = s_t/(p_t c_t + s_t)$ since we cannot set nominal magnitudes) will generate a sequence of δ_t's. Obviously, we know very little, if anything, about the rate at which consumers discount their consumption streams; but we know much more about their savings behavior, since this is (more or less) accurately given by national accounts or consumer surveys. Some numerical experiments with real data have convinced me that it is hard to obtain a nice and realistic sequence of savings rates when the discount rates are chosen exogenously; I

---

6. Except for the oil market for which $p_{T+1} = \lambda p_T + (1 - \lambda)\pi$, π exogenous.

prefer, at least in the calibration phase, to choose σ_t's and compute the δ_t's endogenously.

Of course, this is numerically much more difficult since it forces the modeler to compute a fixed-point of the following Negishi problem (NP):

$$\max \sum_{t=1}^{T} \delta_t u(c_t) + \phi(p_{T+1} k_{T+1}),$$

subject to the following constraints (for $t = 1, 2, \ldots, T$):

$$c_t + Vv_t - y_t \leq 0, \tag{1}$$

$$Ky_t - k_t \leq 0,$$

and

$$k_{t+1} - k_t - v_t \leq 0,$$

with $y_t \in Y_t$, k_1 given, so that for every $t = 1, 2, \ldots, T$, the welfare weights δ_t are such that the savings-investment equality

$$\sigma_t(p_t c_t + s_t) = s_t = p_t Vv_t \tag{2}$$

holds for given σ_t. In (NP), v_t represents the vector of investment by destination, V is a matrix that converts sectors of origin to sectors of destinations, K is a diagonal matrix of capital-output ratios, k_t is the vector of capital stocks at time t, y_t the vector of productions, Y_t a (convex) production set, and finally p_t is the vector of (shadow) prices associated with demand-supply inequalities (1). See Boucher et al. 1987 for technicalities and an existence proof of the fixed point of (NP).

Let me now turn to the terminal conditions issue. The problem can be treated in very much the same spirit; instead of appending to the objective function the term $\phi(p_{T+1} k_{T+1})$, consider appending $\delta_{T+1} \phi(p_{T+1} k_{T+1})$ where δ_{T+1} is also an unknown welfare weight. We now have $T + 1$ unknown welfare weights to be determined so that the T conditions (2) hold; but since the weights may be normalized so that, say $\delta_1 = 1$, there are exactly as many conditions to be fulfilled as there are unknowns, and we have a fixed point problem of dimension T. This procedure, however, does not dispense to exogenously set the price vector p_{T+1} and to specify the function ϕ; but it ensures the last period's savings ratio to be what we want it to be, and it makes the choice of p_{T+1} somewhat less arbitrary and less important. I will come back to this in section 3 when I discuss the terminal conditions' choice under imperfect competition.

I have also tried to force the terminal period to satisfy the golden rule of accumulation; in this case, terminal period's savings should be equal to the terminal period's capital income, that is, $s_{T+1} = r_{T+1} k_{T+1}$, where r_{T+1} is the shadow price of the constraint $Ky_T - k_T \leq 0$.

Imperfect Competition

The first problem that I want to address is normalization. It unfortunately so happens that price normalization matters a lot when there are oligopolistic or monopolistic producers. Not only may the equilibrium allocations change with normalization, but worse than that, there may exist normalization choices that prevent an equilibrium to exist.[7] The nonexistence problem encountered in some cases by BB may thus be due to the algorithm that fails to discover an equilibrium;[8] but we cannot exclude the possibility that, for the implicitly chosen price normalization, the profit functions of the monopolists fail to be quasi-concave, so that no equilibrium exists.

I have constructed an example[9] in which I show that welfare decreases or increases may be larger when normalization is changed than when imperfections (like tariffs or taxes) are removed. In other words, under one normalization, welfare may increase when an imperfection is removed; under another one, welfare may decrease, or increase less. But then, what sort of conclusions can we draw from experiments in which we try to assess the welfare effects of moves to more competition?

My second point is devoted to short- or medium-term imperfections versus long-term perfect markets, and is linked to my introductory remarks. BB compute solutions under perfect competition and under monopolistic behavior in some of their three regions; they also compute solutions for a case in which a cartel of oil producers forms in one of the periods, and only lasts during some time. I find this a very nice idea, but it would even be nicer to endogenize such "switches" (but make sure that after a sufficient length of time, there is perfect competition again). I do not know whether this is possible, and it may be interesting to devote some time to such an issue.

---

7. The normalization issue is discussed in many papers. See, e.g., the seminal paper by Gabszewicz and Vial 1972. On the existence problem, see Dierker and Grodal 1986; they construct an economy in which, for some price normalizations, there exists an equilibrium, while for others, there is no equilibrium.

8. Though BB claim their algorithm necessarily converges.

9. Ginsburgh (this volume).

My last remark is concerned with the choice of terminal conditions under imperfect competition. What BB do is to constrain the solutions to satisfy:

$$k^{nc}_{T+1} = k^{c}_{T+1},$$

where the superscripts nc and c, respectively, refer to the noncompetitive and competitive solution. Thus, when computing equilibria in the noncompetitive case, they set as terminal conditions the ones obtained under perfect competition. This, of course, forces the trajectories to "jump" in the one before the last period. A possibly more smooth trajectory would be obtained by setting, along the lines suggested in Section 2:

$$\sigma^{nc}_{T+1} = \sigma^{c}_{T+1},$$

where σ represents savings rates.

References

Abel, A., and O.-J. Blanchard. 1983. An Intertemporal Model of Saving and Investment. *Econometrica* 51:675–92.

Abreu, D. 1988. On the Theory of Informally Repeated Games with Discounting. *Econometrica* 56:383–96.

Adelman, I., and S. Robinson. 1978. *Income Distribution Policy in Developing Countries: A Case Study of Korea*. Stanford, CA: Stanford University Press.

Adelman, I., D. Roland-Holst, and A. Sarris. 1990. Adjustment Under Uncertainty with Computable General Equilibrium Models: General Theory and an Application to Korea. *International Economic Review* 4 (2): 1–20.

Ahluwalia, M., and F. J. Lysy. 1979. Welfare Effects of Demand Management Policies: Impact Multipliers under Alternative Model Structures. *Journal of Policy Modeling* 1 (3): 317–42.

Anderson, R., and H. Sonnenschein. 1982. On the Existence of Rational Expectations Equilibrium. *Journal of Economic Theory* 26 (2): 261–78.

Armington, P. 1969. A Theory of Demand for Products Distinguished by Place of Production. *IMF Staff Papers* 16 (1): 159–78.

Auerbach, A., and L. Kotlikoff. 1987. *Dynamic Fiscal Policy*. Cambridge: Cambridge University Press.

Bacha, E. 1986. External Shocks and Growth Prospects: The Case of Brazil 1973–89. *World Development* 14 (8): 919–36.

Balassa and Associates. 1971. *The Structure of Protection in Developing Countries*. Baltimore: Johns Hopkins University Press.

Balassa and Associates. 1982. *Trade Strategies for Semi-Industrial Countries*. Baltimore: Johns Hopkins University Press.

Balassa, B., M. Bueno, P. Kuczynski, and M. H. Simonsen. 1986. *Toward Renewed Economic Growth in Latin America*. Washington, DC: Institute of International Economics.

Benjamin, N. 1990. Investment, the Real Exchange Rate, and Dutch Disease: A Two-Period General Equilibrium Model of Cameroon. *Journal of Policy Modeling* 12 (1): 77–92.

Benjamin, N., S. Devarajan, and R. J. Weiner. 1989. The Dutch Disease in a Developing Country: Oil Reserves in Cameroon. *Journal of Development Economics* 30:71–92.

Bergsman, J. 1974. Commercial Policy, Allocative Efficiency and X-Efficiency. *Quarterly Journal of Economics* 88:409–33.

347

Berthélémy, J., and F. Bourguignon. 1984. Le Sud dans le cadre d'un modèle mondial intertemporel à trois zones. *Recherches économiques et sociales* 11–12:163–91.

Bevan, D., P. Collier, and J. W. Gunning. 1990. The Macroeconomics of External Shocks. Working Paper. Oxford University.

Bhagwati, J. N., and S. Chakravarty. 1969. Contributions to Indian Economic Analysis: A Survey. *American Economic Review (Supplement)* 59: 2–73.

Blanchard, O.-J., and S. Fischer. 1989. *Lectures in Macroeconomics*. Cambridge, MA: MIT Press.

Blanchard, O.-J., and J. Sachs. 1982. Anticipations, récessions et politique économique: un modèle de déséquilibre intertemporel. *Annales de l'INSEE* 47–48: 509–36.

Blitzer, C., and R. Eckaus. 1986. Energy-Economy Interactions in Mexico: A Multiperiod General Equilibrium Model. *Journal of Development Economics* 21:259–81.

Blitzer, C. R., R. S. Eckaus, S. Lahiri, and A. Meeraus. 1989. An Economy Wide Energy Policy Model for Egypt. Center for Energy Policy Research, MIT. Photocopy.

Böhm, V. 1990. General Equilibrium with Profit Maximizing Oligopolists. Discussion Paper 414/90. Universität Mannheim.

Boucher, J., V. Ginsburgh, Y. Smeers, and A. Svoronos. 1987. Introducing Realistic Savings Patterns in Intertemporal Models. *Operations Research Letters* 6:211–19.

Bourguignon, F., W. H. Branson, and J. de Melo. 1992. Macroeconomic Adjustment and Income Distribution: A Macro-Micro Simulation Model. *Journal of Development Economics* 38:17–39.

BPS. 1984. *Input-Output Table 1980*. 4 vols. Jakarta: Biro Pusat Statistik.

BPS. 1986. *Social Accounting Matrix 1980*. 2 vols. Jakarta: Biro Pusat Statistik.

BPS. 1987. *Indikator Pemerataan Pendapatan Jumlah dan Persentase Penduduk Miskin di Indonesia, 1976–1984*. Jakarta: Biro Pusat Statistik.

BPS/ISS/SOW. 1986. *Report on Modeling: The Indonesian Social Accounting Matrix, Static Disaggregated Model*. Jakarta: Biro Pusat Statistik.

Brainard, W., and J. Tobin. 1968. Pitfalls in Financial Model Building. *American Economic Review (Papers and Proceedings)* 58:99–123.

Brander, J., and B. Spencer. 1984. Tariff Protection and Imperfect Competition. In *Monopolistic Competition in International Trade*, ed. H. Kierzkowski. Oxford: Oxford University Press.

Bronsard, C. 1971. *Dualité Microéconomique et Théorie du Second Best*. Louvain: Université Catholique de Louvain.

Bruno, M. 1979. Stabilization and Stagflation in a Semi-Industrialized Economy. In *International Economic Policy: Theory and Evidence*, ed. R. Dornbusch and J. A. Frenkel. Baltimore: Johns Hopkins University Press.

Bruno, M., and J. Sachs. 1982. Input Price Shocks and the Slowdown in Economic Growth: The Case of U.K. Manufacturing. *Review of Economic Studies* 49:679–705.

Buffie, E. F. 1984. Financial Repression, the New Structuralists, and Stabilization

Policy in Semi-Industrial Economies. *Journal of Development Economics* 14:305–22.

Burniaux, J.-M., and J. Waelbroeck. 1992. Preliminary Results of Two General Equilibrium Models with Imperfect Competition. *Journal of Policy Modelling* 14 (1): 65–92.

Calvo, G. 1978. On the Time Consistency of Optimal Policy in a Monetary Economy. *Econometrica* 6:1411–28.

Cardoso, E., and A. Fishlow. 1989. The Macroeconomics of the Brazilian External Debt. In *Developing Country Debt and the World Economy,* ed. J. Sachs. Chicago: University of Chicago Press.

Cavallo, D. 1981. Stagflationary Effects of Monetarist Stabilization Policies in Economies with Persistent Inflation. In *Development In an Inflationary World,* ed. M. J. Flanders and A. Razin. New York: Academic Press.

Chenery, H. B., J. D. Lewis, J. de Melo, and S. Robinson. 1986. Alternative Routes to Development. In *Industrialization and Growth: A Comparative Study,* ed. H. B. Chenery, S. Robinson, and M. Syrquin. London: Oxford University Press.

Chiarella, C. 1980. Trade Between Resource-Poor and Resource-Rich Economies as a Differential Game. In *Exhaustible Resources, Optimality and Trade,* ed. M. Kemp and N. Long. Amsterdam: North Holland.

Codognato, G., and J. Gabszewicz. 1990. Cournot-Walras and Walras Equilibria in Exchange Economies: An Example. CORE Discussion Paper 9047. Université Catholique de Louvain.

Cohen, D., and P. Michel. 1988. How Should Control Theory Be Used to Calculate a Time-Consistent Government Policy? *Review of Economic Studies* 55:263–74.

Corden, W. M. 1982. Booming Sector and Dutch Disease Economics: A Survey. Working Paper 79. Faculty of Economics and Research, School of Social Sciences, Australian National University.

Cripps, M. W., and G. D. Myles. 1988. General Equilibrium and Imperfect Competition: Profit Feedback Effects and Price Normalisations. Warwick Economic Research Papers no. 295. Department of Economics, University of Warwick.

Cuddington, J. T. 1987. Macroeconomic Determinant of Capital Flight: An Econometric Investigation. In *Capital Flight and Third World Debt,* ed. D. R. Lessard and J. Williamson. Washington: Institute for International Economics.

Dahl, H., S. Devarajan, and S. van Wijnbergen. 1989. Revenue-Neutral Tariff Reform: Theory and an Application to Cameroon. John F. Kennedy School of Government, Harvard University. Mimeo.

Dasgupta, P., and G. Heal. 1980. *Economic Theory and Exhaustible Resources.* Cambridge: Cambridge University Press.

d'Autume, A., and P. Michel. 1987. Transversality Conditions, Budget Constraints and the Determinacy of a Perfect Foresight Equilibrium in a Monetary Growth Model. *European Economic Review* 31 (7): 1343–67.

Davis, J., J. Whalley, and B. Hamilton. 1989. Capital Income Taxation in a Two-Commodity Life Cycle Model. *Journal of Public Economics* 39:109–26.

de Melo, J., and D. W. Roland-Holst. 1990. An Evaluation of Neutral Trade Policy Incentives Under Increasing Returns to Scale. In *Trade Theory and Economic*

Reform: North, South, and East—Essays in Honor of Bela Belassa, ed. J. de Melo and A. Sapir. Oxford: Basil Blackwell.

de Melo, J., and D. Roland-Holst. 1991. Industrial Organization and Trade Liberalization: Evidence from Korea. In *Empirical Studies of Commercial Policy,* ed. R. Baldwin. Chicago: University of Chicago Press: Cambridge, MA: NBER.

De Janvry, A., and K. Subbarao. 1986. *Agricultural Price Policy and Income Distribution in India.* Delhi: Oxford University Press.

Dervis, K. 1975. Substitution, Employment, and Intertemporal Equilibrium in a Non-Linear Multi-Sector Planning Model for Turkey. *European Economic Review* 6:77–96.

Dervis, K., J. de Melo, and S. Robinson. 1982. *General Equilibrium Models for Development Policy.* Cambridge: Cambridge University Press.

Dervis, K., and S. Robinson. 1978. *The Foreign Exchange Gap, Growth and Industrial Strategy in Turkey: 1973–1983.* World Bank Staff Working Paper no. 306. Washington, DC: World Bank.

Dervis, K., and S. Robinson. 1982. A General Equilibrium Analysis of the Causes of a Foreign Exchange Crisis: The Case of Turkey. *Weltwirtschaftliches Archiv* 118 (2): 259–80.

Devarajan, S., and J. de Melo. 1987. Adjustment with a Fixed Exchange Rate: Cameroon, Côte d'Ivoire and Sénégal. *World Bank Economic Review* 1 (3): 447–88.

Devarajan, S., and J. Lewis. 1988. Structural Adjustment and Economic Reform in Indonesia: Model-Based Policies versus Rules of Thumb. Harvard Institute for International Development. Mimeo.

Devarajan, S., and J. Lewis. 1991. Structural Adjustment and Economic Reform in Indonesia: Model-Based Policies vs. Rule-of-Thumb. In *Reforming Economic Systems in Developing Countries,* ed. D. Perkins and M. Roemer. Cambridge, MA: Harvard University Press.

Devarajan, S., and D. Rodrik. 1989a. Pro-Competitive Effects of Trade Reform: Results from a CGE Model of Cameroon. Working Paper 3176. National Bureau of Economic Research.

Devarajan, S., and D. Rodrik. 1989b. Trade Liberalization in Developing Countries: Do Imperfect Competition and Scale Economies Matter? *American Economic Review (Papers and Proceedings)* 79:283–87.

Dewatripont, M., and S. Robinson. 1985. *The Impact of Price Rigidities: A Computable General Equilibrium Analysis.* Giannini Foundation Working Paper no. 375. Berkeley: University of California.

Dierker, H., and B. Grodal. 1986. Nonexistence of Cournot-Walras Equilibrium in a General Equilibrium Model with Two Oligopolists. In *Contributions to Mathematical Economics in Honor of Gerard Debreu,.* ed. W. Hildenbrand and A. Mas Colell. Amsterdam: North Holland.

Dixit, A. 1984. International Trade Policy for Oligopolistic Industries. *Economic Journal* 94:1–16.

Dixit, A. 1985. Tax Policy in Open Economies. In *Handbook of Public Economics* 1, ed. A. J. Auerbach and M. Feldstein. Amsterdam: North-Holland.

Dixit, A. 1986. Comparative Statics for Oligopoly. *International Economic Review* 27 (1): 107–22.

Dixon, P. B., B. R. Parmenter, J. Sutton, and D. P. Vincent. 1982. *Orani: A Multisectoral Model of the Australian Economy.* Amsterdam: North-Holland.

Dornbusch, R. 1976. Expectations and Exchange Rate Dynamics. *Journal of Political Economy* 84 (6): 1161–76.

Dornbusch, R. 1984. *External Debt, Budget Deficits and Disequilibrium Exchange Rates.* NBER Working Paper 1336. Cambridge, MA: National Bureau of Economic Research.

Dornbusch, R., and S. Fischer. 1980. Exchange Rates and the Current Account. *American Economic Review* 70:960–71.

Dornbusch, R., and A. Reynoso. 1989. Financial Factors in Economic Development. *American Economic Review* 79 (2): 204–9.

Eaton, J. 1989. Foreign Public Capital Flows. In *Handbook of Development Economics* 2, ed. H. Chenery and T. N. Srinivasan. Amsterdam: North-Holland.

Eaton, J., and G. Grossman. 1986. Optimal Trade and Industrial Policy Under Oligopoly. *Quarterly Journal of Economics* 101:383–406.

Edwards, S. 1988. Terms of Trade, Exchange Rates and Labor Market Adjustments in Developing Countries. *World Bank Economic Review* 2 (2): 165–85.

Edwards, S. 1989. Structural Adjustment Policies in Highly Indebted Countries. In *Developing Country Debt and the World Economy,* ed. J. Sachs. Chicago: University of Chicago Press.

Ellis, F. 1988. Future Rice Strategy in Indonesia: Rice Self-Sufficiency and Rice Price Stability. IPU Technical Paper no. 7. Bulog, Jakarta.

Erlich, S., V. Ginsburgh, and L. Van der Heyden. 1987. Where Do Real Wage Decreases Lead Belgium. *European Economic Review* 31:1369–83.

Fane, G., and C. Phillips. 1987. *Effective Protection in Indonesia.* Canberra: Centre for International Economics.

Fargeix, A. 1990. Stabilization Policies and Income Distribution: A Computable General Equilibrium Model for Ecuador. Ph.D. diss. Department of Agricultural and Resource Economics, University of California at Berkeley.

Findlay, R. 1980. The Terms of Trade and Equilibrium Growth in the World Economy. *American Economic Review* 70:211–99.

Fischer, G., K. S. Frohberg, M. A. Keyzer, and K. S. Parikh. 1988. *Linked National Models: A Tool for International Food Policy Analysis.* Dordrecht: Kluwer Academic Publishers.

Friedman, J. 1971. A Non-Cooperative Equilibrium for Supergames. *Review of Economic Studies* 38:1–12.

Friedman, J. 1982. Oligopoly Theory. In *Handbook of Mathematical Economics* 2, ed. K. Arrow and M. Intriligator. Amsterdam: North-Holland.

Frischtak, C., with B. Hadjimichael and U. Zachan. 1989. *Competition Policies for Industrializing Countries.* Policy and Research Series no. 7. Washington, DC: World Bank.

Gabszewicz, J. J., and J.-Ph. Vial. 1972. Oligopoly à la Cournot in General Equilibrium Analysis. *Journal of Economic Theory* 4:381–400.

Gelb, A., and Associates. 1988. *Oil Windfalls: Blessing or Curse?* Oxford: Oxford University Press and the World Bank.

Ginsburgh, V., and J. Mercenier. 1988. Macroeconomic Models and Microeconomic

Theory: The Contribution of General Equilibrium Theory. In *Challenges for Macroeconomic Modelling*, ed. W. Driehuis, M. Fase, and H. den Hartog. Amsterdam: North-Holland.

Ginsburgh, V., and H. Sneessens. 1989. Structural Shocks and Investment Subsidies in an Overlapping Generations Model with Perfect Foresight. CORE Discussion Paper 8931. Université Catholique de Louvain.

Goulder, L., and B. Eichengreen. 1989. Trade Liberalisation in General Equilibrium: Intertemporal and Inter-Industry Effects. Working Paper no. 2814. National Bureau of Economic Research.

Grinold, R. 1983. Model Building Techniques for the Correction of End Effects in Multistage Convex Programs. *Operations Research* 31:407–31.

Harris, R. G. 1984. Applied General Equilibrium Analysis of Small Open Economies with Scale Economies and Imperfect Competition. *American Economic Review* 74 (5): 1017–32.

Harris, R. G. 1988. A Guide to the GET Model. Working Paper 88–10. Queens University.

Harris, R. G. 1989. The New Protectionism Revisited. *Canadian Journal of Economics* 24 (4): 751–78.

Hart, O. D. 1985. Imperfect Competition in General Equilibrium: An Overview of Recent Work. In *Frontiers of Economics*, ed. K. Arrow and S. Honkapohja. Oxford: Basil Blackwell.

Hayashi, F. 1982. Tobin's Marginal q and Average q: A Neoclassical Interpretation. *Econometrica* 50:213–24.

Heady, C. J., and P. Mitra. 1987. Distributional and Revenue Raising Arguments for Tariffs. *Journal of Development Economics* 26:77–101.

Helpman, E. 1989. The Noncompetitive Theory of International Trade and Trade Policy. Proceedings of the World Bank Annual Conference on Development Economics 1989. *World Bank Economic Review (Supplement)*, 193–216.

Higham, D., and J. Tomlison. 1982. Why Do Governments Worry about Inflation? *National Westminster Bank Quarterly Review.*

Hillman, A. L. 1989. *The Political Economy of Protection.* New York: Harwood Academic Publisher.

Horstmann, I., and J. Markusen. 1986. Up the Average Cost Curve: Inefficienct Entry and the New Protectionism. *Journal of International Economics* 20:225–48.

Huarachi, G., and A. Beltran. 1988. *El Modelo Computable de Equilibrio General.* La Paz, Bolivia: UDAP.

Hutabarat, B. 1988. Description of Food Crops Policies in Indonesia. Working Paper no. 6. UNE Armidale, Australia–CAER Bogor, Indonesia.

Ize, A., and G. Ortiz. 1987. Fiscal Rigidities, Public Debt and Capital Flight. *IMF Staff Papers* 34 (2): 311–32.

Johansen, L. 1960. *A Multi-Sectoral Study of Economic Growth.* Amsterdam: North-Holland.

Jorgenson, D. W., and P. J. Wilcoxen. 1989. Environmental Regulation and U.S. Economic Growth. Presented at the MIT Workshop on Energy and Environmental Modeling, Cambridge, MA.

Jorgenson, D. 1963. Capital Theory and Investment Behavior. *American Economic Review* 53 (2): 247–59.

Kehoe, T. J., and D. K. Levine. 1985. Comparative Statics and Perfect Foresight in Infinite Horizon Economies. *Econometrica* 53 (2): 433–54.

Ketkar, S. L., and K. W. Ketkar. 1989. Determinants of Capital Flight from Argentina, Brazil and Mexico. *Contemporary Policy Issues* 7:11–29.

Kemp, M., and N. Van Long. 1980. *Exhaustible Resources, Optimality and Trade.* Amsterdam: North-Holland.

Keyzer, M. A. 1990. Under Imperfect Competition, Price Normalization Should Not Matter. Vrije Universiteit Amsterdam. Typescript.

Keyzer, M. A. 1991. On the Approximation of Infinite Horizon Allocations. In *Applied General Equilibrium Modeling,* ed. H. Don, T. Van de Klundert, and J. Van Sinderen. Dordrecht: Kluwer Academic Publishers.

Khan, M. S., and N. Ul Haque. 1985. Foreign Borrowing and Capital Flight: A Formal Analysis. *IMF Staff Papers* 32 (4): 606–28.

Kharas, H., and H. Shishido. 1987. Forreign Borrowing and Macroeconomic Adjustment to External Shocks. *Journal of Development Economics* 25:125–48.

Koopmans, T. 1957. *Three Essays on the State of Economic Science.* New York: McGraw-Hill.

Kouwenaar, A. 1988. *A Basic Needs Policy Model: A General Equilibrium Analysis with Special Reference to Ecuador.* Amsterdam: North-Holland.

Krugman, P. 1979. Increasing Returns, Monopolistic Competition and International Trade. *Journal of International Economics* 9:469–79.

Krugman, P. 1984. Import Protection as Export Promotion. In *Monopolistic Competition in International Trade,* ed. H. Kierzkowski. Oxford: Oxford University Press.

Kwack, T. 1983. Taxation, Subsidy and Investment in Korean Manufacturing Industry. Ph.D. diss. Department of Economics, Harvard University.

Kydland, F., and E. Prescott. 1977. Rules Rather than Discretion: The Inconsistency of Optimal Plans. *Journal of Political Economy* 85:473–93.

Lave, L.B. 1988. The Greenhouse Effect: What Government Actions Are Needed? *Journal of Policy Analysis and Management* 7 (3): 460–70.

Lewis, J. D. 1985. Financial Liberalization and Price Rigidities in a General Equilibrium Model with Financial Assets. Development Discussion Paper no. 211. Harvard Institute for International Development, Harvard University. Mimeo.

Lewis, J. D. 1992a. Adjustment in a Previously Closed Economy: Turkey, 1973–1981. In *Adjustment in Oil-Importing Developing Countries: 1973, 1979, 1990,* ed. P. Mitra and associates. Cambridge: Cambridge University Press.

Lewis, J. D. 1992b. Financial Repression and Liberalization in a General Equilibrium Model with Financial Markets. *Journal of Policy Modelling* 14 (2): 135–66.

Lewis, J. D., and S. Urata. 1984. Anatomy of a Balance-of-Payments Crisis: Application of a Computable General Equilibrium Model to Turkey, 1978–1980. *Economic Modelling* 1 (3): 281–303.

Lipton, D., and J. Sachs. 1983. Accumulation and Growth in a Two-Country Model: A Simulation Approach. *Journal of International Economics* 15:135–59.

Long, N. Van, and N. Vousden. 1987. Risk Averse Rent Seeking with Shared Rents. *Economic Journal* 97:971–85.

Lora, E. 1989. Real and Financial Interactions in a Computable General Equilibrium Model for Colombia. Fedesarrollo. Mimeo.

Lucas, R. E. 1976. Adjustment Costs and the Theory of Supply. *Journal of Political Economy* 75:321–4.

Lucas, R. E. 1988. On the Mechanics of Economic Development. *Journal of Monetary Economics* 22:3–48.

Manne, A. 1985. On the Formulation and Solution of Economic Equilibrium Models. *Mathematical Programming Study* 23:1–22.

Manne, A. 1988. Unequal Time Intervals in Dynamic Models. Stanford University. Mimeo.

Manne, A., and P. Preckel. 1985. A Three-Region Intertemporal Model of Energy, International Trade and Capital Flows. *Mathematical Programming Study* 23:56–74.

Manne, A., and R. G. Richels. 1989. CO_2 Emission Limits: An Economic Analysis for the USA. Presented at the MIT Workshop on Energy and Environmental Modeling, Cambridge, MA.

McKinnon, R. I. 1973. *Money and Capital in Economic Development.* Washington, DC: Brookings Institution.

McKinnon, R. T. 1984. Comments. In *Applied General Equilibrium Analysis,* ed. H. Scarf and J. Shoven. Cambridge: Cambridge University Press.

McMillan, J. 1988. *Game Theory in International Economics.* Fundamentals of Pure and Applied Economics. Churl: Harwood Economic Publishers.

Mercenier, J. 1987. Tariff Change, Foreign Capital and Immiserization: A General Equilibrium Evaluation of the Latin American Case. *Journal of Development Economics* 26:145–62.

Mercenier, J. 1989. On Wealth Effects in Sticky-Price Exchange Rate Models with Optimizing Agents. Cahier 3689. C.R.D.E., Université de Montréal.

Mercenier, J., and P. Michel. 1991a. A Criterion for Time Aggregation in Intertemporal Dynamic Models. Cahier 0891. C.R.D.E., Université de Montréal.

Mercenier, J., and P. Michel. 1991b. Discrete Time Finite Horizon Approximation of Optimal Growth with Steady State Invariance. Cahier 2091. C.R.D.E., Université de Montréal.

Mercenier, J., and M. Sampaïo de Souza. 1992. A Decentralized Multisector Intertemporal General Equilibrium Evaluation of Brazil's Protectionism. In *International Trade Modelling,* ed. M. G. Dagenais and P. A. Muet. London: Chapman and Hall.

Murtagh, B., and M. Saunders. 1987. MINOS 5.1 User's Guide. Department of Operations Research, Stanford University.

Narayana, N. S. S., and K. S. Parikh. 1987. Rural Works Programmes in India: Costs and Benefits. *Journal of Development Economics* 29 (2): 131–56.

Narayana, N. S. S., K. S. Parikh, and T. N. Srinivasan. 1991. *Agriculture, Growth and Redistribution of Income: Policy Analysis with a General Equilibrium Model of India.* Amsterdam: North-Holland; New Delhi: Allied Publishers.

Negishi, T. 1960. Welfare Economics and Existence of an Equilibrium for a Competitive Economy. *Metroeconomica* 12:92–97.

Parikh, K. S., and T. N. Srinivasan. 1989. Employment vs. Food in Poverty Alleviation: India. Presented at the IFPRI/World Bank Conference.

Pastor, Manuel, Jr. 1990. Capital Flight from Latin America. *World Development* 18 (1): 1–18.

Pearson, S., W. Falcon, P. Heytens, E. Monke, R. Naylor, and P. Timmer. 1988. Rural Income and Employment Effects of Rice Policy in Indonesia. Food Research Institute, Stanford University.

Ramirez-Rojas, C. L. 1985. Currency Substitution in Argentina, Mexico and Uruguay. *IMF Staff Papers* 32 (4): 629–67.

Ratha, D. K. 1987. Planning and Resource Mobilization in a Developing Economy. Ph.D. diss. Indian Statistical Institute.

Ravallion, M., and M. Huppi. 1989. *Poverty and Undernutrition in Indonesia During the 1980s*. PPR Working Paper 286. Washington, DC: World Bank.

Rivera-Batiz, L. A., and P. Romer. 1991. International Trade with Endogenous Technical Change. *European Economic Review* 35 (4): 971–1001.

Roberts, J., and H. Sonnenschein. 1977. On the Foundation of the Theory of Monopolistic Competition. *Econometrica* 45 (1): 101–13.

Robinson, S. 1989. Computable General Equilibrium Models of Developing Countries: Stretching the Neo-Classical Paradigm. University of California at Berkeley. Mimeo.

Robinson, S. 1989. Multisectoral Models. In *Handbook of Development Economics* 2, ed. H. B. Chenery and T. N. Srinivasan. Amsterdam: North-Holland.

Robinson, S. 1991. Macroeconomics, Financial Variables, and Computable General Equlibrium Models. *World Development* 19 (11): 509–26.

Robinson, S., and L. D. Tyson. 1984. Modelling Structural Adjustment: Micro and Macro Elements in a General Equilibrium Framework. In *Applied General Equilibrium Analysis*, ed. H. Scarf and J. B. Shoven. Cambridge: Cambridge University Press.

Robinson, S., and L. D. Tyson. 1985. Foreign Trade, Resource Allocation, and Structural Adjustment in Yugoslavia: 1976–1980. *Journal of Comparative Economics* 9:46–70.

Rodrik, D. 1988. Imperfect Competition, Scale Economies and Trade Policy in Developing Countries. In *Trade Policy Issues and Empirical Analysis,* ed. R. E. Baldwin. Chicago: University of Chicago Press; Cambridge: N.B.E.R.

Romer, P. M. 1986. Increasing Returns and Long-Run Growth. *Journal of Political Economy* 94:1002–37.

Romer, P. 1989. Capital Accumulation in the Theory of Growth. In *Modern Business Cycle Theory*, ed. R. J. Barro. Cambridge, MA: Harvard University Press.

Rutherford T., and S. Winer. 1990. Endogenous Policy in a Computational General Equilibirum Framework. University of Western Ontario. Mimeo.

Ryan, S. M., and J. C. Bean. 1989. Degeneracy in Infinite Horizon Optimization. *Mathematical Programming* 43:305–15.

Sachs, J. 1985. External Debt and Macroeconomic Performance in Latin America and East Asia. *Brookings Papers on Economic Activity* 2:523–64.

Sachs, J., ed. 1989. *Developing Country Debt and the World Economy*. Chicago: University of Chicago Press.

Sampaïo de Souza, C. 1987. Proteçao, Crescimento e Distribuiçao de Renda no Brasil: Uma Abordagem de Equilibrio Geral. *Revista Brasileira de Economia* 41 (1): 99–116.

Sargent, T. J. 1987. *Macroeconomic Theory.* 2d ed. (1st ed. 1979.) New York: Academic Press.

Scarf, H. 1967. The Approximation of Fixed Points of a Continuous Mapping. *SIAM Journal of Applied Mathematics* 15:1328–43.

Scarf, H., with T. Hansen. 1973. *The Computation of Economic Equilibria.* New Haven: Yale University Press.

Scarf, H., and J. Shoven, eds. 1984. *Applied General Equilibirum Analysis.* New York: Cambridge University Press.

Shaw, E. 1973. *Financial Deepening in Economic Development.* Cambridge: Oxford University Press.

Shoven, J., and J. Whalley. 1972. A General Equilibrium Calculation of the Effects of Differential Taxation of Income from Capital in the U.S. *Journal of Public Economics* 1:281–322.

Shoven, J. B., and J. Whalley. 1984. Applied General-Equilibrium Models of Taxation and International Trade: An Introduction and Survey. *Journal of Economic Literature* 22 (3): 1007–51.

Sirohi, A. S. 1984. Impact of Agricultural Subsidies and Procurement Prices on Production and Income Distribution in India. *Indian Journal of Agricultural Economics* 39 (4): 563–85.

Smith, A., and A. Venables. 1988. Completing the Internal Market in the European Community: Some Industry Simulations. *European Economic Review* 32:1501–25.

Smith, A., and A. Venables. 1989. Trade Policy Modelling with Imperfectly Competitive Market Structures. Presented at the conference on General Equilibrium: Theory and Applications. Louvain-la-Neuve: Center for Operations Research and Econometrics.

SOW. 1988. *Agriculture in Repelita V: A Review of Policy Issues in Indonesia Through 1993.* Amsterdam: Centre for World Food Studies.

SOW. 1990a. *Structural Adjustment in Indonesia: A Counterfactual Assessment for the Eighties.* Research Report SOW 90-01. Amsterdam: Centre for World Food Studies.

SOW. 1990b. *Technical Specification of Indonesia Model.* Addendum to Research Report SOW 90-01 and Research Memorandum 90–01. Amsterdam: Centre for World Food Studies.

Srinivasan, T. N. 1989a. Comment on The Noncompetitive Theory of International Trade and Trade Policy by E. Helpman. Proceedings of the World Bank Annual Conference on Development Economics 1989. *World Bank Economic Review (Supplement)*, 217–22.

Srinivasan, T. N. 1989b. Recent Theories of Imperfect Competition and International Trade: Any Implications for Development Strategy? *Indian Economic Review* 24 (1): 1–23.

Stockey, N. L., and R. E. Lucas. 1989. *Recursive Methods in Economic Dynamics.* Cambridge, MA: Harvard University Press.

Summers, L. 1981. Capital Taxation and Accumulation in a Life Cycle Growth Model. *American Economic Review* 71:533–44.

Taylor, L. 1979. *Macro Models for Developing Countries.* New York: McGraw-Hill.

Taylor, L. 1981a. IS-LM in the Tropics: Diagrammatics of the New Structuralist Macro Critique. In *Economic Stabilization in Developing Countries,* ed. W. R. Cline and S. Weintraub. Washington, DC: Brookings Institution.

Taylor, L. 1981b. South-North Trade and Southern Growth. *Journal of International Economics* 11:589–602.

Taylor, L. 1983. *Structuralist Macroeconomics: Applicable Models for the Third World.* New York: Basic Books.

Taylor, L., and J. A. Rosensweig. 1984. *Devaluation Capital Flows and Crowding-Out: A Computable General Equilibrium Model with Portfolio Choice for Thailand.* Boston: Department of Economics, Massachusetts Institute of Technology.

Taylor, L., and J. A. Rosensweig. 1990. Devaluation, Capital Flows and Crowding-Out: A CGE Model With Portfolio Choice for Thailand. In *Socially Relevant Policy Analysis: Structuralist Computable General Equilibrium Models for the Developing World,* ed. L. Taylor. Cambridge, MA: MIT Press.

Timmer, C. P. 1988. Regulation and Deregulation of Rice Markets in Indonesia: Reflections on Bulog's Changing Role and Mission. Harvard University. Mimeo.

Tobin, J. 1969a. A General Equilibrium Approach to Monetary Theory. *Journal of Money, Credit, and Banking* 1 (1): 15–29.

Tobin, J. 1980. *Asset Accumulation and Economic Activity.* Yrjo Jahnsson Lectures. Oxford: Basil Blackwell.

Ulph, A., and M. Folie. 1980. Exhaustible Resources and Cartels: An Intertemporal Nash-Cournot Model. *Canadian Journal of Economics* 4:645–58.

Ulph, A., and D. Ulph. 1982. International Monopoly-Monopsony Power over Oil and Capital. University of Southampton. Mimeo.

van den Boom, G. 1989. A Land Development Model to Maintain, Improve and Expand Cultivable Area with an Application to Public Works Irrigation Systems in Indonesia. Working Paper 89–08. Centre for World Food Studies, Amsterdam.

van Wijnbergen, S. 1982. Stagflationary Effects of Monetary Stabilization Policies: A Quantitative Analysis of South Korea. *Journal of Development Economics* 10:133–69.

van Wijnbergen, S. 1983. Credit Policy, Inflation and Growth in a Financially Repressed Economy. *Journal of Development Economics* 13:45–65.

van Wijnbergen, S. 1985. Oil Discoveries, Intertemporal Adjustment and Public Policy. In *Macroeconomic Prospects for a Small Oil Exporting Country,* ed. O. Bjerkholt and E. Offerdal. The Hague: Martinus Nijhoff Publishers.

Venables, A. 1985. Trade and Trade Policy with Imperfect Competition: The Case of Identical Products and Free Entry. *Journal of International Economics* 19:1–19.

Waelbroeck, J. 1990. Private communication with author.

Whalley, J. 1982. General Equilibrium Modeling of Trade Liberalization Issues among Major World Trade Blocks. In *Global International Economic Models,* ed. B. G. Hickman. New York: Elsevier.

Willig R. D., and E. E. Bailey. 1981. Income Distribution Concerns in Regulatory Policy-Making. In *Studies in Public Regulation,* ed. G. Fromm. Chicago: University of Chicago Press.

World Bank. 1983. *Turkey: Special Economic Report—Policies for the Financial Sector.* Report no. 4459-TU. Washington, DC: World Bank.

World Bank. 1989a. *Indonesia: Strategy for Growth and Structural Change.* Report no. 7758-IND. Washington, DC: World Bank.

World Bank. 1989b. *World Development Report 1989.* Washington, DC: World Bank.

Young, S. 1985. The Role of Trade Policy in Korea's Economic Development and Problems of Import Liberalization. Korea Development Institute, Seoul. Mimeo.

Contributors

Nancy Benjamin, Syracuse University

Jean-Claude Berthélémy, University of Maine and Delta—Joint research unit : CNRS, ENS and EHESS, Paris.

Charles R. Blitzer, The World Bank.

François Bourguignon, University of Maine and Delta—Joint research unit : CNRS, ENS and EHESS, Paris.

Jaime de Melo, The World Bank.

Dominique Desruelle, Université de Montréal.

Shantayanan Devarajan, Harvard University.

Richard S. Eckaus, Massachusetts Institute of Technology.

André Fargeix, University of California at Berkeley.

Victor Ginsburgh, Université Libre de Bruxelles and CORE.

Michiel A. Keyzer, Free University of Amsterdam.

Supriya Lahiri, University of Lowell.

Jeffrey D. Lewis, Harvard Institute of International Development.

Eduardo Lora, Fedesarrollo, Bogota.

André Martens, Université de Montréal.

Gary McMahon, International Development Research Centre, Ottawa.

Alexander Meeraus, GAMS Development Corporation.

Jean Mercenier, Université de Montréal.

Kirit S. Parikh, Indira Gandhi Institute of Development Research, Bombay.

Jacques Robert, Université de Montréal.

David Roland-Holst, U.S. International Trade Commission and Mills College.

Elisabeth Sadoulet, University of California at Berkeley.

Maria da Conceiçao Sampaïo de Souza, Universidade Federal de Pernambuco, Recife.

359

Herbert Scarf, Yale University.

T. N. Srinivasan, Yale University.

Lance Taylor, Massachusetts Institute of Technology.

Ngo Van Long, McGill University.

Wim C. M. van Veen, Free University of Amsterdam.